NN.

3

WITHDRAWN

Japan Faces China

Also by Chae-Jin Lee

Communist China's Policy toward Laos
A Case Study

Political Leadership in Korea
(co-editor, with Dae-Sook Suh)

JAPAN FACES CHINA
Political and Economic Relations in the Postwar Era

Chae-Jin Lee

The Johns Hopkins University Press

Baltimore and London

Manufactured in the United States of America

The Johns Hopkins University Press, Baltimore, Maryland 21218
The Johns Hopkins University Press Ltd., London

Library of Congress Catalog Card Number 75-40408
ISBN 0-8018-1738-2

Library of Congress Cataloging in Publication data
will be found on the last printed page of this book.

Library of Congress Cataloging in Publication Data

Lee, Chae-Jin, 1936-
    Japan faces China.

    Includes index.
    1. Japan–Foreign relations–China. 2. China–
Foreign relations–Japan. 3. Japan–Foreign econom-
ic relations–China. 4. China–Foreign economic
relations–Japan. I. Title.
DS849.C6L33   327.52'051   75-40408
ISBN 0-8018-1738-2

Contents

Illustrations

Tables

Preface

On September 29, 1972, Japan and the People's Republic of China agreed to establish diplomatic relations and to promote political, economic, and cultural cooperation. This development not only opened an exciting new chapter in the long history of intimate contacts between these two Asian neighbors, but also marked an important change in the international order of East and Southeast Asia. Even though diplomatic rapprochement was consummated in a rapid fashion, it was nonetheless a result of the complex events and forces that had taken place both in Japan and in China since 1949.

In order to understand the nature and substance of these events and forces, the present book is mainly designed (1) to describe a broad pattern of political and economic relations between Japan and China from 1949 through 1972, (2) to discuss the politics of linkages that Japan's political and economic groups, especially the ruling Liberal-Democratic Party and the opposition Socialist Party, maintained with China, and (3) to assess the effects of this inter-party competition (and other domestic cleavages) upon the unfolding of Sino-Japanese relations in political, diplomatic, and economic areas. I must point out that the book is somewhat constrained by the asymmetry of accessible sources and information in Japan and China and by the unavailability of relevant archival materials. Consequently, some of my analyses and interpretations remain tentative and suggestive. It is only hoped that my modest scholarly endeavor will stimulate further research on the intricate relationship between Japan and China.

I wish to thank Professor H. Arthur Steiner for his untiring guidance of my studies on China and Japan. In the course of my research over several years, I have been deeply indebted to a large number of Japanese scholars, politicians, diplomats, journalists, and businessmen. I am particularly grateful to Dean Ishikawa Tadao of Keio University, Professor Seki Hiroharu of Tokyo University, Ōkubo Genji, Sakai Yukio of *Yomiuri Shimbun*, Shimizu Minoru of *Japan Times*, Uezumi Minoru of the Japan Socialist Party, Shiranishi Shinichirō of the Japanese Association for Promotion of International Trade, President Tsutsumi Yūji of the Prince Hotels, and Dietmen Eda Saburō, Sasaki Kōzō, Kawakami Tamio, and Kawasaki Kanji. Moreover, I have benefited from discussions with members of the Chinese Embassy at Tokyo. I would also like to acknowledge the assistance given by Leon D. Mayo, Jr., Tsukamoto Masaya, and David H. Cohen.

My research was partially financed by a Fulbright-Hays Faculty Research Fellowship from the Department of Health, Education, and Welfare (1967–68) and by a grant from the Joint Committee on Japanese Studies of the Social Science Research Council and the American Council of Learned Societies (1973–74). At the University of Kansas I have received generous financial and administrative support from the Office of Research Administration, the Graduate Council, the Department of Political Science, and the Center for East Asian Studies. I am also appreciative of the useful facilities provided by the Union Research Institute in Hong Kong, the Diet Library in Japan, the Institute of Oriental Culture at Tokyo University, and the Institute for Comparative and Foreign Area Studies at the University of Washington.

Lawrence, Kansas
May 1975

To my wife and son

Abbreviations

AAPSG	Asian-African Problems Study Group
APSG	Asian Problems Study Group
ASPAC	Asian and Pacific Council
CAPIT	Chinese Association for Promotion of International Trade
CCP	Chinese Communist Party
CEC	Central Executive Committee
CGP	Clean Government Party
CJFA	China-Japan Friendship Association
COCOM	Coordinating Committee
DSP	Democratic Socialist Party
JAPIT	Japanese Association for Promotion of International Trade
JCFA	Japan-China Friendship Association
JCP	Japan Communist Party
JCTPC	Japan-China Trade Promotion Council
JSP	Japan Socialist Party
KMT	Kuomintang
LDP	Liberal-Democratic Party
MITI	Ministry of International Trade and Industry
NCNJCDR	National Council for the Normalization of Japan-China Diplomatic Relations
NCRJCDR	National Congress for the Restoration of Japan-China Diplomatic Relations
PRC	People's Republic of China
ROC	Republic of China

Keidanren	Federation of Economic Organizations
Keizai Dōyūkai	Japan Committee for Economic Development
Sōhyō	General Council of Trade Unions
Zengakuren	All-Japan Federation of Student Self-Governing Associations
Zennichinō	National Farmers' Union

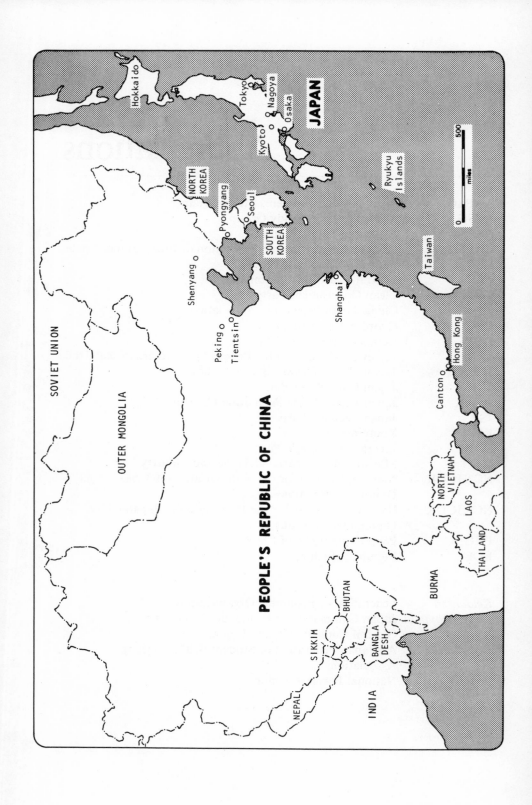

1
Introduction

Under ordinary circumstances one might assume that the combination of close cultural ties, geographic proximity, and economic complementarity between Japan and the People's Republic of China (PRC) would be conducive to the normalization and expansion of their diplomatic, economic, and cultural relations. In particular, Japan was profoundly indebted to the traditional Chinese influences, ranging from its written script and ethical foundations to its educational system and religious practices, all of which led Wilbur to suggest that even the Anglo-American cultural bonds were hardly closer than those linking Japan and China.[1] However, the general pattern of interaction between these two Asian neighbors in the postwar period up until 1972 was characterized by a mixture of diplomatic, ideological, and strategic conflicts and economic and cultural cooperation.

There were a variety of reasons for this extraordinary state of affairs between Japan and the PRC. The record of Sino-Japanese relations over a half century until 1945 was dominated by Japan's armed aggression, territorial expansion, colonial exploitation, and massive atrocities committed against the Chinese people; at the same time many ambitious Chinese youths—Sun-Yat-sen, Chou En-lai, Chiang Kai-shek, Wang Ching-wei, Lu Hsün, and Kuo Mo-jo, to name a few—studied or worked in Japan.[2] At the end of World War II all relations ceased. But then Japan became a thoroughly defeated and totally demoralized nation, subjected to alien military occupation. For the following seven years the U.S. occupation authorities in Japan designed a form of government and promoted a conservative political elite compatible with American economic and ideological interest. The result was to drive Japan into the anti-Communist camp in the ensuing global cold-war structure.[3] Even after Japan regained its political independence in 1952 as a result of the San Francisco peace treaty, the successive conservative governments, still weak and thus unsure of their proper place in the world community, failed to assert an imaginative and autonomous foreign posture, especially in regard to the two rival Chinese regimes, and continued to remain under the shadow of U.S. policy, which attempted to contain the PRC politically and militarily and to isolate it diplomatically and economically.

Not only did postwar ideological developments serve to estrange these two countries in spite of their long and close traditional ties, but scholars became skeptical about the strength and importance of the cultural ties as agents automatically favorable to friendly relations. Regarding the likely determinants of contemporary Sino-Japanese relations, Johnson pointed out that, despite their common cultural heritage, the peoples of Japan and China had responded to the influence of Western imperialism in almost diametrically opposite ways and had approached each other with misleading stereotypes. Hence he asserted in 1972 that "there is little evidence that either country understands the other any better than it did in the past."[4] Jansen, too, noted the decreasing importance of cultural ties and war guilt in Japan's conception of China.[5] He persuasively argued that the fact of geographic proximity made the two countries important to each other, but had no effect upon the warmth between them. A more important factor affecting their relationship was what Jansen called the "contrasting rates of modernization." While Japan was one of the most industrialized countries in the world, China was still a "have-not" nation, thus sharing the problems of economic underdevelopment with many Third World members. Moreover, both Johnson and Scalapino predicted that longstanding rivalry and regional competition rather than cooperation would determine the direction of Sino-Japanese relations during the 1970s.[6]

As the importance of Sino-Japanese relations loomed larger on the Japanese domestic political scene, Japanese political forces, especially the governing Liberal-Democratic Party (LDP) and the opposition Japan Socialist Party (JSP), responded to the Chinese question with varying policies and commitments. The LDP and its predecessors, which had almost single-handedly decided and executed Japan's foreign policies since 1952, continued to honor the Japan-(Nationalist) China peace treaty and to expand diplomatic and economic relations with Chiang Kai-shek's Taiwan until 1972. While upholding the principle of separation between political and economic matters, however, the LDP or some of its parliamentary members were deeply engaged in promoting trade relations with the PRC. On the Chinese question, therefore, the LDP never achieved a complete cohesion among its divergent leaders, but exhibited a growing interfactional cleavage in recent years.

As a radical alternative to the LDP's conservative foreign relations, the JSP advocated a broad policy line of peaceful coexistence, positive neutralism, and total disarmament. It also proposed that Japan should normalize its diplomatic and economic relations with the PRC and conclude both peace treaties and nonaggression pacts with the PRC and the Soviet Union. Though the JSP managed to maintain a reasonable degree of internal consensus on these general foreign policy goals, its leaders and supporters disagreed on their relative priorities and their specific methods of implementation. The problem was compounded by the intensification of socialist factional rivalries, the polycentric tendencies of international Communist movements, the gradual disintegration of the American alliance system, and the LDP's changing external tactics.

Furthermore, the LDP and the JSP represented a bimodal distribution of their orientations on major foreign and strategic issues, particularly in regard to China; thus, both suffered from the substantial discrepancies between their extreme orientations and the unimodal tendency of Japanese public opinion.[7] They were not adequately prepared to adjust their diametrically opposed official policies to the moderate and centrist trends of Japanese political opinion or to the shifting conditions of external political environments. Nor were they effective in mobilizing sufficient domestic political and economic resources against each other's international positions. While the LDP was content to follow an established routine in foreign affairs, the JSP was more interested in challenging the legitimacy of the LDP's governing structure than in changing its specific policies in an incremental, bargaining fashion. Consequently, irreconcilable confrontation rather than compromise and cooperation characterized the LDP-JSP relations, and the JSP was denied a constructive role in influencing normal decision-making procedures with respect to Japan's governmental policy toward China. No doubt this interparty cleavage was a crucial determinant of the development of Sino-Japanese relations until 1972.

In order to conceptualize the functions and effects of the LDP and the JSP in Sino-Japanese relations, it is assumed that the ways in which these two major political parties or their components made and implemented a certain policy decision were determined, separately or jointly, by three main interrelated factors: (1) domestic environment, (2) foreign environment, and (3) each party's internal conditions. The scope and modes of interaction between the domestic and foreign factors influenced each party's attitudes and activities on such issues as diplomatic relations, security interests, and economic exchange. The whole conversion process from environments to policy outputs differed according to the relative saliency of particular issue areas.[8] As crudely illustrated in figure 1, some policy outputs stemming from each party or its constituent elements (such as factions and individual members) exerted a "feedback" effect upon both domestic and foreign environments. Other outputs disappeared without noticeable consequences. The feedback influenced a certain element of the foreign environment such as the PRC, which then reasserted its previous input into the conversion process. One party's action also had an appreciable effect upon a certain aspect of the domestic environment such as the other party, which was forced to adopt either a more negative approach toward the PRC, or a more productive one than it was prepared to take.

Foreign Environment

Much of the external environment for Japanese policy toward China during the 1950s was determined by the loose, bipolar international system

Figure 1. Political Party and Foreign Policy

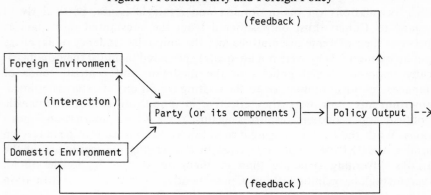

dominated by the two superpowers, the United States and the Soviet Union, but the system gradually collapsed during the 1960s. While both superpowers realized the impracticability of controlling all major global issues, their respective, erstwhile "client-states," Japan and the PRC, began to generate a host of conditions conducive to a readjustment of their own bilateral relations. Even though Japan did not possess significant military power, its foreign trade and economic influence, especially since the early 1960s, already provided some initial signs for viewing it as one of the polar powers in East and Southeast Asia.[9] These signs pointed to a potential regional competition between economically powerful Japan and nuclear-armed China, but it was unrealistic to deemphasize the strong influence of the two superpowers in Asia. Hence the trends of four-power multipolarity or quadrilateral structure, rather than the regional bipolarity, seemed to represent the changing nature of international relations in East Asia during the 1960s and early 1970s.[10]

The emerging Sino-Japanese regional competition was evident in Taiwan, Korea, and parts of Southeast Asia. Viewed from the Chinese perspective, which feared the recurrence of the experiences of recent history, Japan was bent on expanding its enormous capabilities to the rest of Asia through economic aid, foreign trade, direct investment, and multilateral programs; this economic expansion was to be accompanied by Japan's growing political and military involvement in Asia. As evidence of this perceived trend, the Chinese cited Japan's increasing defense expenditure, its active role in the Asian and Pacific Council (ASPAC), and its alleged interest in forming the anti-China collective security system called the Northeast Asia Treaty Organization. According to the Chinese argument, Japan's ultimate foreign policy goal was to revive the defunct design of the Greater East Asia

Coprosperity Sphere. While the LDP denied all these charges, the JSP agreed with some of them concerning the revival of Japan's militarism and expansionism.

Of particular relevance to the development of Sino-Japanese relations and to the LDP's and the JSP's foreign policies was China's evolving relationship with the Soviet Union and the United States. When the PRC concluded a Treaty of Friendship, Alliance and Mutual Assistance with the Soviet Union in 1950, both countries still regarded Japan as a potentially common enemy. The bond of mutual interest linking Peking and Moscow was broken down first by Moscow's unilateral diplomatic recognition of Japan in 1956, and then by the post-1957 Sino-Soviet dispute. Consequently, both the PRC and the Soviet Union competed for influence on Japan's Communists and Socialists as their useful allies. Indeed, Sino-Soviet competition placed Japanese Communists and Socialists in a very awkward position. Even as third parties to the dispute, they were often compelled to choose between Moscow and Peking and to explain their own positions, while the LDP attempted to take advantage of Peking-Moscow conflicts. The JSP, in particular, intended to maintain equally harmonious contacts with both Peking and Moscow, but found it increasingly difficult to strike a judicious, impartial balance between these two Communist powers. And whenever the JSP was driven into a position of ambiguity and ambivalence, its lack of independent political judgment was profusely criticized by the LDP.

As far as the Sino-American conflict was concerned, the LDP faithfully respected and emulated the U.S. policy throughout the 1950s and 1960s, while the JSP was generally supportive of China's contentions. Yet the sudden unfolding of partial Sino-American accommodation in the early 1970s threw both the LDP and the JSP into a state of shock and confusion. Once the initial tidal wave of shock was over, both political parties officially welcomed President Nixon's visit to China, but the JSP used the occasion to dramatize the "bankruptcy" of the LDP government's inflexible foreign policy. Yet the JSP itself was caught in a delicate policy dilemma as the PRC intended to pursue a general political reconciliation with the U.S. and Japan.

After a century of national humiliation and frustration inflicted by European and Japanese imperialists, the Chinese leaders aspired to safeguard their political independence and national security and to achieve territorial reunification. They wished to restore their traditional national grandeur and to assert international status commensurate with their power and pride. At the same time, they appeared to seek political leadership in the Third World, especially in Asia. Whatever differences they exhibited in terms of factional alliances and tactical orientations, the Chinese leaders seemed to espouse basically similar foreign policy objectives. Judged by any conceivable criteria, however, China, unlike Japan, was an immensely dissatisfied country, which, despite nuclear weapons and diplomatic fronts, did not possess all the means and capabilities to fulfill its policy goals. As Wilkinson succinctly puts it, "actual Chinese capabilities are far from sufficient to reunify China, impose local suzerainty, regain lost territory, control the Communist movement, or revolutionize the world."[11]

The most important external factor with which both the LDP and the JSP had to reckon was, of course, China's evolving conception of Japan, for the behavior of a nation was "determined by the way in which the situation is defined subjectively by those charged with the responsibility for making choices."[12] The Chinese conception of Japan, as of other countries, was largely based on a delicate and unstable balance between a professed belief in the "universal truth" of Marxism-Leninism and an ethnocentric pursuit of China's national interest. There was little doubt that Maoist ideology, as a set of internally coherent values and doctrines, theoretically guided the Chinese, thus shaping much of their analytical instruments and policy preferences. They tended to view Japan in the context of universal ideological commitments, and thus believed that since Japan reached a high stage of monopoly capitalism, it developed a potential for imperialistic, militaristic foreign policy. At the same time they argued that this development created some economic conditions and social forces in Japan that could be mobilized against the LDP government's anti-Communist policy. When they placed a top priority on ideologically inspired foreign policy, as they did during the Great Leap Forward and again during the Cultural Revolution, they lost the freedom of political maneuver and limited the range of policy options. However, they also utilized, from time to time, the convenient notion of peaceful coexistence in order to improve their state-to-state relations with Japan.

While they took into full consideration the political conditions of Japan and attempted to capitalize on them, they tended, naturally, to define their national interest toward Japan in the light of their own images, experiences, and expectations. Hence they made political assessments according to Chinese, more than Japanese, experiences and criteria. The manifestation of their national interest was therefore reflected in a reconstruction of China's traditional relations with Japan and a persistent concern with China's national security vis-a-vis both the U.S. forces stationed in Japan and Japan's own military potential. Moreover, China's economic interest in Japan was substantial because Japan was in an excellent position to assist China's industrial development and foreign trade, but the Chinese were apprehensive of excessive economic dependence upon Japan for fear of losing their political flexibility.

Although the Chinese leaders were conscious of their traditional cultural superiority over Japan, they seemed to be obsessed with their traumatic experiences with Japanese imperialistic aggression and exploitation. In their minds, the memory of those experiences was fresh and vivid; and they were constantly mindful of the possibility that Japan might once again become a formidable challenge to China. In view of this historical reconstruction of their experiences, it was not surprising that the Chinese regarded Japan as a potential regional adversary. Further, this Japanese "threat" was made more serious because it defied the standard defects that the Chinese had been used to attacking in other competitors for influence in Asia. It was relatively easy to attack the United States (or even the Soviet Union), a white, non-Asian power, or to mobilize the nationalistic sentiments among Asians against it. Nevertheless, the Chinese found it difficult to expose Japan's gradual and subtle influence over much of Asia that resulted from Japan's past colonial experiences, economic inducements, and low political posture. They were also sensitive to the growing nationalist sentiment among the Japanese people and the increasing military build-up, and to the impact that these, coupled with Japan's economic power, could have on Asian politics in the future.

In the process of realistic strategic assessment, the Chinese established the supremacy of vital security interests over universal ideological commitments, recognized their limited military capabilities, and refrained from provoking a direct armed confrontation with the United States over Japan. Thus, in polemical arguments and declaratory pronouncements about Japan, they at times sounded militant and irresponsible, but in practice they remained generally prudent and reserved in military matters.

It has so far been suggested that China's postwar policy toward Japan was largely determined by a dualistic conceptual scheme in which ideological considerations were often compromised by or subordinated to the realistic requirements of China's national interest. If, indeed, the Chinese were more concerned with their strategic and other practical interests rather than revolutionary ideological commitments in Japan, it was quite natural that, while pledging their long-range desire for communized Japan, they preferred a medium-range solution—namely, Japan's neutralization and concomitant measures. Except for the brief period of their rigid two-camp international outlook (1949–51), their immediate objective in Japan was not geared toward a violent armed insurrection along a Maoist line. While supporting violent demonstrations against the Japanese government and the United States policy in Japan, they seemed to attach a higher priority to mobilizing Japan's domestic forces in an attempt to modify its foreign policy or to change its governing personnel, for the violent method of an outright Communist revolutionary movement in Japan was deemed risky and counterproductive.

Even if Japan were to become a Communist state, there would be no guarantee that the JCP, a very strong advocate of political independence and autonomy, would always respect and promote China's national interests. The neutralization of Japan, which seemed a more popular and practicable goal than that of a Communist revolution, offered the Chinese a combination of pragmatic advantages that could not be expected of a communized Japan. A Japan which would neither allow hostile foreign military forces or bases on its soil, nor maintain military alliances with foreign powers could hardly threaten China's national security in the immediate future or compete with China in the region. This step, they probably hoped, would disrupt what they termed an anti-China "unholy alliance" forged by U.S. imperialists, Soviet revisionists, Indian reactionaries, and Japanese militarists.

In order to achieve their policy objectives in Japan, the Chinese relied upon a variety of means and a complex structure of individual and collective organizational networks. In addition to its open, competitive, and pluralistic political system, Japan, perhaps because of its insularity, had many linkage groups. Holt and Turner suggest that the number of linkage groups is likely to be greater in an insular polity than in a noninsular one, and that the insular polity reacts more frequently, more quickly, and more strongly to inputs from the international system.[13] As far as the Chinese were concerned, some members and factions of the LDP and the JSP, along with trade firms, friendship associations, and other friendly groups, were the principal linkage groups that were useful for promoting their interests in Japan.[14] As to the general expectation for Japan's future development, there was a congruence of common interests between the PRC and the JSP; this congruence was strongly resented by the LDP.

Domestic Environment

While both political parties were constantly required to respond to dynamic political stimuli stemming from Japan's foreign environments, the scope and effectiveness of their international policies were conditioned by a set of domestic political circumstances. These were (1) pluralistic public opinion, (2) competitive interparty relations, (3) vigorous interest articulation, and (4) complex governmental institutions.[15]

Public Opinion As Neumann suggests, the political party in a liberal democracy is supposed to be a "great intermediary" that links social forces and popular opinions to governmental institutions and public policies.[16] Even though the Japanese political system has an open, liberal, and constitutional governmental framework, the tradition of effective links between general populace and public policies is short. Moreover, despite the almost universal literacy rate and the extensive mass communications facilities in Japan, the degree of public awareness of international affairs is not high.

In June 1967, when the various media of Japanese mass communications —television, radio, newspapers, weeklies, and popular magazines—were flooded with reports and comments about the Chinese Cultural Revolution and the Red Guards' activities, the Japanese public demonstrated a surprisingly limited range of cognitive orientations toward their immediate neighbor. As table 1 shows, one out of three persons did not even know of the existence of a Communist government in mainland China, and nearly half of the interviewees were unaware of the absence of diplomatic relations between Japan and the PRC.[17] Only two out of five persons answered all six cognitive questions correctly, whereas one out of eight persons was totally ignorant. If this finding was an accurate measure of Japanese public opinion, it suggested that the probable size of Japan's "attentive public," those who were aware of and concerned with China, was rather limited. Of course, the organized demonstrations and anomic mass explosions also constituted a form of political expression, but they did not easily change the party's substantive policies toward China.

The public's views on foreign policies may also be manifested in electoral contests and legislative processes. As Abbott and Rogowsky suggest, the actualization of this indirect link between opinion and policy via election depends upon several factors, such as "policy-oriented campaigns, candidates with meaningful policy alternatives and voter knowledge of candidates' major issue positions."[18] The candidates for the Japanese National Diet frequently carried on heated debates on foreign policy issues and presented their respective party platforms to the electorate. But a large number of Japanese voters were less concerned with the candidates' issue-orientations or party affiliations than with their personal appeals or local constituency ties. For instance, a nationwide random survey conducted in 1967 showed that 37.2% of the Japanese electorate voted according to their party preferences and 47.3% according to the candidates' personal qualifications, while 11.4% of the answers were "Do Not Know" and 4.2% "Un-

Table 1—Japanese Public Awareness of Mainland China, June 1967

Questions	Correct Answers (percentage)
1. It is a Communist state.	68.1
2. It does not have diplomatic relations with Japan.	54.1
3. It is not a member of the United Nations.	54.1
4. It has exploded nuclear weapons.	80.0
5. It has a conflict with the Soviet Union.	64.1
6. It undergoes the Cultural Revolution.	69.4

SOURCE: *Ajiyakeizai Jumpō* [Asian economic review], August 1967, pp. 22–28

Table 2—House of Representatives—Election Results, 1949-55

Year	(month)	Conservative			Socialist			Communist	Others	Total
1949	(January)	Democratic		Democratic-Liberal	Socialist		Labor-Farmer			
	Votes	14.8%		56.7%	10.3%		1.5%	7.5%	9.2%	100.0%
	Seats	69		264	48		7	35	43	466
1952	(October)	Reform		Liberal	Left	Right	Labor-Farmer			
	Votes	18.2%		51.4%	11.6%	12.2%	0.9%	0	5.6%	100.0%
	Seats	85		240	54	57	4	0	26	466
1953	(April)	Reform	Hatoyama	Yoshida	Left	Right	Labor-Farmer			
	Votes	16.3%	7.5%	42.7%	15.4%	14.2%	1.1%	0.2%	2.6%	100.0%
	Seats	76	35	199	72	66	5	1	12	466
1955	(February)	Democratic		Yoshida	Left	Right	Labor-Farmer			
	Votes	39.6%		24.0%	19.1%	14.3%	0.9%	0.4%	1.7%	100.0%
	Seats	185		112	89	67	4	2	8	467

known."[19] The corresponding figures in 1969 were: 48.8%—party preferences, 22.0%—personal qualifications, 13.2%—"Do Not Know," and 5.1%—"Unknown."[20] Although the role of policy-oriented electoral decisions loomed larger in urban areas and the campaign rhetoric on foreign affairs continued to be flamboyant, much of Japanese voting behavior was still governed by the traditional patterns of communal pressure and hierarchical personal relations. The major foreign-policy controversies that dominated the national elections, such as the Japanese-Soviet diplomatic relations (February 1955), the Japanese-Chinese trade suspension (May 1958), the Japanese-American Security Treaty revision (November 1960), and the Okinawa reversion (December 1969), did not make any significant impact upon the relative parliamentary strengths of the two major political forces.

Interparty Relations The opinion-policy linkage was weak, not only because of the limits of policy-based electoral decisions but also because of the legislators' straight party-line voting behavior in the National Diet. Consequently, the two major political parties enjoyed a degree of freedom from general public opinion in the area of foreign policy. They were not

Table 3—House of Representatives—Election Results, 1958–72

Year	(month)	LDP	JSP	JCP	DSP	CGP	Others	Total
1958	(May)							
	Votes	61.5%	35.5%	0.2%	–	–	2.8%	100.0%
	Seats	287	166	1	–	–	13	467
1960	(November)							
	Votes	57.6%	27.6%	2.9%	8.8%	–	3.1%	100.0%
	Seats	296	145	3	17	–	6	467
1963	(November)							
	Votes	54.7%	29.0%	4.0%	7.4%	–	4.9%	100.0%
	Seats	283	144	5	23	–	12	467
1967	(January)							
	Votes	48.8%	27.9%	4.8%	7.4%	5.4%	5.7%	100.0%
	Seats	277	140	5	30	25	9	486
1969	(December)							
	Votes	47.6%	21.4%	6.8%	7.7%	11.0%	5.5%	100.0%
	Seats	288	90	14	31	47	16	486
1972	(December)							
	Votes	46.9%	21.9%	10.5%	7.0%	8.4%	5.3%	100.0%
	Seats	271	118	38	19	29	16	491

NOTE:
LDP: Liberal-Democratic Party
JSP: Japan Socialist Party
JCP: Japan Communist Party
DSP: Democratic Socialist Party
CGP: Clean Government Party [Kōmeitō]

always sensitive or responsive to the public sentiments and demands that were abundantly investigated and recorded by various opinion research organizations in Japan. Nor were they effective in aggregating and translating expressed public views into specific policy recommendations, especially in regard to foreign affairs. The relative foreign-policy freedom of political parties did not mean that the public tolerance or acquiescence of any partisan international position was unlimited; there was always a possibility that the usually amorphous public opinion could be mobilized against a sufficiently unpopular foreign policy. When its China policy faced a growing national opposition, the LDP, even for the sake of its domestic political consideration, was forced to modify it; hence the realization of "reactive process"—one of three linkage processes identified by Rosenau—was certainly conceivable in the LDP's China policy.[21]

Further, each party's foreign policy was constantly subject to challenges and criticisms from other parties. The JSP, as the principal opposition party, performed the function of checking and balancing the LDP's paramount role in making Japan's official foreign policies. As Ward stresses, the JSP often made use of the traditional Japanese preference for decision by consensus: "When the opposition forces in Japanese politics complain so bitterly against 'tyranny by majority,' they are saying, in effect, that majorities, even when acting by a perfectly legal process, have no right to make a decision which ignores or over-rides the views of the minority."[22] By appealing to the Japanese aversion to the LDP's unilateral decision in the National Diet, the JSP solicited sympathy and support from the voters.

Sometimes a suprapartisan parliamentary coalition was formed on the Chinese questions. For example, a large number of National Diet members from both ruling and opposition parties took part in the Dietmen's League for Japan-China Trade Promotion and in the Dietmen's League for Promoting Restoration of Japan-China Diplomatic Relations. The Diet also adopted a series of nonpartisan resolutions for promotion of Sino-Japanese trade relations. In general, the JSP spearheaded the parliamentary maneuver against the Japanese government's China policy, attempted to stir up policy disputes within the LDP, and formed irregular anti-LDP united fronts with other opposition parties—the Democratic Socialist Party (DSP), the Japan Communist Party (JCP), and/or the Clean Government Party (CGP).

For the first half of the 1960s it was the JCP that assumed an undisputed, commanding role in establishing informal linkages between Japan and the PRC; the LDP's antimainstream factions and the JSP's leftist factions shared the secondary responsibility for promoting Japan's relations with mainland China. Once the Chinese developed a serious dispute with the JCP in early 1966, they promptly isolated it from its hitherto dominant functions of mediation and cooperation with China. Instead, they sought to find an organizational substitute for the JCP in the JSP—and, to a lesser extent, in the LDP's dissident factions—so that their interests and positions could continue to be represented on the Japanese domestic political scene. This change in China's approach was favorably reciprocated by the JSP, which wished to gain a domestic political dividend out of the China issues. When the JSP demonstrated its unique international capabilities, unequaled by either the LDP or the JCP, to maintain important linkages with the PRC, it was able to represent Japanese public opinion desiring Sino-Japanese diplomatic normalization. In fact, the JSP was engaged in an uncomfortable, jealous, and often acrimonious competition with the JCP in dealing with the PRC. Whereas the JSP accused the JCP of selling out Japan's national interest to China, the JCP assailed the JSP's "unprincipled and subservient" attitude toward the Chinese will. This persistent JSP-JCP controversy, coupled with the JCP-CCP feud, was a major stumbling block to the organization of an effective united front among opposition parties against the LDP's official China policy. When the JSP joined the LDP's dissident members and the CGP and DSP in setting up the Dietmen's League for Promoting Restoration of Japan-China Diplomatic Relations in December 1970, the JCP was conspicuously excluded from its leadership positions.

Interest Articulation   Even if the LDP and the JSP managed to de-emphasize the policy relevance of public opinion, they could hardly afford to ignore the international orientations of a number of important interest groups with which they had close political and financial ties. These groups included business, labor unions, trading companies, small-industry associations, friendship societies, peace groups, youth organizations, and other professional and cultural associations. While the LDP attempted to discourage these groups' tangible links with China, the JSP or its individual members sponsored, joined, or financed some of these groups. The JSP also endorsed their programs, represented their interests, and coordinated with them in carrying out common activities, such as mass demonstrations, joint statements, and organizational ties. These groups, by virtue of their own linkages with the PRC, sometimes bypassed the JSP and directly articulated China's interests and wishes in Japan. They undertook the "emulative process" relative to the PRC.[23] Indeed, the possibilities and channels of China's "penetrative process" toward interest groups were abundantly available in an open, plural society like Japan. In particular, Japanese trade and friendship groups were vulnerable to China's direct influence and manipulation, and many of them were heavily penetrated.

Ordinarily, as Eckstein points out, interest groups that pursue favorable policy decisions and administrative dispositions must adjust their activities to the processes by which these decisions and dispositions are made.[24] While wishing to get direct access to the PRC or to influence the Japanese government and the LDP, which made policy decisions about China,

Japan's interest groups sought to take advantage of the JSP's good offices, which assisted the fulfillment of their particular interests. In an open political system such as Japan's, Coplin and Kegley hypothesize, "the role of interest influencer [in foreign policy making] is large because some interest influencers have financial resources or popular appeal to affect the ability of partisan influencers and decision makers to win elections."[25] This hypothesis held true in the LDP's relations with business and other influential groups, but it had a limited applicability to the JSP's relations with interest groups except the *Sōhyō* (General Council of Trade Unions).

As it provided a main organizational and financial support for the JSP's electoral campaigns and developed its own linkages with the PRC and the Soviet Union, the *Sōhyō* exerted significant influence over the JSP's attitude toward foreign countries. The JSP, in turn, was particularly desirous to coordinate its activities with those of the *Sōhyō* in regard to the China question. These two organizations, for example, jointly initiated and led a mass movement called the National Congress for the Restoration of Japan-China Diplomatic Relations. In examining the JSP-*Sōhyō* relations, Langdon notes: "The boundaries between party and pressure group are so weak that the party can be overwhelmed by the group."[26]

The LDP's policy-making process, on the other hand, was substantially influenced by mainstream business circles (*zaikai*), for the LDP business symbiosis was intrinsic and pervasive. In particular, the "big four" business associations—*Keidanren* (Federation of Economic Organizations), *Keizai Dōyūkai* (Japan Committee for Economic Development), *Nisshō* (Japan Chamber of Commerce and Industry), and *Nikkeiren* (Federation of Employers' Organizations)—and the Kansai Economic Federation aggregated divergent business interests and articulated them to the LDP and its government. The leading members of these powerful associations served as advisers to the Ministry of Foreign Affairs, and some of them (led by the *Keidanren* Chairman) joined the LDP's pro-Taiwan Dietmen in organizing the Committee on Japan-(Nationalist) China Cooperation and in sponsoring various anti-Peking activities. Further, the LDP or its factions maintained close financial and policy ties with Japan's major industrial-commercial complexes (*zaibatsu*)—notably, Mitsubishi, Mitsui, Sumitomo, Itōchū, and Marubeni-Iida—that had deep economic involvement in Taiwan. Even though Japan's mainstream business circles did not have a consensus on the Chinese question, their overwhelming pro-Taiwan orientations helped sustain the LDP's anti-Peking policy throughout the 1950s and 1960s. Conversely, a decisive relaxation of these orientations in the early 1970s paved the way for Sino-Japanese diplomatic normalization.

Governmental Institutions   As the ruling party, the LDP controlled the National Diet, the cabinet, and the vast and powerful bureaucratic structure, while the JSP found it difficult to exert effective political pressure upon

these formal governmental institutions. At the beginning of each Diet
session, the prime minister and his foreign minister delivered policy speeches
on Japan's foreign relations, and the JSP's chairman or his representative
presented its alternatives to the LDP's policies. As the largest opposition
party in the Diet, the JSP actively participated in parliamentary committee
work and vigorously interpellated the prime minister and his cabinet
members. In fact, the LDP government's major foreign-policy statements on
China were frequently announced and articulated in the course of parliamentary debates, especially in the Committees on Foreign Affairs and on the
Budget. Occasionally the JSP, in cooperation with other opposition forces,
introduced motions of no confidence against the prime minister or cabinet
members who they accused of making mistakes in foreign affairs. It also
initiated a variety of legislative bills, policy recommendations, and parliamentary measures that had political implication to Sino-Japanese relations.
In reality, however, all these vigorous and dynamic parliamentary activities
of the JSP performed in coordination with other opposition parties did not
have any significant results concerning Japan's foreign policy. There were
two principal reasons for this situation. First of all, the LDP enjoyed a
comfortable working majority in the Diet and managed to preserve a
remarkable level of party discipline and cohesion in important legislative
votes and debates. Second, the JSP was more apt to make a general
statement of desired policies and grandiose principles than to propose a set
of serious legislative demands that would have a realistic chance of adoption
by the Diet.

   Conditioned by the continuation of rigid ideological commitments and
confrontationist parliamentary tactics on major foreign policy issues, the
JSP was, above all, unable to adapt its behavior to political reality and to
carry through pragmatic, piecemeal compromises with the majority party.
Nor was the ruling LDP prepared to entertain any substantive compromise
with the parliamentary opposition; thus, opposition bills or resolutions
rarely passed in either house of the Diet.

   Most important, the prime minister and his cabinet members easily
overrode the opposition parties' vociferous resistance, and still survived
politically. The prime minister was effectively shielded from the immediate
political impact of violent parliamentary clashes or changing public sentiments. Unlike the president of the United States, he was not directly elected
to the executive position by popular vote, but indirectly chosen by the LDP.
So long as he obtained a winning coalition of diverse LDP factions, his
status as the party president and therefore as the prime minister was not
directly threatened. In order to be an effective national leader, of course, he
had to be sensitive to the changing parliamentary and public attitudes
toward the PRC. But Coplin and Kegley suggest that "in an open system, the
ability of partisan influencers to pressure the foreign policy decision maker is

limited by the fact that the executive usually takes the initiative and the demands of security and secrecy often limit opposition."[27] This trend was pronounced in the relationship between the LDP government and the JSP.

Finally, the JSP was even more seriously hampered by the fact that it was denied a meaningful channel of communication with the powerful bureaucratic organizations, such as the Ministry of Foreign Affairs and the Ministry of International Trade and Industry, which often initiated, and ordinarily implemented, the most important foreign-policy decisions on China. Guided and supervised by the prime minister and his political appointees, higher civil servants followed the LDP's broad foreign-policy guidelines, while invoking the principle of political neutrality to guard themselves against the opposition parties' penetration and to protect their vested interests in foreign affairs.

However, the political executives as well as the LDP's policy organs relied heavily on senior career bureaucrats for initiation and implementation of specific foreign policies. Even though civil servants constituted a fairly homogenous, elitist group of their own due to their shared social backgrounds and administrative experience, intrabureaucratic conflicts on foreign affairs were quite evident in the case of Sino-Japanese relations. The Ministry of Foreign Affairs, which did not wish to undermine Tokyo-Taipei diplomatic relations, was frequently in conflict with the Ministry of International Trade and Industry, which intended to facilitate and expand trade with the PRC. Even in the Ministry of Foreign Affairs a difference in policy preferences between hawks and doves was known to exist. Notwithstanding intrabureaucratic conflicts and jealousies, it was extremely difficult for the JSP to cultivate any foreign-policy coordination with Japanese bureaucrats, except on the basis of personal or school ties.

For all practical purposes, then, the LDP monopolized formal governmental institutions for foreign relations, while the JSP, by virtue of its minority parliamentary position and uncompromising tactics, hardly constituted a "veto group" that was powerful enough to prevent or undo the conduct of Japan's official foreign policy.[28] No doubt the Chinese were keenly aware of the inter- and intra-party relations prevailing in Japan. It was clearly evident from their behavior that they frequently sought access to the LDP or its factions in an attempt to set up effective linkages with the Japanese foreign-policy-making process. The evolving pattern of interaction between the PRC and the LDP was therefore carefully observed by the JSP, which intended to use the Chinese issue as a weapon to discredit the LDP's political integrity and external capability. Almost completely alienated from Japan's governmental institutions dealing with foreign affairs, the Japanese Socialists suffered from a lingering nightmare that, just as the Soviet Union had done in 1956, the Chinese leaders, diplomatic realists, might suddenly bypass them by concluding a negotiated diplomatic accommodation with the LDP government. Indeed, the Tokyo-Peking diplomatic rapprochement deprived the JSP of one of its most useful instruments for undermining the LDP, though the JSP reasoned that the opening of diplomatic relations was insufficient to resolve all of the possible differences between Japan and the PRC.

Intraparty Conditions

The manner in which the LDP or the JSP perceived Japan's domestic and foreign environments and translated them into policy output was undoubtedly related to a number of conditions internal to each party, such as (1) its ideological orientation, (2) factional dynamics, (3) organizational channels, and (4) policy-making procedures.

Ideological Orientation   Even though it is not easy to define the LDP's precise ideological commitments, there is little doubt that it espoused a general framework of conservative political philosophy and capitalist economic system and that it opposed all shades of a radical socialism. Attached to the "free world" in the cold-war era, the mainstream of the LDP tended to disfavor China, North Korea, and North Vietnam, but to support the staunch anti-Communist governments—such as Nationalist China, South Korea, South Vietnam, Thailand, and the Philippines. Yet the Chinese, despite their fundamentalist ideological dispositions, usually dismissed the importance of ideological incompatibility in their association with some LDP members; a more pragmatic consideration in the context of peaceful coexistence was given a higher priority in their policy toward the LDP.

At the other end of conservative-progressive ideological continuum stood the JCP and the JSP. Unlike the European Socialist parties, the Japanese Socialists never formed a government nor were members of a governing coalition, except during a brief postwar period (1947-48). This permitted them the luxury of concentrating on the correctness and purity, rather than the practical relevance, of their ideology and programs. As it lost strength at successive national and local elections and drifted further away from the prospect of becoming the governing party, its frustrated radical members were inclined to adopt the familiar, simplistic, and ready-made solutions offered by one of the most extreme brands of Marxism—Maoism. In view of their ideological inferiority complex toward the JCP, they were tempted to articulate or demonstrate the rhetoric of pure revolutionary doctrine. Among all the opposition political parties in Japan, the JSP remained the most conservative in the sense that it was unwilling to recruit youthful leaders or to accept new ideas for innovation and adaptation. All these tendencies notwithstanding, the healthy ideological discussions provoked by

Eda's "vision" in the early 1960s promised to renovate the JSP's doctrinal stand along a more pragmatic line. This promise was quickly smothered by barren factional polemics and deteriorating Sino-Soviet relations.

The toleration of a wide range of ideological inclinations, while attempting to achieve a distinctive Japanese way to socialism, limited the party's capability to present a unified foreign policy. In relation to the PRC, therefore, it was confronted by a peculiar dilemma. On the one hand, the less ideological unity or discipline it revealed, the less effective it became in dealing with the PRC. In fact, the positive correlation between ideological unity and external effectiveness was apparent in other political parties, including the LDP. The lack of ideological unity made it easier for China to penetrate the JSP's internal ideological debates. On the other hand, when the JSP articulated a clearly Japanese way to socialism, it sharpened the ideological difference between the JSP and the PRC as was demonstrated during Eda's heyday.

In general, the greater the ideological distance the JSP maintained from the PRC, the more flexibility it enjoyed in its China policy. The best ideological strategy the party could adopt toward the PRC was a *modus operandi* whereby both sides would recognize their differing social conditions and political aspirations and agree to disagree on controversial ideological issues under the principles of peaceful coexistence and mutual noninterference. This strategy was ineffective partly because ideological issues in the JSP were closely intertwined with factional dynamics. The extent to which ideological orientations were associated with international positions was blurred by the logic of factional rivalries.

Factional Dynamics   It has been claimed that whereas the Liberal-Democratic factions are primarily based on personal loyalties and pecuniary benefits, the Socialist factions are influenced more by ideological and policy considerations. This claim was challenged by the observation that the factions of both parties were characterized to the same degree by traditional sorts of *oyabun-kobun* (boss-follower) behavior. Thus Langdon perceptively argued that "it may even be a kind of traditional personal tie that is being embodied in an ideological form for the purpose of political competition and leadership."[29]

The dynamics of factional competition were not only shaped by the combined effect of hierarchical personal relations and ideological or policy differences, but were also influenced by a sharing of interests in electoral contests, campaign funds, and career backgrounds. More often than not, factional polemics on important foreign policy issues, such as China, tended to lose their policy relevance, and instead became a carefully contrived instrument of interfactional rivalry. At the same time the direction of disputes and alignments among various factions was dictated more by political expediency than by policy consistency. Cole, Totten, and Uyehara suggested that the JSP's position on China was "a barometer of factional influences and trends in party policy."[30]

Irrespective of their policy preferences and political strengths, all these factions maintained a high degree of functional autonomy and constituted an integral part of each party's political processes. Most factions had their own hierarchical leadership structures, ran separate headquarters, and sponsored periodic caucuses and other meetings. They manifested different policy tendencies and issued diverse journals and other factional publications. The degree of internal stability and political cohesion, especially on foreign-policy questions, differed from one faction to the other. Compared with the LDP's official policy, nonmainstream or antimainstream factions that did not participate in the party's leadership coalition tended to be more flexible about the PRC. In the case of the JSP, the left-wing factions were more sympathetic to and cooperative with China than the right-wing and centrist factions. In both the JSP and the LDP, the factions that failed to take part in the dominant coalition or to influence its policies on China were likely to express their own policy preferences through channels other than their party's official organs.

Organizational Channels   The disagreements on foreign policy can be a convenient instrument for the factions to use in their competition to control party organizations that make policies and allocate resources. According to its constitution, the LDP has four formal decision-making organs—the party conference, the Assembly of the Members of the National Diet, the Executive Council, and the Policy Affairs Research Council (PARC). Even though the annual party conference, consisting of all conservative dietmen and four delegates from each prefectural federation, is called "the supreme organ of the party," it did not play an important role in initiating or determining the party's policy on China. Strictly controlled by party officials and factional leaders, the conference merely rubber-stamped the action program prepared by the party leadership. Nor did the Assembly of the Members of the National Diet assume a crucial policy-making role.[31]

As far as the LDP's formal formulation of foreign policies was concerned, the PARC's functional units—the Investigative Committee on Foreign Affairs and the Division on Foreign Affairs—usually initiated, deliberated, and formulated a policy recommendation, which the PARC Deliberation Commission or a meeting of the PARC's chairman and vice-chairmen reviewed and approved. Upon receipt of the PARC's report, the thirty-member Executive Council made an official party decision on the recommended policy. In reality, however, the prime minister, as president of the governing party and as chief of the executive branch of government, exercised a substantial influence over the party's policy-making processes on China. After all, he appointed the LDP's powerful secretary-general (usually from his own faction), vice-president, and chairmen of the Executive

Council and the PARC, and controlled the composition of these two councils. The prime minister's statements and actions were not necessarily synonymous with the LDP's official positions, but in most cases they were mutually compatible and interchangeable.

For the normal conduct of foreign affairs, the prime minister relied upon his foreign minister and senior bureaucrats of the Ministry of Foreign Affairs, but he rarely made a major foreign-policy decision on China unless it was approved by his cabinet and the appropriate party organs. Constrained by interfactional checks and balances both in his cabinet and in the party organs, it was difficult for him to decide upon and implement a bold, innovative policy in regard to highly controversial foreign-policy issues, notably the Chinese question. In the event of serious intraparty disputes or party-cabinet disagreements, the prime minister sometimes convened informal ad hoc decision-making groups, such as the "top six" conference and the party officials' conference.[32]

As the highest decision-making organ of the JSP, the annual party congress adopted basic policies and chose members for other principal party organs. Contrary to the LDP's brief, orderly, and perfunctory national conference, the Socialist congress, heavily represented by local party activists, was an open, free, and lively forum for earnest debates and noisy procedures. The congress delegates interpellated the party leadership, explained their own positions, and adopted an action program that spelled out the party's positions and activities on domestic and foreign issues. The exchange of arguments on the action program therefore revealed much information as to how the local party leaders perceived the party's role in international politics.[33]

Composed of about two dozen members elected by the congress, the Central Executive Committee (CEC) was the supreme executive organ. It had jurisdiction over appointments of party functionaries and nomination procedures for electoral candidates, and it established party policies when the congress was not in session. A clearly differentiated factional distribution in the CEC made it the central arena for intraparty power struggles. Of particular relevance to the party's role in international politics were the Bureau of International Affairs, the Bureau of National Movements, and the Policy Planning Board. Ad hoc committees, such as one on Japan-China relations, also exercised a considerable voice in determining the party's approach toward the given issue.

The chairman of the CEC was no more than *primus inter pares* among its members, but, as the party's nominal head, his ideological tendencies, international outlook, and leadership style exerted an unmistakable influence over the party's approach toward China. The effectiveness of his leadership depended upon the extent to which he obtained cooperation from a majority of the CEC members and, in particular, from the secretary-general, who, unlike his conservative counterpart, was directly elected by the congress. Although both the chairman and the secretary-general were ultimately accountable to the national congress and its Central Executive Committee, the combination of their party posts with their factional support rendered their respective roles a significant variable in the formulation and implementation of the party's foreign policies.

Decisional Situations   Since both major political parties were characterized by factional diversity and organizational diffuseness, the process of making their policies toward China was extremely complex. Added to this complexity was the traditional Japanese system of decision making, which showed preferences for unanimous rather than majoritarian rule, for collective decision rather than individual one, and for blurred compromises rather than forceful decisions. The juxtaposition of these traditional and factional characteristics made it equally difficult for both parties to bring about a decisive reorientation of their China policies. Unlike the JCP, the LDP and the JSP proved incapable of unifying their respective posture on China primarily because they were governed by a built-in system of factional and organizational balances. Consequently, policy *immobilisme* was easily set in these two parties, and they were frequently inclined only to make a routine response to the external political stimuli from China. Any attempted radical change in each party's major position on China provoked an intraparty crisis unless it was approved by more than a majority of its factional leaders.

All other domestic and external conditions aside, a particular foreign-policy decision made either by the LDP or by the JSP was a function of interfactional conflicts and compromises. The types of policy decisions therefore differed according to the three possible interfactional relations: (1) a monopolistic decision made by a preponderant faction or by a top leader, (2) a majoritarian decision made by a coalition of mainstream factions, and (3) a consensual decision reached as a compromise among conflicting factional positions. The first type, which did not take place often in both parties except under extraordinary circumstances, had a dynamic or innovative element, but one faction's monopoly of policy-making procedure easily exacerbated interfactional tensions. Some partisan decisions, especially those made in the JSP's national congress, belonged to the second type, but there was always a danger that the anti- or non-mainstream factions, alienated from the normal policy-making channels, felt free to express their factional views even at the expense of the party's official line. This danger increased the probability that these factions were susceptible to penetration by foreign units, such as the PRC. The third type of decision making minimized the extent of direct inter-factional disagreements because it was a product of suprafactional compromise based on a consensus. This was a common tendency in a small decision-making unit, such as the cabinet, the LDP's councils, and the JSP's Central Executive Committee. By placing a priority on factional harmony rather than on policy innovation, the consensual decision was conveniently ambivalent and unimaginative.

While the complex processes of political estrangement, diplomatic reconciliation, and economic cooperation between Japan and the PRC are discussed in the following chapters, special attention is paid to the manner in which Japan's political and economic groups, particularly the LDP and the JSP, responded to their external environments, especially China's policy shifts, and manipulated a set of domestic political conditions for their respective approaches toward China. In order to explain the different attitudes and policies of both major political parties, the dynamics of inter- and intra-party relations in Japan is taken into full consideration. Most importantly, the developmental pattern of contemporary Sino-Japanese relations from 1949 through 1972 is identified and analyzed in the broad context of Japan's domestic-foreign linkages.

2

The Processes of Political Estrangement

The San Francisco System and its Effects

San Francisco Treaties   The development of Sino-Japanese relations in the immediate postwar period was largely determined by the outcome of the Chinese civil war and the changing U.S. policy in East Asia. Strictly controlled by the MacArthur occupation authorities, the Japanese government lacked both legal ability and psychological readiness to pursue an independent foreign policy toward China. When the Chinese Communist Party (CCP) was about to gain a decisive victory over the Kuomintang troops in 1949, U.S. Secretary of State Dean Acheson admitted in the White Paper on China that the "unfortunate" and "ominous" result in China was the "product of internal Chinese forces, forces which this country tried to influence but could not."[1] Despite mounting congressional criticism against the "loss" of China, President Truman took a flexible wait-and-see position toward China, and he made it clear in January 1950 that the United States would neither use its armed forces to defend Chiang Kai-shek's Taiwan nor to provide military aid or advice to it.[2] This initial attitude, coupled with the U.S. intention to stimulate Japan's economic reconstruction as a prerequisite of political stability, led to a relaxation of restrictions on Sino-Japanese trade.

Yet the Chinese Communists, in cooperation with the Soviet Union, espoused a doctrinaire two-camp international outlook and adopted a hardline policy of extreme hostility toward the United States and Japan. They arrested and detained a U.S. consul-general and his staff at Mukden (now Shenyang) and seized its consular premises and property in Peking. Thus the early possibility of Sino-American diplomatic reconciliation was effectively thwarted. Moreover, they attacked the alleged U.S. plan to protect Taiwan and to remilitarize Japan. The Japanese Communist Party (JCP) was called upon to lead a violent struggle against U.S. and Japanese "reactionaries."[3] In the Treaty of Friendship, Alliance and Mutual Assistance signed at Moscow in February 1950, the People's Republic of China and the Soviet Union undertook to adopt "all necessary measures" for the purpose of preventing the revival of Japanese imperialism and the resumption of aggression on the part of Japan or "any other state that may collaborate with Japan directly or indirectly in acts of aggression."[4] They also expressed their common desire to consult with other allied powers for the purpose of concluding a joint peace treaty with Japan as soon as possible.

The creation of this Sino-Soviet military alliance aroused a great deal of apprehension among U.S. and Japanese leaders, who wished to restructure the occupation system in a manner consistent with the emerging regional reality. This need was made more imperative by the outbreak of the Korean War and the direct military confrontation between the United States and China. To strengthen its position in East Asia in the face of this new threat, the U.S. government outlawed the JCP, released some war criminals from prison, started Japanese rearmament, and accelerated John Foster Dulles's negotiations for a multilateral peace treaty between Japan and allied powers.

Dulles's immediate domestic task was to obtain a bipartisan congressional support for his diplomatic efforts and to seek a compromise between the Department of State and the Department of Defense over the security arrangements in a peace settlement with Japan. As a leading foreign-policy spokesman of the Republican Party, he could neutralize any opposition from his party, but the State-Defense cleavage was deep and fundamental. Whereas the State Department wanted a prompt, nonpunitive peace treaty with Japan, despite Moscow's and Peking's obstructions, the Defense Department considered it premature unless there was an assurance that U.S. troops would continue to remain in Japan and that the Soviet Union and the PRC would sign the peace treaty. As a State-Defense compromise, but with General MacArthur's endorsement, Dulles sought to make a bilateral security treaty with Japan inseparable from any peace settlement and to urge Japan's substantial rearmament at 350,000 men.[5]

One of the thorny international issues faced by Dulles, especially in terms of Anglo-American cooperation, was which of the two contending Chinese governments should be invited to the forthcoming peace conference. The United States continued to regard the Republic of China on Taiwan as the lawful government of China, but Great Britain had already recognized the PRC in January 1950. Caught in between, Japanese Prime Minister Yoshida Shigeru, who was basically pro-British in general foreign-policy outlook, remained noncommittal. However, Chinese Foreign Minister Chou En-lai declared that since the PRC was the only legal government of China, it must take part in preparing, drafting, and signing a peace treaty with Japan; and any treaty concluded without its participation should therefore be considered "illegal" and "void."[6] In June 1951, Dulles and British Foreign Secretary Herbert Morrison reached a compromise formula stating that, while the United States, as a host country, would invite neither Taipei nor Peking to sign the peace treaty at San Francisco, "Japan's future attitude toward China must necessarily be for determination by Japan itself in the exercise of the sovereignty and independent status contemplated by the treaty."[7] It was also decided that Japan should make a simple renunciation of its former sovereignty over Taiwan, the Kurile Islands, southern Sakhalin, and other foreign territories without specifying their recipients.

At the San Francisco peace conference in September 1951, Acheson, in response to Prime Minister Yoshida's worrisome inquiry, suggested that the question of Japan's future relations with China be subjected to deliberate study and careful decisions following the conference.[8] As president of the conference, Acheson utilized parliamentary maneuvers to reject Andrei Gromyko's move to invite the PRC to San Francisco. On the morning of September 8, Yoshida signed the peace treaty, as drafted by the United States and Great Britain, with 48 countries—over the protest of the Soviet Union, Poland, and Czechoslovakia. The afternoon of the same day, he also signed a secretly negotiated mutual security treaty with the United States; this was clearly intended to safeguard an independent Japan and to constitute a countervailing force to the Sino-Soviet alliance.[9]

On many occasions China publicly registered strong opposition to the Anglo-American draft treaty and the San Francisco conference itself. In August 1951, Chou En-lai stated: "(The draft treaty) completely violates international agreements, damages the interests of the allied powers at war with Japan, shows hostility to China and the Soviet Union, constitutes a menace to the peoples of Asia, disrupts the peace and security of the world, and is detrimental to the interests of the Japanese people."[10] As alternatives, he demanded the conclusion of an "over-all and genuine peace treaty" between Japan and all allied powers, the participation of the PRC—"the principal power," which had fought against Japan since 1937—in all phases of peace negotiations, and the return of Taiwan, the Pescadores (Penghu), the Spratly (Nanwei or Nansha) Islands, and the Paracel (Hsisha) Islands to China. Other demands included a ban on the "remnant and reviving militaristic organizations" in Japan, the development of Japan's peaceful economy and normal trade with China and the Soviet Union, and the withdrawal of U.S. occupation forces from Japan, the Ryūkyū Islands, the Ogasawara (Bonin) Islands, and other Japanese territories.[11] On the question of war reparations, Chou declared, "those states which had been occupied by Japan, had suffered great losses, and have difficulties in rehabilitation by themselves should reserve their right of claiming reparation." He did not specify whether or not China belonged to the category of those states. Upon conclusion of the San Francisco conference, Chou issued another angry protest against the peace treaty and the U.S.-Japan security treaty; both treaties of hostility toward China and the Soviet Union, he warned, would drag Japan into a new aggressive war and plunge her into ruin.[12]

Even though Yoshida rejected Dulles's original proposal for Japan's full-scale rearmament, he not only favored a U.S. military guarantee of Japan's external security, but also intended to reorganize and expand the 75,000-man National Police Reserve force for her internal security. One of the main reasons given for his security policy was China's massive armed intervention in the Korean War, but the U.S.-Japan security treaty was primarily thought of as an effective deterrent against a potential attack from the Soviet Union.[13] Yoshida himself dismissed the likelihood of a direct military threat from China because it lacked sophisticated naval and air capabilities and an industrial basis for their development. Yet the security treaty contained some military provisions that China regarded as provocative to its own national security.

As a "provisional arrangement" for Japan's defense, the United States gained the right to retain its armed forces and military bases in and about Japan and assumed a responsibility to protect Japan against external armed attack as well as internal riots and disturbances. Of particular relevance to China's security interest was the provision (Article 1) that allowed the U.S. forces stationed in Japan to be utilized for the "maintenance of international peace and security in the Far East," for the "Far East" undoubtedly embraced the Taiwan area and the Korean peninsula. Moreover, Yoshida, in his exchange of notes with Acheson at San Francisco, agreed to provide the use of Japanese facilities and services in support of any U.N. military action in the Far East.[14] Specifically, it was a commitment to render Japan continuously available as a vital rear area for logistic and other support to the U.S. military activities in Korea. Viewed from the perspective of China's long-range strategic interest, the most crucial aspect of the San Francisco system was the U.S. right to use the Ryūkyū Islands as its anti-Communist military bastion adjacent to the Chinese coast. Hence the Chinese opposition to the U.S.-Japanese security arrangements was more serious than that to the peace treaty per se.

Japan-Taiwan Peace Treaty   Meanwhile, the Japanese National Diet was deeply embroiled in an intense partisan dispute over the ratification of both treaties. The overwhelming majority of conservative dietmen—both "liberals" and "democrats"—were favorable to the San Francisco outcome, despite some democrats' misgivings, but the precariously united Socialist Party was split into two rival factions by policy differences. As a general policy for the peace treaty, the Socialist Party had adopted in December 1949 three principles: that an overall peace treaty with both international camps be concluded, that Japan's neutral status be preserved, and that foreign military bases in Japan be banned. Although it had wavered in the aftermath of the Korean War, it had added another principle in January 1951—namely, its opposition to Japanese rearmament.[15] In their meeting with Dulles in the same month, Suzuki Mosaburō and Asanuma Inejirō of the Socialist Party explained their ideas for an unarmed, neutral Japan, but Dulles rejected them as completely unrealistic, particularly because of the Korean War and the Chinese intervention.[16] The enunciation of these four principles, however, failed to prevent the party's two-way division at its eighth National Congress in October 1951. While the left-wing Socialist Party opposed both treaties, the right-wing Socialist Party decided to approve the peace treaty but to reject the security treaty.

In the course of Diet debates, Prime Minister Yoshida indicated his willingness to set up government overseas agencies—as the highest form of foreign relationship then permitted to Japan—both in Taipei and in China's Shanghai.[17] However, prior to the U.S. ratification of both treaties, fifty-six senators signed a letter to President Truman, in which they expressed a serious concern about Yoshida's possible recognition of the PRC. The letter buttressed the efforts of the U.S. government which, despite the Dulles-Morrison agreement for Japan's sovereign and independent determination of its China policy, was from the beginning determined to bring about a bilateral peace treaty between Japan and the Republic of China.

Against this background, Dulles, accompanied by U.S. Senators H. Alexander Smith of New Jersey and John J. Sparkman of Alabama as a pressure group, visited Japan in December 1951 and strongly urged Yoshida to adopt a foreign-policy posture consistent with the U.S. positions and to commit himself to a clearly pro-Taipei policy as a quid pro quo for regaining Japan's political independence. Accordingly, on December 24, 1951, Yoshida wrote to Dulles a letter that was probably drafted by Dulles himself.[18] The Yoshida letter stated that his government would be prepared as soon as legally possible to conclude a treaty with the Republic of China to reestablish normal relations, and that the treaty would be applicable to "all territories which are now, or which may hereafter be, under the control" of the Republic of China. It was also noted that Japan had already established a government overseas agency in Taiwan but not in mainland China. Most important, Yoshida assured Dulles and skeptical U.S. senators that his government had no intention of concluding a bilateral treaty with the Chinese Communist regime; as reasons for this policy, he said that this regime was condemned by the United Nations as an aggressor, that it supported the JCP's program for a violent overthrow of the constitutional system in Japan, and that the Sino-Soviet military alliance was directed against Japan.[19] Thus the important foreign-policy commitment of an independent Japan was formally declared while Japan was still under U.S. military occupation. The Yoshida letter helped the U.S. Senate's ratification of both treaties but, predictably, displeased the PRC. Vice-

Minister of Foreign Affairs Chang Han-fu assailed the letter as a flagrant act of provocation launched by American "imperialists" and Japanese "reactionaries" against the PRC.[20] He called for the Japanese people's struggle against a prospective peace treaty between Japan and the "remnant Kuomintang reactionaries."

On the same day (April 28, 1952) that both of the treaties concluded at San Francisco came into force, Japan and the Republic of China signed at Taipei a bilateral peace treaty, an accompanying protocol, and other related documents.[21] The Japan-Taiwan peace treaty, which was achieved under intense U.S. pressure, was a logical extension as well as an integral part of the San Francisco system.[22] As stated in the Yoshida letter, both signatories understood that the treaty was applicable to all territories that were then, or that may thereafter be, under the Nationalist Chinese control. The Republic of China gave up its right to demand reparations from Japan and recognized Japan's renunciation of "all right, title and claim" to Taiwan, the Pescadores, the Spratly Islands, and the Paracel Islands. The fact that the legal recipient of these islands was again left ambiguous in the treaty led to a subsequent controversy about their exact status; at the time of Diet considerations, however, Foreign Minister Okazaki Katsuo unequivocally called Taiwan and the Pescadores China's territories.[23] Further, in response to a right-wing Socialist member's question in the House of Councillors, Yoshida made it clear that as the Japan-Republic of China peace treaty would not apply to all Chinese territories, he hoped to conclude a treaty with "one total China" in the future.[24]

While the Japanese Socialists opposed this treaty itself, Secretary-General Miki Takeo of the Democratic Party was critical of the speed with which the Liberal Party government concluded it with Taipei.[25] Obviously the suggestive nuance of Yoshida's subtle legalistic remarks did not impress the Chinese Communist leaders, who regarded the treaty as an "open insult and act of hostility to the Chinese people." Under the U.S. "order," Chou En-lai contended, the Yoshida government had become the "stablemate of the remnant Chiang Kai-shek gang" and had prepared a new aggressive war against China.[26] "The Chinese people," he warned, "will heighten their vigilance and get ready to strike these war provocateurs heavy blows as the occasion demands." While these Chinese claims were exaggerated, the depth of their concern with this estrangement in Tokyo-Peking relations was justified. For once the San Francisco system and its corollary, the Japan-Taiwan peace treaty, became a fait accompli, over Peking's vehement verbal protest, it was destined to govern the basic direction of Japan's policy toward China for the next two decades.

China's Peaceful Overtures   In part due to the new reality in Japan and the failure of the JCP's violent struggle, the Chinese gradually softened their militant posture and assumed a more pragmatic policy of peaceful coexistence toward Japan, especially after the death of Stalin and the armistice agreement in Korea.[27] This shifting coincided with Yoshida's willingness to increase nondiplomatic contacts between Japan and China. Consequently, the Chinese signed the first two unofficial trade accords with Japanese political leaders, started the repatriation of Japanese nationals from China, stopped capturing Japanese fishermen, and promoted various cultural exchange programs with Japan.

The emphasis of the Chinese on "peace and cooperation," instead of "struggle and revolution" harmonized with the peaceful strategy subsequently adopted by the Soviet Union. The decision to alter their policy toward Japan also reflected a reappraisal of their domestic and external conditions. At the international level the Chinese had evidently learned through their recent experience with the Korean and Indochinese conflicts that it was highly risky and costly to assist violent national liberation movements. They apparently believed that any radical attempt to change the world-wide strategic equilibrium would be effectively resisted by the massive retaliatory power of the United States and its allies. The Korean War, in particular, had inflicted great punishment on the Chinese army and had revealed striking shortcomings in Chinese military technology and preparedness. When their national security was directly threatened by MacArthur's proposal to bomb Manchuria, they must have taken stock of their limited strategic capabilities. The Chinese indeed were seriously concerned with the idea that the United States might attack them—possibly with nuclear weapons. And the relative advantages that the United States would have enjoyed in such a conflict were forceful arguments for a softening in foreign policy, which could be expected to remove potential causes of a Sino-American war. Another factor contributing to China's external prudence was its current program of socialist economic reconstruction, political consolidation, and military modernization. The first Five-Year Economic Plan (1953–57) required a concentration of their limited resources, human and material, on the domestic front, to the detriment of external "adventures." Their economic ambitions at home, together with the proven strength of their foreign foes, made it necessary for China to settle for a peaceful international environment.

As part of this global peace offensive, Chou En-lai told Professor Ōyama Ikuo (member of the House of Councillors, chairman of the Japanese Peace Committee, and a recipient of the Stalin Peace Prize) for the first time in September 1953 that China was willing to restore "normal relations" with Japan and to expand mutual trade on the basis of "peaceful coexistence."[28] He added that "an independent, democratic, peaceful, and free Japan" must have her own self-defense forces; of course, Japanese remilitarization under U.S. auspices was opposed. A month thereafter, Vice-Premier Kuo Mo-jo, who had studied medicine at Kyushu Imperial University, indicated the possibility of a Sino-Japanese nonaggression pact.[29] The Chinese also refrained from denouncing Prime Minister Yoshida's decision to conclude a mutual defense assistance agreement with the U.S. and to enact the Defense Agency Establishment Law as well as the Self-Defense Forces Law in the spring of 1954. In order to defend Japan against "direct and indirect aggression" and to maintain "public order," he established the National Defense Agency and strengthened the Ground, Maritime, and Air Self-Defense Forces.

The conciliatory Chinese policy in Asia was further demonstrated at the Geneva Conference on Indo-China in 1954. By making a crucial contribution to the successful negotiations at Geneva, Chou En-lai displayed China's peaceful intentions and enhanced its voice in the management of Asian affairs. In June—during the recess of the Geneva conference—he incorporated the five principles of peaceful coexistence in his separate joint statements with Indian Prime Minister Nehru and Burmese Prime Minister U Nu. The Chou-Nehru statement observed that if these principles were applied in general international relations, they could form a solid foundation for peace and security in the world, replacing the existing atmosphere of "fear and apprehension" with a "feeling of confidence."[30] Subsequently, in his talks with Japanese Diet leaders, Chou emphasized these principles as a basis for normalizing Sino-Japanese relationships. At the same time Mao Tse-tung and Khrushchev expressed their common desire to take steps to improve their relations with Japan under the principle of peaceful coexistence.[31] The principal objective of China's peace offensive in East Asia was to break or loosen Japan's ties with the United States and Taiwan, to prevent Japan from becoming a resurgent militarist force, and to facilitate diplomatic and economic cooperation with Japan.

The Yoshida government, which had never violated its commitments to the United States and Taiwan, remained largely unresponsive to these Sino-Soviet diplomatic overtures, but Prime Minister Hatoyama Ichirō of the Democratic Party, who replaced Yoshida in December 1954, took a more favorable attitude toward Moscow and Peking. After his first cabinet session, he, while noting the U.S. apprehension, stressed the priority of opening peaceful relations and economic intercourse with the Soviet Union and China.[32] The next day his foreign minister, Shigemitsu Mamoru, who had served as Japan's wartime foreign minister and minister of Greater East Asia and ambassador to the Nanking government, London, and Moscow, and who had signed the instrument of Japanese surrender aboard the USS *Missouri* in September 1945, expressed the new government's intention to normalize diplomatic relations with both Communist countries on "mutually acceptable terms."[33] Pleased with Hatoyama's and Shigemitsu's statements, Chou En-lai, in his report to the Chinese People's Political Consultative Conference in December, reiterated his readiness to restore diplomatic relations with Japan provided the Japanese government so desired.[34] In a further attempt to encourage Hatoyama's conciliatory move, the *People's Daily* (December 30, 1954) editorially stated that it was not necessary for Japan to sever its relations with the United States as a condition for normalization of Chinese-Japanese relations, though the notion of two independent Chinese states was absurd.

This indirect exchange of mutually reinforcing declarations and overtures persisted throughout Prime Minister Hatoyama's tenure, but he was restrained by the U.S. government's toughening anti-Peking policy, which was represented by the U.S.-Taiwan mutual defense treaty signed in December 1954 and by the congressional resolution on Formosa passed in January 1955. Secretary of State Dulles argued that the U.S. capabilities of massive retaliation, not diplomatic accords, were the only effective way to rescue from Communist aggression nations unable to defend themselves.[35] Not only did he erect a bilateral and collective system of peripheral military containment against China, but he also strengthened the measures to isolate China in diplomatic and economic areas. It was therefore not surprising that unlike his successful diplomatic negotiations with the Soviet Union, Hatoyama's approach toward Peking was frustrated.

Aware of this potential policy cleavage between Japan and the United States, Chou En-lai accelerated his peace campaign toward the Hatoyama government. When Hatoyama decided, despite Washington's displeasure, to send an official Japanese delegation led by State Minister Takasaki Tatsunosuke (ex-president of Manchurian Heavy Industry) to the Bandung conference in April 1955, Chou praised his courage and used the opportunity to sell China's policy of peaceful coexistence to Asian and African participants. At Bandung he articulated a hope to restore diplomatic relations with Japan in the framework of the five principles of peaceful coexistence.[36] More significantly, in his informal talk with Takasaki—the highest incumbent Japanese official he had ever met, Chou explored the possibility of translating his hope into reality. No diplomatic breakthrough was achieved in their talk, but their friendship paved the way to Takasaki's important role in the subsequent Sino-Japanese trade. A more concrete outcome of Chou's Bandung diplomacy was the opening of Sino-American ambassadorial talks, which started at Geneva in August 1955.[37]

Apparently encouraged by Chou's friendly conversation with Takasaki and his opening of the ambassadorial talks with the United States, the Chinese government initiated a direct diplomatic contact with Japan. Chou was apparently confident that the combination of Japan's domestic political conditions—particularly Hatoyama's favorable disposition—and of an expected new thaw in Sino-American relations would be conducive to the process of this decisive diplomatic step. The channel used for this purpose was an exchange of diplomatic notes between Japanese and Chinese consuls-general at Geneva—Tatsuke Keiichi and Shen Ping, respectively. Even though a spokesman of the Chinese Foreign Ministry publicly refuted Tatsuke's first note to Shen, dated July 15, 1955, in which Japan asked for an investigation of 40,000 Japanese nationals still missing in China, Shen, in his secret reply dated August 17, proposed that, in order to promote normalization of Sino-Japanese relations and contribute to further relaxation of international situations, the Japanese government send a delegation to Peking to discuss trade, exchange of persons, status of overseas residents, and "other important problems" of mutual interest.[38] On the same day, in Peking, Chou indicated to a delegation of Japanese journalists and broadcasters that the immediate abrogation of the Japan-Taiwan peace treaty was not a necessary precondition for the normalization of Sino-Japanese diplomatic relations.[39] The intent of these Chinese overtures, both public and secret, was clear enough, but the Japanese response was less than positive. On August 29 and October 20, Tatsuke delivered other notes to Shen, in which the Japanese government again requested China's humanitarian repatriation of missing Japanese nationals and war criminals. Curiously, however, neither note mentioned anything about the proposed Peking conference. Again, in a secret note dated November 4, Shen invited a Japanese government delegation to Peking and argued that the time was ripe for restoration of diplomatic relations between China and Japan.[40]

The Japanese government remained silent on the repeated invitation, so Chou exerted verbal pressure—at the Chinese People's Political Consultative Conference in January 1956, he stated his regret that the Japanese government had failed to respond to China's two formal proposals for diplomatic negotiations.[41] This public pressure, rather than moving Japan closer to diplomatic relations with China, had exactly the opposite result, however. A few days later, when asked about Chou's statement in the House of Representatives Committee on Foreign Affairs, Foreign Minister Shigemitsu flatly denied such Chinese proposals and ruled out the possibility of diplomatic normalization with China.[42] To substantiate its own position, the Chinese government was therefore forced to publish the full texts of its two notes, which it did on February 11, 1956. So ended the first round of China's serious efforts to normalize diplomatic relations with Japan; it took sixteen more years for China to start the second round.

The important question here is why the Hatoyama government, which had publicly pledged to improve relations with China, failed to accommodate Chinese diplomatic initiative. According to Suzuki Mosaburō (JSP adviser), Hatoyama told him in 1956 that he had failed to establish diplomatic relations with China owing to the strong objection from the United States, and that he felt the JSP should lead a movement for Sino-Japanese diplomatic normalization.[43] Suzuki's statement, with its unmistakable partisan flavor, may not be accepted at face value, but there was little doubt that the United States as well as Taiwan had protested against Hatoyama's initial flirtation with China. Needless to say, the U.S. policy of diplomatic isolation against China was being rigidly enforced in Asia. In addition, there existed the legally binding Japan-Taiwan peace treaty, and the Japanese government, which was striving to enter the United Nations, was reluctant to irritate Taiwan—a veto-equipped, permanent member of the Security Council.

More important, Hatoyama was constrained by a number of other domestic and foreign conditions. No doubt he attached, from the beginning, a higher priority to diplomatic rapprochement with the Soviet Union than with China, but the Chinese initiative came at a time when he was deeply troubled by the deadlocked Soviet-Japanese negotiations over northern territorial issues. The timing was such that he was unable to respond positively to China. Moreover, his conciliatory approach toward the Soviet Union and China confronted a growing opposition within his own cabinet (led by Foreign Minister Shigemitsu) and among conservative dietmen (led by Yoshida's adherents). Since his Democratic Party did not command a majority in the National Diet, Hatoyama had to take into account the Liberal Party's strong anti-Peking orientation. Even after the Liberal-Democratic merger in November 1955, he was inevitably sensitive to the recalcitrant Yoshida faction. Hence his ability to conduct an innovative foreign policy was crippled by his domestic and intraconservative political weakness; understandably, he did not want to aggravate the situation and to spoil the opportunity of Japanese-Soviet accord by introducing yet another thorny external issue. It must be noted here that a sizable number of Yoshida's followers, in protest over Hatoyama's "sell-out" policy, did not take part in the Diet's ratification of the Japanese-Soviet joint declaration. Compared with the Japanese-Soviet diplomatic normalization, the question of Japanese-Chinese diplomatic relations was far more controversial in the LDP due partly to the Japan-Taiwan peace treaty.

Even though the Chinese were disappointed by the Soviet Union, which did not tie its diplomatic normalization with Japan to the similar arrangement between Peking and Tokyo, they continued to suggest diplomatic contacts with Japan throughout 1956.[44] Neither Hatoyama nor his successor Ishibashi Tanzan could offer any encouragement to their hopes for diplomatic normalization. Nevertheless, in nondiplomatic areas, both Hatoyama and Ishibashi were ready and able to assist various types of vigorous interactions between Japan and China. When the Chinese delegation headed by Lei Jen-min visited Japan and concluded the third unofficial trade agreement with Japanese political leaders in May 1955, it was Hatoyama who promised to support its implementation. Other agreements were concluded on fisheries in April 1955, on cultural exchanges in November 1955, and on repatriation of Japanese war criminals in June 1956. By August 1956, China had released

1,062 Japanese war criminals. The volume of two-way trade reached a postwar peak during 1956. The first Chinese commercial exhibit was held at Tokyo and Osaka in the fall of 1955; in return, a Japanese exhibit was held in Peking and Shanghai the following year. Also the exchange of visitors increased rapidly during 1955 and 1956; more than 2,000 Japanese citizens visited China during these two years, and a number of Chinese delegations, though containing only one-tenth of the number of Japanese visitors, came to Japan.[45]

The rise of Kishi Nobusuke (ex-director of the General Affairs Board of Manchukuo and minister of Commerce and Industry in Tōjō's wartime cabinet) to a leading position of Japanese foreign policy—first as foreign minister in December 1956 and then as prime minister (and concurrently foreign minister) in February 1957—contributed to a gradual deterioration in Sino-Japanese relations. With strong personal commitments to the United States and Taiwan, Kishi was instrumental in preventing the establishment of a Chinese resident trade mission in Japan. During his tour of South and Southeast Asia in May 1957, he told Indian Prime Minister Nehru that Japan could not recognize the PRC because the United Nations had condemned it as an aggressor.[46] Furthermore, as the first Japanese prime minister to visit Taiwan, Kishi reportedly confided to Chiang Kai-shek in June that it was necessary for Japan and Taiwan to cooperate for Asian stability and world peace and that he would welcome Chiang's recovery of mainland China.[47] Soon thereafter, he went to the United States and warned against China's efforts to infiltrate the entire region of Asia. Even though the Chinese initially refrained from criticizing the Kishi cabinet in early 1957, they launched open attacks aginst his trips to Taiwan and the United States. In his interview with Japanese broadcasters and correspondents in July, Chou assailed Kishi's "open hostility" and "slanderous statements" toward China.[48] The Chinese attack was soon extended to Kishi's alleged attempt to revise the peace clause in the Constitution, to incorporate Japan in the U.S. nuclear system, and to prepare the revival of Japanese militarism.[49]

Opposition Diplomacy   As the LDP government became increasingly involved in an acrimonious conflict with the PRC, the opposition JSP spearheaded "people's diplomacy" with China and used it as a tool of its anti-Kishi campaign. In April 1957, the JSP dispatched to Peking its first official mission led by Secretary-General Asanuma Inejirō, culminating a gradual, two-year shift in its China policy. When the two rival Socialist Parties decided to form a unified Japan Socialist Party in October 1955, they adopted a broad foreign policy outline on China.[50] They pledged (1) to work for the establishment of diplomatic relations between Japan and the PRC, (2) to seek the early repatriation of Japanese nationals and war criminals from China, and the conclusion of intergovernmental trade agreements, and

(3) to help resolve the international tensions over Taiwan by peaceful means. However, due to factional disagreements, they failed to clarify their official positions on the Japan-Taiwan peace treaty and on "two Chinas." The leftist factions were constantly pressing the party officials to recognize the PRC as the only lawful government of China, but the Central Executive Committee (CEC) formally adopted in May 1956 an unmistakable "two-China" position. It urged the Japanese government to normalize diplomatic relations with the PRC at once, but to preserve Japan's de facto relations with the Nationalist Chinese government on Taiwan.[51] Neither Peking nor Taipei were appreciative of this position, but the pro-Peking sentiment was steadily growing in the JSP.

At the thirteenth JSP National Congress in January 1957, a dominant coalition of leftist factions passed the Action Program, which specifically rejected any form of "two-China" scheme. The JSP was instructed to lead a national movement for the conclusion of intergovernmental trade accords, the exchange of commercial missions, the abolition of COCOM regulations, and the conclusion of agreements on fisheries and cultural exchange.[52] As an organ to carry out these objectives, the CEC set up a twenty-one-member Special Committee for Restoration of Japan-China Diplomatic Relations (Nitchū kokkō kaifuku tokubetsu iinkai) headed by Dietman Katsumata Seiichi.[53] Already, in October 1956, Katsumata had met with Chou En-lai in Peking; Chou had expressed his extreme interest in the JSP's five-year economic plan and fiscal policy, and had invited its delegation to China.[54] Thus the Action Program paved the way for the factionally balanced JSP mission to China, but the CEC decided in March 1957—just prior to the mission's departure—that the restoration of Sino-Japanese diplomatic relations should be unconditional, but added that "in the transition until the ruling power of the People's Republic of China is actually extended to the Taiwan area, Japan's relations with the Taiwanese government will continue as a matter of fact." The last point was in conflict with the Action Program, but the CEC, influenced by its right-wing members, did not wish to initiate the abrogation of the Japan-Taiwan peace treaty or to terminate Japan's de facto relations with Taiwan in nondiplomatic fields.[55] The Kishi government issued passports to the Socialist delegates only after obtaining their written promise that they would not engage in "diplomatic negotiations" with China.[56]

After a series of extensive discussions with Mao Tse-tung, Chou En-lai, and other Chinese officials, Asanuma joined Chang Hsi-jo, president of the Chinese People's Institute of Foreign Affairs, in signing a joint statement on April 22, 1957—the first such statement concluded between China and a Japanese political party.[57] With the agreement that Taiwan was China's internal matter, they declared that "in view of the geographical and historical relations between the two countries and the present situation, the two sides fully agree that the time has come for the governments of Japan and the PRC to restore diplomatic relations as soon as possible, formally and completely." The statement recorded their complete agreement on a number of other issues—such as the PRC's right to representation in the United Nations, the repudiation of any form of "two-China" policy, and the need for the conclusion of intergovernmental accords on economic, technological, and cultural exchange programs. The JSP delegates had a strong impression that China might renounce its right of war reparations at the time of diplomatic negotiations. They also obtained from China some specific concessions and promises in regard to the investigation of missing Japanese nationals, the release of six Japanese war criminals, the drafting of a comprehensive long-range trade plan, and technical exchange programs in textile industries.

Of particular importance to Sino-Japanese strategic relations was a clarification of Mao's and Chou's views on nuclear weapons and on collective peace. The joint statement considered it necessary to effect a drastic reduction in armaments, abolish antagonistic military blocs, and withdraw all troops stationed in foreign countries (meaning U.S. forces in Japan), and to "prohibit the manufacture, stock-piling, and use of nuclear and thermonuclear weapons." They asked the United States, the Soviet Union, and Great Britain to conclude agreements to this effect and to ban nuclear tests. Yet Mao frankly predicted that China, Japan, and India would eventually possess atomic and hydrogen bombs in the future; he argued that since the best situation was no nuclear weapons for any nation, and the worst situation was nuclear possession by "them" only, the inevitable conclusion was nuclear development by both "them" and "us." More important, he concurred with the JSP's proposal for simultaneous abrogation of the Sino-Soviet and U.S.-Japanese security treaties and for the establishment of a new collective security system embracing the United States, the Soviet Union, China, and Japan. He suggested that even prior to the nullification of the U.S.-Japan security treaty, China was willing to conclude a nonaggression pact with Japan; if Japan abrogated its security treaty with the United States and removed the latter's military bases and armed forces, he said, the Sino-Soviet treaty would be revised.[58]

Chou was favorably impressed by the enthusiastic friendship and cooperative spirit shown by the JSP mission. Given its recent gain in the National Diet, he wished to use the JSP, in addition to the JCP, as an institutional device to penetrate into Japan's political processes and to influence the Japanese government's China policy. His strategy was to mobilize and form the broadest possible united front among all Japanese forces that were sympathetic to China's interests. Hence he asked the JSP to enlighten the Japanese people about China and to assume "leadership" in Japanese diplomacy. Indeed he regarded "people's diplomacy" as an important, integral element of China's international relations.[59]

The main motivation of the JSP's delegation diplomacy toward China was three-fold: (1) to realize its policy of peaceful and friendly relations with the PRC and strengthen its socialist solidarity with Chinese people; (2) to demonstrate, in the absence of diplomatic relations between Tokyo and Peking, its capability in conducting external affairs, and thereby to exert political pressure upon the Japanese government for a change in its China policy; and (3) to articulate and mobilize those elements in Japanese society who were favorably disposed toward China and critical of the LDP's foreign policy. As an initial step for these policy purposes, the JSP was satisfied with the success and publicity achieved by its first mission.

But the LDP was quick to minimize the domestic political impact of the JSP's mission. Upon release of the Asanuma-Chang statement, LDP Secretary-General Miki Takeo accused the JSP delegates of having been submissive to Chinese demands and of having violated their written commitment not to engage in diplomatic talks with China.[60] He termed their positions on Taiwan and on an Asian collective security system as "unrealistic." A few days later the LDP issued a formal document on "Our Attitudes toward the Asanuma-Chang Joint Statement."[61] It pointed out, among other matters, that the Republic of China was a member of the United Nations and had concluded a peace treaty with Japan, whereas the PRC had been condemned by the United Nations as an aggressor in the Korean War. It criticized as "imprudent" the JSP pplicy, which disregarded the stark reality of Nationalist China on Taiwan in recognizing Communist China as the only lawful government of China, and which advocated an immediate establishment of diplomatic relations between the latter and Japan. Nevertheless, the LDP added that it would further accelerate its efforts to increase Japan's trade with China. These arguments, constructed on the U.N. status of the two Chinese governments, and on the separation of diplomatic and economic matters, constituted the conceptual basis for subsequent official policy toward China.

Broken Relations The intense LDP-JSP debates, carried out in the context of Japanese domestic political competition, beclouded any prospect of direct diplomatic contacts between Tokyo and Peking during the remainder of 1957. There evolved a vicious circle; the closer the JSP moved toward Peking's embrace, the more remote the prospect for Sino-Japanese diplomatic rapprochement became, and vice versa. The prospect was then completely foreclosed in May 1958 by the flag incident at Nagasaki. On May 2, 1958, a Japanese youth tore down a small PRC flag at the Chinese stamp exhibit show in a Nagasaki department store, but he was charged with destroying Chinese furniture, a light indictment. (A few days earlier the

Nationalist Chinese consul in Nagasaki had asked the city officials to prevent a PRC flag from being displayed; a similar request had been made by the Nationalist Chinese ambassador to the Japanese Foreign Ministry, which had advised Nagasaki's mayor to stop the display of a PRC flag.[62])

The Chinese reaction was prompt and drastic. On May 9, Foreign Minister Chen Yi issued a protest statement in which he criticized Kishi's "hostile," "vicious," and "imperialistic" provocation against 600 million Chinese people.[63] The Japanese Ministry of Foreign Affairs and the LDP, while denying Chen's "distorted" charges, responded with a warning that China should not use the minor incident as an instrument to interfere with Japan's forthcoming general elections.[64] However, in retaliation for the Nagasaki case, which was interpreted to be a symbolic demonstration of Kishi's anti-Chinese stand, the PRC suspended all economic transactions with Japan and broke off other forms of relations, ranging from cultural exchange programs to ongoing negotiations for repatriation of Japanese nationals.

Why did China take such extreme measures of retaliation for the seemingly minor flag incident? It is often suggested that by blaming Kishi for total trade suspension, the Chinese intended to accomplish two main objectives—to mobilize Japanese business circles, especially those engaged in Sino-Japanese trade, against his anti-Peking policy and undermine his leadership, and to help the progressive forces in the forthcoming general elections for the House of Representatives. In fact, Chen Yi specifically lauded the JSP's correct position on China, and noted that some LDP leaders were not in complete agreement with Kishi's hostile policy toward the PRC. In response, Kishi condemned China's support for the JSP's election campaign.

If these had indeed been their only intentions, the Chinese committed an error because they failed to change Kishi's China policy or his subsequent electoral victory two weeks later. But more important than these two objectives was a symbolic demonstration of their indignation of Kishi's growing political cooperation with Taipei and Washington. The Chinese were particularly annoyed by the fact that Kishi had paid the first state visit to Taipei as Japanese prime minister in June 1957 and had at least indirectly supported Chiang's policy of return to the mainland. They therefore interpreted the Japanese government's handling of the Nagasaki incident as a logical consequence of Kishi's longstanding record of willing subservience to Taipei and Washington.

It is also important to note that the episodes described above took place at the time when the Chinese pursued an assertive posture in foreign affairs and showed an excessive confidence in their own economic capabilities. Upon the Soviet Union's successful tests of an intercontinental missile and the Sputnik, Mao Tse-tung offered a new appraisal of the balance of international forces in November 1957. The east wind, he declared at Moscow, was now prevailing over the west wind.[65] He clearly meant that the balance was tilted decisively in favor of the Socialist camp. This view departed substantially from the idea of strategic balance between East and West, the underlying assessment that had sustained China's policy of peaceful coexistence in the early and middle parts of the 1950s. And on the domestic scene, after some initial gains made for their ambitious "Great Leap Forward" movement during the winter of 1957, the Chinese were preparing, in May 1958, a nationwide campaign of a people's commune movement. They were overly confident that through self-reliance and ideologically inspired mass efforts, they would be able to catch up with the British industrial production level in fifteen years. This change in China's world outlook and domestic politics may have precipitated China's fundamentalist hard line on Japan. Indeed, Chen Yi and Nan Han-chen reminded Kishi that the PRC, unlike old China of twenty years ago, was a powerful state capable of achieving rapid economic progress without depending on trade with Japan.[66]

The unilateral termination of Sino-Japanese relations meant a collapse of the gradualist "people's diplomacy" that the Chinese had patiently pursued under the principle of peaceful coexistence with Japan. It was a vivid expression of their frustrations about the lack of any tangible breakthrough in establishing diplomatic relations with Japan. The *People's Daily* (July 7, 1958) claimed, for example, that the Kishi cabinet was the most reactionary of all the cabinets formed since 1945 and that it was "a concentrated representation of the interests of the most aggressive magnates of Japanese monopoly capital who have close ties with the U.S." It made a cutting attack against Kishi's "latent" militarist ambitions for constructing a new "Greater East Asia Coprosperity Sphere," which was supposedly manifested in Japan's alleged anti-Communist military alliance with Chiang Kai-shek, Syngman Rhee, and Ngo Dinh Diem. The Chinese found an additional symptom of Japanese militarism in the projected revision of the U.S.-Japan security treaty. Chen Yi expressed "grave concern" over Kishi's negotiations for its revision, already underway in 1958, and charged that Kishi was concocting a hostile military plot against China in collusion with the United States.[67] Even though the Japanese Ministry of Foreign Affairs promptly denied Chen's accusations and defended the equal and defensive nature of the treaty revision, it failed to prevent China from encouraging and assisting the gathering storm over the treaty crisis in Japan.[68]

Meanwhile, the JSP dispatched Dietman Sata Tadataka to Peking in August 1958 to resume trade with China; and in September it joined the JCP, the *Sōhyō*, the Japan-China Friendship Association, and other "democratic organizations" in setting up a secretariat for the National Conference for Restoration of Japan-China Diplomatic Relations (*Nitchū kokkō kaifuku kokumin kaigi*).[69] This was the first major JSP-JCP united action in regard to China, and the JSP also adopted a comprehensive seven-point platform on China.[70]

On the heels of the JCP-CCP conference at Peking in March 1959, the JSP sent to China its second official mission, again headed by Secretary-General Asanuma Inejirō.[71] In his speech, delivered on March 12 at the auditorium of the Chinese People's Political Consultative Conference, Asanuma, while referring to the U.S. military presence in Okinawa and Taiwan, made the celebrated, but highly controversial, statement that "U.S. imperialism is a common enemy of the peoples of Japan and China."[72] His Chinese hosts applauded the statement that was to become a useful catch phrase, frequently quoted in Chinese documents, but it stirred a great deal of commotion on the domestic Japanese political scene. The right-wing Socialist factions, spearheaded by Nishio Suehiro, were openly critical of the statement, and LDP Secretary-General Fukuda Takeo, in consultation with the Kishi government, cabled a protest message to Asanuma at Peking.[73] The LDP regretted Asanuma's vilification of the U.S., and used this provocative utterance as a fortuitous device to attack the JSP's "pro-Communist" tendency before the upcoming general elections.

Compared with the first Asanuma-Chang joint statement, the second one signed on March 17, 1959 was more militant in tone, and more comprehensive in its contents.[74] The first statement, two years ago, had carefully avoided any concrete references to imperialism, the U.S.-Japan security treaty, neutralization of Japan, liberation of Taiwan, and the Japan-Taiwan peace treaty. "At the present moment," they now declared, "the forces against imperialism and colonialism are growing daily stronger throughout the world." They considered this trend highly favorable both to the Japanese people in their efforts to defeat the U.S.-Japanese security system and to China in her efforts to liberate Taiwan. The neutralization of Japan and the nullification of the Japan-Taiwan peace treaty were specifically called for; the Chinese side endorsed and announced its respect for the JSP's policy of "unarmed neutrality" (*hibusō chūritsu*). In order to remove the "artificial barriers" against diplomatic normalization, Asanuma and Chang reaffirmed China's "three political principles" and the inseparability of political and economic issues.[75] On strategic questions both sides agreed to support an "unconditional" prohibition of the testing, manufacture, stockpiling, and use of nuclear weapons, and to form a nuclear-free zone in Asia and the Pacific.

The Nishio and Kawakami factions opposed Asanuma's acceptance of the extreme leftist phraseology and "non-neutral" positions in the joint statement; the JSP, they insisted, should be genuinely neutral by being friendly toward all major powers including the United States. The CEC, however, easily ratified the Asanuma-Chang joint statement, and JSP Chairman Suzuki conveyed this decision to Mao and Chou.

Encouraged by the ascendancy of progressive movements in Japan, especially against the National Police Law in late 1958, Chou apparently hoped that the JSP-JCP united action, strengthened by their common bonds with China, would develop into the leadership elements of a mass movement both for Sino-Japanese diplomatic normalization and against the security treaty revision. At the First Session of the Second National People's Congress in April 1959, Chou stated:

The Chinese people cannot sit idly by while Japanese militarism is being revived, nor can they tolerate the continued hostile policy of the Kishi government toward China. The Chinese people welcome the great efforts made by the Japanese people to advance friendly relations between the two peoples. We regard as entirely correct the series of proposals for improving Sino-Japanese relations and resuming diplomatic relations between China and Japan which were put forward recently by the delegation of the Japan Communist Party and that of the Japan Socialist Party during their successive visits to China. We are confident that the Japanese people will ultimately break down all obstacles and develop peaceful and friendly relations with the Chinese people.[76]

Emphasis on opposition diplomacy did not mean the absence of China's contacts with the governing LDP. Even though they flatly rebuked Foreign Minister Fujiyama Aiichirō's proposal for ambassadorial talks as a deceptive election gimmick, the Chinese did cultivate their cooperation and friendship with the LDP's antimainstream factions led by Ishibashi Tanzan, Matsumura Kenzō, Miki Takeo, and Kōno Ichirō.[77] This move, which was designed to broaden a pro-Peking united front in Japan and to undermine the Kishi leadership in the LDP, was derived from their assessment that these "far-sighted" and "sensible" members of the LDP had favored the idea of Sino-Japanese cooperation and had expressed great discontent with Kishi's "reactionary policy," especially in regard to the security treaty revision.[78]

Fully aware of the intricate interfactional dynamics in the ruling party, Chou En-lai invited to China ex-Prime Minister Ishibashi Tanzan (and Dietmen Utsunomiya Tokuma and Kato Tsunetarō) in September 1959.[79] The following month ex-Minister of Agriculture and Education Matsumura Kenzō, who had lost to Kishi in the LDP's presidential contest in January 1959, made a trip to China. It was true that both Ishibashi and Matsumura were reluctant to follow the Kishi leadership in revising the U.S.-Japan security treaty, but they wished to assure their Chinese hosts that the revised treaty would not permanently damage the prospect of Sino-Japanese cooperation. Matsumura, in particular, dismissed the relevance of the U.S.-

Japanese security arrangements to Sino-Japanese relations.[80] They were more interested in promoting a gradual accumulation of close, friendly ties, which they hoped would ultimately lead to diplomatic normalization between Japan and China. Yet any remaining hope for direct Sino-Japanese diplomatic contacts was to be irrevocably dashed by the crisis over the security treaty revision in Japan.

Dimensions of Assertive Confrontation

Ikeda's "Low Posture"   The security treaty crisis provided the Chinese with a unique opportunity to take part in Japan's dynamic political process. They actively supported the violent antitreaty movement with extensive propaganda, financial aid, and sympathetic mass demonstrations throughout China.[81] In the process they gained a valuable insight into Japanese politics; while they were impressed by the strength of mass actions led by progressive parties, trade unions, and radical student groups, they were also reassured of the importance of deep factional and policy cleavage in the LDP itself. This experience, coupled with the inauguration of Prime Minister Ikeda Hayato as Kishi's successor, set the new stage for Sino-Japanese relations in the 1960s.

In a conscious attempt to relax the pent-up tensions built up at home and abroad, Ikeda professed to take a "low posture" (*teishisei*) in domestic politics and a "friendly diplomacy" (*zenrin gaikō*) with all countries, including China and the Soviet Union.[82] At first the Chinese cautiously avoided any adverse comment on the Ikeda government, and gradually amended the state of their relations with Japan. In July 1960 Liu Ning-yi, president of All-China Federation of Trade Unions, led the first Chinese delegation to Japan since the Nagasaki flag incident. The following month Chou En-lai, in his talks with Suzuki Kazuo, managing director of the Japan-China Trade Promotion Council, initiated what was known to be a friendship method for trade resumption, a method of trading with Japanese companies that China specifically recognized as "friendly" toward its policy positions. However, China's initial wait-and-see attitude toward Ikeda was unmistakably over by October. They openly denounced his "reactionary" and "hostile" policy against China; in fact, the *People's Daily* (October 11, 1960) found no difference between Ikeda and Kishi in so far as their China policies were concerned. The catalog of their complaints against Ikeda was long, but familiar in its essential implications: (1) by sending Matsuno Tsuruhei, speaker of the House of Councillors, to Taiwan in August and Foreign Minister Kosaka Zentarō to Seoul in September, Ikeda had adopted and implemented Kishi's old plan to form a Northeast Asian military alliance; (2) by supporting the U.S. policy to impose a moratorium on the Chinese question at the United Nations and to adopt the Tibetan question as its agenda item, he had interfered in China's internal affairs and followed Washington's "two-China" conspiracy; and (3) by a substantial increase in defense expenditures he had attempted to revive Japanese militarism.

Like Fujiyama, Ikeda made a secret proposal for ambassadorial talks with China, but it was rejected on the ground that since the nature of Sino-Japanese relations was different from that of Sino-American relations, a comprehensive political settlement should be negotiated at the ministerial level, not in peripheral ambassadorial talks.[83] Yet Ikeda made it clear at the National Diet in December 1960 that he was opposed to diplomatic normalization or intergovernmental agreements with China.[84] The Chinese rather hardened their antagonism toward the Ikeda government during 1961 and 1962. Viewed from their perspective, Ikeda took a series of steps to solidify his anti-China stand; for example, he reaffirmed the unsettled legal status of Taiwan, held a summit meeting with President Kennedy to strengthen the U.S.-Japanese military alliance, accepted the notion of "successor states" for dual Chinese representation at the United Nations, and refused to let the CCP delegation (headed by Peking Mayor Peng Chen) attend the eighth JCP Congress. Moreover, according to China's top-secret military publication (*Tsan-kao Hsiao-hsi* or *Bulletin of Activities*), Ikeda sent Kishi to Taipei to cement Tokyo-Taipei solidarity and carried out an anti-China campaign in Southeast Asia through economic expansion and peace corps.[85] Nothwithstanding China's angry accusations, Ikeda, unlike his predecessor, did not respond in a tit-for-tat fashion, but practiced a low posture toward China. The LDP's "interim report," prepared in May 1961 by a subcommittee on China (under Chairman Matsumoto Shunichi), also recommended a cautious approach toward China, but ruled out immediate diplomatic contact between Japan and China.[86]

Tokyo-Peking relations sank to a new low in December 1961, when the question of Chinese representation was debated at the sixteenth U.N. General Assembly. Ever since its admission to the United Nations in 1956, Japan had consistently supported the U.S. strategy to impose a moratorium on the question of Chinese representation at each General Assembly seesion. As only 43% of the U.N. members voted for moratorium in 1960, Japan decided in 1961 to join the United States, Australia, Colombia, and Italy in cosponsoring a resolution that any proposal to change the representation of China was an "important question" under Article 18 (2) of the U.N. Charter, which required a two-thirds rather than a simple majority vote.[87] This resolution was intended to make it difficult for the PRC to replace the Republic of China in the United Nations, but the Ikeda government called it a transitional measure for admitting the PRC to the General Assembly with a permanent seat in the Security Council, while retaining the Republic of China in the General Assembly.

In his carefully worded thirty-five-minute speech at the U.N. General Assembly on December 6, 1961, Ambassador Okazaki Katsuo (ex-Foreign Minister in the Yoshida cabinet) explained his government's stand on China.[88] His arguments may be summarized as follows:

1. Japan and China share geographic proximity, racial affinity, and linguistic similarities based on a 2,000-year history of close cultural ties;

2. Japan's present relations with the PRC are limited to a bare minimum because the latter emphasizes "political principles and objectives" in its foreign policy, while Japan has enjoyed an extremely close and friendly relationship with the Republic of China (ROC) since their bilateral peace treaty was concluded in 1952;

3. There now exist the two competing Chinese authorities separated by the Taiwan Straits; while the PRC exercises effective control over more than 600 million people on the mainland, the Republic of China is in effective control of 10 million people who have a high standard of living and a strong aversion to Communism, on Taiwan and its adjacent islands;

4. The ROC is one of the founders of the United Nations and a permanent member of the Security Council; it has faithfully fulfilled its obligations under the Charter;

5. On the other hand, the General Assembly, in a resolution adopted on February 1, 1951, denounced an aggressive act of the PRC in the Korean War; according to the Charter, however, a member of the United Nations must be a peace-loving state that is able and willing to carry out the obligations under the Charter and to resolve international disputes by peaceful means;

6. The United Nations, since its inception, has recognized the ROC as a government representing China, and therefore any move to replace the ROC by the PRC amounts in effect to an expulsion of a member, which is an important question.

These arguments became Japan's main policy theme to be repeated for a decade in the United Nations. Okazaki's speech was, however, much milder than that of U.S. Ambassador Adlai E. Stevenson, who contended that if China were admitted to the United Nations, it would favor atomic testing, advocate the "rule of the gun," and exert a "demoralizing effect" upon the United Nations itself.[89] The General Assembly adopted the five-nation resolution by a vote of 61 to 34, with 7 abstentions and 2 absent, and rejected a Soviet proposal to seat the PRC by a 36 to 48 vote with 20 abstentions. It also adopted the resolution (cosponsored by Malaya, Thailand, El Salvador, and Ireland) that accused China of "depriving the Tibetan people of their fundamental human rights and freedoms." (Japan voted for the resolution.)[90]

The JSP promptly attributed Okazaki's lack of an autonomous policy to the Ikeda government's submissive attitude toward the United States, but, ironically, the Nationalist Chinese press complained about Okazaki's reference to the PRC's effective control in the mainland.[91] More serious than these responses was the strong protest that the Chinese lodged against Japan's role in the U.N. decisions. They had apparently expected that Japan would at least abstain in voting on both the "important question" resolution and the Soviet proposal, and they were disappointed by Japan's willingness to go all the way in the anti-Peking campaign at the United Nations.[92] In a Foreign Ministry statement they defined the issue of Chinese representation as a "purely procedural question" (namely, that of credentials), and declared that the five-nation resolution that "tramples upon the U.N. Charter and infringes on China's sovereignty" was totally illegal, null and void.[93] They understood and excused some member-states that were coerced by the U.S. to vote against China, but they singled out the Japanese delegates as the most unabashed and active servants of the U.S. conspiracy. The denunciation of Ikeda's U.N. policy was therefore particularly bitter and acrimonious.

The more diplomatic confrontations the Chinese had with the Japanese government, the closer the ties they sought to develop with those "far-sighted" persons in the LDP. The security treaty crisis demonstrated to them that the LDP's interfactional differences in personalities and policies were more substantial than they had expected. Mao Tse-tung himself showed a keen interest in the LDP's internal rivalries and specifically identified Ishibashi, Matsumura, Miki, Kōnō, and Takasaki Tatsunosuke as his "indirect allies" in Japan. His "direct allies" included the JSP and the JCP. Comparing the mainstream-antimainstream cleavage in the LDP to the rift between the United States and Western Europe, Mao told JSP Dietman Kuroda Hisao, in January 1961, that "it is beneficial to the people if both sides widen their gaps and fight against each other."[94]

The LDP's mainstream factions were unhappy with the visits of antimainstream members to China, and wished to inculcate a unified party-line position on China among LDP dietmen. In order to confine the discussions and activities concerning China to its regular organizations, such as the Committee on Foreign Affairs, the LDP requested the dissolution of the pro-Peking Japan-China Problem Study Group (*Nitchū mondai kenkyū-kai*), which had been set up in December 1960 as a product of the merger between the Study Group for the Improvement of Japan-China Relations (*Nitchū kaizen kenkyūkai*, organized by Utsunomiya Tokuma and Ishibashi faction members) and the China Problem Study Group (*Chūgoku mondai kenkyūkai*, organized by Matsumura-Miki faction members).[95] Yet it could not prevent pro-Peking dietmen from visiting the PRC or issuing statements critical of the LDP's official policy. In October 1960, LDP Dietman Takasaki Tatsunosuke led a group of visitors to China, and he was soon followed by a number of influential conservative legislators, including Utsunomiya Tokuma.[96]

In September 1962, Matsumura Kenzō had a discussion with Chou En-lai (and Chen Yi and Liao Cheng-chih) and set the stage for long-term memorandum trade between Japan and China. The Matsumura mission enjoyed an explicit, wholehearted endorsement from Prime Minister Ikeda, who was anxious to expand Sino-Japanese trade for his "income-doubling" policy. It included Dietman Ogawa Heiji of the Ikeda faction and Ikeda's key advisor, Tabayashi Masayoshi—in addition to Dietmen Furui Yoshimi (Matsumura faction), Tagawa Seiichi (Nakasone faction, Kōno Ichirō's nephew, and Matsumura's former secretary), and Fujii Katsushi (Miki faction). In the informal minutes of their talks, Matsumura and Chou stressed the desirability of a gradual and cumulative method (*zenshinteki katsu tsumikasane no hoshiki*) for normalization of economic and diplomatic relations between their two countries.[97] At first Chou prepared a draft of the formal joint statement upholding the inseparability of economic and political matters, but Matsumura successfully insisted that they should forego this reference and use the informal minutes so as not to give a weapon to anti-Peking forces in the LDP.[98] They also agreed to exchange trade liaison agencies between Tokyo and Peking and to use a method of deferred payment for Japan's plant exports. As political guarantors of this commercial arrangement, they appointed Liao Cheng-chih (deputy chief of the Foreign Affairs Staff Office in the State Council and vice-chairman of the China Committee for Afro-Asian Solidarity and of the China Peace Committee, who was born in Tokyo and educated at Waseda University) for China and LDP Dietman Takasaki Tatsunosuke or Okazaki Kaheita (president of All-Nippon Airways and ex-bank official in China) for Japan. All these agreements were specifically incorporated in the Takasaki-Liao accord reached two months later; Takasaki was accompanied by Okazaki, and LDP Dietmen Matsumoto Shunichi (ex-ambassador to Great Britain and principal negotiator for Japanese-Soviet diplomatic normalization), Noda Takeo, and Takeyama Yūtarō.[99]

At Peking Matsumura explained to his Chinese hosts that Prime Minister Ikeda, unlike Kishi, had no hostile attitude toward China, and Chou went as far as to say that he would welcome the visit of Prime Minister Ikeda or his new Foreign Minister Ōhira Masayoshi to China. It is difficult to assess how serious Chou's diplomatic overture was, but Ikeda simply and quietly decided not to follow it up. Instead, Ikeda, in an exchange of letters with Indian Prime Minister Nehru in November 1962, regretted China's military action along the Sino-Indian border, which he considered a threat to the peace in Asia.[100] He was, however, prepared to honor and implement the Matsumura-Chou and Takasaki-Liao agreements. The United States, Taiwan, and some powerful pro-Taipei LDP dietmen such as Kaya Okinori (chairman of the Policy Affairs Research Council) asked Ikeda not to provide any form of "foreign aid" to China, but, in accordance with the Matsumura-Chou accord, in August 1963 Ikeda permitted the Kurashiki Rayon Company to use the Export-Import Bank's fund for exporting a $22-million vinylon plant to China.[101] Moreover, despite Foreign Minister Ōhira's objection, in September 1963 he allowed two officials of the Ministry of International Trade and Industry to accompany the Okazaki Kaheita delegation to China.[102]

Despite China's verbal abuse, Prime Minister Ikeda thus managed to have the best overall relations with the PRC since the Hatoyama government. The Kurashiki Rayon decision, together with the Chou Hung-ching case, suggested to the Chinese that they could expand their notion of "intermediate zone" from France to Japan.[103] A *People's Daily* editorial (January 21, 1964), noting the imbalance of world capitalist development, raised and encouraged the possibility that Japan might follow President Charles de Gaulle in asserting its independent posture from the United States. Yet the Tokyo-Peking reconciliation strained diplomatic and economic relations between Tokyo and Taipei in early 1964. Chiang Kai-shek announced the resignation of his ambassador to Japan (Chang Li-sheng), recalled other top diplomats to Taipei, and threatened to take a drastic retaliatory economic policy against Japan. Further, pressures caused by the Tokyo-Taipei tension and the French recognition of the PRC aroused a serious debate on China in the LDP, which led both the Ministry of Foreign Affairs and the LDP's Committee on Foreign Affairs to clarify, in March 1964, their identical official positions on China.[104] They argued, *inter alia*, that for Japan to follow French example in recognizing the PRC would terminate Japan's present relations with Taiwan and would endanger Asian peace and security as well as the unity of the free world. It was noted that the United States and almost every member of NATO had criticized the French decision. Furthermore, since any attempt to replace the Republic of China by the PRC in the United Nations would have a grave effect on Asian peace and the world situation, they maintained, Japan must seek a fair solution to the Chinese question that was acceptable to international public opinion. The LDP, in particular, declared that the JSP, the JCP, and other leftist groups had an ultimate goal of destroying the U.S.-Japan security treaty by advocating Japan's recognition of the PRC and the abrogation of the Japan-Taiwan peace treaty. It was a frontal rebuttal of the public appeal that JSP Chairman Kawakami Jōtarō, JCP Chairman Nosaka Sanzō, *Sōhyō* Chairman Ōta Kaoru, and twenty-two other prominent Japanese leaders had signed in February. They had urged the Japanese government to normalize diplomatic relations with China, nullify the Japan-Taiwan peace treaty, and restore China's legitimate status in the United Nations.[105] The appeal had stimulated a nationwide campaign to collect thirty million signatures for these diplomatic objectives, and a growing number of prefectural assemblies and municipal councils had passed resolutions favorable to the appeal.

Unmoved by the mass movement spearheaded by the JSP and the JCP during 1964, Ikeda instead took a few concrete steps to ease the Tokyo-Taipei strains. He encouraged ex-Prime Minister Yoshida Shigeru, who had just completed his Taiwan trip, to send his conciliatory "private letter" to Chiang Kai-shek's Chief Secretary Chang Chün (graduate of the Japanese Imperial Military Academy) in May, dispatched Foreign Minister Ōhira to Taipei in July, and conferred with Chang Chün in Tokyo in August. These overtures toward Taipei notwithstanding, he was still ready to accommodate Matsumura's efforts for exchanging memorandum trade liaison missions between Tokyo and Peking in 1964. The mission was the first significant breakthrough made by China in its long maneuver to establish de facto diplomatic presence in Tokyo, but the Japanese Ministry of Foreign Affairs made it clear in July 1964 that Japan did not recognize China's trade liaison personnel as representatives of the PRC government, and that they would not be allowed to engage in Japan's domestic political affairs.[106] Their activities in Japan were to be governed by a set of specific regulations—such as forty-eight-hour advance notification of their local travels and a ban on their propaganda operations. The clarification was obviously designed to reiterate Japan's continuing adherence to the separation of commercial and diplomatic matters and, more important, to mitigate an expected protest from Taipei and pro-Taiwan LDP dietmen. The absence of diplomatic relations, however, insured that the respective liaison offices in both capitals were staffed by government officials, and that they would assume a wide range of quasi-diplomatic functions, ranging from diplomatic receptions and consular activities to intelligence-gathering operations and political articulation. In fact, the Japanese government assumed all the expenses, including salaries, for Japan's trade liaison representatives stationed in Peking.

About the time that the exchange of liaison offices was agreed on, Chou En-lai evidently proposed to Kitamura Tokutarō a meeting of Chinese and Japanese government officials in France or another third country. Upon receipt of this proposal, Foreign Minister Ōhira instructed his staff to consider its merits, but Ikeda and Ōhira presumably failed to accept Chou's proposal.[107] Conceivably, Chou En-lai wished to explore the possibility of expanding the agreement on liaison offices to a more formal diplomatic arrangement, or of applying the precedent of Sino-French diplomatic rapprochement to Japan. Still constrained by their domestic and foreign consideration, Ikeda and Ōhira felt that the exchange of resident trade offices was the maximum option they could afford at the moment.

Conservative Cleavage   When Satō Eisaku replaced Ikeda as Japanese prime minister in November 1964, the Chinese had a reason to expect a positive, favorable policy from his new cabinet. As a candidate for the LDP presidency, he had publicly stated that it was urgent for Japan to pursue an independent diplomacy without relying on the United States and the Soviet Union, and to restore diplomatic relations with China.[108] He had apparently given a similar policy commitment to Nan Han-chen during their talks at Tokyo in April 1964; Nan was so favorably impressed by State Minister Satō's "far-sighted" wisdom that he expected to enter an era of diplomatic thaw under Satō's leadership—despite the pro-Taiwan pressure from his brother and political adviser, Kishi Nobusuke.[109]

The expectation was short-lived, however, and the Chinese were quickly disappointed by what they regarded as his definitely anti-China decisions. As examples of these decisions made from late 1964 to early 1965, they cited Satō's denial of an entry visa to the CCP delegation (headed by Peng Chen) to the ninth JCP Congress, his attack against China's first nuclear explosion, and his reiteration of the unsettled legal status of Taiwan; and they alleged that, in his summit talk with President Johnson, Satō agreed to make Japan a "willing tool" of U.S. imperialist policies in Asia.[110] It is true that at Washington, Satō, in view of China's nuclear development, obtained President Johnson's commitment to defend Japan from "any outside attack," but Japan maintained an unmistakably mild attitude toward China in the Satō-Johnson joint communique of January 13, 1965.[111] Whereas Johnson branded China's "militant policies and expansionist pressures" against its neighbors, Satō declared a policy of promoting trade with China under the principle of separation of political from economic matters. On top of all these developments was Satō's pronounced adherence to the Yoshida letter in February 1965, which the Chinese took as an extremely hostile blow to their national pride and economic interests.[112] They were further irritated by the disclosure of Japan's top-secret military contingency plan called the "Three Arrow Study" (*Mitsuya Kenkyū*). According to JSP Dietman Okada Haruo, who exposed this plan at the National Diet, the Japanese self-defense forces, in the event of another Korean War, were supposed to take at least indirect armed action (as a reserve force) against China and North Korea; they were also expected to be trained jointly with U.S., South Korean, and Nationalist Chinese troops.[113]

Not satisfied with Satō's deteriorating relations with China, a number of powerful pro-Taiwan LDP dietmen organized, in December 1964, the Asian Problems Study Group (*Ajiya mondai kenkyūkai*) to check the probability of his pro-Peking decisions in the future. Led by such staunch anti-Communist warriors as Kaya Okinori (ex-finance minister in Tōjō's wartime cabinet), Funada Naka, Ishii Mitsujirō, and Nadao Hirokichi, this group originally contained ninety-eight conservative parliamentary members, with heavy representation from the Satō, Kishi-Fukuda, Ishii, and

Ikeda factions.[114] Although not all of its members shared a complete policy consensus on China, they tended to favor the status quo of Japan's intimate ideological, diplomatic, and economic links with Taiwan.[115] While they were not categorically opposed to the exchange of nondiplomatic contacts between Japan and China, they cautioned that Japan should not offer any diplomatic or political concessions to China for the sake of trade expansion or depend too much upon China for vital raw materials. Closely associated with the Satō cabinet and Japanese *zaikai*, the group emerged as a powerful interfactional coalition for articulating Taiwan's interests in Japan and for counterbalancing any pro-Peking pressure in the LDP. Not only did they play a leading role in various organizations promoting Japan-Taiwan cooperation, but they also extended their role to promoting the regional anti-Communist cause through organizations such as the Asian People's Anti-Communist League, the Asian Parliamentary Union, and the Committee on Japan-(South) Korea Cooperation.

As a rival of the Asian Group, some antimainstream LDP leaders—Matsumura, Utsunomiya, Ishibashi, Fujiyama, to cite a few—gathered seventy-seven dietmen in January 1965 to set up the Asian-African Problems Study Group (*Ajiya afurika mondai kenkyūkai*). For all practical purposes it was a successor to the defunct Japan-China Problem Study Group. Notwithstanding the lack of cohesive attitudes and concrete policy alternatives, it became a catalyst in advancing the broad goal of peaceful coexistence and cooperative relations between the two Asian neighbors. Occasionally, its members, collectively or individually, urged Prime Minister Satō to adopt a "forward-looking" posture toward China, and they sponsored a variety of educational activities and economic interchanges. For example, they assumed top positions in the two principal organizations for Sino-Japanese trade: Ishibashi and Utsunomiya were president and vice-president, respectively, of the Japanese Association for Promotion of International Trade; and Matsumura, Furui Yoshimi, and Tagawa Seiichi became political advisers to the Japan-China Overall Trade Association (or the "Takasaki Office").

Why were Matsumura, Ishibashi, Utsunomiya, and other leaders of the Asian-African Problems Study Group so favorably inclined toward China? There must have been a multitude of diverse personal, political, and psychological reasons, but the most important common determinant of their attitudes seemed to be their search for Asian consciousness and an autonomous diplomacy (*jishu gaikō*), especially free from the U.S. containment policy. They manifested the tradition of Pan-Asian solidarity and the notions of *"dōbun dōshu"* (common script and common race) and "brotherhood" between Japan and China. The restoration of Japan's traditional ties with China was for them a way to reassert their Asian identity and to demonstrate their autonomous diplomatic direction.[116] They regarded Mao's China not as a vanguard of violent international Communist conspi-

Table 4—Factional Composition of the Asian Problems Study Group and
Asian-African Problems Study Group in the LDP, 1965

Faction	APSG	AAPSG
Satō	27	9 (3)
Kōno	2	17
Ikeda	12 (1)	8
Miki	9 (2)	18 (3)
Fujiyama	9 (2)	10 (1)
Ōno	9 (2)	13 (1)
Kawashima	4	1
Ishii	10	0
Kishi-Fukuda	13	0
Others	3	1
Total:	98	77

SOURCE: Sadako Ogata, "Japanese Attitude toward China," *Asian Survey*, August 1965,
p. 395.
NOTE: Number in parentheses shows members of the House of Councillors; otherwise,
members of the House of Representatives.

racy, but as an incarnation of China's legitimate nationalist aspirations
compatible with the security and prosperity of Japan. In fact, Ishibashi and
Matsumura suggested that the security of Asia should be protected by a
concerted effort of Japan and China. Added to this mixture of Japanese
nationalism and Asian regionalism was their personal commitment to
redeem a "China guilt" and to accomplish a "historic mission" for Sino-
Japanese cooperation. No matter how sanguine it may sound, material
incentives and individual political interests, too, cannot be ruled out in their
motivations. Later, in February 1968, they organized a New Policy Discussion Group (*Shinseisaku kondankai*) as a loose coalition of factions critical
of Satō's domestic and foreign policies.[117]

These two rival study groups—the APSG and the AAPSG—carried on a
running battle over a number of China-related issues during the latter half of
the 1960s. Let us examine briefly the extent to which the leading spokesmen
of both study groups differed on China. A fundamental cause of their policy
cleavage centered around the status of the Nationalist Chinese government
on Taiwan. From the perspective of political realism, Utsunomiya and other
spokesmen of the AAPSG considered it "fictitious" and "absurd" for Japan
to have recognized the Republic of China as representing 700 million people
on mainland China; in 1966 he even compared its insignificant, but trouble-
some status to a rival Japanese government hypothetically established on
Oshima Island in Itsu Bay.[118] He also talked about the advisability of CCP-
KMT reconciliation by offering Chiang Kai-shek vice-chairmanship of the
PRC or governorship of an autonomous Taiwan Province; Chiang could

Table 5—Factional Composition of the New Policy
Discussion Group in the LDP, 1968

Faction	Total members in the House of Representatives	Members in the New Policy Discussion Group
Satō	50	0
Kishi-Fukuda	27	0
Ishii	14	0
Funada (ex-Ōno)	13	3
Murakami (ex-Ōno)	10	3
Kawashima	17	4
Maeo (ex-Ikeda)	42	17
Miki	37	13
Nakasone (ex-Kōno)	23	21
Matsuda (ex-Kōno)	11	1
Fujiyama	13	10
Matsumura	4	4
Others	12	5
Total	273	81

SOURCE: *Asahi Shimbun*, July 19, 1968.

then retain his troops only if their insignia were changed to those of the Chinese People's Liberation Army.

On the other hand, the APSG's Kaya, whose personal and political attachments to Chiang's government were absolute, and thus not negotiable, told LDP members and Kansai businessmen in 1966 that "from the points of view of international justice and logic," it was impossible to "deny the existence of a country (the Republic of China) which has righteous qualifications as a state and has not committed any violation of the rules as a member of the U.N."[119] He listed four basic reasons for Japan's "indebtedness" to Nationalist China: (1) among the allied powers Chiang alone had opposed the idea of abolishing the emperor system in Japan toward the end of World War II; (2) at the end of the war Chiang had issued "strict but generous" instructions to guarantee the safe repatriation of two million Japanese nationals—both military and civilian—out of China; (3) he had helped save Japan from a tragedy of being divided into several occupied zones; and (4) he had magnanimously given up his right of war reparations from Japan, while Communist China had claimed reparations of $60 billion—five times as much as the annual Japanese national budget.[120] In addition, he argued that Taiwan was important for the regional security of Asia and for the free passage off its eastern shores of Japanese ships with petroleum and iron ore.

While Kaya and Funada contended that the Japan-Taiwan peace treaty had already terminated the state of war between Japan and China, because the Nationalist Chinese government had ruled China during the war, Utsunomiya and Tagawa took the opposite view—that, legally, the state of war between Japan and mainland China was not over, and that Japan, as a nation, had a "moral obligation" to redeem its past crimes committed against the Chinese people.[121]

Another major area of disagreement arose as to how Japan should assess the PRC's might. While the AAPSG emphasized the defensive nature of China's military policy and dismissed China's intentions to attack Japan, the APSG tended to stress the lack of China's capabilities to do so. Fujiyama denied any danger of military attack by China or territorial expansion against Japan, and Furui argued that Japan's collusion with the U.S. war policy, particularly in Indo-China, presented a military threat to China.[122] Utsunomiya, too, suggested that China was a "peaceful cow" with no aggressive intentions, but that the United States had acted like a "bull-fighter" to provoke her into becoming a beast. Hence he argued that the Japanese government should assume a mediatory role between the United States and China.[123] He shared the view of Kosaka Zentarō who, as acting chairman of the LDP's Committee on Foreign Affairs in 1966, regarded the relaxation of Sino-American conflicts as essential to Sino-Japanese cooperation.[124] The rightist LDP members opposed this view, however. Defining Mao's nationalism as expansionism, Kaya in 1966—and Director-General of the Defense Agency Masuda Kaneshichi in 1967—pointed out China's direct armed aggression against Korea, Tibet, and India, and indirect subversive operations in Indonesia, Thailand, Malaysia, and the Philippines.[125] In light of China's alleged public pledges to liberate other nations by military means, Kaya contended that even if China wanted to attack Japan, it could not bring its massive army across the sea because its air and naval power was limited. Furthermore, he was confident that the U.S.-Japan security treaty constituted an effective deterrent against China's nuclear threat. Yet, as late as 1968, some members of the APSG—notably, ex-Director-General of the Defense Agency Matsuno Raizō (Matsuno Tsuruhei's son and close confidant of Yoshida and Satō)—found a "potential threat" against Japan in the Sino-Soviet treaty as well as in China's nuclear capabilities.[126]

However, it was widely felt by the members of both study groups that, as Chief Cabinet Secretary Suzuki Zenkō and a spokesman of the Japanese Ministry of Foreign Affairs had commented on China's first atomic test in October 1964, China's nuclear weapons, in the absence of sophisticated delivery vehicle, were incapable of threatening Japan's security so long as the U.S. nuclear shield was in effect.[127] Likewise, the LDP's Security Problems Research Committee, which was dominated by those members closely associated with the APSG, dismissed in late 1964 the possibility of a Chinese nuclear attack. "Even if the Chinese do, after several years, succeed in developing some kind of nuclear weapons system," it contended, "this will increase only slightly the threat to which Japan has been previously exposed by Soviet military might."[128] The same conclusion was reached in the committee's interim report prepared two years later. Furthermore, just as Kaya argued, the interim report pointed out that China's conventional military power was even more limited than its nuclear force because of China's poor military equipment, antiquated naval and air forces, and backward industrial conditions.[129]

The LDP government, unlike the JSP, disregarded Premier Chou En-lai's proposals for a world-wide summit conference on total nuclear disarmament or for a denuclearized zone of the Asian and Pacific region, including the United States, the Soviet Union, Japan, and China.[130] As a matter of policy, rather than a constitutional requirement, Prime Minister Satō adopted the "three non-nuclear principles"—namely, that Japan will refuse to manufacture, possess, or permit the entry of nuclear weapons into its soil. In fact, no responsible leader of the LDP openly advocated the option of developing Japan's indigenous *force de frappe à la* General Pierre Gallois. This was attributable to a variety of reasons, but they included the adequacy of U.S. deterrence, the economic cost of nuclear programs, the counterproductive strategic effects of Japan's nuclear development, and, above all, the pervasive "nuclear allergy" among Japanese people. As table 6 indicates, the number of those Japanese favoring Japan's nuclear possession dropped to 14.8% in 1961 (following the security treaty crisis), but rose to 26.4% in 1964. Even after China's nuclear tests, the number in 1967 tapered off to pre-1961 levels. The antinuclear sentiment was particularly strong among Japanese intellectuals and scientists, whose cooperation was indispensable to Japan's nuclear programs.

The fact of China's nuclear armament did not seriously alarm the anti-Peking forces in the LDP, but rather bolstered an argument in favor of Sino-Japanese political and diplomatic accommodation. As a result of China's atomic explosions, said Matsumura Kenzō, "the necessity of normalizing Sino-Japanese relations has become greater than ever."[131] Instead of strengthening the U.S. nuclear umbrella over Japan, Utsunomiya urged, the Japanese government should initiate *hanashiai* (consultations) with China to reduce mutual hostilities and to create the regional environment mitigating against the use of nuclear weapons.[132] Emphasis on diplomatic reconciliation and economic interdependence, rather than Japan's military preparedness, was seen as the best defense policy for Japan vis-a-vis Chinese nuclear might.

The most specific diplomatic issue over which the LDP was deeply divided was Japan's policy toward Chinese representation at the United Nations. The AAPSG—and the New Policy Discussion Group—formally requested the Satō government in 1968 not to cosponsor the "important

Table 6—Japanese Public Opinion on Nuclear Weapons, 1954-67
(percentage)

"Do you favor or disfavor Japan's possession of nuclear weapons?"

	Favor	Disfavor	Other Answers	Do Not Know
1954	23.5	65.2	0	11.3
1960	24.8	63.2	0	12.0
1961	14.8	69.8	0	15.4
1964	26.4	53.2	0.4	20.0
1967	24.7	54.6	0	20.7
1967 Subgroups				
LDP Supporters	31.2	50.7	0	18.1
JSP Supporters	25.5	68.3	0	6.2

SOURCE: *Chōsa Geppō*, July 1968, p. 18.

question" resolution, but to vote to admit the PRC to the United Nations. In this request, the future status of the Republic of China in that organization was left conveniently vague.[133] Fujiyama and Kawasaki simply defined the issue of Taiwan as China's "internal matter" into which Japan should not interfere, but some moderate members of both study groups were favorably inclined toward the "one China and one Taiwan" solution.[134] The APSG, on the other hand, was solidly behind Satō's intention to cosponsor the "important question" resolution. Kaya bluntly stated that Communist China, as an "aggressive state," was not qualified to join the United Nations, and that it was a "silly idea" to have China as a permanent member of the Security Council.[135] If China were admitted, he predicted, it would inevitably destroy the already partially paralyzed United Nations. The APSG saw no reason to change Satō's policy of nonrecognition and no admission regarding China, but the AAPSG favored an opening of ambassadorial or ministerial talks between Tokyo and Peking.

As far as the issue of Chinese representation in the United Nations was concerned, the Japanese people tended to be more sympathetic to the AAPSG than to the APSG. According to table 7, 46% of Japanese interviewees—including 49% of LDP supporters and 61% of JSP supporters—favored in 1967 the PRC's representation in the world organization, and only 8% was negative. There appeared no decisive public view on the "one China and one Taiwan" proposition. Moreover, table 8 shows that in 1968 although 47% of the Japanese people favored Japan's recognition of the PRC with 17% opposed, there was a substantial partisan cleavage in their attitudes. Yet a large majority of them (85%), irrespective of their partisan preferences, did not wish to see a drastic termination of Japan-Taiwan relations.

The opposing views articulated by the outspoken leaders of both study groups did not necessarily reflect a consensus among their associates, but the LDP could not afford to ignore them. In order to iron out these disagreements within the LDP, moderate party officials, such as Vice-President Kawashima Shōjirō, in the late 1960s arranged for discussions between the two rival study groups in the Committee on Foreign Affairs. No tangible policy compromise resulted, however. Much of this conservative policy cleavage, which also took place in the context of interfactional rivalries, was not entirely substantive. For it did not entail a basic transformation of Japan's overall foreign policy—such as rejection of a neutral status, military alliance with the United States, and preservation of Japan's economic relations with Taiwan. Unlike their JSP counterparts, even the most liberal, pro-Peking members of the AAPSG and the NPDG did not—at least up until 1969—publicly ask the Japanese government to abrogate the Japan-Taiwan peace treaty, to sever all relations with Taiwan, or to nullify the U.S.-Japan security treaty. And while the continuing friction between these policy coalitions did not produce an immediate change in the LDP's or the

Table 7—Japanese Public Opinion on China, 1961-67
(percentage)

(A) "Do you favor or disfavor Japan's support for the PRC's representation at the United Nations?"

	Favor	Disfavor	Other Answers	Do Not Know
1961	45.2	9.7	2.2	42.9
1964	44.6	11.8	1.9	41.7
1967	46.0	7.8	1.7	44.5
1967 Subgroups				
LDP Supporters	49.1	9.7	1.6	39.6
JSP Supporters	61.4	7.6	2.8	28.3

(B) "Do you favor or disfavor 'one China and one Taiwan' solution at the United Nations?"

	Favor	Disfavor	Other Answers	Do Not Know
1964	27.3	26.2	2.0	44.5
1967	26.1	22.5	1.7	49.7

SOURCE: *Chōsa Geppō*, July 1968, pp. 12–13.

Table 8—Japanese Public Opinion on China, 1966-68
(percentage)

(A) "Do you favor or disfavor Japan's recognition of China?"

	Favor	Disfavor	Do Not Know
November 1966	44	14	42
December 1968	47	17	36
1968 Subgroups			
LDP Supporters	36	22	42
JSP Supporters	58	14	28

(B) "Should Japan continue or cancel her relations with Taiwan?"

	Continue	Cancel	Do Not Know
November 1966	76	6	18
December 1968	85	3	12
1968 Subgroups			
LDP Supporters	87	2	11
JSP Supporters	85	3	12

SOURCE: Douglas H. Mendel, Jr., "Japanese Opinion on Key Foreign Policy Issues," *Asian Survey*, August 1969, pp. 625–39.

Japanese government's China policies, the gradual intensification of the LDP's internal cleavage on China helped eventually to undermine the conservative basis of Prime Minister Satō's foreign policy. Aware of this intraconservative conflict, the Chinese were eager to encourage and exploit it as an effective device for their penetration into the LDP's factional affairs.

Confrontation at the U.N   As the Japanese government had to make and execute a concrete decision on the question of Chinese representation at every U.N. session, its effect on the LDP loomed larger each year. This was particularly so because Prime Minister Satō professed to conduct a U.N.-centered diplomacy and used Nationalist China's original membership of that organization as a major rationale for his nonrecognition of the PRC. The implication was that only if the PRC were admitted to the United Nations, would he then begin to consider the question of recognizing it. Moreover, although the Chinese issue was debated and decided far away from East Asia and without Peking's direct participation, it constituted a symbolic demonstration of Sino-Japanese diplomatic confrontation.

Mindful of the growing intraparty debates on China, Prime Minister Satō explained his policy before the National Diet in January 1966. He said:

In the present international situation, the problem of China is taking on more and more importance in the sense that it is inseparably related to the peace and stability not only of Asia but of the whole world. . . . (T)he Japanese people, who have long had close relations with the people of China, earnestly desire the relaxation of international tensions, so that they can live in peace and harmony with all the Chinese people. However, as long as Communist China persists in its present rigid attitude and maintains a policy which might lead only to shutting its own gateway to the international community, we cannot deny that many difficulties still stand in the course of the development of the situation. The government, while maintaining its traditional friendly relations with the Republic of China, will deal cautiously with Communist China on the basis of not interfering with each other's domestic affairs and of ascertaining scrupulously our national interests.[136]

The Diplomatic Blue Book (1966), too, observed that China was further being isolated by a series of recent international events—the abortive military coup in Indonesia, the failure of the second Bandung conference, and China's diplomatic strains with some African countries and Cuba.[137] Above all, it noted the deterioration of Sino-Soviet relations due to their "fight for hegemony" among Communist states and Asian-African nations and to their differences over the Vietnam War and the Indo-Pakistani border dispute. It was a widely shared view in the Japanese Ministry of Foreign Affairs that the debates on Vietnam had precipitated the Cultural Revolution in China.[138] While upholding Japan's regular diplomatic relations with the Republic of China, the book stated that the issues concerning China must be settled "in a fair manner consistent with world opinion."

The notions of China's self-isolation and rigid attitude and Japan's vague references to "cautious" and "fair" approach were an underlying verbal theme that characterized Satō's China policy. For the Japanese the United Nations decisions on China were a principal measurement of the "world opinion," though they themselves were actively engaged in influencing these decisions. Earlier, at the twentieth U.N. General Assembly in November 1965, Ambassador Matsui Akira (Prime Minister Yoshida's secretary at the San Francisco peace conference) had noted no basic change in the factors concerning China since the 1961 decisions, but he had strengthened the Japanese stand favoring exclusion of the PRC with two additional arguments—namely, the unrealistic attitude of China toward the United Nations and the adverse regional consequence of China's representation at the United Nations.[139] If the General Assembly attempted to replace the ROC by the PRC, he warned, "no one can doubt that the present balance of forces in the area would be upset and that tensions would be unnecessarily increased." Citing Foreign Minister Chen Yi's recent press conference in which he criticized the Soviet-American domination in the United Nations and demanded the nullification of the U.N. resolutions condemning the PRC and North Korea as aggressors, Matsui expressed doubt as to whether China had any intention of recognizing the authority of the United Nations and of participating in its works.[140] The General Assembly, once again, passed the "important question" resolution by a vote of 56 to 49, with 11 abstentions and 1 absent, but for the first time the Albanian resolution for the PRC's sole representation at the United Nations received a tie vote (47 to 47, with 20 abstentions and 3 absent). Demonstrably happy with this voting record, the Chinese called it a "humiliating setback" to the U.S. and criticized "a very few countries such as Japan and Thailand" that openly echoed the United States abuse against China.[141]

At the twenty-first General Assembly in September 1966, Foreign Minister Shiina Etsusaburō complained about China's position on Vietnam as "conspicuously lacking in flexibility," and urged the PRC to show a "cooperative attitude" for peace and security in Asia and in the world.[142] Speaking at the First Committee two weeks later, Matsui repeated Shiina's earlier protest against the atmospheric nuclear tests conducted by China and France and urged them to listen to the "voice of reason" and to adhere to the partial nuclear test ban treaty. Further, he argued in November that the PRC had never extended its control to the Island of Taiwan, while the Republic of China had established a "free and democratic system which is totally different from that on the mainland."[143] The Albanian resolution, he said, was a complete denial of the indisputable facts about Taiwan and would result in "a serious state of affairs which might endanger peace and security in Asia and the Pacific." The General Assembly adopted the "important question" resolution by a 66 to 48 vote, with 7 abstentions, but defeated the Albanian resolution by a 46 to 57 vote (with 17 abstentions and 1 absent). Japan then voted for the Italian resolution, which would have set up a special committee to study the Chinese question, but the resolution was defeated.[144]

The official Japanese position on China was manifested in the LDP's ":ten-point platform" issued in December 1966, prior to the general elections for the House of Representatives.[145] It pledged to pursue an "independent foreign policy" dedicated to world peace on the basis of the U.N. Charter, to expand Japan's cooperation with the free world, and to strengthen friendly relations with Asian countries. As to China, it stated that: "The party will strive to expand economic and cultural exchanges with Communist China on the basis of the principles of mutual respect and non-interference in internal affairs. With regard to the problem of admitting Communist China to the U.N., the party will treat this problem carefully bearing in mind the existence of the Japan-(Nationalist) China peace treaty."

At the Extraordinary Diet session following the general elections, Prime Minister Satō noted the uncertain direction of China's Cultural Revolution, but observed that the Chinese situation would have "profound influence" on peace not only in Asia, but also in the world.[146] However, he made a round of visits to Taiwan and five Southeast Asian countries in September, to Australia, New Zealand, and three more Southeast Asian countries in October, and then to the United States in November 1967. His Taiwan visit, accompanied by LDP Dietman Matsuno Raizō and Vice-Minister of Foreign Affairs Mori Haruki, was the first by a Japanese prime minister since his brother's visit in 1957. At Taipei he twice conferred with Chiang Kai-shek, and joined Vice-President and Premier Yen Chia-kan in stressing their common goal of strengthening their solidarity for the maintenance of peace and prosperity in the Asian and Pacific region.[147] Satō and Yen also agreed to accelerate their bilateral cooperation in political, economic, and cultural fields. Satō's visit was soon reciprocated by Chang Chün, who was Chiang's special envoy at the funeral of Yoshida Shigeru in October, and later, by Chiang's son and Defense Minister Chiang Ching-kuo in November 1967.

Prime Minister Satō's extensive foreign trips were not only a reflection of his desire for anti-Communist regional solidarity, especially in relation to China and North Vietnam, but also a prelude to his determined negotiations with President Johnson for the reversion of the Ryūkyū and Bonin Islands. Noting China's nuclear programs, Satō and Johnson, in their joint communique of November 15, 1967, agreed on the importance of "creating conditions wherein Asian nations would not be susceptible to threats from Communist China."[148] They also hoped that China would cast aside its "intransigent attitude" and would seek to live in peace. Satō reported to Johnson that he had found widespread support for free world efforts to cope with "Communist intervention and infiltration" in Southeast Asia, and he promised to make a positive contribution to the peace and stability of Asia. This promise for Japan's regional role was offered at least in part to expedite the return of the Bonin and Ryūkyū Islands. For the same purpose he stated at the National Press Club in Washington that security in the Far East was of vital concern to Japan, and that Japan recognized the continuing role of the Ryūkyūs in maintaining that security. Furthermore, in his address given in New York, Satō specifically denounced China's nuclear weapons development and its "dogmatic and selfish way" of interfering in the affairs of its neighboring nations.[149]

The Chinese reaction to Satō's foreign ventures was predictably prompt and bitter. "Satō's trip to Taiwan," declared an angry editorial of the *People's Daily* (September 10, 1967), "is a component part of a big anti-China, anti-Communist, anti-people and counter-revolutionary conspiracy that is being vigorously hatched by the U.S. imperialists and Soviet revisionists in Asia." Moreover, a commentator in the *People's Daily* (November 21, 1967) claimed that the Satō-Johnson meetings meant "a serious step by the U.S. imperialists and Japanese reactionaries in their total collaboration—political, economic, and military—to carry on their policy of aggression and war in Asia more energetically."

While Prime Minister Satō manifested his extremely unfriendly attitude toward China, Foreign Minister Miki Takeo, who had succeeded Shiina in December 1966, deliberately attempted to take a little more conciliatory posture toward China, at least in the subtle nuances of his public remarks. This posture was related to his forthcoming bid to unseat Prime Minister Satō on the basis of their foreign policy differences. Sympathetic to the Asian-African Problems Study Group, Miki had frequently professed to seek good-neighbor relations and *kyōzon kyōei* (coexistence and coprosperity) with China—irrespective of its political system. Thus, in March 1967, he expressed at the National Diet his intentions to keep open a door to intergovernmental contacts with China and to take into account the changing international situation.[150] Although he viewed diplomatic normalization with China as premature, Miki was nonetheless enthusiastic about the expansion of economic, cultural, and personal exchanges between Japan and China. During the second ministerial meeting of the Asian and Pacific Council (ASPAC) held at Bangkok in July, it was Miki who restrained the extreme anti-Communist positions of Nationalist China and South Korea and inserted a moderate line of peaceful coexistence in the joint communique.[151] Likewise, at the twenty-second U.N. General Assembly in September, he refrained from repeating Shiina's earlier complaint about China's inflexible position on Vietnam, and explained that his support of the "important question" resolution was not meant to exclude the PRC from the United Nations.[152] He appealed to China and France to show a "cooperative attitude" toward the partial test ban treaty and the upcoming nuclear nonproliferation treaty. Miki's manifest attitude toward China was moderate and conciliatory, but he was unable to change the substance of Prime Minister Satō's China policy.

Meanwhile, the violent Cultural Revolution and its external effects damaged China's diplomatic image and strengthened the anti-Peking arguments at the United Nations. At the twenty-second General Assembly on November 10, 1967, Ambassador Tsuruoka Senjin, perhaps in the light of China's domestic political turmoil, no longer used the adjective "effective" in describing the PRC's control over mainland China, and questioned "whether that government is in fact willing to carry out the obligations and responsibilities enjoined by the Charter and whether its membership in the U.N. would be a positive factor in enhancing the prestige and authority of our organization."[153] Stripped of the diplomatic circumlocution, Tsuruoka's statement, in effect, denounced China's irresponsible and disruptive international behavior; but his statement was still far more restrained than the devastating charges made by the U.S. delegates. For example, L. H. Fountain contended that "there cannot be any more widely known fact in international affairs today than the warlike and aggressive manner in which the Peking regime has conducted itself all around its periphery from Tibet to Korea."[154] In response to Albania's defense of China's peaceful policy, he asked a rhetorical question: Can this possibly be said of the regime that committed or assisted an aggressive act in Korea, India, Laos, and Vietnam and that intervened to promote subversion as far away as Africa and Latin America? Citing the abuses of China's diplomatic behavior, he urged the member states to reject "this rigidly fanatical and violence-prone regime" at the United Nations. Undoubtedly as a result of the trouble cited by Fountain, Tsuruoka, and other pro-Taiwan spokesmen, the relative strength of pro-Peking forces declined at the United Nations for two years in a row; the margin of victory for the "important question" resolution rose from 7 votes in 1965 to 18 in 1966, and then to 21 in 1967, while the Albanian resolution, which had obtained a 47 to 47 tie in 1965, fell by 46 votes to 57 in 1966, and by 45 to 58 in 1967.

Extremely frustrated by these undesirable trends, a correspondent for the *People's Daily* (November 30, 1967) branded the United Nations as "nothing but an instrument of the U.S. in pushing its policies of aggression and war."[155] He also called Japan an American stooge and the Soviet Union an "insidious and despicable ally" of the United States in opposing China's representation. However, he added, the Chinese people were not at all interested in sitting in the United Nations—a place for playing power politics and striking political bargains. Again at the twenty-third General Assembly, Japan continued to cosponsor the "important question" resolution, though the AAPSG and the NPDG had specifically requested otherwise. Foreign Minister Miki simply hoped for the day when the PRC would willingly come

Table 9—U.N. Votes on China, 1961–68

Year		For	Against	Abstain	Absent	Total
1961:	A	61	34	7	2	104
	B	36	48	20	0	104
1962:	B	42	56	12	· 0	110
1963:	B	41	57	12	1	111
1965:	A	56	49	11	1	117
	B	47	47	20	3	117
1966:	A	66	48	7	0	121
	B	46	57	17	1	121
	C	34	62	25	0	121
1967:	A	69	48	4	1	122
	B	45	58	17	2	122
	C	32	57	30	3	122
1968:	A	73	47	5	1	126
	B	44	58	23	1	126
	C	30	67	27	2	126

NOTES: A To decide the "important question" resolution
B To replace the Republic of China by the PRC
C To set up a special committee on China (Italy)

to play a "constructive role for world peace."[156] Without much prodding from the United States or Japan, the United Nations resoundingly voted against the PRC in November 1968.

No doubt the erosion of pro-Peking sentiment in the United Nations was a direct result of China's extremely xenophobic and erratic foreign relations during the Cultural Revolution. The rampaging Red Guards attacked and harassed the premises and personnel of foreign diplomatic establishments in China and paralyzed the Ministry of Foreign Affairs and other governmental agencies. All but one of China's ambassadors were recalled to Peking, and China's diplomatic representatives in foreign countries continued to reflect an unstable, isolationist mood. The Japanese Diplomatic Blue Book (1968), while noting China's preoccupation with domestic political problems, observed that it would take some time before China could resume full-scale diplomatic activities.[157] In fact, the Cultural Revolution served to justify Prime Minister Satō's lack of an innovative policy toward China. The Chinese issue was used by Miki and his followers to challenge Satō for the LDP presidency in late 1968, but Satō easily won his third consecutive term at the first ballot.

Yet the growing intraparty pressure against Satō's policy at the United Nations, together with the closing phase of the Cultural Revolution, somewhat mellowed his stand on China. Speaking before the National Diet in January 1969, he said: "Although the Cultural Revolution is beginning to taper off, Communist China today is still beset with a number of problems, both domestic and external, and has not yet taken any initiatives in external relations based on international understanding and cooperation with all the countries of the world. The government, for the present, will keep the various doors for contact open as heretofore in the expectation of the change in Communist China's attitude."[158]

These "doors" were opened a bit wider in early 1969 when Japanese diplomatic agencies in France and other third countries asked their Chinese counterparts to hold negotiations about thirteen Japanese nationals detained in China, and about other related matters, but with no avail.[159] As far as the Chinese were concerned, they were in no mood to respond to Japan's limited diplomatic overtures, which they regarded as a deceptive maneuver. They were also reluctant to make a major diplomatic decision just prior to the ninth CCP National Congress, and they were irritated by Prime Minister Satō's and Foreign Minister Aichi Kiichi's unequivocal statements that the Republic of China was the only sovereign government of the entire Chinese territories and that the Japan-Taiwan peace treaty was applicable to mainland China.[160] Against this background they found it unrealistic to have fruitful diplomatic negotiations with the Satō government. Nevertheless, despite China's determined coolness, Aichi confidently asserted in *Foreign Affairs* (October 1969) that "the Communist Chinese will have to take more notice of Japan as our national influence, in keeping with our responses to new challenges, continues to rise."[161]

Problems of "People's Diplomacy"

The JSP and China   The irreversible alienation of first Ikeda and then Satō from the PRC did not always result in mutually beneficial cooperation between the JSP and China during the 1960s. As an extreme alternative to the LDP's China policies, the JSP proposed that Japan should abrogate the peace treaty with Taiwan, establish diplomatic relations with the PRC, and support the latter's exclusive representation in the United Nations. It also advocated the conclusion of a nonaggression pact and other intergovernmental agreements between Japan and China. However, the JSP, like the LDP, suffered from an intensifying interfactional policy cleavage on China, especially during the Cultural Revolution. Moreover, it was unable to adjust its radical policy to the moderate tendency of Japanese voters or to the rapid change of external political environments.[162]

In retrospect, it is evident that the Chinese pursued throughout the 1960s an explicit policy to undermine a coalition of moderate Socialist factions led by Eda Saburō and to tilt the factional balance in favor of Sasaki Kōzō. As Eda—first acting chairman and then secretary-general—solidified his control of the JSP in the aftermath of the security treaty crisis and Asanuma's assassination (in October 1960), the Chinese launched a systematic and extensive campaign against his "revisionist" concepts of structural reform, positive neutrality, and total disarmament. For though Eda regarded China as an important problem of Japanese foreign policy that needed to be resolved, he was firmly committed to the JSP's "autonomous" and "neutral" posture in international politics. Critical of the "Asanuma statement," he recognized a distinct difference between Japan and China in their respective antiimperialist struggles; in essence, he wished to dissociate the JSP from the CCP and the JCP, and to seek a Japanese way to socialism.[163]

As early as the summer of 1961, Chou En-lai conveyed to Tanaka Toshio (ex-dietman of the JSP and member of the extremist *Heiwa Dōshikai*) his dissatisfaction with Eda's structural reformism and with his "smile" toward the United States.[164] Chou's acceptance of the JSP's third official mission headed by Suzuki Mosaburō (former JSP chairman) in December 1961 was probably timed to publicize China's criticism of Eda's leadership and thus to bolster Sasaki's challenge against Eda at the forthcoming twenty-first JSP National Congress.[165] At the first reception held in Peking for the Suzuki mission, Chang Hsi-jo expressed his appreciation to Suzuki, Sasaki, and other Socialist leaders for their criticism of the "erroneous theory" (meaning Eda's structural reformism).[166] Mao Tse-tung, too, praised the unique quality of the JSP's militant tradition, thus implying his disapproval of Eda's policy which violated that tradition.[167]

The Suzuki-Chang joint statement issued on January 13, 1962 reaffirmed the correctness of the Asanuma statement and echoed Mao's declaration that the east wind was prevailing over the west wind.[168] It profusely accused the U.S. "imperialists" of reviving Japanese militarism, intensifying tensions all over the world, and suppressing national liberation movements in Asia, Africa, and Latin America. The Ikeda government was assailed for its hostile policy toward China and its behavior at the sixteenth U.N. General Assembly. Within the JSP, the moderate Kawakami and centrist Wada factions were openly critical of the reaffirmed Asanuma statement, while it was enthusiastically endorsed by the Suzuki faction and the *Heiwa Dōshikai*.[169] And the militant contents of this joint statement and China's overt interference into the JSP's internal matters backfired at the twenty-first National Congress a week later; by a 323 to 260 vote Eda defeated Sasaki for the post of secretary-general and the congress ratified his structural reformist platform.

The LDP promptly responded to the Suzuki-Chang joint statement with a massive counterattack that was far more vigorous than its previous reactions to the JSP-China joint statements. Secretary-General Maeo Shigesaburō denounced the JSP's lack of autonomy and the falsehood of the statement.[170] Further, the LDP organized a number of protest rallies in Tokyo, Osaka, and other metropolitan centers, where LDP officials and cabinet ministers spoke against the joint statement.[171] Their message was simple and clear—the JSP had shamefully sold out Japanese national interests by accepting China's irrational and militant foreign policy. Embarrassed by the sustained attack from within the JSP and without, Suzuki submitted a secret letter to JSP Chairman Kawakami Jōtarō in July to exonerate himself in relation to the controversial joint statement. He explained that although the Suzuki mission had originally decided not to reiterate the Asanuma statement, its members—Hozumi Shichirō and Hososeki Kanemitsu of the *Heiwa Dōshikai*—had privately expressed at Peking their support of the Asanuma statement; despite Suzuki's reluctance, it thus crept into the Suzuki-Chang joint statement. Since the CEC had already approved the joint statement, Kawakami quietly returned the letter to Suzuki without further action and subsequently explained his decision to the CEC.[172] But it was suspected that it was the Eda faction that leaked the letter to the press in August, in an effort to break up the leftist political alliance between the Suzuki (and Sasaki) faction and the *Heiwa Dōshikai*.[173]

Eda's conflict with China came to a direct and decisive confrontation at the eighth World Conference Against A- and H-Bombs in August 1962. While the JSP opposed the resumption of nuclear tests by the Soviet Union and the United States, the JCP and the Chinese delegates argued that the nuclear tests by Socialist states were meant to protect world peace against U.S. imperialism. (They also insisted that the conference should single out U.S. imperialism as the "enemy of peace," refrain from seeking total disarmament, and integrate the antibomb movement with national liberation struggles. Eda, however, demanded the broadest possible antibomb movement irrespective of class differences and political beliefs.) The dispute threw the conference into confusion, and the departing Chinese delegates attacked "a few JSP and *Sōhyō* leaders headed by Eda Saburō" for having obliterated a distinction between "enemies" and "friends" and for having slandered China's position at the conference.[174] On his part Eda criticized China's sectarian and divisive policy and stressed the JSP's "autonomous line" in anti-bomb movements.[175]

Speaking at the second anniversary of Asanuma's death in October 1962, Chang Hsi-jo equated Japanese "right-wing social democrats" with Tito and accused them of being agents of U.S. imperialism and modern revisionism.[176] The same charge was repeated two days later in the joint communique signed by the Chinese People's Institute of Foreign Affairs and the JSP's "*Anpokai*" (Group on the Security Treaty, which consisted of the first-term dietmen who were elected in the year of the security treaty crisis).[177] Moreover, when Sasaki submitted a critique of the "Eda vision" to the CEC just before the twenty-second National Congress, Hsieh Nan-kuang, director of the China-Japan Friendship Association, bolstered it by writing an article in Peking's *Takung-pao* (October 22, 1962), which condemned Secretary-General Eda's structural reformism and his alleged collusion with U.S. Ambassador Edwin O. Reischauer.[178] Eda was further blamed for his failure to follow the Asanuma spirit and for his inability to recognize the close relationship between national liberation movement and peaceful coexistence. In order to isolate Eda in the JSP, Hsieh praised Chairman Kawakami, Sasaki, the Suzuki faction, the *Anpokai*, and the *Heiwa Dōshikai*. When the twenty-second National Congress narrowly passed in November the Sasaki faction's resolution censuring the "Eda vision," Eda relinquished his secretary-generalship to his close ideological comrade, Narita Tomomi, but he kept his influence over the party almost intact.[179] The Chinese attack against Eda was not only intended to promote the leftist ascendancy in the JSP but was also designed to enhance the JCP's leadership in Japanese progressive movements. In fact, the Chinese were at this time earnestly wooing the JCP in their ideological disputes with the Soviet Union as indicated by the fact that they invited to China increasing numbers of JCP leaders and members in the first half of the 1960s.[180]

As the JSP began to be torn apart in the strong crosscurrents of the Sino-Soviet dispute, which was further supplemented during 1963 by the partial nuclear test ban treaty and by the divided anti-bomb movement, its leaders, particularly Secretary-General Narita, suggested that "we must preserve our basic policy of positive neutralism and peaceful coexistence and pursue friendly relations with both Communist countries."[181] The CEC followed with a "unified view" in August 1963 that the JSP must (1) avoid its involvement in the ideological conflicts of Communist states, (2) support Moscow's peaceful coexistence policy and the test ban treaty, and (3) sympathize with China's international positions.[182] This view represented a conscious effort among JSP leaders to maintain their internal unity and to show their neutral stand in the Sino-Soviet polemics.

Yet, on March 2, 1963, Radio Peking broadcast to Japanese listeners a Hsinhua News Agency report criticizing the right-wing Socialists, who had completely dominated the CEC posts in the twenty-third JSP National Congress held ten days previously. These leaders were accused of conniving to insure the success of the "two-China" plot and of colluding with U.S. imperialism and modern revisionism.[183] The JSP denied China's charges and suggested that China must cease its interference into the party's internal affairs.[184]

The fact that Eda and other moderate leaders had difficult relations with the PRC from 1961 to 1964 was a salient issue that the left-wing factions led by Sasaki adroitly exploited in their attacks on the moderate party leadership. The logic of factional dynamics and the conflict between "ins" and "outs" in the JSP's leadership structure magnified factional differences on foreign policies. This, in turn, led to a closer association between the left-wing factions and the PRC.

A day after the JSP dispatched an official goodwill delegation, headed by Secretary-General Narita, to the Soviet Union and East European states in June 1964, Sasaki and other left-wing Socialist dietmen departed for China. In his talks with Sasaki, Kuroda, and other JSP and Sōhyō leaders at Peking, Mao Tse-tung played up to Japanese nationalism by supporting Japan's claims to the Kurile archipelago, while he singled out for ridicule the JSP's policy of structural reformism, which he called "nonsensical." Chou En-lai added that structural reformism in the JSP and modern revisionism in the JCP were identical twins. If the left-wing Socialists persisted in their struggle for the Asanuma spirit, Chou encouraged, they would eventually capture a majority in the JSP.[185]

The growing power of the left-wing factions in the JSP was demonstrated when, under strong pressure from the Sasaki faction, Narita reluctantly led the JSP's fourth official mission to Peking amidst China's first nuclear explosion. As JSP Chairman Kawakami Jōtarō sent a cable to Premier Chou En-lai in which the JSP protested against China's explosion, Narita ran into a heated debate on nuclear issues with his Chinese hosts and barely averted an open rupture with China. The Narita-Chang joint statement of October 29, 1964 reaffirmed their common commitment to the Asanuma statement, but noted their differences on nuclear weapons.[186] It was noted, however, that both sides reached an agreement on the necessity of total and complete nuclear disarmament and the establishment of a nuclear-free zone in the Asian and Pacific region, including Japan, China, the Soviet Union, and the U.S.

Upon his assumption of the party chairmanship in 1965, Sasaki radicalized the JSP's international position along a pro-Peking orientation, but Eda raised the question of Sasaki's close identity with China to challenge his political integrity.[187] Eda preached an independent and creative Japanese road to socialism, but he was basically sympathetic to Moscow's peaceful policy and was unmistakably critical of Peking's militant tactics. By emphasizing the great promise of peaceful coexistence in world politics, he denounced the leftist Sasaki faction's pro-Peking outlook that the focus of international contradictions was shifting from U.S.-Soviet conflict to U.S.-Chinese confrontation and that the Vietnam War was only an extension of such a broad U.S.-Chinese relationship.[188]

Evidently influenced by Peking's arguments used in its anti-Soviet polemics, Sasaki argued that the JSP should simultaneously attack Japan's monopoly capitalists and the international imperialist forces headed by the United States. He declared that U.S. imperialism was not only the common enemy of Japanese and Chinese peoples but also the main enemy of the whole world.[189] In line with Peking's rhetoric he pointed out the illusion of those moderate Socialists who expected an era of peaceful coexistence to result from a Washington-Moscow détente. The articulation of Sasaki's radical and doctrinaire arguments against Eda and Moscow reflected his growing sympathy with Peking's foreign policy. In general, the international positions of Eda and Sasaki became divergent almost in direct proportions to the intensity of their factional struggles in the JSP and to the deterioration of Sino-Soviet relations. And adding to this divergence were their diametrically opposing assessments of the Chinese Cultural Revolution.

The Cultural Revolution became a major subject of debates among delegates at the twenty-eighth JSP National Congress in December 1966. The Eda faction was most distressed not only because an alliance of left-wing factions reelected Sasaki as chairman over Eda, but also because "there was a considerable increase in the number of deputies who rejected the party's line of positive neutrality, admired Mao Tse-tung's thought, and demanded a favorable appraisal of the Cultural Revolution."[190] Indeed, a radical pro-Peking deputy boldly stated at the Congress: "The Great Proletarian Cultural Revolution is a great cause which has no precedent in history. Mao Tse-tung's thought, which guides this Revolution, is the summit to Marxism-Leninism in our era. We must make conscious efforts to creatively study and apply Mao Tse-tung's thought."[191] Another added that nobody could grasp the international situation if he did not correctly understand the Cultural Revolution and the Soviet revisionism. Still another delegate criticized the Soviet Union's détente policy.[192] Obviously delighted with these statements made at the JSP congress, the Chinese concluded that these "mirrored the recent growth of the progressive forces within the (JSP)."[193]

Asked to clarify the party's position on the Cultural Revolution, Secretary-General Narita refused to give a definitive answer. But Chairman Sasaki was much less cautious in suggesting that "we need not be afraid of being called pro-China." His faction had already recognized the "great historical importance" of the Cultural Revolution, and some of its members had publicly praised the Chinese development and had sponsored the first Japanese edition of "Quotations from Chairman Mao Tse-tung."[194] When the JSP lost the general elections in January 1967, Sasaki was challenged by many defeated Socialist candidates, who attributed their failure to the party's ambiguous attitude toward the Cultural Revolution. Moreover, the Eda faction argued that this ambiguity created doubts among the Japanese people, who feared a similarly brutal situation might take place under a Socialist government in Japan.[195] The Kōno (ex-Kawakami) faction demanded the JSP's denunciation of the Red Guards' violent methods and of Mao's personality cult.[196] As the Cultural Revolution grew into a principal issue of interfactional controversies and its ugly features were prominently depicted in Japanese mass media during 1967, Sasaki became aware that his close identification with the PRC was a serious political liability. More importantly, his own faction was divided on the Cultural Revolution—between radical admirers and skeptical realists.

While the Sasaki faction remained relatively reticent on the Cultural Revolution, and the Kōno and Katsumata (ex-Wada) factions restrained their critical comments, the Eda faction stepped up its biting condemnation against the PRC's latest mass campaign. It was openly critical of the Red Guard's outrageous activities against foreign diplomats stationed in China, particularly those of the Soviet Union and East European countries; this "overflow of madness" or "xenophobic hysteria," it insisted, cast doubts on China's declared adherence to "proletarian internationalism."[197] It also warned the left-wing Socialists that they would repeat their electoral defeats unless they regarded China's extremist policy as harmful to the JSP's progress. Moreover, the Eda faction severely assailed the PRC's recent behavior toward its neighbors, charging that China was exporting the Cultural Revolution to Burma, India, and Indonesia and supporting armed revolutionary movements in these countries. The egocentric, great-nation chauvinism, it claimed, was amply manifested in China's insistence that Mao's thought was the only truth and that all those who did not respect that truth were reactionaries, fascists, or revisionists.[198] This outspoken diatribe by Eda was far more damning than Kaya Okinori's assessment of the Cultural Revolution.[199]

After a series of factional maneuvers resulted in the resignation of Chairman Sasaki and Secretary-General Narita at the twenty-ninth National Congress in August 1967, a precarious coalition of all major factions took over the party leadership with Katsumata Seiichi as chairman, Yamamoto Kōichi (Sasaki faction) as secretary-general, and Eda Saburō and Kōno Mitsu as vice-chairmen. As this leadership structure was based on a compromise of factional differences, it carefully avoided any action that might jeopardize the foundation of factional harmony. On such sensitive issues as the Cultural Revolution, therefore, both Katsumata and Yamamoto were reluctant to clarify their positions on China. Nevertheless, they took a few marginal initiatives to assume the leadership of a nationwide movement for Sino-Japanese cooperation. They proposed that a National Conference for the Restoration of Japan-China Diplomatic Relations be established by all those who could support its basic purpose—irrespective of political belief and affiliation. They also set up an informal policy discussion unit under the CEC to study the problems of Sino-Japanese relations and the shape of China's policy following the Cultural Revolution.[200] At the same time the JSP's Special Committee for Restoration of Japan-China Diplomatic Relations (chaired by Kuroda Hisao) drafted in May 1968 a position paper that suggested that the Cultural Revolution was an inevitable development necessary for all socialist countries and a major blow to the JCP "revisionists."[201] As these recommendations infuriated many moderate Socialists, Katsumata simply tabled them at the Central Executive Committee.

Dissatisfied with Katsumata's indecisive posture, the Chinese not only declined to accept any official mission that the JSP wished to send to China but also failed to welcome his proposal that a top-level supraparty Japanese delegation visit China.[202] It was indeed difficult for Katsumata to satisfy Peking's stubborn demand that the JSP formally declare its support of the Cultural Revolution. Like other small decision-making groups in Japan, the CEC, which consisted of divergent factional leaders, failed to make a major policy decision on China in the absence of a consensus among its members. The problem was further complicated by a JSP crisis in the latter half of 1968. After its disastrous defeat in the House of Councillors elections, the JSP elected Narita Tomomi and Eda Saburō as chairman and secretary-general, respectively.[203]

The revival of Eda's party leadership constituted a serious setback to the Sasaki faction and to China, both of which had long carried out a joint campaign against his "revisionist" influence in the JSP. Moreover, a segment of the Sasaki faction led by Yamamoto Kōichi defected and formed a Socialist Policy Discussion Group in December 1968. This protofaction, despite its leaders' hitherto pro-Peking orientation, came to espouse a general foreign-policy outlook that supported Soviet policies and opposed those of Peking.[204] It was Sasaki who had urged the JSP to recognize the success of the Cultural Revolution and to lead a national movement for Sino-Japanese diplomatic normalization, but he had failed to persuade his new political ally, Narita Tomomi.[205] As an independent-minded leader, Narita refused to identify himself with either Peking or Moscow, and had to maintain harmonious working relations with Secretary-General Eda and other moderate leaders whose critical views on the Cultural Revolution were unquestionable.

The *Heiwa Dōshikai* still constituted a tiny but militant minority that continued to articulate a pro-Peking line within the JSP, while the larger Sasaki faction was too divided to play an influential function in Japanese-Chinese relations. The Eda, Kōno, and Katsumata factions remained critical of the Cultural Revolution, and Narita and Eda did not attach a high policy priority to the Chinese question. The JSP's electoral failure led to more intense factional divisions, which in turn generated a profound dilemma in its relations with China. Crippled by internal disharmony and external ambivalence, it was unable to spearhead a popular movement for Sino-Japanese diplomatic normalization or to exert concerted pressure upon the LDP government's China policy.

Tactics of "People's Diplomacy"   Inspite of, or perhaps because of, the absence of diplomatic relations between Tokyo and Peking, a broad range of Japanese individuals and groups—in addition to the political parties and

Table 10—Socialist Factional Distribution in the House of Representatives, 1963–69

Faction:	1963[1]	1967[1]	1969[2] (preelection)	1969[2] (postelection)
Sasaki	39	44	33	17
Narita	–	–	6	6
Yamamoto	–	–	6	4
Eda	16	26	24	16
Kōno (ex-Kawakami)	22	19	13	14
Katsumata (ex-Wada)	44	31	28	22
Heiwa Dōshikai	9	8	(5)[3]	(1)[3]
Nōmin Dōshikai	3	3	4	3
Unaffiliated	8	9	15	7
Total:	141	140	134	90

SOURCES:
1. Hans H. Baerwald, "Japan: New Diplomatic Horizons, Old-Style Domestic Politics," *Asian Survey*, January 1968, p. 48.
2. Hans H. Baerwald, "Ittō-Nanaraku: The 1969 General Election in Japan," *Asian Survey*, March 1970, p. 187.
3. Adjusted from other sources, including *Kokkai Binran* (1970).

business circles—conducted various types of "people's diplomacy" with their Chinese counterparts. The activities ranged from cultural exchanges and mutual visits to joint declarations and political rallies. In the process, they served, intentionally or not, as important instruments for forging China's desired links with the Japanese body politic. As Herbert Passin suggests, the Chinese attached a particular political importance to playing on the susceptibilities and dispositions of responsive individuals and strata in Japan.[206] They appealed to the Japanese people's prevailing desire to be independent of foreign political influence, to become good neighbors of Asian nations, and to enjoy a peaceful and prosperous life. Even though the Japanese in general were known to espouse an ambivalent cultural orientation toward China—namely, a mixture of disdain and respect—they had historical and psychological reasons that rendered them susceptible to the lure of "people's diplomacy" with China. The tradition of cultural association between Japan and China is long, and an overwhelming majority of Japanese people felt their cultural indebtedness to China.[207] About one out of ten Japanese adults had the experience of visiting mainland China, Taiwan, or Hong Kong, and a large number of them shared a feeling of guilt toward China because of Japan's brutal aggression and exploitation of the Chinese people.[208] Many also had a nostalgic or sentimental attachment to China, where they had worked or stayed before the end of World War II. Still others, especially progressive intellectuals and students, tended to develop a new sense of admiration for what they regarded as the united, disciplined, and powerful government in China. Moreover, Japan, as an open competitive political system, was ideal for the shrewd tactics used by China in its penetrative process.

The Chinese conception of "people" as differentiated from "government" had a revolutionary implication in countries like Japan, whose governments did not, at least in the Chinese interpretation, correspond to the basic interests and aspirations of "people." The operational principle of the Chinese "people's diplomacy" was therefore to cultivate and mobilize friendly relations with as many "people" as possible so that they would be able to change the personnel or policies of the "government." It was also intended to help develop a people's revolutionary culture and to broaden the antiimperialist, patriotic united front in Japan.[209]

Much of "people's diplomacy" was carried out through elaborate and complex networks linking Japanese and Chinese "people's organizations." The Japanese proclivity to organize groups was an ideal setting for these networks. No doubt China's "people's organizations" were strictly controlled by the CCP; many leaders of these organizations enjoyed an overlapping membership in the CCP and/or the government bureaucracy. As Ross Terrill states, the personnel of these semiofficial "people's organizations," which are invisible within China, circulate like satellites in the outer orbit of the Ministry of Foreign Affairs and perform an able, flexible, and sometimes mysterious diplomatic function as integral parts of Chinese foreign-policy instruments.[210] The Sino-Japanese organizational linkage as of March 1966 is exemplified in chart 1. This linkage underwent a drastic change during 1966 and 1967 as a result of the CCP-JCP conflict and of the Cultural Revolution. Most Japanese organizations (e.g., the Japan-China Friendship Association) were split into two rival factions—pro-Peking and pro-Yoyogi, but others (e.g., the Japan-China Cultural Exchange Association) were purged of pro-JCP members. The JCP's subsidiary organizations (e.g., the Democratic Youth League) were completely excluded from the "people's diplomacy" with China. The revised organizational linkage as of June 1967 is illustrated in chart 2.

Of particular importance to the regular and comprehensive conduct of "people's diplomacy" were the Japan-China Friendship Association (JCFA), the Japan-China Cultural Exchange Association (JCCEA), the Chinese People's Association for Cultural Relations with Foreign Countries (CPACRFC; renamed in 1966 the Chinese People's Association for Friendship with Foreign Countries), and the China-Japan Friendship Association (CJFA). The JCFA was set up in 1950 under Matsumoto Jiichiro's leadership (JSP member of the House of Councillors) by the JCP, the JSP, labor unions, trade organizations, and cultural groups; the JCCEA was organized in 1956 under the leadership of former Prime Minister Katayama Tetsu (JSP member of the House of Representatives). The CPACRFC (under President Chu Tu-nan) was established in 1954 as a nongovernmental agency for administering cultural exchange programs with those countries with which China did not have diplomatic relations. The CJFA was the first binational friendship association organized for a country that did not establish diplomatic relations with China—an exceptional circumstance indicative of the high priority that China assigned to its "people's diplomacy" with Japan.

The CJFA was founded in October 1963 under the auspices of nineteen "people's organizations." They included the CPACRFC, the Chinese People's Institute of Foreign Affairs, the All-China Federation of Trade Unions, the Chinese Association for Promotion of International Trade, the Chinese Committee for Afro-Asian Solidarity, the China Peace Committee, the All-China Federation of Democratic Women, the All-China Federation of Democratic Youth, the Chinese Academy of Sciences, and the Chinese Red Cross.[211] Foreign Minister Chen Yi, Chu Tu-nan, and Li Te-chuan (president of the Chinese Red Cross) attended the inauguration meeting; also present were Ishibashi Tanzan, Suzuki Kazuo (vice-president of the JCFA), and Saionji Kinkatsu (a grandson of the late *genro* Saionji Kimmochi and ex-member of the House of Councillors, who had moved to Peking in 1958 as deputy secretary-general of the Peace Liaison Committee of the Asian and Pacific Regions). The officers were: honorary president—Kuo Mo-jo

Figure 2. Organizational Linkages between China and Japan: March 1966

Chinese Party	Chinese Government	Chinese "People's Organizations"	Japanese Organizations
Foreign Affairs Department	Ministry of Foreign Affairs	CPIFA	Japan Socialist Party
Foreign Affairs Staff Office of the State Council	Ministry of Foreign Trade	Liao Cheng-chih Office	Takasaki Office
	CERFC	CAPIT	JAPIT
			JCTPC
			JCEIU
			JCCEA
	CCRFC	CPACRFC	JCFA
		CJFA	
International Liaison Department	Bureau of Broadcasting	Radio Peking	RPLG
	Bureau of Foreign Publications	Foreign Languages Press	Bookstores
		Peking Review	Japan Press Service
			Ajiya Tsūshinsha
CCP			Japan Communist Party
Young Communist League	Bureau of Travel and Recreation	China International Travel Service	Democratic Youth League
			Travel Agencies
	COCA	All-China Federation of Returned Overseas Chinese	Tokyo Overseas Chinese Association
	Hsinhua News Agency	All-China Federation of Overseas Chinese	Japanese Journalists' Association
		All-China Federation of Newspaper Workers	
		All-China Federation of Trade Unions	Sōhyō
		All-China Students' Federation	Zengakuren, Shaseidō, and other youth groups
		All-China Federation of Democratic Women	Women's groups
		China Peace Committee	Japan Peace Committee
			Gensuikyō
		China Committee for Afro-Asian Solidarity	Japan's Afro-Asian Solidarity Committee

Notes:

CCP—Chinese Communist Party
CERFC—Commission for Economic Relations with Foreign Countries
CCRFC—Commission for Cultural Relations with Foreign Countries
COCA—Commission for Overseas Chinese Affairs
CPIFA—Chinese People's Institute of Foreign Affairs
CAPIT—Chinese Association for Promotion of International Trade
CPACRFC—Chinese People's Association for Cultural Relations with
  Foreign Countries

CJFA—China-Japan Friendship Association
JAPIT—Japanese Association for Promotion of International Trade
JCTPC—Japan-China Trade Promotion Council
JCEIU—Japan-China Export-Import Union
JCCEA—Japan-China Cultural Exchange Association
JCFA—Japan-China Friendship Association
RPLG—Radio Peking Listeners' Group
Sōhyō—General Council of Trade Unions
Zengakuren—All-Japan Federation of Student Self-Governing Associations
Shaseidō—Socialist Youth Alliance
Gensuikyō—Japan Council Against Atomic and Hydrogen Bombs

Figure 3. Organizational Linkages between China and Japan: June 1967

Chinese Party	Chinese Government	Chinese "People's Organizations"	Japanese Organizations
	Ministry of Foreign Affairs	CPIFA	Japan Socialist Party
Foreign Affairs Department — Foreign Affairs Staff Office of the State Council	Ministry of Foreign Trade	Liao Cheng-chih Office	Takasaki Office
	CERFC / CCRFC	CAPIT / CPAFFC[1] / CJFA	JAPIT / JCCEA / JCFA (OH)[2]
	Bureau of Broadcasting	Radio Peking	
	Bureau of Foreign Publications	Foreign Languages Press / Peking Review	Bookstores / Tōhō Tsūshinsha[3] / Chūgoku Tsūshinsha[4] / Pro-Peking Splinter Groups of the JCP[5] / Travel Agencies
CCP — International Liaison Department	Bureau of Travel and Recreation	China International Travel Service	
	COCA	All-China Federation of Returned Overseas Chinese	Tokyo Overseas Chinese Association
	Hsinhua News Agency	All-China Federation of Newspaper Workers	Japanese Journalists' Congress[6]
		All-China Federation of Trade Unions	Sōhyō
		All-China Students' Federation	Rōdō Shūhōsha / Anti-JCP Zengakuren
		All-China Federation of Democratic Women	Shaseidō / Women's groups
		China Peace Committee	
		China Committee for Afro-Asian Solidarity	Japan Committee for Afro-Asian Solidarity[7]

Notes:
1—Chinese People's Association for Friendship with Foreign Countries (renamed in April 1966 for the CPACRFC)
2—Japan-China Friendship Association (Orthodox Headquarters) (split in October 1966)
3—Split from the Japan Press Service in October 1966; under Satō Shigeo
4—Split from the Ajiya Tsūshinsha in March 1967
5—Include Yamaguchi Prefectural Committee(Leftist), which was organized in August 1966; Research Institute on Mao Tse-tung Thought(organized in October 1966); Japan Communist Party(Liberation Front), which had existed prior to the CCP-JCP conflict; and Zenshin Group(Osaka), which was set up in November 1966
6—Reorganized in November 1966 under Kobayashi Yuichi
7—Reorganized in November 1966 under Sakamoto Tokumatsu

(president of the Chinese Academy of Sciences, chairman of the China Peace Committee, and former vice-premier); president—Liao Cheng-chih (chairman of the Chinese Committee for Afro-Asian Solidarity); vice-presidents—Nan Han-chen (chairman of the Chinese Association for Promotion of International Trade), Chao Pu-chu (vice-president and secretary-general of the Chinese Buddhist Association), and Chou Erh-fu (vice-president and secretary-general of the CPACRFC); secretary-general—Chao An-po (director of the CPIFA); deputy secretaries-general—Lin Lin, Sun Ping-hua, and Wang Hsiao-yün.[212] In a telegram sent to the JCFA, the new association promised to pursue four objectives: to develop friendly and brotherly relations between the Chinese and Japanese peoples, to expand their cultural and economic exchanges, to normalize diplomatic relations, and to safeguard peace in Asia and in the world.[213]

Japan-China Friendship Association(s) Among all the Japanese organizations linked to China, the JCFA was the most important one for demonstrating the functions and problems of Sino-Japanese "people's diplomacy" in the 1960s. It assumed a wide range of functions designed to promote people's friendship and cooperation between two countries. Political representation and mobilization were its primary functions in Japan, for its faithfully and actively articulated and supported China's diplomatic and political interests. Through statements and mass demonstrations it exerted popular pressure upon the LDP government to nullify the Japan-Taiwan peace treaty, to establish diplomatic relations with the PRC, and to admit the latter to the United Nations. For example, the association cosponsored in 1964 a nationwide campaign to collect thirty million Japanese signatures on a petition favoring PRC representation and joined in 1965 the Liaison Committee for Promotion of Japan-China Diplomatic Restoration. Further, it organized protest rallies against Prime Minister Satō's journey to Taipei, and against Nationalist Chinese leaders' visits to Japan. And it unconditionally endorsed the Chinese positions on such controversial issues as nuclear tests, territorial disputes (with India, the Soviet Union, and even Japan), and the Cultural Revolution.[214] The association did not exercise an appreciable influence over the LDP and its government, but its membership grew from several hundred persons in 1950 to 51,500 in 1965.[215] Most of these members were drawn en masse from the JCP, the JSP, *Sōhyō*, trading firms, and other progressive cultural groups. Until mid-1966, members of the JCP and JSP dominated the association's central leadership posts.

Together with the Japan-China Cultural Exchange Association, the JCFA played a major role in negotiating and arranging cultural and personal exchange programs with China. The delegations of assorted functional, geographic, and cultural groups, from scientists and writers to dancers and sportsmen, were exchanged, and Chinese movies, paintings, pictures, stamps, sculpture, and artifacts were displayed in Japan. The association also sponsored public lectures, seminars, and language institutes to introduce China to the Japanese people, and held semidiplomatic receptions for visiting Chinese delegations or meetings for celebrating Chinese national days. It also saw that Chinese periodicals and other publications in Japanese—notably, "Quotations from Chairman Mao Tse-tung" (little red book), Mao's "Selected Writings," *Pekin Shūhō* (Peking Review, weekly), *Jinmin Chūgoku* (People's China, monthly), and *Chūgoku Gahō* (China Pictorial, monthly)—were widely disseminated.[216] The literary and historical writings, especially those by Kuo Mo-jo and Lu Hsün, were popularized in Japan. The Radio Peking Listeners' Group was organized to encourage and reward Japanese listeners to Peking's radio programs broadcast toward Japan for seven hours a day; at one time in the mid-1960s the group claimed 100,000 regular Japanese fans. The association sent a study group and other delegations to China, and set up in 1964 a Japanese-Chinese tourist company to organize all sorts of Japanese visitors to China. Table 11 demonstrates that a large number of the Japanese people visited China during the 1960s, though the number somewhat tapered off as a result of the Cultural Revolution. The Japanese visitors enjoyed warm receptions, guided tours, political talks with their Chinese hosts, and audiences with Chinese leaders; Chou En-lai alone met several hundred Japanese visitors during the 1960s. On these occasions the Chinese showed their socialist achievements and articulated their attitudes toward diplomatic and other relations with Japan. They utilized all these cultural and personal exchange programs to gain supporters and to neutralize skeptics and potential opponents.

In addition, the association provided direct services and supportive functions for humanitarian matters between Japan and China. The repatriation of Japanese nationals and the release of Japanese war criminals were supported, and the association helped repatriate to mainland China those Chinese workers who had been brought to Japan during World War II. Sometimes it held memorial services for those who had died in Japan and returned their remains to their relatives in China. Moreover, the association recommended about 20% of all "friendly" trading firms to China and assisted with China's economic and scientific exhibits held in Japan. In fact, many Japanese companies engaged in Sino-Japanese trade became corporate members of the association, thus providing a financial basis for its activities.

The CCP-JCP conflict, which started as a result of the abortive Mao-Miyamoto meeting in March 1966, caused a shock wave of confusion and disintegration in all major Japanese organizations, including the JCFA. This wave also intensified an already competitive relationship between the JCP and the JSP, and with this intensified competition Sino-Japanese "people's diplomacy" found itself in deep trouble. A number of JCFA leaders,

Table 11—Exchange of Visitors between Japan and China, 1949-69

Year	Japanese Visitors to China[1]	Chinese Visitors to Japan (Number of Groups)
1949	6	0
1950	0	0
1951	9	0
1952	50	0
1953	139	0
1954	192	10 (1)
1955	847	106 (4)
1956	1,204	144 (8)
1957	1,255	146 (19)
1958	589	93 (5)
1959	222	0
1960	595	18 (2)
1961	440	86 (12)
1962	613	78 (10)
1963	1,831	281 (24)
1964	1,924	493 (61)
1965	4,472	454 (62)
1966	3,844	486 (59)
1967	2,778	142 (25)
1968	2,228	10 (2)
1969	2,547[2]	6 (1)[3]

SOURCES: *Nitchū kankei kihon shiryōshū* (Tokyo: Kasumiyamakai, 1970); and Suga Eiichi, Yamamoto Tsuyoshi, and Shiranishi Shinichiro, *Nitchū mondai* (Tokyo: Sanseidō, 1971).

NOTES: 1. Excludes Japanese participants in Canton fairs
2. Up until October 1969
3. Up until November 1969

together with some influential JSP and *Sōhyō* members, were active in assisting the CCP's determined campaign against Miyamoto's leadership of the JCP. On September 26, 1966, for example, Miyazaki Seimin (JCFA chairman), Kuroda Hisao (JCFA vice-president and JSP adviser), and Itō Takeo (JCFA vice-president and chairman of the Chinese Research Institute) joined Sasaki Kōzō (JSP chairman), Horii Toshikatsu (*Sōhyō* chairman), Iwai Akira (*Sōhyō* secretary-general), and other prominent civic leaders in issuing a "32-person appeal," in which they stressed the importance of unity and friendship between Japanese and Chinese peoples.[217] They also suggested that the obstacle to this friendship in Japan (implying the JCP) should be overcome.

In response to this Japanese appeal, fifty-two Chinese leaders—including Kuo Mo-jo, Liao Cheng-chih, Chang Hsi-jo, and Liu Ning-yi—issued a welcoming congratulatory statement on October 5. They denounced the anti-China positions adopted by U.S. imperialists, the Satō government, Soviet revisionists, and their "old and new followers" (meaning the JCP).[218]

The identification of these "four enemies" became a major policy line employed by China in Sino-Japanese "people's diplomacy." The CJFA and seven other Chinese organizations sponsored a rally of 1,500 people in Peking to support the "32-person appeal." Liao, Kuroda, and Saionji spoke at the rally.[219] A week thereafter, the delegation of the JCFA headed by Miyazaki Seimin issued a joint statement with Liao Cheng-chih.[220] The statement expressed their support for the "32-person appeal" and the "52-person statement," pointed out the danger of Japan's revived militarism, and attacked the further degeneration of the Soviet revisionism. The Japanese side noted that the Cultural Revolution was an important process for guaranteeing China's correct revolutionary progress and pledged to fight against all the obstacles that were developing in Japan against the goal of Sino-Japanese friendship and cooperation.

When the Board of Standing Directors of the JCFA met on October 25, 1966, some members, especially those belonging to the JCP, refused to ratify the Miyazaki-Liao joint statement on the ground that it contained a transparent attack against the JCP. Although a majority of the board members supported the statement, they decided to leave the JCP-dominated JCFA and to set up a new rival organization. The following day the Japan-China Friendship Association (Orthodox Headquarters) was established under Miyazaki Seimin (chairman), Matsumoto Jiichirō (president), Kuroda Hisao (one of three vice-presidents), and Miyoshi Hajime (secretary-general).[221] The situation was similar to the two-way split of the Japan-Soviet Friendship Association that had taken place in the 1964-65 period. The CJFA promptly recognized the new Orthodox Headquarters and denounced the JCP-controlled JCFA. In a telegram sent to Miyazaki and Kuroda, Chao An-po (CJFA secretary-general) expressed his support and appreciation of their professed struggle against "modern revisionists and splitters."[222]

The JSP confronted a difficult problem of choice between the two rival friendship organizations. Even though it had never assumed a position of commanding leadership in the JCP-controlled JCFA, it was reluctant to endorse the Orthodox Headquarters because the latter's unabashed pro-Peking position might tarnish the party's image in domestic politics. Yet some members of the Sasaki faction and the *Heiwa Dōshikai*, including Matsumoto Jiichirō and Kuroda Hisao, took leading positions in the Orthodox Headquarters. When the JCFA and the JCP were directly involved in a bloody incident with radical overseas Chinese students at the *Zenrin* (Good Neighbor) Student Hostel in Tokyo in late February and early March 1967, the JSP was compelled to clarify its position on the incident, which was a CCP-JCP confrontation by proxy. As soon as the CEC decided to conduct an investigation of the incident, the JCP presented its own version and threatened that should the JSP's investigation make any accusation against the JCP's activities, it would adversely affect their united action in local elections, particularly in the contest for the Tokyo governorship.[223]

Meanwhile, the JCFA (Orthodox Headquarters), the Japanese Association for Promotion of International Trade, and the Japan-China Cultural Exchange Association jointly sponsored a meeting which 250 politicians, businessmen, labor leaders, and cultural persons attended to discuss the *Zenrin* incident; it was held in response to the protest meetings and demonstrations organized by the JCP and the JCFA.[224] Kuroda, Kaneta Tomitarō (*Sōhyō* vice-chairman and chairman of the All-Japan Dock Workers' Union), and Sun Ping-hua (head of the Liao Cheng-chih Liaison Office in Tokyo) denounced what they called the JCP's deliberate persecution of overseas Chinese students at *Zenrin*. LDP Dietman Utsunomiya Tokuma, a spokesman of the Asian-African Problems Study Group, also joined the meeting and spoke against the JCP. Ultimately, the meeting adopted a resolution deploring the JCP's and JCFA's anti-China policy.[225] The *Zenrin* episode was a decisive turning point in the deteriorating relations between the JCP and the CCP. The Chinese expressed strong indignation and protest against the JCP's "atrocities" at *Zenrin* and its leaders' alleged racial slur against the Chinese people (as "chankoro"), while the JCP attacked the CCP's "ultra-leftist opportunism" and "big-nation chauvinism."[226]

Once the local elections were over, the JSP sent instructions to its local organizations in May 1967; it held the JCP responsible for the *Zenrin* incident and formally endorsed the Orthodox Headquarters.[227] The instructions explained that the JCP's change in its international positions had caused friction with China and that the JCFA had been ineffective in promoting friendly cooperation between the Japanese and Chinese peoples. The JCP's reaction was immediate and bitter.[228] JCP Chairman Nosaka Sanzō and Secretary-General Miyamoto Genji met with Sasaki and Narita and protested against the JSP's decision, but to no avail. In a series of ensuing *Akahata* editorials and articles, the JCP launched a direct attack against the JSP's lack of independent judgment. Like the JCP, the Eda and Kōno factions criticized the instruction and asked Sasaki and Narita to rescind it at once. The JSP's interfactional disputes were thus revitalized by the question of the Sino-Japanese friendship movement, although its twenty-ninth National Congress held in August 1967 in effect accepted the party's association with the Orthodox Headquarters.[229]

While the JCP continued to control the weakened JCFA (with a reduction of membership from 50,000 to 30,000), which had an extremely unfriendly attitude toward the PRC, the Orthodox Headquarters suffered from a low membership (only several thousand members) and an internal power struggle—particularly between the ex-JCP members of Yamaguchi

Prefecture and the radical Marxist-Leninist faction of the *Zengakuren* (All-Japan Federation of Student Self-Governing Organizations). One aspect of their struggle was their competition to show that they were more Maoist than Mao Tse-tung. The struggle, which developed into direct physical confrontations in the spring of 1969, caused a split between Miyazaki and Kuroda, who headed the rival offices for the Orthodox Headquarters.[230] Much to the disappointment of the Chinese, these confrontations threw the Orthodox Headquarters into a state of utter confusion and decay. Given its factional infighting and its total submission to Chinese policy, the Orthodox Headquarters, already in tough conflict with the JCFA, failed to foment a broad united action on China's behalf or to lead a viable friendship movement between the Japanese and Chinese peoples. This situation was to persist until 1971, when the Chinese finally persuaded Kuroda and Miyazaki to merge their rival factions into the unified Orthodox Headquarters.[231]

The disintegration of pro-Peking political forces in Japan, including the JCFA and the JSP, demonstrated the failure of China's "people's diplomacy" during the Cultural Revolution. Since the Chinese had already suffered an irrevocable political estrangement from the LDP government as well as the JCP, they had no effective organizational instrument for influencing Japan's domestic politics and foreign affairs. Hence they were clearly incapable of achieving their primary objectives in Japan—namely, to mobilize a broad pro-Peking united front in Japan and to undermine Japan's support for the United States policy of military containment and diplomatic isolation against the PRC.

Like his conservative predecessors from Yoshida to Ikeda, Prime Minister Satō steadfastly refused to deviate from the San Francisco system and its corollaries. If Japanese prime ministers had followed an unimaginative and passive policy toward China during the 1950s because they lacked an economic and psychological basis for autonomous foreign policy and because they were sufficiently constrained by external pressures from Washington and Taipei, Satō presided over the period of Japan's unprecedented economic growth and witnessed the increase in Japan's national self-confidence. Yet he failed to take any bold initiative for improving the political context of Sino-Japanese relations, but rather decided, despite the LDP's internal disagreements, to pursue an increasingly assertive and hostile policy toward the PRC. Consequently, there appeared no immediate prospect for relaxation of political tensions between Tokyo and Peking.

3
The Making of Diplomatic Rapprochement

Erosion of the Containment Structure

Controversy over Japanese Militarism About the time that the ninth National Congress of the CCP, which was held in April 1969, concluded one phase of the tumultuous Cultural Revolution and solidified the Maoist political order, the PRC started to retreat from the militant and xenophobic foreign policy that it had pursued for nearly three years. The Ministry of Foreign Affairs resumed its normal diplomatic functions, and Chinese ambassadors were sent abroad for the first time since the Cultural Revolution. This relaxation of China's external posture led to substantial increase in economic and personal exchanges between Japan and China. Various "people's organizations" in Japan were thus encouraged to expect a new blossoming of intimate Sino-Japanese relations in the post-Cultural Revolution era, but the LDP government asserted that because of the increased power of military leaders in the ninth CCP Central Committee, China would continue to maintain a rigid diplomatic posture for some time to come.[1]

The JSP, unlike the LDP or the JCP, promptly recognized the legitimacy of the ninth National Congress and prepared itself for leading a movement for Sino-Japanese diplomatic normalization.[2] This followed its introduction to the National Diet in March 1969 of a resolution calling on the Japanese government to normalize diplomatic and economic relations with China and to restore its lawful rights in the United Nations.[3] And even though the governing LDP majority had easily blocked this parliamentary maneuver, it failed to discourage the JSP's other activities in support of China in the following months.

Another political development, perhaps far more significant in the long run than the JSP's activities, was taking place in the LDP. The pro-Peking dietmen of the Asian-African Problems Study Group seized on the passing of the Cultural Revolution as an opportunity to reassert their positions more boldly than ever before. The mood was symbolically reflected in the joint communique on memorandum trade that Dietman Furui Yoshimi signed with China's Liu Hsi-wen (assistant deputy vice-minister of foreign trade) in April 1969.[4] The Chinese denounced the Satō government "for stepping up its efforts to follow U.S. imperialism, for participating in the conspiracy to create 'two Chinas' and for barefacedly adopting a policy of hostility toward China." Furui admitted that (1) the Japanese government was responsible for the deterioration of Sino-Japanese relations; (2) the Japan-Taiwan peace treaty was illegal; and (3) the U.S.-Japan security treaty constituted a threat to China and thus an important obstacle to Sino-Japanese cooperation. He also stated "that the Government of the People's Republic of China is the only legitimate government representing the Chinese people, that Taiwan Province is an inseparable part of China's territory, that this must be the basis for understanding the promotion of the normalization of diplomatic relations between Japan and China, and that it opposes the conspiracy of creating 'two Chinas' in any form."

Furui explained to his Chinese counterparts that while he himself was opposed to the U.S.-Japan security treaty, it was not an aggressive pact. Yet the Chinese insisted on Furui's public and explicit opposition to the treaty because they were aware of, and hopeful for, a possible domestic crisis in Japan during 1970 over its status.[5] The JSP promptly hailed the communique as a "programmatic document" for normalizing Sino-Japanese relations, and declared that the Satō government had a political and moral obligation to respect the trade agreement negotiated and signed by the LDP dietman.[6]

Neither the Japanese government nor the LDP formally refuted the charges contained in the communique. At the House of Councillors a few days later, Prime Minister Satō simply denied his "hostility" toward China, but instead stressed the mutual benefits of continuing trade relations. Moreover, Minister of International Trade and Industry Ōhira Masayoshi expressed his appreciation for Furui's difficult efforts to preserve memorandum trade, though LDP Vice-President Kawashima Shōjirō dissociated the party from the communique.[7]

Further evidence of divisions within the LDP was provided by a wide range of divergent individual comments offered by LDP dietmen. While Matsumura, Fujiyama, Miki, Maeo Shigesaburō, Nakasone Yasuhiro, and Kōno Yohei were supportive of Furui's efforts, Kaya Okinori accused him of having committed a discourteous act against Nationalist China and the United States for the sake of "subservient trade" with China, and Funada Naka criticized Liu's and Furui's attack on the U.S.-Japan security treaty. A few pro-Taiwan LDP dietmen, notably Nakano Shirō of the Satō faction and Kikuchi Yoshirō of the Kawashima faction, demanded that the party institute strict disciplinary measures against Furui.[8] These controversies not only demonstrated a growing policy cleavage in the ruling political party, but also reflected Satō's basic political friction with the PRC.

The Tokyo-Peking friction was further aggravated by Satō's visit to the United States in November 1969, which provoked China's vociferous attack against the revival of Japanese militarism. The primary purpose of his visit was to expedite the Okinawa reversion, but, as a price tag for this purpose, he was prepared to make a public commitment for Japan's broad security interest in Asia. In a joint communique issued on November 21, 1969, Satō and President Nixon stated:

The President and the Prime Minister specifically noted the continuing tension over the Korean peninsula. The Prime Minister deeply appreciated the peace-keeping efforts of the United Nations in the area and stated that the security of the Republic of Korea was essential to Japan's own security. The President and the Prime Minister shared the hope that Communist China would adopt a more co-operative and constructive attitude in its external relations. The President referred to the treaty obligations of his country to the Republic of China which the United States would uphold. The Prime Minister said that the maintenance of peace and security in the Taiwan area was also a most important factor for the security of Japan.[9]

Nixon agreed to return to Japan the administrative rights over Okinawa by 1972 so long as it constituted no detriment to the security of the Far East. The United States was allowed to retain its military facilities in Okinawa on the same level as Japan proper, but without nuclear weapons. In turn, Satō promised to assume the responsibility for the defense of Okinawa, to extend the U.S.-Japan security treaty indefinitely, and to make "further active contributions" to the peace and prosperity of Asia.

Moreover, in his address delivered at the National Press Club, Satō declared, in effect, that if Taiwan or South Korea were under an armed attack from the outside, Japan would regard the situation as a threat to the peace and security of the Far East, including Japan, and would take prompt and positive measures so that the United States would use its military bases and facilities within Japan to meet the armed attack.[10] As part of what he termed a "New Pacific Age," Satō asked China to revise its rigid posture and to carry out its international responsibilities in a constructive manner.

While the Soviet Union was pleased with the Nixon-Satō joint communique because it was expected to prevent the development of a unilateral strategic force by Japan and to contain China's regional military temptations, China's reaction was swift and acrimonious.[11] "The Nixon-Satō talks," asserted the Chinese, "are an important step by the U.S. and Japanese reactionaries in intensifying their military collaboration and hatching a new war plot."[12] At the diplomatic reception given by the Albanian ambassador to China on November 29, Chou En-lai commented on the Nixon-Satō statement. He argued that the Okinawa reversion was a fraud, because while Nixon agreed to return Okinawa to Japan, Satō in fact agreed to turn the whole of Japan into another Okinawa—namely, the U.S. base for aggression in Asia. Thus the Okinawanization of Japan became China's chief propaganda theme. "Abetted by U.S. imperialism and drunk with rabid ambition," said Chou, the Satō government was attempting to "step up the revival of militarism and realize its old dream of a Greater East Asia Coprosperity Sphere."[13] He also argued that the Soviet Union was actively wooing the Satō government and was trying to make use of the U.S.-Japanese military alliance in isolating China and sabotaging Korea's reunification. This argument was probably intended to discourage Japan's acceptance of Brezhnev's plan for an Asian collective security system (proposed in June 1969) and to drive North Korea out of Moscow's embrace.

Even though Prime Minister Satō and Foreign Minister Aichi Kiichi, in view of the renewed Sino-American diplomatic talks at Warsaw, suggested in December 1969 (before the general elections) that they were willing to open intergovernmental negotiations with China, the latter's anti-Satō rhetoric did not subside. Instead, the Chinese launched a vigorous campaign against the revival of Japanese militarism, which reached a climax during Premier Chou's state visit to North Korea in April 1970. The joint communique signed by Chou and Kim Il-song on April 7 declared:

Actively shielded by U.S. imperialism, Japanese militarism has revived and has become a dangerous force of aggression in Asia. . . . The Japanese militarists are directly serving U.S. imperialism in its war of aggression against Vietnam, actively taking part in the U.S. imperialist new scheme of war in Korea and widely attempting to include the Chinese people's sacred territory Taiwan in their sphere of influence.[14]

The communique was soon followed by Chou's enunciation of "four conditions" for Sino-Japanese trade relations.[15]

The Chinese thesis that "Japanese militarism has already revived" was not a new phenomenon in 1970, but it had been asserted on previous occasions—for example, on January 14, 1960, when the Chinese Foreign Ministry denounced the revised U.S.-Japan security treaty, and on November 21, 1967, when the *People's Daily* criticized the Johnson-Satō joint communique. What made the Chinese thesis particularly important in 1970 was the fact that during the 1960s Japan had established a powerful economic base for potential military expansionism. Further, despite the alleged collusion between U.S. imperialism and Japanese militarism, the Chinese seemed to change their conception of Japanese-American relations in the 1969-70 period; Japan was not viewed as a hitherto subservient dependency of the United States, but as an increasingly competitive economic rival of the United States.

As Okabe's content analysis of the *People's Daily* shows, the Chinese tended to pay more sensitive attention to Japanese militarism than to U.S. imperialism and to blame the Japanese ruling elite for anti-China activities, arms expansion, economic aggression, foreign military ambitions, and militaristic propaganda.[16] Table 12 demonstrates that out of the total number of paragraphs (488) which the *People's Daily* devoted to Japan in the first quarter (January-March) of 1969, 20 paragraphs (4.1%) referred to Japanese militarism, but 102 paragraphs (20.9%) to U.S. imperialism. In the third quarter (July-September) of 1970, however, the *People's Daily* allocated more paragraphs to Japanese militarism than to U.S. imperialism (46.5% vs. 35.5%). Likewise, in table 13, we can find a considerable increase in *People's Daily* reports on the Japanese ruling elite (from 60.9% in the first quarter of 1969 to 86.5% in the third quarter of 1970) and on their general aggressiveness (from 19.9% to 59.9% for the same duration). As the Japanese ruling elite's behavioral attributes in the third quarter of 1970, the *People's Daily* most frequently discussed their anti-China activities (23.1%) and economic aggression (15.0%). Moreover, whereas the Chinese had been mainly concerned with the issue of Japanese-Taiwanese cooperation in the 1960s, in 1970 they were more vocal about Japan's alleged efforts to strengthen economic control over Taiwan, to assist the Taiwanese independence movement, and to reannex Taiwan itself.[17]

Table 12—*People's Daily* Reports on Japan, 1967-70

	1967	1968				1969				1970			Total
	IV	I	II	III	IV	I	II	III	IV	I	II	III	
Total Number of Paragraphs on Japan	367	332	462	477	427	488	302	470	468	440	398	355	4,986
Paragraphs on Japanese Militarism	21	24	25	32	17	20	5	32	45	47	118	165	551
(%)	5.7	7.2	5.4	6.7	4.0	4.1	1.7	6.8	9.6	10.7	29.6	46.5	11.1
Paragraphs on American Imperialism	82	81	148	97	79	102	63	77	128	84	173	125	1,239
(%)	22.3	24.4	32.0	20.3	18.5	20.9	20.9	16.4	27.4	19.1	43.5	35.5	24.8

SOURCE: Okabe Tatsumi, *Gendai chūgoku no taigai seisaku* [Modern Chinese foreign policy] (Tokyo: Tokyo daikaku shuppankai, 1971), p. 32.
NOTES: I   January-March
       II   April-June
      III July-September
      IV October-December

Table 13—People's Daily Reports on Japan, 1967-70

	1967 IV	1968 I	1968 II	1968 III	1968 IV	1969 I	1969 II	1969 III	1969 IV	1970 I	1970 II	1970 III	Total
Total Number[1] of Paragraphs on Japanese Ruling Elite	172	164	234	280	183	297	193	330	343	267	267	307	3,037
(%)[2]	46.9	49.4	50.6	58.7	42.9	60.9	63.9	70.2	73.3	60.7	67.1	86.5	60.9
Aggressiveness	51	53	69	62	26	59	48	85	129	110	160	184	1,036
(%)	29.7	32.3	29.5	22.1	14.2	19.9	24.8	25.8	37.6	41.2	59.9	59.9	34.1
Arms Expansion	2	20	20	27	12	10	11	53	47	65	27	34	328
(%)	1.2	12.1	8.5	9.6	6.6	3.4	5.7	16.1	13.7	24.3	10.1	11.1	10.8
Foreign Military Dispatch	4	0	0	2	3	1	0	12	29	31	27	11	120
(%)	2.3	0	0	0.7	1.6	0.3	0	3.6	8.5	11.6	10.1	3.6	4.0
Economic Aggression	6	1	30	27	15	14	19	39	48	44	28	46	317
(%)	3.5	0.6	12.8	9.6	8.2	4.7	9.8	11.8	14.0	16.5	10.5	15.0	10.4
Militaristic Propaganda	0	8	2	11	3	1	8	14	3	16	9	35	110
(%)	0	4.9	0.9	3.9	1.7	0.3	4.1	4.2	0.9	6.0	3.4	11.4	3.6
Anti-China Activities	72	13	30	52	30	35	37	78	67	69	50	71	604
(%)	41.9	7.9	12.8	18.6	16.4	11.8	19.2	23.6	19.5	25.8	18.7	23.1	19.9

SOURCE: Okabe Tatsumi, *Gendai chūgoku no taigai seisaku* [Modern Chinese foreign policy] (Tokyo: Tokyo daikaku shuppankai, 1971), p. 33.

NOTES: 1. References to the Japanese ruling elite include "Japanese reactionaries," "Japanese government," "Satō government," "Japanese militarists" and "Japanese monopoly capitalists."

2. Percent of total paragraphs on Japan

Quoting Lenin's dictum that "modern militarism is the result of capitalism," the Chinese constructed an economic determinism of Japanese militarism. Underlying this notion was their apparently genuine fear that the rapid growth of Japanese economic power might be inevitably accompanied by political and military expansionism. They were aware of the fact that the Japanese *zaikai* (especially, *Keidanren* Chairman Uemura Kogorō and Mitsubishi) were exerting a strong pressure upon their government to increase domestic production of armaments and to allow military sales to foreign countries.[18] Yet the military-industrial complexes were far from solidified in Japan, and defense industries occupied less than 1% of Japan's total industrial outputs. As table 14 reveals, it is true that Japan's defense budget had increased nearly five-fold over a decade (FY 1960-71), but the Chinese failed to note that contrary to their own high military expenditures, which shared about 10% of China's Gross National Product, Japan's relatively modest expenditures were less than 1% of its GNP and only about one-fifth of China's defense budget in 1970. The size of the Japanese Self-Defense Forces had remained almost steady during the 1960s, but there was

Table 14—Japanese Defense Expenditure and Self-Defense Forces, 1954-72

Year	Defense Expenditure (in million dollars)	Percent of National Budget	Percent of Gross National Product	Authorized Size of the SDF (in thousands)	Actual Size of the SDF (in thousands)
1954	375	13.51	1.73	152	146
1955	375	13.31	1.52	180	178
1956	397	13.11	1.44	197	188
1957	399	13.11	1.28	214	211
1958	412	11.14	1.26	222	214
1959	432	10.29	1.14	231	215
1960	444	9.07	.99	231	206
1961	510	8.71	.92	242	209
1962	594	8.34	.99	244	216
1963	688	8.10	.97	244	213
1964	780	8.41	.95	246	216
1965	846	8.16	.94	246	226
1966	957	7.71	.91	246	227
1967	1,075	7.74	.86	250	231
1968	1,172	7.13	.80	250	235
1969	1,375	7.14	.79	258	236
1970	1,640	7.16	.81	259	236
1971	2,252	–	.88	259	–
1972	2,601	–	.88	263	–

SOURCES: 1. *Nihon no bōei* [Japanese national defense] (Tokyo: Bōeichō, 1970).
2. Kunio Muraoka, *Japanese Security and the United States* (London: International Institute for Strategic Studies, 1973, Adelphi Paper No. 95).
3. *Japan Report*, February 16, 1972.

a marked improvement in their training programs and sophisticated weapons. Still, table 15 illustrates a tremendous disparity between China and Japan both in strategic capabilities and in conventional armament.

The vigorous Chinese attack against Japanese militarism aroused a great emotional commotion among the LDP leaders, especially when it was incorporated in another Furui-Liu joint communique on memorandum trade issued in April 1970.[19] The communique condemned the Nixon-Satō summitry, U.S.-Japan military cooperation, and the deceptiveness of the Okinawa return. Furui further expressed his "determination to make greater efforts to renounce and smash the revival of Japanese militarism and to oppose wars of aggression." It is difficult to imagine how a responsible parliamentarian of the conservative ruling party could have accepted the extremely harsh attacks against his own government. In fact, during his long and tortuous political debates with his Chinese counterparts, Furui had made a serious attempt to resist their fundamentalist terms, especially in regard to the "fraud" of the Okinawa reversion and the "facts" of revived Japanese militarism. But after he was directly accused of being a Satō apologist, Furui was even forced to make a "self-criticism" before his Chinese negotiators. Although LDP Dietman Tagawa Seiichi in Peking advised him to call off the trade negotiations, Furui decided to swallow a bitter pill, namely most of the Chinese terms, in a desperate effort to save memorandum trade.[20] On his part, Furui felt that he had invested too much

Table 15—Military Balance—A Comparison, 1970

	Army		Navy		Air Force	
	Number of Troops (in thousands)	Number of Divisions	Number of Ships	Tonage (in 10,000 tons)	Combat Aircraft	Percent[1]
Japan	179	13 divisions	210	12.5	450	1.0
China	2,450	118 divisions	940	20	2,800	1.8
U.S.A.	1,363	16 divisions 5 brigades 5 regiments 45 battalions 200 independent aviation units	2,200	790	6,500	8.5
Soviet Union	2,000	157 divisions	2,000	240	10,200	6.9

SOURCE: 1. *The Military Balance, 1970–1971* (London: International Institute for Strategic Studies, 1970); *The Military Balance, 1971–1972* (1971).
2. *Nihon no bōei* [Japanese national defense] (Tokyo: Bōeichō, 1970).
NOTE: 1. Total regular forces as percent of serviceable population

of his energy and political career in the continuation of memorandum trade to abandon it. He also hoped that the Japanese people would understand his serious, though largely wasted, efforts to resist the Chinese imposition.

Even those Japanese who were usually sympathetic to the PRC were disturbed by its hard line manifested in the Furui-Liu joint communique. Still, the intensity of its anti-Satō tirade was less severe than that of the joint communiques on friendship trade issued by the Chinese and Japanese Associations for Promotion of International Trade.[21] Unlike Furui, Japan's friendship trade negotiators were ready to accept whatever their Chinese hosts wanted to incorporate in the communiques. Thus there was readily produced a profusion of China's vituperation against Japanese militarism designed to demonstrate their indignation against the Nixon-Satō collusion over Taiwan and to have an unnerving effect on Satō's foreign policy. (Later, when discussing the danger of Japanese militarism, Chou En-lai explained to James Reston of the *New York Times* that "when you oppose a danger, you should oppose it when it is budding. Only then can you arouse public attention."[22]) It was also intended to dispel the complacent notion prevailing in Japan that irrespective of Satō's policy, trade with China was bound to increase, mainly because China badly needed it. The Chinese were particularly annoyed by Satō's repeated public pronouncements that the Japanese government was diligently striving to expand trade with China through memorandum trade.

Contrary to their calculated self-restraint shown in regard to the 1969 Furui-Liu communique, Satō and his associates decided to launch a direct counter-attack against the intolerably provocative contents of the 1970 communique. Initially, Sato said at the House of Councillors Committee on the Budget meeting that Japan was not on the road to militarism and imperialism, nor was she an agent of U.S. policy. He regretted the existence of misunderstanding and mistrust between China and Japan, but upheld the importance of Japan's international credibility in preserving her diplomatic commitment with Nationalist China.[23] The following day, in view of the prolific reactions of LDP dietmen, his cabinet issued a "unified view" contending that since Japan had the Peace Constitution, China's references to Japanese militarism (as well as to the Okinawanization of Japan) stemmed from its distortions and misunderstanding.[24] The view also argued that it was legitimate for Japan to express in the Nixon-Satō statement its concern with the security problems of Taiwan and South Korea. The mild tone of this unified view failed to satisfy the irritated hawks in the LDP, who demanded the party's tit-for-tat rebuttal of China's unilateral denunciation and of Furui's "submissive diplomacy."

On the recommendation of the joint session of the Committees on Foreign Affairs (Chairman Kosaka Zentarō) and on National Defense (Chairman Akagi Munenori), the LDP's Executive Council released an official party statement on April 28.[25] The statement drafted by Kosaka and Akagi included the following points: (1) the LDP's efforts to establish friendly relations with China on the basis of mutual respect and noninterference in domestic affairs were misunderstood by China, and its "unilateral criticism and attack" against Japan was regretted; (2) the Chinese denunciation of Japanese militarism was nothing but a "vicious slander" to the Japanese people, who were seeking to build a peaceful state; (3) the Chinese distorted the defensive nature of the U.S.-Japan security treaty, and Japan had the right to pursue whatever bilateral relations it wished to have with the United States; (4) the Okinawa reversion was not a fraud, but a goal of the entire Japanese people; (5) it was natural for Japan to regard the peace and security in the Taiwan area as important to her own security; (6) the communique on memorandum trade had been designed to drive a wedge between the Japanese people and their chosen government, and China must understand that any attack against the Japanese government was an insult to the Japanese people. The statement was the most vindictive, angry, and direct counterattack ever made by the LDP in response to the Chinese condemnation, but it did not censure or criticize Furui's activities.[26] Nor did it assail China's enormous defense budget, nuclear programs, verbal bellicosity, and the like.

While the JCP disputed the Chinese contention on the ground of its own effective struggle against the LDP government's reactionary policies, the JSP was in complete agreement with the Chinese position. The Central Executive Committee was quick to criticize the LDP Executive Council statement, which it said denied the clearly established reality of Japanese militarism; it also demanded the abrogation of the U.S.-Japan security treaty, the unconditional Okinawa reversion, and the immediate normalization of diplomatic relations between Japan and the PRC.[27] Yet there was a considerable factional cleavage of opinions about Japanese militarism within the JSP. The Sasaki faction and other leftist groups were unreservedly supportive of the Chinese arguments, but a coalition of moderate factions tended to perceive of Japanese militarism more as a militaristic state of mind than as the Japanese government's explicit policy.[28]

Even with the JSP's public support, the Chinese failed to make a significant impact upon the minds of the Japanese people. According to the *Yomiuri Shimbun* survey conducted in May 1970, only 22.6% of the Japanese public felt that Japanese militarism had already revived, while 50.5% flatly denied it. Table 16 indicates an appreciable difference between conservative and socialist voters, but still the JSP's official position was not fully accepted by 65.7% of its own supporters.

Party Politics on China   Soon thereafter, at the invitation of the China-Japan Friendship Association, ex-JSP Chairman Sasaki Kōzō visited China and conferred with Premier Chou En-lai. Chou expressed a keen interest in

Table 16—Japanese Public Opinion on Militarism, 1970
(percentage)

"Do you think that militarism has already revived in Japan?"

	Yes	No	DK/NA
Nationwide	22.6	50.5	26.9
LDP	15.8	61.3	22.9
JSP	34.3	45.0	20.7
CGP	30.8	46.2	23.1
DSP	19.8	63.4	16.8
JCP	55.4	26.8	17.9
Nonpartisan	27.2	42.5	30.3

SOURCE: Opinion Research Section of *Yomiuri Shimbun*.
NOTES: DK Do not know
         NA No answer

the links between Japanese monopoly capital and militarism, the degree of Japan's economic, military, and political cooperation with the United States, and the contradictions among Japanese and American monopoly capitalists as manifested in textile negotiations.[29] The Chou-Sasaki meeting paved the way for the JSP's fifth official mission, which Chairman Narita Tomomi himself led to China from October to November 1970. It was the first official delegation sent to China by any Japanese political parties since the Miyamoto-Mao meeting in early 1966. In a joint statement signed on November 1, 1970, by Narita and Kuo Mo-jo (honorary president of the China-Japan Friendship Association), both sides pointed out that "the movement for Japan-China friendship and restoration of diplomatic relations between Japan and China is a component of the Japanese people's struggle against U.S. imperialism and the revival of Japanese militarism by the U.S. and Japanese reactionaries."[30] The JSP reiterated China's contention that Japanese militarism had already revived. Upholding the Asanuma spirit, it also pledged to "make an effort to unite on a broad scale with all the forces in Japan that are truly for Japan-China friendship and for the restoration of diplomatic relations between Japan and China." The joint statement emphasized a common struggle against "U.S. imperialism and its collaborators, running dogs and accomplices" and, in its English version, attacked the "super-powers" (meaning both the United States and the Soviet Union). The JCP perceived these references as a transparent confirmation of China's "four-enemy" thesis, but the JSP denied any such intention.[31] The moderate Socialist factions, too, objected to Narita's acceptance of Chinese demands and the excessive ideological overtone of the joint statement, especially in regard to the notion of forming an antiimperialist united front.[32]

In order to translate the joint statement into the mass movement for Sino-Japanese diplomatic normalization, the JSP decided to revive the Dietmen's League for Japan-China Trade Promotion, which had been virtually dormant since the Nagasaki flag incident, and to organize the National Congress for the Restoration of Japan-China Diplomatic Relations (*Nitchū kokkō kaifuku kokumin kaigi*). The congress, formally inaugurated in February 1971, included members from the JSP, *Sōhyō*, the JCFA (Orthodox Headquarters), the Japan-China Cultural Exchange Association, the Japanese Association for Promotion of International Trade, the Japan-China Memorandum Trade Office, the National Farmers' Union (*Zenni-chinō*), the Japan Socialist Youth Alliance (*Shaseidō*), and other progressive groups and individuals. It was headed by Chairman Nakajima Kenzō (chairman of the JCCEA) and Secretary-General Iwai Akira (former *Sōhyō* secretary-general); its directors included JSP Chairman Narita, Sasaki, *Sōhyō* Chairman Ichikawa, Yokohama Mayor Asukada Ichio, Kuroda Hisao, Mrs. Asanuma Inejirō, Okazaki Kaheita (head of the Japan-China Memorandum Trade Office), and Hagiwara Teiji (managing director of the Japanese Association for Promotion of International Trade).[33]

The CGP, too, sponsored a similar organization called the National Council for the Normalization of Japan-China Diplomatic Relations (*Nitchū kokkō seijōka kokumin kyōgikai*); it was headed by Professor Rōyama Michio of Sophia University. The two organizations sought to achieve the same diplomatic goal, but they were competitive in aspiring for a role of leadership in mass movements for Sino-Japanese diplomatic normalization.

The JSP and the CGP also strengthened interparty cooperation with the DSP and the LDP's antimainstream factions. The secretaries-general of the three opposition political parties held a couple of meetings in November 1970 and decided to form a new suprapartisan Dietmen's League for Promoting Restoration of Japan-China Diplomatic Relations (*Nitchū kokkō kaifuku sokushin giinrenmei)* as a successor to the old league. LDP Dietman Fujiyama Aiichirō, whom Matsumura Kenzō had designated as his successor in regard to Sino-Japanese cooperation, headed the new Dietmen's League established in December, and four vice-chairmen were selected from the JSP, the CGP, the DSP, and the LDP.[34] Its membership, consisting of 255 representatives and 124 councillors—95 from the LDP, 154 from the JSP, 71 from the CGP, 37 from the DSP, 21 from the JCP, and one independent dietman, surpassed a simple majority of all dietmen. All legislators of the JSP, the CGP, and the JCP joined the league, but a few DSP dietmen, including Nishio Suehiro and Sone Eki, did not because of their concern with the Taiwan question. (The league excluded the JCP, in view of its conflict with the CCP, from its vice-chairmanship and from its board of directors). A large number of the league's members had already visited China or were about to do so. The Dietmen's League adopted a resolution deploring the Japnese government's "anachronistic" ties with Taiwan and contending that, despite the Japan-Taiwan peace treaty, the state of war had not legally been terminated between Japan and China. Further, it stressed the urgency of achieving Japan's diplomatic normalization with China.[35]

The fact that one-fifth of the LDP dietmen, despite the party's formal objections, cooperated with the opposition political parties against Prime Minister Satō's China policy was an unprecedented development. It suggested, among other things, that an increasing number of the LDP's antimainstream leaders were willing to revolt against Satō's foreign policy. In fact, the Asian-African Problems Study Group had set up a Consultative Group on China and had gotten fifty-five LDP dietmen to sign the petition asking the Satō government not to cosponsor the "important question" resolution at the forthcoming twenty-fifth U.N. General Assembly.

Prime Minister Satō was not entirely unconcerned about the growing domestic challenge to his China policy. In an attempt to counterbalance this petition and the Dietmen's League, the LDP formed a forty-five-member Subcommittee on China in its Committee on Foreign Affairs (under Chairman Noda Takeo). But Satō's China problems were far from being confined to the manifest attraction to the PRC shown by members in his own party and in the parliamentary opposition; in fact, a large number of

Table 17—Number of Japanese Dietmen Visiting China, 1955-71

Year	LDP	JSP	JCP	Others	Total
1955	29	43	2	4	78
1956	7	12	1	1	21
1957	7	27	1	1	36
1958	2	7	1	1	11
1959	7	14	2	1	24
1960	1	4	0	0	5
1961	4	8	5	1	18
1962	10	18	0	0	28
1963	6	13	1	2	22
1964	11	33	0	0	44
1965	5	1	0	0	6
1966	18	9	0	0	27
1967	1	3	0	0	4
1968	2	2	0	0	4
1969	3	2	0	0	5
1970	7	10	0	0	17
1971*	19	11	0	12**	42

SOURCE: *Nitchū kankei shiryōshū, 1945-1971* (Tokyo: Nitchū kokkō kaifuku sokushin giinrenmei, 1971), pp. 637– 46.
NOTES: *Up until October 1971
          **They included 9 from the CGP and 3 from the DSP.

Japanese people were becoming increasingly unhappy with his inability to improve Sino-Japanese relations. According to a survey conducted by *Yomiuri Shimbun* in May 1970, 27.9% of nationwide interviewees—and 20.1% of LDP voters—agreed with the view shared by China and the JSP that their government had a hostile policy toward the PRC. Further, 54.0% of them, including an almost identical percentage of LDP voters, favored, with varying degrees of intensity, China's representation at the United Nations. On top of the rapid rise in China's international status following the Cultural Revolution, the strong shift in favor of the PRC demonstrated in public opinion and within the LDP contributed greatly to Satō's changed thinking about Sino-Japanese relations.

Speaking for the first time before the U.N. General Assembly in October 1970, Satō did not specifically discuss the Chinese question, but referred to the general problems of "divided states," which he hoped would be resolved by peaceful means.[36] A month later, Japanese Ambassador Tsuruoka Senjin made a brief eight-minute speech on China, but the tone

Table 18—Japanese Public Opinion on China, 1970
(percentage)

(A) "Do you think that the Japanese government has a hostile policy toward China?"

	Yes	No	DK/NA
Nation-wide	27.9	36.3	35.9
LDP	20.1	45.1	34.8
JSP	43.7	28.5	27.7
CGP	33.3	37.2	29.5
DSP	29.7	43.6	26.7
JCP	57.1	23.2	19.6
Nonpartisan	33.0	30.5	36.5

(B) "Do you support or oppose China's representation at the United Nations?"

	Oppose		Support		
	Strong	Moderate	Moderate	Strong	DK/NA/OA
Nationwide	2.8	5.5	26.3	27.7	37.7
LDP	3.3	6.6	30.4	23.3	36.4
JSP	3.1	5.0	26.2	36.6	29.1
CGP	3.8	3.8	14.1	47.4	30.9
DSP	4.0	8.9	40.6	26.7	19.8
JCP	1.8	3.6	19.6	57.1	17.9
Nonpartisan	2.0	4.9	24.3	30.1	36.7

SOURCE: Opinion Research Section of *Yomiuri Shimbun*.
NOTES: DK Do not know
NA No answer
OA Other answer

of his remarks was markedly milder than his previous speeches at the United Nations. He no longer expressed doubt about China's ability to carry out its U.N. responsibilities, though he did invoke the principle of universality against ousting the Republic of China from the United Nations.[37] This speech was a clear sign of Satō's inclination to pursue a "two-China" solution, but he was to be compelled to moderate his China policy even further in the face of the facts that the Albanian resolution obtained a plurality at that General Assembly and that NATO members such as Canada and Italy were switching their diplomatic relations from Taipei to Peking.

Satō and his Foreign Minister Aichi shared the view that since the prospect of passing the "important question" resolution was bleak at the next U.N. General Assembly, Japan should adopt a different strategy on the Chinese issue. At the same time, a meeting of China specialists in the Ministry of Foreign Affairs, plus Japanese ambassadors in West Europe and the Middle East, recommended a change in Japanese policy toward China. In his address at the National Diet in January 1971, therefore, Satō, for the first time, used the "People's Republic of China" instead of his usual references—"Communist China," "mainland China," or "Peking government."[38] The semantic change may sound trivial, but it was suggestive of the beginning of his new outlook and tactics toward China. He also stated:

It is our sincere wish to positively promote our interchange with mainland China, and to improve our relations with it. The fundamental basis for establishing Sino-Japanese relations is without doubt the mutual understanding of the two peoples. To this end, for the purpose of dissolving the unnatural situation between our country and mainland China, our government, from the long-term point of view, is prepared to make various contacts on the governmental level, and strongly hopes for increased interchange in such matters as the expansion of private trade and the smooth exchange of press reporters. At the same time, it is our hope that efforts to meet us halfway will also be made by the government of the People's Republic of China.

Elaborating on Satō's suggestion, Aichi stated his wish for a formal dialogue with the PRC. Likewise, the LDP adopted a positive policy line on China in its 1971 Action Program.[39]

The subtle change in the LDP government's policy toward China was evident, but it is difficult to ascertain whether it took any meaningful initiatives for lowering the "unnatural" barriers or opening intergovernmental talks with the PRC. The LDP elevated and expanded its Subcommittee on China to a full-blown committee with 101 members, and Satō urged its Chairman Noda Takeo to visit China as his emissary.[40] However, Satō's flexible public utterances were considered by the Chinese to be a deceptive smokescreen to cover up his unchangeable hostility toward China. Chou En-lai complained to Japanese visitors that Satō even lagged behind Nixon in appreciating the changing international environments regarding China.[41] Given their basic distrust of Satō's intentions, it was almost unthinkable for the Chinese to meet Satō even halfway. They made it clear in the joint statement signed on July 2, 1971 by the China-Japan Friendship Association and the Clean Government Party that only if the Japanese government accepted the CGP's five-point demand, would the PRC end the state of war, restore diplomatic relations, and conclude a peace treaty with Japan.[42] The Satō government failed to notice that, unlike the JSP-China joint statement issued eight months ago, this statement, prepared just a week before Kissinger's secret arrival at Peking, revealed a marked softening of the Chinese attack on U.S. imperialism, and a shift in priority to the question of Taiwan. Just as it had done in response to the JSP-China joint statement, the LDP leadership chose to take exception publicly with the CGP-China joint statement, by accusing the CGP of submitting itself to Chinese demands and thus of betraying Japan's national interest.[43]

The Nixon Shock   The sudden news of President Nixon's forthcoming visit to the PRC produced a profound and pervasive shock throughout Japan. A few hours before Nixon's televised announcement at San Clemente in the evening of July 15 (morning of July 16 in Japanese time), Satō convened his early morning cabinet meeting at Tokyo and ironically discussed a draft of his planned speech to be delivered at the sixty-sixth National Diet session. Significantly, the draft dropped a customary reference to Japan's cooperation with Nationalist China and South Korea, but included a general statement for promoting Japan's "friendly relations" with her neighboring countries (including the PRC). It was supported by Director-General of the Economic Planning Agency Kimura Toshio (who was also acting foreign minister because of Aichi's visit to Manila) and Minister of Agriculture Akagi Munenori, while cabinet members of the Nakasone and Funada factions opposed it and Minister of Justice Maeo Shigesaburō remained neutral.[44] As a result of the intracabinet disagreement, Satō decided to exclude the general statement, and to restore the specific reference to Nationalist China and South Korea in his speech. The strict adherence to a consensual policy-making tradition led to Satō's option for nondecision on the Chinese question. While this debate was going on in Satō's cabinet, Secretary of State Rogers, upon his arrival at San Clemente, attempted to call Japanese Ambassador Ushiba Nobuhiko in Washington and to deliver a prior notice of Nixon's forthcoming announcement. The attempt was in vain because Ushiba was unreachable. When Ushiba finally received Rogers's message and conveyed it to his home ministry, Satō's morning cabinet meeting was about to adjourn; this was shortly before the national television broadcast an Associated Press news bulletin on Nixon's statement.

Upon receiving word of the shift in American policy on China, Satō and his associates experienced mixed emotions of envy for Nixon's diplomatic breakthrough and of bitterness toward his neglect of their domestic and external prestige. As Halperin correctly observed, the frank and intimate consultations Satō thought he was having with the United States on China were exposed as a sham.[45] This was particularly so because Satō and Nixon had agreed in October 1970 to maintain close mutual consultations on China, and because, as late as June 9, 1971, Rogers and Foreign Minister Aichi had affirmed this same agreement at Paris. Three weeks before Nixon's announcement, Satō was reassured by the U.S. ambassador to Japan that the United States would make no move toward recognition of China without prior consultation with Japan.[46] It is most likely that the absence of adequate prior consultation and notification reflected Nixon's propensity for dramatic diplomatic announcements as much as China's request for absolute secrecy. As Tang Tsou suggests, the Chinese were perhaps afraid that any premature leak by Japanese sources might provoke opposition among domestic critics and among American allies. Moreover, the United States kept preliminary diplomatic negotiations secret to build mutual trust with China.[47]

At any rate some members of the LDP and senior officials of the Ministry of Foreign Affairs suspected that the United States might strike a diplomatic bargain with China at the expense of Japan's interests; a Sino-American conspiracy to "stop Japan" as an economic superpower was also feared. Nor were the leaders of the Asian-African Problems Study Group and of opposition political parties, who had long warned that they would wake up one morning to discover a Sino-American diplomatic accommodation, comforted by their prophecy. The Nixon move signaled an erosion of the U.S. policy of diplomatic isolation and military containment against China which Japan had faithfully followed since the San Francisco conference. It was a difficult challenge for the Satō government to adjust its posture to the evolving Sino-American détente. Although it did not cause an immediate movement for Sino-Japanese diplomatic normalization within the government, it certainly added a new momentum to that movement in Japan. Its supporters were tremendously encouraged, and a growing number of hitherto uncommitted political and economic leaders were stimulated to jump on the China bandwagon.

The day following the Nixon announcement, Satō, still embarrassed by the shock, spoke before the sixty-sixth National Diet session.[48] He welcomed Nixon's China visit as a measure to ease world tensions, and stated:

It is most important for our country to maintain and promote friendly and amicable relations with the Republic of Korea, the Republic of China, and other neighboring countries. In particular, the China problem is one of the biggest issues facing our country's diplomacy in the 1970s. . . . Recently, exchanges between Japan and China have also shown signs of becoming more active; it is strongly hoped that in the future, these will develop into intergovernmental talks.

Notwithstanding his mellowed posture, Satō came under heavy attack from all opposition political parties and the LDP's antimainstream dietmen.

JSP Secretary-General Ishibashi Masashi, too, welcomed Nixon's visit as a contribution to the peace in Asia and in the world.[49] At the same time he seized on the opportunity to assail Satō's "non-policy" regarding China. While pointing out the bankruptcy of Satō's foreign policy, he demanded Japan's "independent" and "positive" approach toward the PRC. If Satō failed to do so, he warned, the JSP would request his resignation. A week thereafter, the Dietmen's League introduced to both Houses of the National Diet a resolution urging the Japanese government to establish diplomatic relations with the PRC and to restore its lawful status at the upcoming twenty-sixth U.N. General Assembly.[50] About 230 members of the House of Representatives, including 54 LDP members, originally cosponsored the resolution, but the LDP used all conceivable persuasive tactics to reduce the conservative cosponsors to 21 die-hard liberal dietmen. They included the leaders of the Asian-African Problems Study Group—such as Fujiyama, Utsunomiya, Kawasaki, Furui, and Tagawa. And though the resolution failed to reach the floor in both Houses due to the LDP's parliamentary control, it clearly demonstrated the stiffening of the pro-Peking LDP dietmen's protest against Satō's China policy.

The Nixon shock wave was not confined to the political and economic communities, and it influenced a vast number of Japanese people in all walks of life. According to a public opinion survey conducted by *Sankei Shimbun* a few days after Nixon's announcement, 73% of Japanese adults expected that Nixon's visit to China would contribute to the relaxation of international tensions, while 15% expressed a negative assessment and 12% responded with "do not know" answers.[51]. A month later, *Asahi Shimbun* found a lessening of public excitement about Nixon's visit, but reported that 43% of Japanese people still regarded it as a good thing for the relaxation of international tensions, with 22% giving a negative response.[52] Further, 63% of the interviewees favored Satō's visit to China, while 13% opposed it, with 24% in other categories. Asked whether they supported Japan's immediate negotiations with China for diplomatic normalization, 63% said "yes," but 11% answered "no." Yet only 21% of them felt that Satō would be able to change his China policy.

The first Nixon shock, which was further amplified by his decision to impose a 10% import surcharge and a strict textile import quota, affected Satō's immediate thinking about China in opposite directions. Unrestrained by the U.S. containment policy and hurt by Nixon's snub, he wished to assert an independent course of action toward the PRC . But at the same time his protective role for Taipei's diplomatic interests, especially at the United Nations, grew stronger in direct proportion to the United States rapprochement with Peking. When Wang Kuo-chuan (ex-ambassador to East Germany and Poland and vice-president of the China-Japan Friendship Association) visited Japan to attend the funeral of Matsumura Kenzō in August 1971, Chief Cabinet Secretary Takeshida Nobaru greeted his arrival at Haneda Airport. Since he was the first Chinese leader to visit Japan after Nixon's announcement, Wang's activities aroused a sensational interest among Japanese politicians and businessmen; every detail of his daily operations was prominently reported in Japanese press. At the funeral service Satō shook hands with Wang and expressed his appreciation for his presence. Satō asked him to send his "yoroshiku" (best regards) to Premier Chou En-lai, but Wang simply replied with "hsieh, hsieh" (thank you). Politely, but firmly, Wang refused to entertain Satō's direct, personal overtures for Sino-Japanese contacts.[53] However, he strengthened China's growing links with influential Japanese businessmen, some anti-Satō LDP dietmen—such as Speaker of the House of Councillors Kōno Kenzō, Miki, and Fujiyama, and opposition party leaders, including JSP Chairman Narita Tomomi, CGP Chairman Takeiri Yoshikatsu, and DSP Chairman Kasuga Nikkō. In view of the JSP's particular apprehension about Nixon's China visit, Wang assured Narita and other JSP leaders that China was not going to make a deal with the United States on matters of principle.[54] He also attended the national unity conference of the Japan-China Friendship Association (Orthodox Headquarters), where the conflict between Kuroda Hisao and Miyazaki Seimin was resolved to mutual satisfaction. The Chinese leaders, too, attached a great and urgent political importance to Wang's mission to Japan; as soon as he returned to Peking, Wang rushed to make a direct report to Chou En-lai.

Effects of the U.N. Decisions   Satō's conciliatory gesture toward China, which was promptly resisted by the Asian Problems Study Group, was in sharp contradiction with his policy at the U.N.[55] The United States which along with Japan, had already decided to implement a "one-China, one-Taiwan" solution at the United Nations, asked the Satō government to cosponsor the two U.S.-drafted resolutions at the twenty-sixth General Assembly—one (commonly known as the "reverse important question" resolution) for defining the expulsion of the Republic of China as an important question and the other for making the PRC a U.N. member-state with a permanent seat in the Security Council, while affirming the right of the ROC for continued representation in the General Assembly. Since the Japanese cabinet and the appropriate LDP organs were seriously divided over the U.S. request, Prime Minister Satō was left to reach an official decision by himself and to assume the political responsibility for its consequences. When Satō announced in September 1971 his decision to cosponsor both U.N. resolutions, he brought about quite a public uproar, not only from opposition political parties and business circles but also from within his own cabinet and from the LDP. A long list of LDP dietmen—Fujiyama, Furui, Tagawa, Kawasaki, Miki, and Ōhira Masayoshi, to name a few—joined the chorus critical of Satō's policy, as did Minister of Agriculture Akagi and Minister of Justice Maeo.

Nor were the Chinese happy with his decision. The Satō decision, commented the *People's Daily* (September 26, 1971), "has further exposed his reactionary features as a docile accomplice of U.S. imperialism"; he was also blamed for playing a "very vicious role" of offering the United States advice and of acting as go-between in the United Nations. Meanwhile, at Peking, Chou En-lai, Kuo Mo-jo, and Wang Kuo-chuan were entertaining a nonpartisan delegation of the Japanese Dietmen's League. Headed by Fujiyama, it consisted of 19 dietmen—six each from the LDP and the JSP, four from the CGP, and three from the DSP.[56] The joint statement signed on October 2, 1971 by Fujiyama and Wang stipulated four principles, acceptance of which was required for establishing Japan-China diplomatic relations: (1) that there is only one China, and that the PRC is the sole legal government representing the Chinese people; (2) that Taiwan Province is an inalienable part of the territory of the PRC; (3) that the Japan-Taiwan peace treaty is illegal and invalid and that it must be abrogated; and (4) that all the lawful rights of the PRC should be restored in all organs of the United Nations.[57] The principles were essentially a repetition of the CGP's five-point position, but the Fujiyama-Wang statement did not specifically demand the withdrawal of U.S. forces out of Taiwan and the Taiwan Straits area. The league's delegation also pledged to struggle against the revival of Japanese militarism, and expressed its regret over Satō's decision to cosponsor the two resolutions against China at the United Nations. (Later, on the grounds of the positions that he took in the communique on Japanese militarism and the Japan-Taiwan peace treaty, Fujiyama was subjected to a disciplinary action by the LDP.)

Under mounting pressure from all directions, Satō, in his address to the National Diet on October 19, reiterated his determination to take every possible opportunity to open intergovernmental contacts with the PRC.[58] And Foreign Minister Fukuda, perhaps mindful of his bid to succeed Satō, added that the trend of history required the normalization of Japanese-Chinese diplomatic relations. Yet, both attached to their China policy a clear condition—namely, the commitment to respect "international faith" (meaning that Japan should not compromise its diplomatic ties with Taiwan). "If we easily fail to keep international faith," said Fukuda, "we cannot expect to receive any trust from Taiwan with its 14,000,000 population, from the people of mainland China or from the world as a whole."[59] All these remarks were interpreted by the Chinese as shrewd political maneuvers designed by

Satō to hoodwink public opinion at home and abroad; thus there appeared no change in their assessment of Satō's "hostile" and "hypocritical" policy.[60]

At the United Nations, the Japanese delegation headed by ex-Foreign Minister Aichi made strenuous efforts in a vain attempt to retain the Republic of China in the General Assembly. They employed all the force at their disposal, as if the Chinese question was a Maginot Line for their diplomatic interests in Asia. On Taipei's behalf Satō reportedly wrote personal letters to leaders in some ten key countries that remained indecisive on the Chinese question, and Aichi conferred with more than forty U.N. delegates in a week during October.[61] He also delivered a long, ardent, and detailed speech in favor of the two resolutions cosponsored by the United States, Japan, Thailand, the Phillipines, Australia, New Zealand, and other pro-Taiwan members. He welcomed the PRC as a member of the General Assembly and the Security Council, but advanced a number of legal and political arguments to oppose the Albanian resolution, which he called "irrational," "irresponsible," and "cruel."[62] He contended, *inter alia*, that the expulsion of the Republic of China would violate the principle of universality, upset a balance of power in the Far East, set a bad precedent to be abused by others, and deal a blow to the prestige of the United Nations. The Republic of China, he argued, was a founding member of the United Nations, had faithfully fulfilled its international obligations, and had exercised effective control over Taiwan for more than a quarter of a century.

On October 25, 1971, by a vote of 61 to 53, with 15 abstentions, the General Assembly supported the United States and Japan in deciding to vote first on the "reverse important question" resolution, but rejected an ill-timed Saudi Arabian motion to postpone the voting until the next day, by a vote of 53 to 56, with 19 abstentions. The latter decision became a test case showing a relative numerical superiority of pro-Peking forces in the United Nations. Much to the chagrin of the Satō government, the crucial "reverse important question" resolution was then defeated by the narrow margin of 4 votes (55 to 59, with 15 abstentions and 2 absent). The pro-Taipei strength eroded further when the General Asembly, by a 10-vote margin, denied the U.S. motion, which requested a separate vote on the clause expelling the Republic of China as contained in the Albanian resolution, by a vote of 51 to 61, with 16 abstentions. Sensing an imminent defeat, the Nationalist Chinese delegation, after Foreign Minister Chou Shu-kai's brief remarks, walked out of the Assembly Hall. Finally, an overwhelming majority (76 to 35, with 17 abstentions and 3 absent) voted for the Albanian resolution. Thus the PRC succeeded in its twenty-two year campaign to join the organization; and the Japanese delegates, who had fought an all-out diplomatic battle for Taiwan, suffered one of the major diplomatic setbacks in their postwar experience.

The voting procedures at the United Nations were widely televised live in Japan, and Prime Minister Satō and Foreign Minister Fukuda, who had been confident about the combined diplomatic capabilities of the United

States and Japan, were stunned by the unexpected outcome in New York. They were also most unhappy about the timing of Kissinger's second Peking visit amidst the U.N. debates on China, which might have had an adverse psychological effect upon a few wavering delegates at the United Nations. The U.N. decision, which came three months after the Nixon shock, undermined one of Satō's main justifications for nonrecognition of the PRC. In fact, the Chinese, while welcoming the U.N. votes as an "irresistible historical trend," were far more critical of Japanese delegates' "deceptive" and "desperate" vote-canvassing tactics against China in the United Nations than those of the United States.[63] The United States adopted the Moorsteen-Abramowitz strategy that it accepted the possibility of a voting defeat in the United Nations, but refrained from making a too strong effort to keep Taiwan's seat in the General Assembly.[64] Thus, while Nixon, in anticipation of his forthcoming journey to China, could sigh with relief, Satō had suffered irreparable damage to his domestic political leadership.

The LDP responded to the U.N. decision with an ostensibly calm denial that it would immediately change Japan's foreign policy, and Secretary-General Hori Shigeru expressed his party's intention to resolve the question of bilateral diplomatic relations with the PRC on the basis of Japanese national interest.[65] Prime Minister Satō, too, in response to a pointed question by Kawasaki Kanji (head of the JSP's Bureau of International Affairs) in the House of Representatives, welcomed China's entrance into the United Nations, but added in a declaratory vein that the Japan-Taiwan peace treaty "should not be abrogated in a simple way."[66] Yet, within seventy-two hours after the Albanian resolution passed, the JSP, together with the CGP and the DSP, had hastily submitted to the House of Representatives a no-confidence resolution against Foreign Minister Fukuda in connection with Japan's failure at the United Nations. The resolution was defeated by a 169 to 274 vote, but the so-called twelve samurai of the governing LDP, including Fujiyama, Utsunomiya, Furui, Tagawa, and Kawasaki, were conspicuously absent from the Diet out of sympathy for the resolution.[67] Through the unusual method of symbolic absence, they registered their unmistakable protest against Satō's and Fukuda's foreign policy, and they organized themselves into a group for their common political actions.[68] The conservative hawks demanded the LDP's disciplinary action against these twelve recalcitrant legislators, but no official reprimand was made. Indeed, the deepening disagreement on the Chinese question was beginning to threaten the LDP's strict partisan control over parliamentary matters.

The U.N. decision also increased the popular demand for a change in Japan's policy toward China. As table 19 shows, 57.8% of the Japanese public in November 1971 asked their government to establish, either at once or as soon as possible, diplomatic relations with the PRC; this was a modest

3% increase in seven months. More significant was a considerable change, from 8.7% to 19.0%, in the number of those favoring Japanese-Chinese diplomatic normalization, even at the cost of severing Japanese-Taiwanese relations. The expulsion of Taiwan from the United Nations seemed sufficient to effect such a change in the minds of the Japanese people.

Soon thereafter, three opposition political parties, the JSP, CGP, and DSP, jointly introduced another parliamentary resolution similar to the Dietmen's League's abortive attempt made in July. This time, however, the resolution specifically spelled out acceptance of the Fujiyama-Wang Kuo-chuan joint statement in regard to the principles for Sino-Japanese diplomatic normalization.[69] On the same day the LDP submitted a rival resolution, which recognized the PRC as a government representing China and called on the Japanese government to take appropriate measures for normalizing diplomatic relations with the PRC. This was more ambiguous than the original draft prepared by Noda Takeo (chairman of the LDP's Committee on China) and endorsed by Secretary-General Hori; since it had failed to satisfy either pro-Taipei or pro-Peking dietmen in the LDP, the original draft with specific contents was revised into a conveniently vague version.[70]

In addition, the three opposition parties cosponsored a no-confidence resolution against the Satō cabinet, citing its glaring failures in domestic and foreign affairs, particularly its China policy. The conservative majority, this time including the "twelve samurai," defeated the no-confidence move by a 178 to 283 vote in December; and the two rival resolutions of China died, as

Table 19—Japanese Public Opinion on China, 1971
(percentage)

(A) Normalization of Diplomatic Relations with China

	April	November
1. Normalize at once	10.7	13.6
2. Normalize as soon as possible	44.1	44.2
3. Do not hurry	12.9	13.3
4. Do not normalize	1.3	1.2
5. Do not know	31.0	27.7

(B) Diplomatic Relations with Taiwan

	April	November
1. Sever diplomatic relations	1.8	4.5
2. Sever relations only if necessary	6.9	14.5
3. Have relations with both of them	33.9	28.3
4. Other answers	0.9	0.5
5. Do not know	11.3	10.0

SOURCE: Seron Chōsa, January 1972, p. 80.

the Diet, which was preoccupied with the forcible passage of the Okinawa reversion treaty, went into recess at the end of December.[71] However, public approval of Prime Minister Satō's leadership continued to sag. Whereas 37.0% of Japanese public, according to the Jiji News Agency's monthly survey, had supported Satō in January 1971, the figure had dropped to 26.6% in August after the news of Nixon's planned visit to China, and then to 20.7% in November after the U.N. decision on China. It was to hit an all-time low at 19.4% in March 1972, in the aftermath of Nixon's well-publicized journey to China. The decline in Satō's popularity was not entirely attributable to his foreign-policy failure, but it reflected, in a large part, a public mood critical of his international performance.

Processes of Diplomatic Contacts

Satō's Abortive Diplomacy   Amidst diplomatic setbacks and domestic pressures, the Satō government did not stand idle, but adopted what Foreign Minister Fukuda termed *ahiru gaikō* (duck diplomacy); just as a duck may outwardly look serene while it busily uses its feet under water, the Japanese government, despite its calm appearance, busily made behind-the-scene overtures toward the PRC. According to Fukuda's recollection, it relied upon a variety of intermediary *ahiru*, both Oriental and Occidental, to send to China a message of sincere Japanese hopes for diplomatic negotiations.[72] The best-known *ahiru* was Tokyo Governor Minobe Ryōkichi, who person-

Table 20—Popular Support for Prime Minister Satō and
Two Major Political Parties, 1971–72
(percentage)

Year	Month	Pro-Satō	Anti-Satō	DK	Pro-LDP	Pro-JSP
1971	January	37.0	34.6	28.4	33.2	13.8
	July	31.0	35.5	33.5	29.1	17.3
	August*	26.6	47.1	25.3	27.9	16.2
	September	24.4	49.2	26.4	28.3	17.7
	October	27.1	48.8	24.1	29.7	14.6
	November	20.7	52.6	26.7	26.4	16.1
	December**	19.6	51.4	29.0	26.3	13.9
1972	January	23.4	47.8	28.8	28.6	14.1
	February	21.8	52.9	25.3	28.6	17.7
	March***	19.4	52.8	27.8	28.1	14.4

SOURCE: *Seron Chōsa*, March 1971–May 1972.
NOTES: *Survey conducted after the announcement of Nixon's China visit
      **Survey conducted after the U.N. decision on China's representation
      ***Survey conducted after the conclusion of Nixon's visit to China

ally carried in October 1971 a letter brush-written by LDP Secretary-General Hori (one of Satō's closest confidants) to Chou En-lai. In consultation with Satō and Fukuda, Hori explained his position was that there was only one China, that Taiwan was a Chinese territory, and that the PRC represented China (but not as the sole lawful government of China).[73] He then expressed his willingness to visit China to negotiate the establishment of diplomatic relations between Japan and China. When Chou En-lai met with Minobe and a delegation of the National Congress for the Restoration of Japan-China Diplomatic Relations (led by Yokohama Mayor Asukada Ichio) in November, he dismissed the Hori letter as a deceptive one, primarily because it failed to recognize the PRC as the only lawful government of China and failed to specify Hori's position on the Taiwan question.[74] Minobe was as disappointed as the LDP leadership, but he was more annoyed by the JSP and the JCP, which, despite their alliance for his electoral success in Tokyo, criticized his "careless" mediatory role for the LDP.[75] Even in the LDP, some pro-Peking dietmen complained that Hori failed to use their established contacts with the PRC. The Satō government also proposed through various messengers (including Tagawa Seiichi) to dispatch Noda Takeo to China as a Japanese Kissinger, but the proposal was flatly rebuked.

Direct diplomatic contacts were also attempted at the United Nations. Upon the arrival of the Chinese delegation, led by Vice-Minister of Foreign Affairs Chiao Kuan-hua in November 1971, Nakagawa Toru, a Japanese permanent representative to the United Nations, extended a "warm welcome" and added: "My delegation looks forward to close contacts between our two delegations and through them to the development of friendly relations between our two countries."[76] No apparent diplomatic breakthrough was achieved in New York. Finally, when Satō and Nixon, meeting in January 1972 at San Clemente, concentrated much of their discussion on China and agreed "to consult closely on their respective Asian policies," Satō may have asked Nixon's assistance in explaining to Chou Japan's genuine desire for diplomatic normalization with the PRC.[77] However, all of Satō's *ahiru gaiko* for diplomatic negotiations with the PRC bore no concrete results.

Why did the Chinese so adamantly refuse to entertain a seemingly sincere peace feeler from the Satō government? The most important reason appeared to be their continuing suspicion of the intentions behind Satō's diplomatic overtures. In fact, Satō and Fukuda had never publicly accepted the Chinese principles for diplomatic normalization, but, rather, maintained that these were matters to be negotiated between the two governments. And the Chinese leaders' distrust was not abated by Fukuda's formal apology to China for Japan's past aggression and exploitation against the Chinese people.[78] As the joint communique on memorandum trade issued in

December 1971 pointed out, they felt that the Satō government's words about improving Japanese-Chinese relations, without explicit acceptance of the three principles, were an "out-and-out deceptive gesture to extricate itself from a predicament."[79] In view of his numerous commitments given to Taiwan and of his inseparable political ties with Kishi and other pro-Taiwan LDP leaders, they did not consider it possible for him to make concessions on the Taiwan issue. Another reason why the Chinese felt Satō was not likely to change his China policy was his history of greater eagerness for cooperation with the Soviet Union than with China. The Soviet Union let it be known to Satō and Fukuda during Foreign Minister Gromyko's visit to Japan in January 1972, that it would be gravely concerned with any Sino-Japanese diplomatic accommodation made at the expense of its interest. In a subtle attempt to prevent Japan's possible drift toward China and to counterbalance the Sino-American détente, Gromyko displayed a considerable flexibility on northern territorial issues and Siberian development programs.[80]

Moreover, fully aware of Satō's plan to step down after the reversion of Okinawa in 1972, the Chinese were reluctant to establish a long-range political understanding with a lame-duck prime minister of Japan. Even though they were afraid that Fukuda might succeed Satō, they considered it easier to deal with a new Japanese prime minister, who, compared with Satō, might be less self-confident in domestic politics, but more flexible in foreign policy. The adamant manner with which they were rebuffing Satō's *ahiru gaikō* was probably intended to serve notice on his successor that if he were serious at all about diplomatic reconciliation with China, he should, first of all, accept their three political principles. Also, they expected to extract a better bargain from his successor than they could expect from Satō. Whenever the Chinese had an opportunity to talk with LDP dietmen in Peking from December 1971 to early 1972, invariably they asked detailed questions about the personalities of LDP presidential candidates, their relations with Kishi and the *zaikai*, and the direction of interfactional alignments in the LDP.

Another factor which contributed to aggravating Satō's already acrimonious relations with China was a new territorial dispute over a group of small uninhabited islands known as the Senkaku or the Tiaoyü (in Chinese) Islands in the China Sea. The first sign of the Sino-Japanese territorial dispute surfaced in the latter half of 1970. As Japan was planning to investigate and exploit seabed oil resources deposited near these islands, which had been placed under U.S. administration since the San Francisco peace treaty, both the PRC and the Republic of China claimed their traditional sovereignty over them. The PRC, in particular, stepped up its claim in June 1971, when the United States and Japan agreed to include the Senkaku Islands—as part of the Nansei Shoto—among those to be returned to Japan in the Okinawa reversion treaty. On December 30, 1971, the Chinese Foreign Ministry declared the agreement "utterly illegal."[81] It stated that the Tiaoyü and other islands appertained to Taiwan and that "like Taiwan, they have been an inalienable part of Chinese territory since ancient times." The Chinese cited the Ming Dynasty records on Chinese control over these islands, and argued that the Ching government had been forced to cede them to Japan in the unequal Shimonoseki peace treaty of May 1895. Indeed, as a matter of policy, the PRC had consistently refused to recognize territorial concessions made, under duress, in the unequal treaties by the Imperial Chinese government.

The Japanese government—and the LDP—responded that after having ascertained that the islands were not only uninhabited, but that they were without any trace of Chinese control, the Japanese government under Prime Minister Itō Hirobumi had decided in January 1895 to incorporate them as part of the Ryūkyū Islands and to set up posts there to manifest Japan's sovereign territorial control.[82] The JSP, like the JCP, supported the Satō government's position on the Senkaku Islands (as well as on northern territorial issues), but suggested that Japan should seek a peaceful territorial settlement with the PRC and exempt these islands from the application of the U.S.-Japan security treaty.[83]

The territorial dispute produced an angry verbal confrontation between Japanese and Chinese representatives at the U.N. Committee on the Peaceful Uses of the Seabed and the Ocean Floor Beyond the Limits of National Jurisdiction, in March 1972. Chinese Representative An Chih-yuan went as far as to declare that "the Japanese government's wild attempt to occupy China's territory of Tiaoyü and other islands and plunder the seabed resources in the vicinity of these islands is a glaring act of aggression, to which we of course cannot remain indifferent."[84] The combination of conflicting nationalist aspirations, economic interests, and historical inter-pretations rendered the Senkaku Islands a particularly acute and potentially explosive point of contention between Japan and China. Although the dispute stopped short of military clashes, it certainly hurt the chances of Satō's diplomatic approach toward the PRC.

Conspicuously unable to break the diplomatic ice with the PRC, Satō remained ruefully envious of Nixon, whose historic China visit in Feburary 1972 aroused mounting domestic political pressure on Satō's own China policy. On the day the Nixon-Chou joint communique was issued in Shanghai, Satō, adroitly interpellated by CGP Secretary-General Yano Junya in the House of Representatives Committee on the Budget meeting, surprised his audience by conceding for the first time that Taiwan was a territory of the PRC.[85] But confronted with strong protest from pro-Taipei dietmen and senior Foreign Ministry officials on that afternoon, Satō agreed to Foreign Minister Fukuda's retraction of his statement. This episode of policy confusion was indicative of Satō's overly impatient desire, even in the face of seemingly insurmountable obstacles, to open a Nixon-style dialogue with the PRC.

Equally confused by the sudden unfolding of U.S.-Chinese détente were the JSP's leaders, especially those from its left-wing factions. Since one of its main foreign-policy guidelines had been the Asanuma spirit, which identified U.S. imperialism as a common enemy of the Japanese and Chinese peoples, they were unable to get rid of quickly this ideological fixture and to adjust themselves to the rapidly changing international trends. They were at loss to explain how they should unite with China in their common struggle against U.S. imperialism at a time when the Chinese—with some fanfare—were welcoming the visit of the foremost "imperialist." The Sino-American thaw therefore had a far more profound and divisive effect upon the JSP than Secretary-General Ishibashi's initial approval of the Nixon announcement indicated. After a more careful assessment of this external development, they resumed their attack against the United States. They portrayed Nixon's China visit as indicative of a complete failure of his containment policy and as the last weapon to rescue U.S. imperialism, which was beleaguered by economic crisis, the Vietnam War, and antiwar movement.[86] Ishibashi even agreed with Kim Il-song's comment that Nixon was going to China with a white flag in his hand. The Nixon move was viewed as an attempt to replace the containment policy with the Nixon Doctrine, which was suspected to be the basis for a new regional collective security system with Japan as a center. Yet, because of their ideological and international constraints, the JSP's spokesmen failed to discuss why China, after all, had decided to accept Nixon's visit—they especially avoided any indication that they suspected China's concern with the Soviet threat as an underlying motive of its diplomatic about-face.

Upon release of the Nixon-Chou communique, the JSP welcomed it as a sign of transition from direct confrontation to peaceful coexistence between China and the U.S.[87] The resultant easing of international tensions was expected to help solve the problems in Korea and Indo-China. A positive credit was given to China's use of the five principles of peaceful coexistence as a weapon against the Nixon Doctrine in Asia. Most important, the JSP insisted, Japan was left an orphan in Asia due to Satō's reactionary and anachronistic foreign policy.

On the basis of this dire conclusion, the JSP joined other opposition political parties in requesting Satō's resignation, and, together with the CGP, the Sōhyō, the NCRJCDR, the NCNJCDR, and dissident LDP legislators (Fujiyama, et. al.), held a mass rally demanding immediate Japan-China diplomatic normalization. The rally received an encouraging message from the China-Japan Friendship Association. Later, in April, the JSP helped set up a broad liaison committee for the purpose of coordinating all movements for Sino-Japanese diplomatic normalization. The committee embraced twenty-two organizations—such as the JSP, the CGP, the DSP, the *Sōhyō*, the *Chūritsu Rōren* (National Liaison Council of Independent Unions), the *Zennichinō*, the Dietmen's League, the NCRJCDR, the NCNJCDR, the Japan-China Friendship Association (Orthodox Head-quarters), the Japan-China Cultural Exchange Association, the Japan-China Memorandum Trade Office, the Japanese Association for Promotion of International Trade, and the National Association of Progressive May-ors.[88] It represented the broadest possible united front of Japanese political, economic, and cultural groups—except the JCP and its front organizations—which desired the achievement of Japan-China diplomatic relations.

The ultimate effect of Nixon's China trip was to stimulate and spread an irresistible China boom in Japan, which no responsible Japanese leader could afford to ignore. The prevailing public mood set a basic political limit upon the freedom of Satō's successor in dealing with the Chinese question. In anticipation of the decisive turning point at the time of political succession in Japan, the Chinese were carefully and diligently preparing for a favorable turn in Sino-Japanese relations; they amassed and analyzed a vast amount of intelligence reports on Japanese political affairs, especially the LDP's interfactional dynamics, dispatched to Tokyo the best Chinese experts on Japan, and invited to China a variety of Japan's political and business leaders. They also effectively compelled major Japanese newspapers and other mass media to accept their political conditions and to disseminate reports and editorials favorable to their interests.[89] And while continuing to rebuff any *ahiru* sent by the Satō government, the Chinese dropped unmistakable hints to Japanese visitors that they would be most anxious to start a productive diplomatic dialogue with Satō's successor, provided he accepted their three principles.

Tanaka's Policy   As Prime Minister Satō was expected to relinquish his eight-year rule in the summer of 1972, all four candidates for the LDP presidency—Tanaka Kakuei, Fukuda Takeo, Ōhira Masayoshi, and Miki Takeo—committed themselves to a "forward-looking" posture toward the issue of Japanese-Chinese diplomatic relations, because they regarded it as an urgent, popular, and vote-getting task that had to be resolved. The issue was no longer a losing cause in the governing party's leadership contest; indeed, in view of the shifting intraparty politics and the public mood, the candidates vied to appeal to the LDP members of the Dietmen's League and the Asian-African Problems Study Group, which had decided in March 1972 to support a candidate clearly pledged to establish diplomatic relations between Japan and the PRC.[90] Thus Miki had already conferred with Chou En-lai in April and had accepted China's three principles, while Ōhira publicly criticized Satō's China policy. And even Minister of International Trade and Industry Tanaka and Foreign Minister Fukuda (Satō's favorite), the two principal pillars of the Satō cabinet, had subtly maneuvered to demonstrate their distance from Satō's discredited record on China. It was quite clear by June 1972 that any one of them, if elected, could not resist a set of political circumstances that demanded Japan's direct governmental negotiations with the PRC.

Tanaka, Ōhira, and Miki formed an anti-Fukuda alliance and they agreed to attach a high priority to the conclusion of diplomatic relations and a peace treaty between Japan and the PRC.[91] Fukuda, too, promised to visit Peking for the purpose of establishing diplomatic relations with China.[92] The only question left ambiguous by these candidates was Japan's future relations with Taiwan; Miki alone demanded the outright abrogation of the Japan-Taiwan peace treaty. All these maneuvers were followed with utmost interest by the Chinese, whose trade representatives in Tokyo had since April maintained close consultation with the pro-Peking LDP dietman such as Furui and Tagawa and had even held secret meetings with the key lieutenants of Tanaka and Ōhira.[93]

And lest the eventual winner of the LDP leadership contest forget his election promises, the opposition political parties drummed up a concerted campaign against Satō's China policy by introducing yet another no-confidence resolution in June. The resolution, as expected, was defeated in both Houses of the National Diet, but it was an advance warning to Satō's successor that they would continue to press him if he did not move fast in the direction of Japanese-Chinese diplomatic normalization.[94]

The Chinese issue was a contributing factor for Tanaka's electoral victory, but it is important to note that while the *Keidanren* leadership supported Fukuda's candidacy because of his "correct" educational and bureaucratic background and right-wing foreign policy, Tanaka was endorsed by a group of influential *zaikai* leaders, especially those of the *Sangyō mondai kenkyūkai* (Industrial Problems Study Group), and the *Keizai Dōyūkai*, who were active in Sino-Japanese trade.[95] Once Tanaka was installed as a new prime minister in July 1972, with Ōhira as foreign minister and Miki as deputy prime minister, the Chinese showed a serious interest in Tanaka's and Ōhira's remarks on the question of Sino-Japanese relations. A particularly favorable Chinese reaction was given to Tanaka's first press conference on July 5, in which he said that "the time is ripe for Japan to tackle the task of normalizing relations with the PRC."[96] At the first cabinet session on July 7, Tanaka again stated that "on diplomacy, I will expedite the normalization of Japan's relations with the PRC and promote peaceful diplomacy in this fast changing world situation." Ōhira further argued that "the days are over for Japan to follow in the footsteps of the United States," and that the Japan-Taiwan peace treaty would disappear after the normalization of Japanese-Chinese diplomatic relations.[97] These statements also received a prompt and positive response from China.

Speaking at the banquet held on July 9 in Peking for the delegation of the People's Democratic Republic of Yemen, Chou En-lai conspicuously made his first public comment on the new Japanese development. He said: "In Japan, the Satō government which long remained hostile toward China was eventually forced to step down ahead of time. The Tanaka cabinet was formed on the 7th of this month, and on diplomacy a statement was made that normalization of relations between China and Japan would be expedited. This merits welcome."[98] Even though Tanaka and Ōhira had not specifically satisfied China's three principles, the speed and enthusiasm with which Chou responded to their initial statements suggested his readiness to seek a diplomatic settlement with them. It was undoubtedly clear to the Chinese leadership that the occasion of the political transition from Satō to Tanaka presented the best opportunity for China to open direct communications with the Japanese government, especially before Tanaka hardened his position on Taiwan. Chou En-lai was also acutely wary of the possiblity that the Soviet Union might move to make a major policy initiative toward the Tanaka government.[99] Moreover, he may have needed a demonstrable diplomatic achievement for consolidation of his domestic political power in the aftermath of the Lin Piao affair; or, he may have wished to conclude a diplomatic rapprochement with Japan before the leftist swing of China's internal political conditions might start.[100]

Tanaka, for his part, intended to resolve the chronic Chinese question in his typical bulldozer style. Unlike his predecessors, he was prepared to offer a necessary concession on the Taiwan question; he also considered it better to deal with Mao and Chou than with their unknown successors. Given the altered outlook on both sides, the exchange of mutually reinforcing statements between Japanese and Chinese leaders, in fact, further brightened the prospect for their direct diplomatic negotiations. In view of these sudden developments, JSP Chairman Narita Tomomi held a news conference on July 10 and promised to cooperate with the Tanaka government's policy toward China if it accepted the three principles and seriously implemented them.[101] At the same time he warned Tanaka against any "deceptive gesture" or "election gimmick" that might be involved in his moves toward China. This statement was intended to push Tanaka forward despite the strong resistance of pro-Taiwan forces in the LDP and the *zaikai*. The JSP Central Executive Committee, which was afraid that it would be completely left out in the process of Japanese-Chinese diplomatic negotiations, endorsed Sasaki Kōzō's role of mediation and communications between Tanaka and Chou En-lai. After a meeting with Prime Minister Tanaka and Foreign Minister Ōhira, Sasaki visited China on July 14 to 20 at the invitation of the China-Japan Friendship Association. The Chinese apparently wished to benefit from Sasaki's frank assessment of Tanaka's China policy; and the invitation was also a calculated gesture to express their gratitude for his persistent support of their diplomatic cause, and perhaps to boost his political status in the JSP.

Sasaki told Chou En-lai that Tanaka and Ōhira were sincere in their intentions to resolve the Taiwan issue, to accept China's three principles, and to normalize diplomatic relations with the PRC. In response to this message, on July 16 and 19, Chou told Sasaki—and JSP Dietman Matsuzawa Toshiaki—that Tanaka was welcome to visit China.[102] Henceforth, Sasaki assumed a role of guaranteeing the positive merits of Tanaka's China policy. And even though Sasaki found this role in contradiction to his opposition to the LDP government, he was extremely proud of having used it to achieve his diplomatic dream.[103] In addition to Chou's informal invitation of Tanaka, Sasaki obtained a few other personal assurances from Chou, specifically that: (1) China would be satisfied if Japan expressed a "full understanding"—short of acceptance—of the three principles; (2) China would accord the same protocol to Tanaka's visit as it did to Nixon's; (3) an arrangement would be made for Tanaka's direct flight from Tokyo to Peking; (4) China understood that Tanaka, in the light of his intra-party problems, needed a lot of time to deal with the question of the Japan-Taiwan peace treaty; (5) China would take a flexible position on the issue of war reparations.[104]

Upon his return to Japan, Sasaki advised Tanaka and Ōhira as to how they should approach the PRC. Narita, too, had a "summit meeting" with Tanaka on July 21, and urged him to start governmental negotiations with the PRC on the basis of the three principles.[105] Tanaka was also asked by Narita to meet with the two leading Chinese specialists of Japanese politics and business: Sun Ping-hua and Hsiao Hsiang-chien. Sun (ex-chief of the Tokyo Liaison Office and deputy secretary-general of the China-Japan Friendship Association) had come to Tokyo, five days after Tanaka's victory, as head of the visiting Shanghai Dance-Drama Troupe, and Hsiao had recently arrived at Tokyo as chief of the Tokyo Liaison Office of the China-Japan Memorandum Trade Office. Hsiao, who had studied at Tokyo's Higher Normal School as a student-athelete, was standing director of the China-Japan Friendship Association and deputy secretary-general of the Chinese People's Institute of Foreign Affairs. Already, at Fujiyama's reception held in the Hotel New Japan on July 20, Sun and Hsiao had met with Foreign Minister Ōhira, Minister of State Miki, Minister of International Trade and Industry Nakasone, JSP Chairman Narita, CGP Chairman Takeiri, DSP Chairman Kasuga, and top *zaikai* leaders. Other LDP leaders present included Kōno Kenzō (speaker of the House of Councillors), Hashimoto Tomisaburō (LDP secretary-general), Suzuki Zenkō (chairman of the Executive Council), Sakurauchi Yoshio (chairman of the Policy Affairs Research Council), and Kosaka Zentarō. The reception was an unprecedented gala event to honor the two unofficial envoys from a foreign country, but it was a clear reflection of the changing political climate in Japan.[106] On July 22, Sun and Hsiao formally conferred with Ōhira and Hashimoto Hiroshi (chief of the China Section of the Ministry of Foreign Affairs) at the Hotel Okura, and told them that Chou would welcome Tanaka's visit to China. They agreed to use the liaison offices of memorandum trade as a regular channel of intergovernmental communications between Tokyo and Peking.[107] Soon thereafter, Ōhira set up an ad hoc task force in his ministry (under Vice-Minister Hōgen Shinsaku), which was entrusted to prepare diplomatic negotiations with China.

In order to reach an intraparty consensus on the Chinese question and to mobilize its dietmen's support for Tanaka's policy, the LDP in July transformed its Committee on China into a National Council for Japan-China Diplomatic Normalization (*Nitchū kokkō seijōka kyōgikai*); the council was chaired by Kosaka Zentarō (ex-foreign minister and member of the Ōhira faction) and placed directly under Prime Minister Tanaka's supervision.[108] This ad hoc device was instituted to bypass the LDP's normal policy-making organs, such as the Policy Affairs Research Council and the Executive Council. The council, whose voluntary membership quickly totaled 287 dietmen, became a principal forum for heated debates and compromises between the doves and the hawks within the ruling party. At its first general meeting on July 24, Tanaka and Ōhira explained their determination to pursue diplomatic normalization with China; and the council in turn adopted a resolution endorsing their efforts despite passive resistance by the hawks, such as Kishi, Ishii, Kaya, and some youthful, nationalistic dietmen.[109] Since the council itself was too large to work out an effective policy consensus, it relied upon a meeting of its chairman and twelve vice-chairmen for much of its detailed policy deliberation, or on the decisions of its thirty-nine-member executive committee. The executive committee was factionally balanced, while the chairmen's meeting was tilted in favor of pro-Peking forces.[110]

When Ōhira confirmed in early August the Japanese government's "basic positions" that Japan "fully understands" China's three principles, and approves the discontinuance of Japan-Taiwan diplomatic relations while seeking to maintain economic and other relations with Taiwan, he did so at the expense of incurring the wrath of the hawks in the council's executive committee, who attacked his submissive diplomacy and total surrender toward the PRC.[111] Unmoved by the opposition from his party's right-wing, however, Tanaka, at his press conference on August 7, himself reaffirmed Ōhira's positions.[112] This clarification of Tanaka's position on the Taiwanese question satisfied China and thus eliminated the last remaining hurdle to the creation of Sino-Japanese diplomatic relations. On August 11 Sun Ping-hua and Hsiao Hsiang-chien conveyed to Ōhira an official message from Foreign Minister Chi Peng-fei that "Premier Chou En-lai welcomes and invites

Prime Minister Tanaka Kakuei to visit China."[113] At his meeting with Sun and Hsiao on August 15 at the Imperial Hotel, Tanaka, accompanied by Chief Cabinet Secretary Nikaidō Susumu and Hashimoto Hiroshi, accepted Chou's invitation with gratitude and discussed the specific procedures for his trip to China.[114] Soon thereafter, Hashimoto led the Japanese government's thirteen-member advance party to Peking.

After a series of tense discussions and maneuvers that took place over a month, the LDP's council finally passed, on September 8, a compromise five-point platform with regard to the issue of Japan-China diplomatic normalization, in which it endorsed the following positions: (1) normalization of diplomatic relations on the basis of the U.N. Charter, the ten principles of the Bandung Conference, and the five principles of peaceful coexistence; (2) respect by the two sides for each other's relations with other friendly countries; (3) mutual forbearance from using or threatening to use force against each other; (4) promotion of equal economic and cultural relations among all nations; and (5) cooperation for the peace and prosperity of Asia.[115] The preface to this platform emphasized that the Japanese government "must" conduct negotiations with China in such a way that it can maintain its "hitherto existing relations" with the "Republic of China." This was intended to soothe the dissatisfaction of the hawks in the LDP. In fact, the pro-Taiwan dietmen led by Kaya, Ishihara Shintarō, Nakagawa Ichirō, and Aikawa Katsuroku had insisted that the preface should specifically include the words, the "Republic of China" (not "Taiwan" as expressed in the draft), "must" (not "is expected to"), and "hitherto existing relations including diplomatic exchange." The last phrase was rejected, but the council accepted the other two.[116]

No longer were the LDP hawks opposed to the notion of diplomatic normalization with the PRC, although they resisted its implementation at the expense of Taiwan's diplomatic interest. Why had they given in? First, they were not prepared to offer a frontal challenge to the new Prime Minister Tanaka, who, after all, had to assume the responsibility for his foreign policy. More importantly, since 1971 when the international acceptance of the PRC had become an almost universal tendency, the balance between the hawks and the doves within the LDP had reversed in favor of the pro-Peking forces; and as of mid-1972, the hawks could command less than 40% of LDP dietmen in regard to their old pro-Taiwan position.[117] However, unlike Hatoyama's intraconservative weakness seventeen years ago, Prime Minister Tanaka now achieved a substantial support from the LDP dietmen for his China policy.

Preliminary Diplomatic Contacts In the meantime, Tanaka and Ōhira relied upon a few pro-Peking political leaders as their agents to carefully prepare the diplomatic groundwork with their Chinese counterparts. The best known examples of these intermediary agents were CGP Chairman Takeiri Yoshikatsu and LDP Dietman Furui Yoshimi. On July 25, a day after the first plenary session of the LDP's council, Takeiri, who had recently discussed the Chinese question four times with both Tanaka and Ōhira, visited China—his second visit in a year—and engaged in intimate conferences with Chou En-lai and Liao Cheng-chih, for a total of ten hours in three days. Just as Sasaki had done ten days previously, Takeiri explained to his Chinese hosts how sincere Tanaka and Ōhira were in their commitments for diplomatic normalization with China. Surprisingly, it was during these meetings that Takeiri received what amounted to the first Chinese draft of the expected Chou-Tanaka joint statement. The draft, which Chou read from a typewritten text, and which Takeiri copied down, was thought to be a flexible and practicable proposition, which easily satisfied Tanaka and Ōhira. Upon his return to Japan, Takeiri prepared a detailed memorandum for Tanaka's diplomatic scenario toward the PRC.[118] It was also Takeiri who informed Tanaka that Chou had agreed to give up China's right for war reparations, and that he had considered the U.S.-Japan security treaty, the Satō-Nixon joint statement of 1969, and the Senkaku Islands dispute irrelevant to the opening of Sino-Japanese diplomatic relations.

The question here is, why did Chou En-lai choose Takeiri as a crucial go-between in preliminary diplomatic negotiations? Chou En-lai apparently assigned a high priority to boosting Takeiri's ego—perhaps more than he did to boosting Sasaki's—as a token of political reward for the untiring efforts that the CGP had made to organize a mass movement for Sino-Japanese diplomatic normalization (as exemplified in its sponsorship of the NCNJCDR). Indeed, due in part to his pro-Peking tendency, Takeiri had almost been assassinated in September 1971. And added to the CGP's demonstrable contribution was the fact that Chou appreciated Takeiri's political reliability and his close personal friendship with Tanaka and Ōhira. (Chou may have overestimated the political capability of the CGP—and the Sōka Gakkai—in mobilizing public sentiments in Japan, however).

If Takeiri performed the role of a trusted personal intermediary between Tanaka and Chou, Furui, who had in the long process of trade negotiations accumulated a great deal of first-hand knowledge on China's thinking and negotiating patterns, became a principal element of Ōhira's brain trust, as well as a confidential messenger in the execution of Ōhira's diplomatic strategy toward China. Since Tanaka lacked adequate experience in diplomatic matters, he entrusted his foreign policy to Ōhira, who, as a veteran in diplomacy and a perfectionist on every minute detail, determined Japan's specific approach with China in close consultation with Furui.[119] It was, however, Tanaka's own political decision that he himself should lead the Japanese government's delegation to China and establish diplomatic relations with China before—not after—Japan's general election.

On September 9, 1972, a day after the LDP council's adoption of its five-point platform, Furui, together with Tagawa Seiichi and Matsumoto Shunichi (who, as Japanese ambassador to Great Britain, had assumed a vital role in Japanese-Soviet diplomatic negotiations during the 1955-56 period), departed for China under the ostensible purpose of memorandum trade negotiations. Furui's real purpose, however, was to deliver in person Ōhira's proposals for the Chou-Tanaka statement and to discuss them with Chou En-lai and Liao Cheng-chih. The secret cover was used to successfully conclude preliminary diplomatic negotiations and, more importantly, to foreclose an opposition from the LDP's pro-Taiwan dietmen, who were suspicious of Furui's and Tagawa's possible mediatory roles between Tokyo and Peking. Hence it appeared to be a follow-up of the Takeiri mission. According to Furui's subsequent revelation, the main contents of Ōhira's proposal on the statement's format, preamble, and text were as follows:

A. Format: The outcome of the Tanaka-Chou summit talks should be recorded in the form of a joint statement—not a treaty or joint declaration—so that the legal and political complications of the Diet's ratification could be averted.

B. Preamble: (1) Japan would express its self-reproach for the past war; (2) diplomatic normalization would be cited as a common desire of the Japanese and Chinese peoples, and it would be noted as making a contribution to peace in Asia and in the world; (3) Japan and China would promise to coexist peacefully.

C. Text: (1) Japan and China would confirm—not declare (as China desired)—the termination of the state of war between them (for it was a consistent view of the Japanese government that Japan had legally terminated its war with China in the Japan-Taiwan peace treaty); (2) Japan would recognize the PRC as the only lawful government of China and would state its understanding and respect—not acceptance—of the Chinese stand that Taiwan is a part of China; (3) Japan and China would establish diplomatic relations and exchange ambassadors; (4) both sides would negotiate a treaty of peace and friendship; (5) Japan's foreign minister would issue a unilateral declaration—but not in the joint statement—that the Japan-Taiwan peace treaty ceases to be effective; (6) China would renounce its claims for war reparations.

Chou-En-lai was agreeable to most of these points, but he opposed C. (1) on the grounds that both sides must formally terminate the state of war. And he called on the Japanese government to clarify in the preamble its general stand on China's three principles. He also proposed to specify that Sino-Japanese diplomatic normalization was not directed against any other country or countries.[120] Extremely sensitive to the absolute secrecy of preliminary negotiations, Chou En-lai asked Furui not to make a long-distance telephone call to Foreign Minister Ōhira or to send a cable to him; thus Furui recorded the results of his negotiations, as well as Chou's positions, in a lengthy personal letter, which Hashimoto Hiroshi delivered in person from Peking to Tokyo.

Evidently, before Tanaka's voyage to China, both sides reached a comprehensive agreement on all major issues, except on the controversy over the state of war. Sasaki, Takeiri, and Furui performed a useful intermediary function for both sides, but it is conceivable that Chou and Tanaka may have used other Japanese and Chinese envoys and channels, or even mutual foreign friends, as their additional messengers and negotiators from July 7 to September 25, 1972. However, the LDP's first twenty-two-member delegation, which Kosaka Zentarō led to China on September 14 to 20 (during Furui's presence in China), achieved no significant result. Originally conceived as a partisan effort to neutralize the adverse domestic political effects of Sasaki's and Takeiri's well-publicized meetings with Chou En-lai, the Kosaka delegation, consisting of both doves and hawks, was politely received, but was regarded as a necessary nuisance by the Chinese. They felt it necessary to soothe the pro-Taiwan members of the LDP, but flatly rebuked any oblique suggestion for a "two-China" solution.

Just as Chou En-lai bypassed his Ministry of Foreign Affairs and used Liao Cheng-chih and other nonofficial experts of Japanese affairs, who often conducted preliminary diplomatic negotiations with their Japanese counterparts in Japanese, Tanaka and Ōhira relied more heavily on their personal emissaries than on senior governmental bureaucrats, for they did not have a high opinion of policy innovation, albeit technical expertise, among the ranking officials in the Japanese Ministry of Foreign Affairs. Some of these officials were extremely reluctant to compromise Japanese diplomatic relations with Nationalist China and to nullify the Japan-Taiwan peace treaty. In particular, Administrative Vice-Minister Hōgen Shinsaku (a specialist of Soviet and European affairs), Fukuda's protégé, was known to favor Japan's rapid reconciliation with the Soviet Union as an attempt to restrain China's growing international influence. The task force, under Hōgen's leadership, was therefore utilized not to initiate a basic policy line but to recommend the technicalities for its implementation. Among all Japanese Foreign Ministry officials, Hashimoto Hiroshi, who had articulated a minority view in the ministry favoring a flexible policy toward China, played the most active role in Japan-China negotiations. In a span of less than a month, he visited China three times and took part in all major meetings both in Tokyo and Peking.

While Tanaka and Ōhira were seeking a policy consensus in the governing party and sponsoring preliminary bilateral diplomatic negotiations with China, they did not neglect to consult with their foreign political allies, especially the United States, the Republic of China, and the Republic of Korea. During his talks with Nixon in Honolulu on August 31 to September 1, Tanaka reportedly confided to his host that Japanese public opinion, aroused by the Sino-American accommodation, might cause his new cabinet to collapse if it failed to establish diplomatic relations with China. Nixon expressed his sympathy for Tanaka's internal problem.[121] And, so long as Sino-Japanese diplomatic rapprochement did not undermine the U.S.-Japanese security relations, Kissinger added, the United States would not take a quixotic action against Tanaka's China policy.[122] (Earlier in June, Chou En-lai had asked Kissinger at Peking not to oppose his planned search for diplomatic normalization with Satō's successor; Kissinger had twice indicated his support for Chou's intentions.)[123] Thus Nixon and Tanaka, while praising the president's visits to Peking and Moscow as "a significant step forward," expressed their hope that the prime minister's upcoming China visit "would also serve to further the trend for the relaxation of tension in Asia."[124]

A day after his return from Honolulu, Ōhira left for Seoul to attend the sixth Japanese-(South) Korean ministerial conference. He apparently gained a manifestation of understanding from President Park Chung-hi in regard to Japanese-Chinese diplomatic negotiations. A far more difficult task of foreign consultation fell on the LDP Vice-President Shiina Etsusaburō (ex-foreign minister in the Ikeda and Satō cabinets), who, along with fifteen LDP dietmen, carried Tanaka's personal letter to President Chiang Kai-shek. The Shiina mission, unlike the Kosaka mission to Peking, suffered an unfriendly public reception. When Shiina arrived at Taipei on September 17, he was surrounded and harassed by an angry Chinese mob, who protested Tanaka's new China policy. He then met with Premier Chiang Ching-kuo, Vice-President Yen Chia-kan, and Foreign Minister Shen Chang-huan, but he failed to appease them; he was not permitted to see Chiang Kai-shek, who was ill at that time.[125] In spite of the bitter reaction from the Nationalist Chinese leaders, the Japanese refused to budge from the substance of their message: that a diplomatic break was inevitable, and that for the future the best Japan would be able to offer would be to reverse the principle of separation between political and economic matters and to continue to maintain all relations, except the diplomatic one, with Taiwan. Thus Tanaka was able to withstand the pressures that had frustrated Hatoyama in his 1955-56 attempt to improve Japan's relations with the PRC because: (1) the pressure from Washington to maintain relations with Taipei had disappeared in light of the emerging Sino-American rapprochement; (2) Japan's self-confidence in foreign affairs (not to mention its economic power) had grown tremendously in the intervening years; (3) Taiwan's influence in global, Asian, and Japanese politics had declined; and (4) Tanaka found domestic political support for diplomatic relations with the PRC, especially in his own party and in the National Diet, that Hatoyama had not been able to find. Moreover, unlike the foreign-policy cleavage between Hatoyama and his Foreign Minister Shigemitsu, Tanaka enjoyed a comfortable, complete cooperation from Foreign Minister Ōhira both in intraparty politics and in foreign affairs.

Normalization of Diplomatic Relations

Summit Meetings   On September 25, 1972, Tanaka, Ōhira, and Chief Cabinet Secretary Nikaidō Susumu, along with an entourage of forty-nine aides and other personnel, made the historic journey to the PRC, having been seen off at the airport by a large number of well-wishers, who included cabinet members, LDP officials, opposition party leaders, and *zaikai* representatives.[126] At the airport in Peking they were greeted by Premier Chou, Yeh Chien-ying (vice-chairman of the Military Commission and vice-chairman of the National Defense Council), Kuo Mo-jo (vice-chairman of the Standing Committee of the National People's Congress and honorary president of the China-Japan Friendship Association), Chou Chien-jen (vice-chairman of the Standing Committee of the National People's Congress), Chi Peng-fei (foreign minister), Wu Teh (chairman of the Peking Municipal Revolutionary Committee), Fang Yi (minister of Economic Relations with Foreign Countries), Pai Hsiang-kuo (minister of Foreign Trade), Liao Cheng-chih (adviser to the Foreign Ministry and president of the China-Japan Friendship Association), Han Nien-lung (vice-minister of Foreign Affairs), Wang Kuo-chuan (president of the Chinese People's Association for Friendship with Foreign Countries and vice-president of the China-Japan Friendship Association), and Chang Hsiang-shan (adviser to the Foreign Ministry).[127]

On the afternoon of his arrival, Tanaka had the first of his four summit sessions with Chou En-lai. The Japanese side was represented by Tanaka, Ōhira, Nikaidō, Yoshida Kenzō (director of the Bureau of Asian Affairs), Takashima Masuo (director of the Bureau of Treaties), Kiuchi Akitane (Tanaka's secretary), Hashimoto Hiroshi (chief of the China Section), Kuriyama Takakazu (chief of the Treaties Section), and Hatakenaka Atsushi (staff member of the China Section); their Chinese counterparts included Chou, Chi, Liao, Han Nien-lung, Chang Hsiang-shan, Lu Wei-chiao (director of the Department of Asian Affairs), Wang Hsiao-yün (deputy director), and Chen Kang (division chief).[128]

On that evening, in honor of the Tanaka party, Chou held at the Great Hall of the People an elaborate, colorful banquet replete with maotai toasts, warm cheers, and popular Japanese and Chinese songs.[129]

In his welcoming speech, Chou said:

Prime Minister Tanaka's visit to China opens a new page in the history of Sino-Japanese relations. Friendly contacts and cultural exchanges between our two countries have a history of two thousand years, and our two peoples have forged a profound friendship; all this we should treasure. However, in the half-century after 1894, owing to the Japanese militarists' aggression against China, the Chinese people were made to endure tremendous disasters and the Japanese people, too, suffered a great deal from it. The past not forgotten is a guide for the future.[130]

Yet, while expressing a warning against the "very few militarists" in Japan, he was optimistic about the future of peaceful and good-neighborly relations between China and Japan, irrespective of their different social systems. He wished to seek common ground with Tanaka on major issues, but to reserve differences on minor points.

Prime Minister Tanaka responded with a reference to his "profound self-examination" of the fact that Japan had caused *meiwaku* (a mild form of trouble or nuisance) to the Chinese people during several decades in the past. He also added:

We should not forever linger in the dim blind alley of the past. In my opinion, it is important now for the leaders of Japan and China to confer in the interest of tomorrow . . . despite the fact that some minor differences exist between the positions and views of the two sides, I believe it is possible for Japan and China to overcome their divergence of views and reach agreement in the spirit of seeking common ground on major questions and of mutual understanding and mutual accommodation.[131]

The term *meiwaku* (whose Chinese pronunciation, *mi-huo*, means confusion) was translated into Chinese as *ma-fan* (trouble), but those Chinese leaders who understood the subtle nuance of Tanaka's less than sincere apology suddenly stopped their applause and turned visibly cold. Obviously, they were disturbed by Tanaka's evasiveness about Japan's past crimes committed against the Chinese people. At subsequent meetings, the Chinese, including Mao, complained about Tanaka's usage of *meiwaku*, but Tanaka took great pains to explain that the term in Japanese meant a genuine apology. This episode vividly demonstrated the limited political utility of cultural affinity between China and Japan.

The ceremonial highlight of Tanaka's China journey was his talk with Mao at *Chungnanhai* for an hour in the evening of September 27. The talk was officially described as an "earnest and friendly conversation" (in contrast to a description of the Mao-Nixon talk as a "serious and frank exchange of views"), though in fact they only chatted casually about a number of largely apolitical subjects that ranged from Chinese classics, wine, and cooking, to Mao's childhood rebellion against his father and Tanaka's headache with electoral and parliamentary procedures.[132] According to Nikaidō, some of their conversation went as follows:

Mao: "Did you have a fight with Premier Chou (at their summit meetings)?"
Tanaka: "No, I had a smooth discussion with him."
Mao: "Only after a real fight can you (Tanaka and Chou) become good friends."
Mao: "He (pointing to Liao Cheng-chih) was born and raised in Japan. Why don't you take him to Japan with you?"

Tanaka: "Mr. Liao is very popular in Japan, and he may be easily elected to the House of Councillors from a national district."

In fact, the contents of their one-hour conversation were less important than the very fact of Mao's meeting with Tanaka. It bestowed his authoritative approval, especially in the context of Chinese domestic politics, on the Chou-Tanaka summitry itself.[133]

Joint Statement   After a series of top-level meetings, Tanaka and Chou agreed to declare in their joint statement, signed on September 29, that:

China and Japan are neighboring countries separated only by a strip of water, and there was long history of traditional friendship between them. The two peoples ardently wish to end the abnormal state of affairs that has hitherto existed between the two countries. The termination of the state of war and the normalization of relations between China and Japan—the realization of such wishes of the two peoples will open a new page in the annals of relations between the two countries.[134]

The Japanese side stated that it "deeply reproaches itself" for having caused enormous damages in the past to the Chinese people through war. It also accepted the stand of "fully understanding" China's three principles. The nine points of the agreement were as follows:

(1) The "abnormal state of affairs" between China and Japan is declared terminated. (As a compromise of Japanese and Chinese positions, this conveniently avoided the legal issue as to whether the state of war had already terminated or not.) The preamble, quoted earlier, was the first formal agreement between Japan and China to put an end to the state of war.

(2) Japan recognizes the PRC as the sole legal government of China. (It was an absolute Chinese demand accepted by Japan.)

(3) China reaffirms that Taiwan is an "inalienable part" of its territory, and Japan "fully understands and respects" this stand in accordance with Article 8 of the Potsdam Proclamation.[135] (The reference to the Potsdam Proclamation [July 26, 1945] was not included in the Chinese draft handed to Takeiri, but Japan followed the Dutch precedent in understanding and respecting the Chinese stand—rather than the Canadian precedent that just took "note" of the Chinese stand. The Nixon-Chou communique stated that the United States "acknowledges" and "does not challenge" the position that Taiwan is part of China.[136] Japan did not fully *accept* the Chinese claim partly because the acceptance might weaken Japan's arguments about northern territorial disputes with the Soviet Union; however, by adopting this formula, Tanaka did manage to circumvent the San Francisco peace treaty, wherein Japan renounced a right to Taiwan without specifying its recipient.)

(4) Both sides agree to establish diplomatic relations and to exchange ambassadors to their capitals.

(5) China renounces its "demand"—not "right"—for war indemnities from Japan. (The Japanese government contended that since the Republic of China, representing China, had already renounced a right for war reparations in the protocol of the Japan-Taiwan peace treaty, the PRC was not legally entitled to that right. As hinted to Sasaki and Takeiri, China made a concession in renouncing its "demand" for war reparations.)

(6) Both sides agree to establish peaceful and friendly relations on the basis of the five principles of peaceful coexistence and to settle all disputes by peaceful means without resorting to the use or threat of force, in accordance with the U.N. Charter. (The agreement, in effect, amounted to a nonaggression pact, and it is expected to be applicable to their pending territorial dispute over the Senkaku Islands.)

(7) The normalization of their relations is not directed against third countries: while "neither of the two countries should seek hegemony in the Asia-Pacific region, and each country is opposed to efforts by any other country or group of countries to establish such hegemony." (As an attempt to dispel any misgivings felt by third countries, Chou proposed this to Furui—its implications are identical with those of the Nixon-Chou joint communique. Even though Japan is agreeable to this principle against hegemony, she is bound by the Constitution as well as by limited military power to implement it to the fullest extent. The agreement may give rise to a suspicion that Japan and China have a tacit political understanding for their common opposition to other major powers, especially the Soviet Union, in the Asia-Pacific region.)

(8) Both sides agree to conclude a "treaty of peace and friendship."

(9) Both governments hold negotiations to conclude agreements on trade, navigation, aviation, fishery, etc.[137]

The Tanaka-Chou joint statement was not a legally binding agreement in a strict sense, but it was essentially a political document that recorded the basic understanding and commitments made at the highest levels of both governments. On the same day it was signed, Foreign Minister Ōhira held a press conference in Peking and unilaterally declared that as a result of the joint statement, the Japan-(Nationalist) China peace treaty was terminated.[138] He did not abrogate or dispute the prior legality of this peace treaty, but Taiwan lost, among other things, the most-favored-nation status as granted in a protocol of the treaty. In response to Ōhira's announcement, the Nationalist China Foreign Ministry promptly declared a termination of its diplomatic relations with Japan, and it accused the Tanaka government of having betrayed its treaty obligation.[139]

While the question of Japanese-Taiwanese relations was an emotional issue in Taipei, it was handled with much less contention in Peking. During their discussions with Chou, Tanaka and Ōhira made it clear (by repeating their written statement) that Japan would continue to have nondiplomatic relations with Taiwan. They cited the fact that during the previous year Japan had conducted a $1.2 billion trade relationship with Taiwan, that 180,000 Japanese had visited Taiwan (with 50,000 Taiwanese persons visiting Japan), and that there were 3,900 Japanese residents in Taiwan.[140] Chou did not raise a serious objection to their policy intentions on Taiwan.

Apparently Chou and Tanaka did not dwell on the issues of Japan's revived militarism or defense expenditure, which had been a principal theme in China's anti-Tokyo propaganda since 1969. Nor did they disagree on the U.S.-Japan security treaty, which Chou presumably recognized as a necessary arrangement to counterbalance the Soviet influence in East Asia and to constrain Japan's independent nuclear development. Another issue that could have been expected to cause the trouble in Peking was the territorial dispute, but it was de-emphasized in the Chou-Tanaka talks. Tanaka insisted on Japan's traditional sovereignty over the Senkaku Islands, but Chou, while maintaining that these islands did not even appear on an ordinary world map, proposed not to discuss the issue at that time. The dispute was therefore left unresolved. Further, Chou asked Tanaka to send his best wishes to the Japanese emperor, whom he had publicly identified as a symbol of Japanese militarism.[141]

With his historic task accomplished in six days, Tanaka and his party took a brief nonstop flight from Shanghai to Tokyo on September 30. Cheering crowds of several thousand Chinese students and foreign diplomats greeted Tanaka at both Peking and Shanghai, and a great number of Japanese leaders welcomed him back at Haneda Airport. Again, this occasion brought out Japanese cabinet ministers, LDP officials, and opposition party chiefs, including JSP Chairman Narita, CGP Chairman Takeiri, and DSP Chairman Kasuga.[142]

Effects of Diplomatic Normalization   The successful summitry was a tribute both to Tanaka's political decisiveness and to Chou's diplomatic skill. Even though the combined effects of external stimuli, party politics, business pressure, and public mood determined much of his foreign policy outlook, it was after all Tanaka's characteristic decisiveness that set the timing and pace for resolving Japan's major postwar diplomatic dilemma—a dilemma that his predecessors, from Yoshida and Hatoyama to Ikeda and Satō, had been unwilling or unable to deal with. His total personal confidence in, and intimate cooperation with, Foreign Minister Ōhira, an experienced diplomatic negotiator, had also made it easy for the latter to devise a specific course of action toward the PRC.

In order to achieve China's diplomatic breakthrough with Japan, which had eluded him for nearly a quarter-century, Chou En-lai had, himself, conducted a complex, but well-coordinated diplomatic orchestration with

Table 21—Chronological Summary of Major Events
from July to September 1972

July

5. Tanaka, following his election to the LDP presidency, expresses his determination to normalize diplomatic relations with China.
7. Tanaka and Ōhira reiterate the same determination after their first cabinet session.
9. Chou welcomes Tanaka's and Ōhira's statements.
14. Sasaki visits China (and returns to Japan on July 20).
20. Fujiyama holds a reception for Sun and Hsiao, who meet Ōhira, Miki, Nakasone, and other Japanese political and business leaders.
22. Ōhira meets Sun and Hsiao and receives an informal invitation for Tanaka's visit to China.
24. LDP's Council opens its first plenary meeting on China.
25. Takeiri visits China (and returns to Japan on August 3).

August

3. The Japanese Ministry of Foreign Affairs reveals its "basic positions" on China.
7. Tanaka holds his press conference to endorse these positions.
11. Ōhira meets Sun and Hsiao, who deliver Chou's formal invitation for Tanaka's state visit to China.
15. Tanaka meets Sun and Hsiao and accepts Chou's invitation.
19. Tanaka and Ōhira discuss the China question with Kissinger at Tokyo.
31. The Japanese government's advance party leaves for China.

September

1. Tanaka and Nixon reach an understanding on China at Honolulu.
4. Ōhira arrives at Seoul for policy consultation.
8. LDP's Council adopts a five-point platform on China.
9. Furui visits China (and returns to Japan on September 23).
14. Kosaka leads the LDP mission to Peking (and returns to Japan on September 20).
17. Shiina leads the LDP mission to Taipei (and returns to Japan on September 19).
25. Tanaka arrives at Peking and opens the first summit meeting with Chou; Chou holds a banquet for Tanaka.
26. Ōhira holds his first session with Chi Peng-fei, and Tanaka holds his second meeting with Chou.
27. Tanaka visits the Great Wall and the Ming Tombs, holds the third meeting with Chou, and meets Mao for one hour; Ōhira has the second session with Chi.
28. Tanaka visits the Palace Museum, has the fourth meeting with Chou, and holds a return banquet.
29. Tanaka and Chou sign a joint statement; they leave for Shanghai.
30. Tanaka departs Shanghai and arrives at Tokyo.

patience and finesse. The multiple linkages of communications and intermediaries were diligently cultivated and then utilized, first, to get an accurate view of the changing Japanese political reality, and second, to exchange a series of personal assurances and commitments with the Japanese decision makers. Assisted by China's able and seasoned experts on Japanese affairs, particularly Liao Cheng-chih, he provided many Japanese leaders (Sasaki,

Takeiri, Furui, Fujiyama, and others) and organizations with a sense of participation in historic events. And the cumulative political effects of "people's diplomacy," especially opposition diplomacy and the friendship movement, in Japan had been put to good use for China's diplomatic goal. In recognition of this, at the reciprocal banquet held on September 28, both Chou and Tanaka expressed their thanks to many persons of all walks of life in Japan and China for their contributions to paving the way for Sino-Japanese diplomatic normalization.[143]

It had not been necessary, though it was useful, for Chou En-lai to rely on Sasaki for extending an informal invitation to Tanaka or on Takeiri for delivering the first Chinese draft to the Japanese government. Nor had Furui been indispensable for the conduct of preliminary diplomatic negotiations between Tokyo and Peking. The prominent role assigned to these and other Japanese politicians and businessmen was a part of Chou's shrewd political tactics. Sometimes he was stubborn in insisting on a tough, principled position (on Taiwan, for example), but at other times, he was extremely flexible and willing to offer generous concessions (on war reparations and the state of war) and attractive promises (on trade). In the process Chou, a Japanophile (who had twice visited Japan in 1917 and 1919), demonstrated a keen sensitivity to the Japanese psychology and a masterful manipulation of Japan's political and economic forces. As the *People's Daily* (September 30, 1972) editorially put it, Chou and his associates were rejoicing over the complete success of an objective and "irresistible historical tide," but they did not forget to recognize the importance of conscious human effort on both sides.

The Tanaka-Chou joint statement, despite some of its vague elements, was widely acclaimed both at home and abroad. The LDP was pleased with Tanaka's "epoch-making" diplomatic achievement, and all opposition political parties, including the JCP, invariably welcomed it. On the day it was issued, Narita cabled a congratulatory message to Chou En-lai and Liao Cheng-chih, in which the JSP stressed its own foresight in the contribution toward Sino-Japanese cooperation.[144] While the CGP and the DPS fully cooperated with Tanaka's China policy, the JSP had wished to score a domestic political point by inviting a big delegation of the China-Japan Friendship Association to Japan prior to Tanaka's China visit. The Chinese decision to decline the invitation—a correct consideration not to embarass or spoil Tanaka's visit—deprived the JSP of a coveted opportunity to demonstrate its international status.[145] The JSP saved its face by Sasaki's well-publicized visit to China, but it lost a potent foreign-policy issue whereby the LDP government's incompetence had been attacked.

Only the JCP was conspicuously absent in the China bandwagon; thus no JCP members were present at Haneda Airport for Tanaka's departure and arrival. And Chairman Nosaka Sanzō criticized China's rapprochement with Tanaka as an attempt to join the United States and Japan in encircling the Soviet Union and to isolate the JCP in Japanese politics; the worldwide trend of big-power dealings was also condemned.[146] But it could not afford to oppose the establishment of Sino-Japanese diplomatic relations, which it had long advocated. At the same time, however, the JCP called upon China to follow the principle of mutual noninterference in interparty relations.[147] It was proud of its autonomous policy, which was not subjected to China's unilateral terms.

A vexing political problem raised by all opposition political parties was their request that the National Diet should ratify the Tanaka-Chou joint statement.[148] Given the nature of the joint statement, which in effect amounted to a peace treaty, the request, though politically motivated, was legitimate, but Tanaka rejected it because the Diet's ratification might precipitate a legal controversy over the Japan-Taiwan peace treaty and because some pro-Taiwan LDP legislators might oppose or boycott the ratification just as Tanaka and Ōhira, along with Satō and Ikeda, had refused to take part in the Diet's ratification of the Japanese-Soviet joint declaration in 1956. In fact, Tanaka was seriously concerned with a potential political revolt of the pro-Taiwan LDP dietmen, such as Kishi, Kaya, Ishii, and Nadao. These powerful leaders contended that Tanaka had violated the LDP council's five-point platform and that no one but the Diet could nullify the Japan-Taiwan peace treaty.[149] On the very afternoon that they returned from Shanghai, Tanaka and Ōhira had explained their experiences and accomplishments before the joint session of LDP members of both Houses. And expectedly, a number of disgruntled pro-Taiwan dietmen, mostly from the Fukuda, Shiina, and Mizuda factions, had complained about Japan's concessions on the Taiwan question, which they considered a violation of the LDP's "free-world" diplomacy and of the Japanese Constitution.[150] They were suspicious of a secret agreement that Tanaka might have concluded with China in regard to war reparations, but this was flatly denied by Tanaka.

Another criticism directed against Tanaka's reconciliation with China was the rapid speed with which it was consummated. According to this criticism, he should have pursued a deliberately protracted program of diplomatic negotiations in order to extract a Chinese concession on Taiwan or a Soviet concession on the northern territories.[151] Ōhira responded to this attack with a justification based on the claim that the public demand for diplomatic normalization had been so overwhelming in Japan that the new Tanaka cabinet could hardly have avoided fulfilling the political obligation to accommodate that demand. If the demand had been left unresolved, he contended, Japan might have undergone a serious, unhealthy condition of "political constipation."[152] Notwithstanding the lingering complaints and suspicions in the LDP, Tanaka managed to keep a lid on the intraparty disagreements on China at least for the time being. But having been confronted with his diplomatic fait accompli, his opponents were quietly preparing themselves to counterbalance Tanaka's "sell-out" policy toward China. Subsequently, 152 LDP legislators, 99 representatives and 53 councillors, formed a Dietmen's Consultative Association for Japan-(Nationalist) China Relations (*Nikka kankei giinkondankai*) under Chairman Nadao Hirokichi.[153] It embraced many members of the Asian Problems Study Group, and Nadao led a friendly delegation to visit Taiwan. The Chinese question, too, stimulated the birth of the *Seirankai* (Blue Storm Group) by thirty-one youthful, intensely nationalistic, and staunchly anti-Communist LDP dietmen. These two organizations constituted a powerful intraparty pressure force that was expected to check and balance Tanaka's willing cooperation with China.[154]

Although Tanaka's diplomatic rapprochement with China did not prevent a controversy within the LDP, his political fortune soared appreciably as an overwhelming majority of the Japanese people, regardless of their partisan preferences, approved of his China policy. According to a Jiji News Agency survey, 85.8% of nationwide random interviewees endorsed, either strongly or moderately, Tanaka's diplomatic normalization with the PRC.[155] Only 2.7% disapproved with 11.5% responding "Do Not Know." Asked to give the reasons for their support, 45.3% answered that it would strengthen good-neighborly relations between Japan and China. Other reasons most often expressed were the relaxation of tensions in Asia (25.0%), the restoration of historical ties (18.8%), and the promotion of trade relations (15.4%).

As table 22 shows, the *Sankei Shimbun* survey revealed a higher percentage of public approval (97.8%), and this almost universal approval naturally cut across party lines. More important, almost nine out of ten Japanese interviewees also accepted, though mostly in a reluctant fashion, Tanaka's decision to sever diplomatic relations with Taiwan—11.4% answered that the decision was natural, and 77.0% considered it regrettable, but unavoidable. Interestingly, whereas JSP supporters were the least sympathetic toward Taiwan, a slightly higher percentage of voters for JCP and DSP candidates expressed a sympathetic attitude. (A few Japanese Sinologists, notably Professor Ishikawa Tadao of Keiō University, lamented the pervasive lack of sympathetic feeling toward Taiwan among the Japanese people.)[156]

The right-wing reaction within the LDP notwithstanding, Tanaka and his conservative party were ready to translate his diplomatic success into a personal and partisan advantage. During his talks with opposition political leaders, Tanaka appealed for a one-year political truce to carry out his nonpartisan China policy.[157] As a compromise to the opposition parties' request for the Diet's formal approval of the Tanaka-Chou joint statement,

Table 22—Japanese Public Opinion on Diplomatic Normalization, 1972
(percentage)

(A) Approval of Diplomatic Normalization with China

	Approve strongly	Approve moderately	Do not care	Disapprove	Do not know
Nationwide	58.9	38.9	1.6	0.2	0.4
LDP	63.2	34.6	1.7	0.4	0
JSP	52.9	47.1	0	0	0
CGP	62.9	35.5	1.6	0	0
DSP	66.7	30.0	0	0	3.3
JCP	47.8	47.8	4.3	0	0
Nonpartisan	61.1	36.6	1.7	0	0.6

(B) Severance of Diplomatic Relations with Taiwan

	Natural	Regrettable, unavoidable	Impermissible	Do not know
Nationwide	11.4	77.0	10.5	1.1
LDP	9.1	77.1	13.0	0.9
JSP	12.6	79.8	5.9	1.7
CGP	14.5	69.4	12.9	3.2
DSP	6.7	76.7	16.7	0
JCP	30.4	52.2	17.4	0
Nonpartisan	6.9	81.7	9.7	1.7

SOURCE: *Chōsa Geppō*, January 1973, pp. 28–29.

he accepted the idea of a Diet resolution, rather than ratification or approval, which would express a parliamentary consent to his policy. Both Houses of the National Diet unanimously passed the resolution, jointly sponsored by the LDP, the JSP, the CGP, and the DSP, which welcomed the Tanaka-Chou joint statement and urged the Japanese government to conclude a peace treaty with China.[158] This paved the way for the Dietmen's League, with its primary goal achieved, to reorganize itself into a Dietmen's League for Japan-China Friendship (*Nitchū yūkō giinrenmei*) under Fujiyama's continuing leadership; it remained a nonpartisan parliamentary umbrella for promoting Japan-China cooperation. The new league attracted 411 members—38 more than its predecessor, but this time the JCP, critical of its "submissiveness" to China, did not join the league.[159]

In the meantime, Tanaka decided to dissolve the House of Representatives and to hold general elections before the end of 1972. Undoubtedly this was a move designed to increase the LDP's majority—and his factional strength—in the Diet. Just as Nixon had effectively used the television films of his China visit and of Chou En-lai's smiling face as a device for his presidential campaign, Tanaka adopted as his party's campaign symbols a pair of Chinese pandas (named Lanlan and Kangkang) given by Chou En-lai.[160] All opposition political parties, including the JCP, joined the LDP in using the China issue to their best advantage, a boasting of their respective contributions to Sino-Japanese diplomatic normalization. Ironically, however, the Tanaka trip itself seemed to make no appreciable impact upon the LDP's subsequent election outcome; in the year of China, Furui Yoshimi, Kawasaki Hideji, and Kuroda Hisao, all of whom emphasized their prominent roles in Japan-China relations, lost their parliamentary seats. The moral of their electoral failure seems to be that there was a weak association between their international functions and their indigenous electoral strengths. This is not to mean that an activist role in the move toward Sino-Japanese diplomatic normalization was not a political asset, for Fujiyama, Utsunomiya, Tagawa, and other pro-Peking LDP dietmen were reelected, and Okada Haruo and Ishino Hisao, members of the JSP's pro-Peking *Anta Dōshikai* (ex-*Heiwa Dōshikai*), returned to the House of Representatives after a one-term hiatus.

As agreed in the Tanaka-Chou joint statement, Japan and China soon exchanged their respective embassies, staffed by capable and experienced persons. The Japanese pundits who had expected to see either Liao Cheng-chih or Wang Kuo-chuan as China's first ambassador to Japan were completely surprised by the choice of Chen Chu, deputy representative under Ambassador Huang Hua to the United Nations since 1971. Chen was an unknown name in Japan, but he had accumulated an impressive record of diplomatic activities, which ranked him among a dozen leading diplomatic veterans of China. With a background as a revolutionary journalist, he had directed the departments of Public Information, Soviet Union and East European Affairs, and West Asian and African Affairs in the Ministry of Foreign Affairs.[161] He had also served as counselor at the embassy in Moscow and as ambassador to Ghana. And if Chen's experience in Japanese affairs per se was limited, most of his aides at the embassy in Tokyo—notably, Counselor Mei Kuo-chün, First Secretary Sung Wen, and Second Secretary Li Meng-ching—had a variety of prior involvement in Sino-Japanese relations.[162] Moreover, the embassy absorbed all five representatives of the Tokyo Liaison Office of the China-Japan Memorandum Trade Office—Hsiao Hsiang-chien as counselor, Hsü Tsung-mao as second secretary, and the three other representatives as third secretaries.[163] (After presenting his credentials to the Japanese emperor, Chen met with JSP Chairman Narita Tomomi and expressed his appreciation of the JSP's role in Sino-Japanese cooperation.)

It was widely expected that Ogawa Heishirō, one of the most knowledgeable and experienced specialists on China in the Japanese Ministry of Foreign Affairs, would be the logical person to head the embassy in the

PRC. A fifty-six year old Tokyo University graduate and prewar foreign service trainee at Peking, Ogawa had served as consul-general in Hong Kong, director of the Bureau of Asian Affairs, and director of the Ministry's Training Institute.[164] His foreign tour included assignments as counselor in the United States and Indonesia and as ambassador in Denmark; he had not served in Taiwan. His older brother, LDP Dietman Ogawa Heiji (ex-minister of Labor), was an influential member of Foreign Minister Ōhira's faction, and played an important role in improving Tokyo-Peking relations; he had accompanied the Matsumura mission to Peking in 1962, and became a vice-chairman of the LDP's National Council for Japan-China Diplomatic Normalization. At Peking, Ambassador Ogawa was joined by a number of capable career diplomats with backgrounds in Chinese or Asian affairs. They included Ministers Hayashi Yūichi and Yanagiya Kensuke (ex-counselor in the Bureau of Asian affairs), and Counselors Hashimoto Hiroshi (ex-chief of the China Section), Munakata Yoshitoshi, and Horino Shigeyoshi.

While this exchange of Japanese and Chinese diplomatic personnel was under way, Foreign Minister Ōhira made it clear in October 1972 that the Japanese government was prepared to take "any necessary measures" for promoting and guaranteeing economic, cultural, personal, and other forms of nongovernmental exchange between Japan and Taiwan.[165] In fact, he actively encouraged and partially financed a quasi-diplomatic arrangement with Taipei. For this purpose the pro-Taiwan "Interchange Association" (Kōryu kyōkai) was set up in December under President Horikoshi Teizō (Keidanren vice-chairman and standing director of the Committee on Japan-[Nationalist] China Cooperation) and Chairman Itagaki Osamu (ex-ambassador to Taipei, 1969-71).[166] While Horikoshi had intended to call this association "Nikka kōryu kyōkai" (Japan-[Nationalist] China Interchange Association), the Ministry of Foreign Affairs, fearful of its irritating Peking, suggested "Nittai kōryu kyōkai" (Japan-Taiwan Interchange Association). Since the latter was not acceptable to Taipei, no country name was attached to the Interchange Association.[167] The association and its Nationalist Chinese counterpart—the East Asian Relations Association headed by Chang Yen-tien (ex-vice minister of Economic Affairs)—agreed to establish their respective branch offices in Tokyo, Osaka, and Fukuoka and in Taipei and Kaohsiung.[168] Staffed by governmental officials on leave, these branch offices, a functional equivalent of the memorandum trade liaison offices exchanged between Tokyo and Peking, assumed the principal institutional responsibility for consular, commercial, and cultural exchange programs.[169]

The making of Japanese-Chinese diplomatic relations not only marked an important new chapter in the long history of close interactions between these two Asian neighbors but also signaled the gradual emergence of a new international order in East and Southeast Asia. It was more than a mere extension of Sino-American accommodation. In an effort to explain Japan's new China policy to her suspicious neighbors, Tanaka dispatched his personal envoys, ex-Foreign Minister Aichi, ex-State Minister Kimura Toshio, and Parliamentary Vice-Minister of Foreign Affairs Aoki Masahisa, to several Asian capitals, while Ohira himself visited the United States, the Soviet Union, Australia, New Zealand, and U.N. Secretary-General Kurt Waldheim.[170] This effort did not completely dispel the apprehension felt by some countries, especially the Soviet Union, which considered the diplomatic accommodation between nuclear-armed China and economically powerful Japan harmful to their vital national interests.

As far as Japan's long-range foreign policy was concerned, the accommodation contained some significant implications. Viewed from a historical perspective, it signified a beginning of Tanaka's and Ohira's conscious attempt to outgrow the postwar San Francisco system and to de-emphasize the cold-war aspects of world politics. Emphasis was placed on their process of adjustment to the trends of a multipolar international system and of complex regional power realignments. They were prepared to become an active participant, rather than a passive victim, of the balance-of-power game as it was practiced by Chou En-lai and Kissinger. Specifically, they were anxious to lessen their hitherto heavy dependence on U.S. leadership in international politics; and although they did not intend to weaken their security arrangements with the United States, they wished to reorient U.S.-Japanese relations, preferably along a genuinely equal partnership in diplomatic and economic areas. Speaking before an extraordinary session of the National Diet in October 1972, both Tanaka and Ohira proudly stated that with the normalization of Japanese-Chinese relations, Japan's diplomacy had been expanded to global scale, and that with the growth of its national strength, Japan's responsibility and role in international society were becoming greater year after year.[171] In the aftermath of Sino-Japanese diplomatic normalization, they intended to assume an assertive and confident global approach, commensurate with Japan's growing economic power.

4
The Politics
of Economic
Cooperation

The combination of complementary economic conditions and geographic proximity between Japan and China created an ideal setting for the substantial growth of their trade. While China could be both a useful market of manufactured goods and a major source of raw materials for Japan, the latter was in a position to assist the former's industrialization.[1] This promise of mutual benefits, however, was undermined until recently by a number of economic as well as noneconomic factors, including the absence of diplomatic relations and political harmony. Further, the freedom and flexibility of Japan's trade policy were limited by domestic and foreign constraints, while China used, or sometimes abused, trade as a primary, material instrument of its political operations in Japan.[2]

As the volume of two-way trade increased appreciably in the 1960s and early 1970s, its political utility loomed larger in China's foreign policies. Especially, during the height of the Cultural Revolution, China applied the slogan "politics in command" in all dimensions of Sino-Japanese trade, even to the extent of disregarding the elementary requirements of economic rationalism. Hence an editorial in the *Japan Times* (March 8, 1968) bluntly complained that "the Chinese Communists are so completely swayed by political feelings that they have allowed their distrust of Japan to enter into their consideration of commercial matters." Even though this extreme tendency was somewhat mitigated by the passing of the Cultural Revolution, the Chinese continued to emphasize the political functions of trade in several notable ways until 1972. They maximized the quasi-diplomatic activities of their liaison office in Tokyo and manipulated the competitive relationship between "friendship trade" and "memorandum trade" for the purpose of political mobilization in Japan. They also attempted to penetrate into Japan's mainstream business community (*zaikai*)—a backbone of the Japanese power structure—and to influence the factional dynamics and international positions of Japanese political parties. The ultimate political goal of these varied efforts was to force the Japanese government into concessions in its China policy.

The availability of trade for China's political exploitation not only reflected a particular nature of China's policy toward Japan but also stemmed from a unique set of economic and political circumstances that rendered Japan vulnerable to China's shifting tactics. Unlike China's tightly-controlled socialist foreign trade and closed political order, Japan had a loosely structured capitalist economic basis and an open competitive political system. The issue of Sino-Japanese trade and other related matters were a major bone of contention in inter- and intra-party relations in Japan. The governing LDP intended to promote trade with China, but refused to make any compromise in Japan's diplomatic relations with Taiwan. This separation of economic and diplomatic matters was subject to China's severe attacks, but the LDP's growing internal policy disagreements played into China's attentive and skillful hands. As a radical alternative to the LDP government's China policy, the opposition JSP proposed a variety of specific measures to normalize and expand Sino-Japanese economic cooperation and used trade as a potent tool to discredit the LDP and its government in domestic political contests. The dynamic competition between the two major parties, and among their factions, added a complicated political element to economic relations between Japan and China.

The Rise and Collapse of Trade Relations

The Opening of Postwar Trade   Even before the establishment of the PRC government was formally proclaimed in Peking, both China and Japan carefully laid a foundation for resuming their normal trade relations that had been disrupted in the immediate postwar period. At the Second Session of the Seventh Central Committee of the Chinese Communist Party in March 1949, Mao Tse-tung expressed his intention to take a pragmatic and positive policy toward foreign trade by transcending ideological and diplomatic constraints. He declared that "wherever there is business to do, we shall do it. . . . So far as possible, we must first of all trade with the socialist and people's democratic countries; at the same time we will also trade with capitalist countries."[3] The same policy was reiterated at the Preparatory Committee of the Chinese People's Political Consultative Conference in June.[4]

Meanwhile, a number of Japanese political and business leaders, despite the United States government's displeasure, launched a movement for renewed contacts with mainland China. They felt that trade with China was essential for their economic recovery because Japan had relied heavily upon the traditional China market, with which it had traded 21.6% of its total volume of exports and 12.4% of its imports in the 1930s.[5] Already in May 1949 some members of the Japanese National Diet, conservative and progressive, set up a nonpartisan Dietmen's League for China-Japan Trade Promotion. The league helped organize a civilian China-Japan Trade Promotion Council in August.[6] The council was instrumental in reopening trade with China, but the volume of initial transactions during 1949 involved only $3.1 million in Japanese exports and $21.8 million in imports.

The political climate for trade expansion improved in the first half of 1950; the U.S. State Department officially permitted Japan to establish economic relations with the PRC in March, and this decision prompted the Japanese House of Councillors to pass a nonpartisan resolution in April that asked the Japanese government to facilitate trade expansion with "new China."[7] Consequently, in 1950, the volume of Japanese exports, which were composed of electric motors, mining tools, pumps, steel, x-ray equipment, and the like, rose more than six times over the previous year; and the imports of soybeans, rice, salt, coal, iron ore, and other Chinese goods nearly doubled. Japan also imported from Hong Kong $26 million worth of items produced in China, which constituted 62% of Japan's total imports from Hong Kong.

The optimism for revitalized Sino-Japanese trade was short-lived, however, as the Korean War thwarted the opportunities of détente in East Asia. As a result of China's direct military engagement in the war, the United States adopted, in December 1950, a policy of total trade embargo against China, and a similar economic measure was recommended by the United Nations General Assembly in the following May. The U.S. occupation authorities imposed a strict restriction on Japanese exports to China; in response to a petition filed by the China-Japan Trade Promotion Council, General Douglas MacArthur argued that it was morally wrong for Japan to seek a market in a China which denied human rights.[8] In 1952, Japan was compelled to join the Coordinating Committee (COCOM) for export control and its China Committee (CHINCOM), which were set up to control and regulate exports of strategic goods to the Communist bloc.[9] China, too, tried to punish Japan economically, because it was serving as a military base for the U.S. war effort in Korea and was accepting the San Francisco system without China's participation.[10] Under these political conditions, Sino-Japanese trade inevitably suffered a drastic decline in 1951 and 1952. Ironically, however, the principal economic beneficiary of the Korean War was Japan. After having suffered from economic devastation and an inflationary spiral, efforts for Japanese economic recovery were handsomely boosted by its special procurement arrangements and other service contracts with the U.N. forces in Korea.

Although Japan regained the status of political and diplomatic independence from the United States in April 1952 when the San Francisco peace treaty came into effect, its China policy, especially in regard to trade relations with the PRC, was stringently bound by the COCOM and

CHINCOM regulations and by the bilateral peace treaty concluded with Taiwan. While the Japanese government committed itself to an unmistakable pro-Taiwan policy in diplomatic and economic areas, there emerged a new effort among some Japanese politicians and businessmen to expand trade with China in 1952. The Association for Japan-China Trade Promotion was established in May as a broad nonpartisan liaison group for promoting the growth of Sino-Japanese trade.

Private Trade Agreements   The following month Hōashi Kei, a leader of the association and an ex-dietman of the left-wing Socialist Party, and two conservative dietmen (Miyakoshi Kisuke of *Kaishintō* and Kōra Tomi of *Ryokufūkai*), who were on their way back from Moscow, signed at Peking the first private Sino-Japanese trade agreement with Nan Han-chen (chairman of the Chinese Association for Promotion of International Trade).[11] The agreement received a tacit blessing from the Japanese government, and it was consistent with the desires of the *Keidanren* (Federation of Economic Organizations), whose report published in July urged a reassessment of Japan's economic dependence on the United States and an improvement of Sino-Japanese trade.[12]

In the four private trade accords concluded from 1952 to 1958, the Chinese gradually introduced a series of political demands and successfully obtained concessions and promises from the Japanese negotiators, who were in the most cases influential members of the reorganized Dietman's League for Japan-China Trade Promotion (reorganized in 1952 with 309 participants, including members of the ruling political parties).[13] The political and parliamentary status of Japanese negotiators was useful to the Chinese as a way to get the Japanese government directly involved in trade arrangements. In addition to its intrinsic economic value, the Chinese regarded this trade from the beginning as an effective and practical step toward ultimate diplomatic normalization between Peking and Tokyo. The direction of their trade policy stemmed from what might be called a functionalist approach toward economic and political affairs.

Indeed, the Chinese obtained an agreement in 1953 to exchange resident trade representatives between Japan and China, and extracted from the Japanese an additional understanding in 1955 that these representatives must enjoy diplomatic privileges. This was an obvious maneuver to establish the precedent of China's de facto diplomatic presence in Tokyo. Moreover, they demanded that the Japanese government should take part in the signing of trade agreements and guarantee their implementation. As a compromise, the Japanese delegates pledged to campaign for the conclusion of intergovernmental trade accords. They also obtained a commitment from Prime Minister Hatoyama Ichirō in May 1955 that his government would "support and assist" the private trade agreements.[14] The Japanese government, however, refused to allow the exchange of trade missions between Tokyo and Peking on the grounds that Japan had no diplomatic relations with the PRC. Likewise, when the LDP was formed in November 1955, it adopted an official policy of promoting trade with China, but left no room for changing Japan's diplomatic ties with Taiwan.[15]

Even though the Japanese government and the LDP stubbornly upheld a policy of separating trade from political and diplomatic issues concerning the PRC, the method of unofficial trade agreements, bolstered by a series of resolutions by the Japanese Diet, and Japan's liberalization of trade restrictions, contributed to a modest, albeit slow, increase in Sino-Japanese trade. Only a negligible proportion of the first agreement, which set the amount of two-way transactions at 30 million pounds sterling on a barter basis, was implemented by the end of 1953—4% of Japan's projected exports to China and 6% of expected imports—but the achievement of the second agreement improved to 28% and 41% respectively, of Japan's planned exports and imports with China, by May 1955. The trade reached a postwar peak in 1956, when the targets set in the third accord were well met—37% of exports and 91% of imports by April 1956; and 118% of exports and 181% of imports by March 1957. This expansion of trade relations was also accompanied by an agreement on fisheries, the exchange of commodity exhibits, and the visits of cultural and other delegations.[16]

While the Japanese government, especially under Prime Minister Hatoyama, helped implement the private trade pacts during this period, the Chinese, too, had their own reasons to favor increased economic relations with Japan. In addition to their political and diplomatic maneuvers mentioned earlier, the Chinese were anxious to improve foreign trade for their first Five-Year Economic Plan (1953-57). They were also encouraged by Hatoyama's decision to normalize Japan's diplomatic relations with the Soviet Union.

However, in 1957, the Japanese negotiators had an extremely difficult time preparing the fourth trade agreement at Peking, because their Chinese counterparts adamantly demanded the sensitive political conditions that the Japanese government was unwilling to accommodate.[17] At last, in March 1958, both sides signed the agreement, in which they agreed "to obtain the concurrence of their respective governments to insure the security of their commercial agencies (to be exchanged between Tokyo and Peking) and their personnel and facilities for carrying out their work."[18] Specifically, the members of these agencies were to enjoy the privileges of expedient entrance, favorable customs clearance, unrestricted travel, the right to fly their national flags over their facilities, and the exemption from fingerprint requirements. If they were involved in legal disputes, these were expected to be resolved on the basis of procedures agreed upon by both sides.

Although LDP Dietman Ikeda Masanosuke, head of the Japanese negotiating team and chairman of the LDP's Special Committee for Japan-

China Trade Promotion, reluctantly accepted these Chinese conditions only for the sake of continuing trade, the LDP leadership officially decided to oppose his efforts. On the recommendation of the LDP's Committee on Foreign Affairs, the six leaders' meeting, an ad hoc group of top LDP officials, while recognizing the need of trade, adopted a four-fold policy: (1) not to accord any diplomatic privileges to Chinese trade representatives in Japan, but to govern their legal status according to Japanese laws; (2) to deny them the right to use their national flags in Japan; (3) to limit their numbers to the necessary minimum; and (4) not to give the Japanese government's "concurrence" to the private trade agreement.[19]

Behind the LDP decision was the fact that the Kishi Nobusuke government confronted pressures from the United States and Nationalist China. The Chiang government issued a statement protesting the fourth private trade agreement and suspended all business negotiations with Japan; the Nationalist Chinese ambassador had a direct talk with Prime Minister Kishi and Foreign Minister Fujiyama Aiichirō. Kishi attempted to soothe Chiang's anger by sending a letter to him with a commitment that Japan would not recognize the PRC in any form.[20] The Kishi government stated in April 1958 that, while favoring the expansion of Sino-Japanese trade and respecting the "spirit" of the fourth agreement, it would not allow any special privileges to Chinese trade personnel, including the "right" to fly their national flags in Japan.[21] The Nationalist Chinese Foreign Ministry expressed its satisfaction with the Japanese government's repeated assurances. But Nan Han-chen, in his telegram sent to Ikeda, severely attacked Kishi's submission to Washington's and Taipei's anti-Peking pressure. Kishi was accused of destroying the fourth trade agreement and of using trade for the purpose of reviving Japan's dream of a "Greater East Asia Coprosperity Sphere."[22] Nan also criticized Kishi's earlier statement (made in response to JSP Dietman Hozumi Shichirō's question at the Committee on Foreign Affairs of the House of Representatives) that in the event of desecration of a PRC flag in Japan, the case would not be treated as a usual defamation of foreign national flags (under Article 92 of the Criminal Law), but as a damage to private property.[23]

Trade Suspension   The extreme anger with which Nan Han-chen assailed Kishi's China policy meant a virtual abandonment of the fourth trade agreement. Soon thereafter, as discussed in Chapter II, relations were further complicated by the flag incident in Nagasaki. Emphasizing the principle of inseparability between economic and political matters, Chinese Foreign Minister Chen Yi cancelled all economic and cultural relations with Japan.[24] The ongoing trade negotiations in Tokyo were suspended, and the renewal of the fishery agreement was denied. These actions were reminiscent of China's prewar boycotts of Japanese goods. Whereas the trade suspension in the 1951-52 period stemmed from an external event, namely, the Korean

War, and its initiator was the United States, the 1958 case was at least in part China's response to what they considered to be an insult to their national self-esteem.

As China's ultimate political maneuver, the method of trade suspension was less than effective in Japan, because Japan's dependence on the China market was not substantial and because Japan's mainstream business circles, which had close ties with the LDP government, were not yet enthusiastic about the prospect of Sino-Japanese trade. Moreover, China's unilateral, dramatic decision failed to arouse a nationwide public outcry in Japan against Prime Minister Kishi's China policy.

The Dietmen's League expressed regret over the Nagasaki incident and resolved to get the government's "support and assistance" for the fourth trade agreement.[25] The LDP instead decided to remove its members from the Dietmen's League, which entered into a long hiatus, and the Kishi government, despite its efforts for direct diplomatic contacts with the PRC, took a passive attitude toward trade resumption. The JSP promptly seized this opportunity to attack the government's ineptitude in China policy; it suggested that the government should prevent the flag incident from recurring in the future and compensate those trade firms that were adversely affected by trade suspension.[26]

In an attempt to probe the possibility of renewed economic relations with China and at the same time to demonstrate his party's ability in external affairs, Secretary-General Asanuma of the JSP dispatched in August 1958 Dietman Sata Tadataka (former head of its Bureau of International Affairs) to Peking. As a vehicle for trade resumption and conflict resolution between Tokyo and Peking, the Chinese officials presented to him "three principles" and "three conditions."[27] The three political principles (which were first enunciated in the *People's Daily* editorial of July 7, 1958) asked the Kishi government (1) not to adopt a policy inimical to China, (2) not to join a plot to recognize two Chinas, and (3) not to hamper attempts for normalization of Sino-Japanese relations. The Japanese government was further requested to fulfill three specific conditions as follows: (1) that it send an official to Nagasaki to raise the PRC flag, punish the Japanese youth according to the Chinese law of flag desecration, and send an official mission to China to apologize for the Nagasaki incident; (2) as an assurance that it opposed any two-China scheme, it should publicly announce that "the Japanese government wishes and tries to restore normal relations with the PRC"; and (3) if all these measures were taken, then, it would send a delegation to China to discuss matters of mutual interests.

The Japanese government was not at all prepared to consider these terms of total surrender, and the Sata report itself was subject to much criticism by the LDP and by some factions of the JSP. The right-wing Nishio faction, in particular, argued that Sata, perhaps inadvertently, acted as a spokesman for China in presenting these unreasonable demands and in the process damaged the JSP's public image as an independent party.[28] The JSP Central Executive Committee decided in August to dissociate itself from the Sata report, which had become a liability in domestic political maneuvers, but in the following month it adopted a comprehensive seven-point policy on China.[29] Among other things, the JSP demanded, much to China's satisfaction, that the Japanese government apologize to China for the Nagasaki incident, take all measures to guarantee the sanctity of China's national flags, stop all activities supportive of a two-China policy, normalize diplomatic relations with China, consider Taiwan China's internal matter, and faithfully implement the fourth private trade accord. As an opposition party, the JSP failed to exert any appreciable pressure on the Kishi government's China policy, while the Chinese continued to take the position that their three principles and three conditions, as explained in the Sata report, were absolutely not negotiable.

On the requests of the JSP and the General Council of Trade Unions (Sōhyō), the Chinese granted in early 1959 a special trade concession to small and medium-sized Japanese companies, which suffered most from trade termination and which opposed Kishi's anti-China policy.[30] The step was taken in appreciation of the JSP's and Sōhyō's pro-Peking activities; it was also a material incentive for encouraging such activities among other Japanese industrial and trading firms. The total volume of this special trade reached only about $1 million, but it was a hopeful prelude to the subsequent resumption of full-scale commercial transactions between Japan and China.

Expansion of Friendship and Memorandum Trade

Methods of Friendship and Memorandum Trade The drastic decline in Sino-Soviet economic relations (see table 23), coupled with the failure of the Great Leap Forward, forced Chou En-lai to redirect China's foreign trade and to initiate a new form of trade with Japan in 1960. The crisis over the U.S.-Japan security treaty and the replacement of Kishi by a new prime minister, Ikeda Hayato, who took a low-posture policy at home and abroad and attached a top priority to economic growth, made it easier for Chou to forego his hitherto rigid demands about the Nagasaki indicent and related issues, and to take a pragmatic posture toward urgent economic matters. In August 1960, in his talks with Suzuki Kazŭo, managing director of the Japan-China Trade Promotion Council (JCTPC) and director of the Japan Committee for Asian-African Solidarity, Chou presented his three principles of trade relations with Japan: (1) the conclusion of intergovernmental agreements is most desirable for resumption of Sino-Japanese trade; (2) pending such developments, China is willing to accept civilian trade agreements; and (3) China would trade with individual Japanese companies on the basis of special considerations.[31] This policy signaled the beginning of "friendship trade" between Japan and China.

On the recommendations of the JCTPC, the Japanese Association for Promotion of International Trade, the Japan-China Friendship Association, or the Japan Socialist Party, the Chinese first traded with a few "friendly" Japanese companies, which pledged to respect Chou's three political principles (1958) and three trade principles (1960) and to oppose the security treaty. These political qualifications were soon relaxed so as to increase the number of Japanese trading partners, including the "dummies" of Japanese industrial giants that were conveniently designated as "friendly" toward China. The "friendly companies" were limited to 11 in 1960, but their numbers grew to 100 in 1961 and 190 in 1962. This device facilitated China's pragmatic dealings with Japanese "monopoly capitalists," but left its political stand outwardly unblemished. It was not based on "ideological kinship" between China and the Japanese companies involved, but on China's political and economic expediency.[32] Since the Chinese held the ultimate right to recognize or reject Japan's "friendly companies," they could easily obtain favorable commercial terms in such specific arrangements as pricing, inspection, insurance, arbitration, and shipping. These terms were far more beneficial to China than what it had gained from the past four private trade agreements.[33]

In spite of the advantages China enjoyed in the friendship trade, it was hampered by the fact that most of the friendly companies were small-sized

Table 23—Trends in Sino-Soviet Trade, 1950–62
(in million dollars)

Year	Total Volume	Chinese Exports	Chinese Imports	Chinese Balance
1950	579	191	388	-197
1951	808	332	476	-144
1952	964	414	550	-136
1953	1,181	475	706	-231
1954	1,337	578	759	-181
1955	1,391	643	748	-105
1956	1,497	764	733	31
1957	1,282	738	544	194
1958	1,515	881	634	247
1959	2,055	1,100	955	145
1960	1,665	848	817	31
1961	918	551	367	184
1962	742	511	237	280

SOURCE: Takase Kiyoshi, *Nitchū bōeki* [Japan-China trade] (Tokyo: Ashibe Shōbō, 1964).

and therefore economically weak. They lacked large capital reserves, long commercial experience, or organic connections with Japanese *zaibatsu*. They were often subject to collapse in times of economic turmoil, which forced China to suffer adverse effects. Hence they failed to satisfy China's mounting demands for long-term credits, complete industrial plants, and a stable supply of machinery, steel, and chemical fertilizers that were badly needed for its economic programs. Most importantly, the Chinese realized that these companies were unable to influence the LDP government's policy-making process.

As seen in Chapter II, Chou consulted with LDP Dietman Matsumura Kenzō in September 1962 in an attempt to seek a more effective approach toward the political power structure of Japan. They agreed to open memorandum trade as a gradual and cumulative method for normalization of economic and diplomatic relations between Japan and China.[34] According to the Chou-Matsumura accord, LDP Dietman Takasaki Tatsunosuke and Liao Cheng-chih signed in November 1962 a memorandum on "over-all trade" for the period 1963-67. They agreed to conduct an average two-way trade at about $100 million per year, to exchange trade liaison personnel between Tokyo and Peking, and to apply the method of deferred payment and medium-term credit to China's purchases of Japanese industrial plants.[35] This L-T trade (named after the initials of Liao and Takasaki) was characterized by a long-term, large-scale, overall, barter-based transaction. Unlike friendship trade, it contained a semi-official element because it was accepted by some members of the governing LDP and was expected to be partially financed by the government-controlled Export-Import Bank. While both conservative and progressive members of the Japanese National Diet had jointly taken part in negotiations for the four earlier private trade agreements from 1952 to 1958, the L-T trade was exclusively negotiated by LDP Dietmen in cooperation with businessmen. The Chinese had learned in the 1950s that a suprapartisan Japanese negotiating team was politically meaningful, but economically inefficient because Japanese negotiators had suffered from their own partisan infighting. The political accountability of a nonpartisan agreement had not been clear. Moreover, the Chinese had become somewhat disillusioned with the JSP, which was now dominated by a coalition of moderate factions led by Chairman Kawakami Jōtarō and Secretary-General Eda Saburō.

Whereas the terms of friendship trade agreements were individually negotiated by each Japanese trading firm (mainly at the biannual Canton Export Commodities Fairs but sometimes at Peking or through telegrams), details of the L-T trade agreements were collectively negotiated each year at Peking or Tokyo by a group of representatives of Japanese companies and industries that belonged to the Japan-China Over-all Trade Liaison Office. The Chinese Association for Promotion of International Trade, a non-governmental agency for trading with countries having no diplomatic relations, was responsible for friendship trade, but Liao Cheng-chih's office took care of the L-T trade. The execution of specific transactions for both forms of trade was entrusted to China's foreign trade corporations under the Ministry of Foreign Trade.

As table 24 shows, Sino-Japanese trade during the period 1963-67 increased sharply both in terms of total turnover and in comparative significance. In 1965, for example, Japan's share of $470 million trebled the earlier postwar peak attained during 1956. This amount surpassed both the shrinking Sino-Soviet trade ($417 million) and the moderately rising Japanese-Soviet trade ($408 million). Despite the ensuing controversy over the Yoshida letter, U.S. war efforts in Vietnam, and the normalization of Japanese-South Korean diplomatic relations, the figure jumped by 32% in 1966. It then accounted for 14% of China's estimated total foreign trade and made China Japan's fourth largest trading partner after the United States, Australia, and Canada. Even when trade dropped to $558 million in 1967, Japan still remained China's number one trading country.

The practice of a balanced trade, especially in the L-T arrangements, helped ease China's problem of foreign exchange reserves and made Japan more attractive than Canada and Australia, which did not offer comparable markets for Chinese exports of raw materials. The main Chinese exports to

Table 24—Trends in Sino-Japanese Trade, 1950–67
(in million dollars)

Year	Japanese Exports	Japanese Imports	Total Volume	Annual Change (percentage)	Percentage of China's Total Foreign Trade
1950	19.6	39.3	58.9	–	4.8
1951	5.8	21.6	27.4	–53.5	1.4
1952	0.6	14.9	15.5	–43.5	0.8
1953	4.5	29.7	34.2	120.9	1.5
1954	19.1	40.8	59.9	74.9	2.5
1955	28.5	80.8	109.3	82.6	3.7
1956	67.3	83.6	150.9	38.1	4.5
1957	60.5	80.5	141.0	–6.6	4.3
1958	50.6	54.4	105.0	–25.5	2.6
1959	3.6	18.9	22.5	–78.5	0.5
1960	2.7	20.7	23.4	3.9	0.5
1961	16.6	30.9	47.5	103.1	1.5
1962	38.5	46.0	84.5	77.7	2.8
1963	62.4	74.6	137.0	62.2	4.4
1964	152.7	157.8	310.5	126.2	9.6
1965	245.0	224.7	469.7	51.3	12.7
1966	315.2	306.2	621.4	32.3	14.1
1967	288.3	269.4	557.7	–10.2	14.4

SOURCE: *Chūgoku Yoran* [China almanac] (Tokyo: Jiji tsūshinsha, 1973).

Japan were agricultural products (soybean, rice, fruits, vegetables), minerals (coal, pig iron, iron ores), and other raw materials; in return, China imported from Japan fertilizers, steel, machinery, textiles, chemicals, and other manufactured goods. These commercial transactions were accompanied by the exchange of economic delegations, technical experts, and industrial and scientific exhibits between China and Japan.[36]

The growth of Sino-Japanese economic ties, however, gave rise to a complicated quadrangular political relationship among Peking, Tokyo, Taipei, and Washington. When the Kurashiki Rayon Company, in accordance with the Liao-Takasaki agreement, requested to use the Export-Import Bank's fund for exporting to China a $22 million vinylon plant on deferred payment terms, the Ikeda government was hard pressed not to permit the request. Internally some pro-Taipei members of the LDP, including Kaya Okinori, chairman of the Policy Affairs Research Council, opposed the request. More significantly, the U.S. State Department let it be known that Japan's allowance of the deferred payment method to China amounted to a form of foreign aid to the "enemy."[37]

These pressures notwithstanding, the Ikeda government granted the request in August 1963, defending its decisions through a public clarification of its trade policy toward China: (1) it continued to separate trade from the diplomatic issue; (2) the method of deferred payment over five years was declared not to be a form of foreign aid, but a device for export promotion; (3) the terms of deferred payment used in trade with China were not better than those offered by Western European countries to China; and (4) the grant of credit to China was not unlimited.[38] On the same day the Foreign Ministry cabled this policy to Japanese ambassadors in Taipei and Washington so that they could explain it to their host countries.

Just as it had protested the fourth private trade agreement, the Nationalist Chinese government lodged a strong protest against Ikeda's decision and threatened to sever economic and diplomatic relations with Japan. As examined in Chapter II, Tokyo's relations with Taipei were further complicated by the Chou Hung-ching incident, and in January 1964 Chiang Kai-shek recalled his ambassador and other senior diplomatic personnel from Tokyo and suspended all new government procurement of Japanese goods. Since Japan had both commercial and political reasons to avert an open breach with Taipei, in May 1964 Ikeda encouraged Yoshida Shigeru to send a secret "private letter" to Chang Chün giving assurances that the Japanese Export-Import Bank would no longer be used to finance Japan's industrial exports to China.[39] The Yoshida letter, plus Foreign Minister Ōhira's visit to Taipei in July, helped relax tensions between Tokyo and Taipei, but when the contents of the letter were revealed in February 1965, Peking demanded its immediate nullification. It regarded the letter as a symbolic manifestation of the Japanese government's anti-Peking policy. In retaliation to the letter and the new Satō government's decision to honor its contents, the Chinese cancelled their plans to import a large synthetic textile plant ($26 million) from the Nichibō Company, a 12,4000-ton freighter ($3 million) from the Hitachi Shipbuilding and Engineering Company, a urea fertilizer plant from the Tōyō Engineering Company, and about forty other plants for producing steel, freighters, automobiles, paper, and food-processing that were being negotiated.[40] The Japanese Foreign Ministry, along with the *zaikai*, was relieved by China's contract cancellation, but the Ministry of International Trade and Industry was worried about the decline in Sino-Japanese trade and the loss of the China market.[41] In fact, the Chinese promptly purchased various industrial plants from Great Britain, France, West Germany, and other West European countries. At the same time they intensified a propaganda campaign against Prime Minister Satō Eisaku's anti-China policy and also made it clear that his support for the U.S. war policy in Vietnam would have an adverse effect on Sino-Japanese trade.[42]

Trade Liaison Offices   Although the Chinese had long attempted in the four private trade accords to exchange trade missions with Japan as a step toward de facto diplomatic relations, it was only in the L-T trade formula and under Prime Minister Ikeda that their goal was achieved. In April 1964, details had been worked out for the exchange of trade liaison personnel and resident correspondents between Japan and China.[43] As head of the Liao Cheng-chih Liaison Office in Japan, Sun Ping-hua, a well-known specialist on Japanese affairs, arrived at Tokyo in August 1964 with his staff. The office personnel consisted of three representatives, two assistants, their families, and a few local overseas Chinese who were recruited for clerical and driving responsibilities. Sun himself, a former student of the Tokyo Engineering College, was fluent in Japanese, and he had visited Japan on numerous occasions (as deputy secretary-general of the China-Japan Friendship Association). In addition, Sun was director of the Chinese People's Institute of Foreign Affairs and deputy secretary-general of the Chinese People's Association for Cultural Relations with Foreign Countries. His counterpart, Sōma Tsunetoshi, who had just resigned from the Ministry of International Trade and Industry, assumed direction of the three-man Takasaki Liaison Office in Peking. Later, his staff was composed of persons on leave from the Ministry of International Trade and Industry, the Foreign Ministry, the Ministry of Agriculture, or the Bank of Japan.

In addition to the management of trade relations, Sun was also in charge of keeping close contacts with Japanese politicians and businessmen and of supervising pro-Peking overseas Chinese communities in Japan. On economic matters, he was assisted by Wu Shu-tung (former Japan expert at the Ministry of Foreign Trade and standing director of the China-Japan Friendship Association) and on political issues, by Chen Kang (director of the China-Japan Friendship Association and secretary of the Japan Section

of the Chinese People's Institute of Foreign Affairs). Chen remained relatively obscure publicly, but he appeared to be a "political commissar"
whom the PRC and the CCP empowered to make local political decisions at
the Liaison Office and to direct anti-JCP activities in Japan.[44]

When the Takasaki office applied for visas for these Chinese personnel, it
submitted to the Ministry of Justice a legal affidavit guaranteeing that they
would abide by Japanese laws and refrain from interfering in the domestic
affairs of Japan. Once admitted to Japan, however, they gradually engaged
in a wide range of open political activities against the Japanese government
and later against the JCP. In July 1966, for example, Sun Ping-hua issued a
statement criticizing the Japanese government's decision not to admit the
Chinese delegation (headed by Liu Ning-yi) to the twelfth World Conference
Against A- and H- Bombs. After violent clashes, which took place between
radical Chinese students and Japanese Communists at the *Zenrin* (Good
Neighborhood) Hostel in Tokyo during February 1967, Sun bitterly attacked the JCP's "anti-China conspiracy." He claimed that the JCP had
formed a counterrevolutionary alliance with imperialists, reactionaries, and
revisionists. The inadequacy of the Japanese police's precautionary measures at the hostel was also pointed out.[45] And while the JCP's official organ,
Akahata (March 17, 1967), accused Sun of "subversive activities" against
democratic movements in Japan, the Chinese Liaison Office freely distributed various anti-JCP newspapers, pamphlets, and letters to those Japanese
who were considered friendly toward Peking. Again, when Prime Minister
Satō visited Taiwan in September 1967, Wu Shu-tung held a news conference at Tokyo to declare that the visit constituted a criminal interference in
China's domestic affairs. On the day of Satō's departure a violent demonstration was staged at Haneda Airport by the Japanese Association for
Promotion of International Trade, the Japan-China Friendship Association
(OH), and the extreme anti-Yoyogi *Zengakuren* students. Wu was immediately warned that the Japanese Ministry of Justice might take "necessary
measures" against him should he continue to engage in political activities
and thereby violate the conditions of his entrance into Japan.[46]

After a series of complications involving the Liaison Office, particularly
the Chinese personnel's physical confrontation with members of the ultra-
rightist Japan Patriotic Party, who blared anti-Peking speeches in front of
the office, Wu asserted that the Japanese police, in collusion with Japan's
right-wing elements, persecuted Chinese personnel at the office. Through
the Takasaki office in Japan, he asked the Satō government to admit its
mistakes publicly, to punish Japanese policemen who had allegedly as-
saulted Chinese staff members, and to assure that similar incidents would
not recur. The following day the Chinese Foreign Ministry announced its
decision to expel three resident Japanese correspondents (for *Mainichi
Shimbun, Sankei Shimbun,* and *Tokyo Shimbun*) from China on the

ground that they encouraged "the reactionary Satō government's anti-Communist, anti-China and anti-people criminal activities."[47] While the JSP supported the Wu statement, the Japanese government refused to accept Wu's extraordinary demands, though it promised LDP Dietmen Furui Yoshimi and Tagawa Seiichi that all necessary measures would be taken to protect the security of Chinese trade representatives in Japan.[48] None of these controversies deterred the Chinese Liaison Office in Japan from functioning more as a political agency than as a normal commercial mission. This trend simply confirmed China's contention that trade was an extension of politics, a position that was further amplified by the fervor of the Cultural Revolution.

Added to China's problem of continuing disputes over the Liaison Office and the Yoshida letter was the growing awareness that major Japanese firms and industries involved in the L-T trade were economically useful but politically uncontrollable. Compared with friendship trade companies, most of the L-T trade industries were large and conducted trade on the basis of long-term agreements with China; therefore, they were less dependent on China's good will and less susceptible to China's political pressures. Hence pro-Peking Japanese analysts openly denounced "political indifference" or "opportunistic attitudes" of the L-T trade organizations.[49] It was in this political context, which was exacerbated by difficulties in importing factories and exporting rice and meat, that the Chinese de-emphasized the L-T trade and attached a higher priority to friendship trade. Consequently, the share of the L-T trade in total Sino-Japanese trade gradually declined from 46.7% during 1963 to 27.5% during 1967.

New Memorandum Trade   Even though Liao Cheng-chih and Matsumura Kenzō had agreed in May 1966 to extend the L-T trade beyond its original five-year limit, the prospect of its actual extension was clouded during 1967 by the intensifying political friction between Peking and Tokyo and by the pervasive effects of the Cultural Revolution in China.[50] The Japanese government imposed strict COCOM restrictions on seventeen items to be displayed at the Japanese Scientific Exhibit, which was held in Tientsin in June 1967. In protest, about 100 Japanese participants of the exhibit held an anti-Satō demonstration in Tientsin, and they were rewarded in profitable trade contracts with China.[51] (About ninety Japanese trade representatives from forty companies, who were stationed in a Peking hotel, went so far as to hold sessions of self-criticism or on Mao's political thought so as to have their precarious visas extended.) Satō also refused to permit the prolonged stay of six Chinese technical trainees in Japan. The extreme acrimony with which the Chinese perceived Satō's foreign policy, especially his state visit to Taipei in September 1967, contributed to blocking negotiations on the L-T trade throughout 1967.

At last, in January 1968, at Peking, Chou En-lai told JSP Dietman Ishino Hisao (of the *Heiwa Dōshikai*) that a small group of Japanese delegates would be welcome to visit China for trade negotiations.[52] Encouraged by this invitation, LDP Dietmen Furui and Tagawa, and Okazaki Kaheita (chairman of the Japan-China Over-all Trade Liaison Office or the Takasaki office) went to China in the following month with the best wishes of Prime Minister Satō and Foreign Minister Miki. After a tense month-long political discussion, which almost collapsed, both sides agreed to extend the L-T trade (totaling slightly over $100 million) for one more year.[53] As discussed in Chapter III, in a joint statement issued in March 1968, the Japanese delegates recognized Peking's three political principles and reaffirmed their acceptance of the principle of inseparability of economic and political matters.[54] The latter reference was specifically intended to rebuke the Satō government for its policy, which continued to permit economic relations with China without granting diplomatic recognition. The Chinese negotiators led by Assistant Deputy Vice-Minister of Foreign Trade Liu Hsi-wen insisted upon Furui's acceptance of these political principles, because there had appeared during the Cultural Revolution a strong criticism against Liao Cheng-chih and other "old Japan hands," who were accused of aiding the Japanese government by sustaining the unprincipled L-T trade.[55] While praising the positive contribution made by friendship trade organizations, the Chinese asked Furui and Tagawa to demonstrate their anti-Satō and pro-Peking activities. At a reception held for the departing Japanese negotiators, Liu ominously stated that the escalation of Satō's reactionary foreign policy would greatly endanger the future of Sino-Japanese trade.[56] On the same day Chou told members of the Japanese Association for Promotion of International Trade that the United States had used Japanese trade representatives and correspondents as agents of its espionage operations in China.[57]

Subsequently, on China's request, both sides changed the names of their trade organizations—from the Liao Cheng-chih Liaison Office to the China-Japan Memorandum Trade Office, and from the Takasaki Liaison Office (or Japan-China Overall Trade Liaison Office) to the Japan-China Memorandum Trade Office. The signing of a one-year trade memorandum, despite Furui's proposal for another five-year agreement, eliminated the long-term aspect of this economic intercourse. With the trade missions kept intact, however, the new memorandum trade formula preserved a useful semiofficial pipeline between Peking and Tokyo. The Japanese side also accepted China's request that Japanese newspapers whose correspondents were stationed in Peking would be asked to respect and follow China's three political principles.

Meanwhile, a variety of political activities had been sponsored by friendship trade organizations to denounce the Yoshida letter and COCOM regulations and to normalize economic and diplomatic relations between Japan and China. During 1967, for example, these groups had staged demonstrations against Satō's trips to Taipei, Southeast Asia, and Washington, and against the Dalai Lama and the Nationalist Chinese Defense Minister, Chiang Ching-kuo, both of whom visited Japan.[58] Participation in these political demonstrations appeared to be a more important factor than judgments of economic benefits in influencing the Chinese decisions on their trade with each Japanese company. For example, they drastically lowered the volume of their trade contracts with the apathetic Daiichi Trading Company (Mitsui), but strengthened their economic ties with the politically valuable Meiwa Trading Company (Mitsubishi). Whereas they gave a favorable consideration to Japanese fertilizer industries, which, despite their continuing trade with Taiwan and South Korea, took positive steps to improve Sino-Japanese relations, they downgraded the politically inactive steel industries. Conspicuously, those Japanese firms that had assisted Peking's recent campaign against the JCP were given profitable terms of trade at Canton fairs. These tactics of tangible economic reward and punishment were deliberately employed by the Chinese to maximize the political dividends accruing from trade with Japan.

Trade and Political Parties   For many years the JCP exercised great control over Sino-Japanese relations by means of the powerful Japan-China Trade Promotion Council. Evidently, the party had received a substantial amount of financial contributions from many friendly trading companies. Such small firms as Mutsumi, Haga, and Sanshin, which were directly linked with the JCP, shared almost 20% of the total Sino-Japanese trade during 1965.[59] Other companies closely associated with the JCP, too, enjoyed a special privilege in friendship trade arrangements with China. However, after the unsuccessful Mao Tse-tung-Miyamoto Kenji meeting in the spring of 1966, the JCP began to lose its influence over trade with China. The abovementioned three firms, which were considered to be unfriendly, were completely excluded from commercial negotiations in July 1966 and from the privilege of stationing their representatives in China. And the JCP-dominated JCTPC was not allowed to coordinate any shipping procedures or technical exchange programs with China. Against this development in trade with China, *Akahata* (September 13, 1966) carried an article "Toward Correct Movement for East-West Trade," in which the JCP indirectly criticized the "great-nation chauvinism" manifested in China's trade policy toward Japan. It suggested the correct principles of East-West trade —namely, respect for sovereign independence, mutuality of economic benefits, and noninterference in domestic affairs.

The intensifying CCP-JCP rift caused serious division and confusion in Japanese trade circles as well as in other areas. By the fall of 1966 the Chinese had compelled the JCTPC to dissolve itself and terminated trade with all pro-JCP companies. Some of these companies promptly accepted Moscow's trade offers, while others were anxious to dissociate themselves from the JCP. Meanwhile, the Chinese made the Japanese Association for

Promotion of International Trade (led by President Ishibashi Tanzan and Vice-President Utsunomiya Tokuma) a principal tool of their economic policy in Japan. They recognized a number of new trading firms closely linked to the pro-Peking Communist organizations. Among about 280 Japanese companies that were trading with China at the end of 1967, one-fourth of them were set up after October 1966. Almost 200 of them, as "corporate members," joined the pro-Peking Japan-China Friendship Association (Orthodox Headquarters).[60] Later, in 1968, the Chinese helped destroy the government-financed Japan-China Export-Import Union on the ground that it was heavily infiltrated by Japanese Communists.

Nowhere was Peking's anti-JCP trade policy more emphatically incorporated than in a series of friendship trade agreements and minutes signed by the Chinese and Japanese Associations for Promotion of International Trade during 1967 and 1968.[61] These documents, more like a revolutionary manifesto than a trade agreement, unreservedly praised the Cultural Revolution and Mao Tse-tung's political thought, called the Soviet Union an accomplice of U.S. "imperialists" in Vietnam, and declared a struggle against "four common enemies"—U.S. imperialists, Soviet revisionists, Japanese reactionaries, and JCP revisionists. The most devastating attack was directed against the Miyamoto leadership, which they claimed had degenerated into an "anti-people and anti-China special detachment of the U.S.-Japanese reactionaries."[62] As a result of these trade protocols, the Soviet Union formally terminated its relations with the Japanese Association in April 1967.[63]

The Chinese negotiators even stated that "politics is a basis, life, and spirit of economics" and thus suggested that Mao's political doctrine should be the foundation of Sino-Japanese trade.[64] Indeed, Japanese trade representatives who participated at Canton fairs during 1967—850 persons from 250 companies in the spring, and 930 from 282 companies in the fall—were required to study and recite "Quotations from Chairman Mao Tse-tung" before each trade negotiation session, to sing Chinese revolutionary songs, and to take part in demonstrations by the Red Guards. During the *Zenrin* conflict about 125 Japanese trading companies mobilized more than 2,000 persons to join the anti-JCP movement. It was also revealed in *Akahata* (March 10 and 25, 1967) that the JAPIT had asked each company to contribute 10,000-20,000 *yen* to the anti-JCP struggle fund, and that some companies had paid their employees to support the radical overseas Chinese students at *Zenrin*. The Chinese Red Cross reportedly sent 1.5 million *yen* each to the pro-Peking Overseas Chinese Association of Tokyo and to the Japan-China Friendship Association (Orthodox Headquarters).[65]

The fact that most Japanese trading companies obediently followed Peking's anti-JCP campaign was not because they particularly revered Mao or China, but because they simply aspired to bigger commercial opportunities in China.[66] The priority of opportunistic economic pragmatism that China had encouraged among Japanese companies was precisely what the Maoists attempted to eradicate in their domestic economic practices during the Cultural Revolution. This "ironic" and "unprincipled" convergence of Japanese economic opportunism and Chinese political considerations was profusely attacked by the JCP in an extensive *Akahata* article entitled "Mao Tse-tung's Present Line and International Communist Movement" (October 10, 1967). It charged, among other things, that the Maoists had colluded with Japanese monoploy capitalists to betray the interests of the Japanese working classes and had abused their socialist state power and trade instruments to subvert the JCP and other democratic movements in Japan. The Maoists, it insisted, had organized in Japan an unjust united front with anti-JCP renegades, social democrats, business leaders, and bourgeois elements, who were all forced to accept Mao's "fanatic" and "despotic" directives in order to do business.[67] While the ensuing dispute over trade deprived the JCP of a hitherto useful source of financial contributions and further drove the party closer to the Soviet Union, it left Japanese trading circles highly confused—a condition detrimental to the promotion of Sino-Japanese economic cooperation.

The ruling LDP, too, was deeply troubled by the issue of Sino-Japanese trade. Since it was unified in November 1955, the LDP had consistently maintained an official policy that Japan should be prepared to promote trade with the PRC, but without compromising her normal diplomatic and economic relations with Nationalist China. When a growing number of local legislatures adopted in 1964 a resolution favoring diplomatic and economic normalization between Japan and China, the LDP reiterated its policy for separating economic and diplomatic matters and blamed China and the JSP for attaching political conditions to trade. Again, in a ten-point policy statement issued during the general elections in 1966, it pledged to seek economic and cultural exchange with China under the principles of respect for mutual positions and of noninterference in domestic affairs.[68] All these official statements and directives, however, did not achieve a workable consensus on China among LDP dietmen. The trade issue, in particular, threw them into serious disarray due to the combination of their financial, factional, and personal considerations.

As discussed in Chapter II, such influential conservative leaders as Kishi Nobusuke, Ishii Mitsujirō, Kaya Okinori, and Fukuda Takeo constituted a powerful "Taiwan Lobby" to protect the continuity of Japan's political and economic links with Nationalist China. They formed the Asian Problems Study Group in December 1964, and assumed leading roles in the Committee on Japan-(Nationalist) China Cooperation (*Nikka kyōryoku iinkai*), at whose suggestion the Association for Japan-(Nationalist) China Trade Promotion was established in 1967. They successfully attempted to constrain the Japanese government in regard to economic and technical cooperation with the PRC.

On the other hand, a number of antimainstream LDP members criticized Prime Minister Satō's China policy and sponsored various organizations and activities to promote Sino-Japanese trade. Most important, both the Asian-African Problems Study Group and the New Policy Discussion Group proposed in 1968 that the Export-Import Bank's funds be effectively utilized to finance Japan's export of industrial plants to China and that the Kennedy Round tariff cuts be applied to the China trade.[69]

In contrast to their use of subversive activities against the JCP in trade matters and their efforts directed toward exacerbating factional disagreements over China within the LDP, the Chinese attempted to solidify a common antiimperalist bond with the JSP, whose platform advocated the expansion of Sino-Japanese trade so as to lessen Japan's heavy economic dependence on the United States. The JSP, together with the Sōhyō, assumed a leading role in the resumption of trade in the early 1960s; it not only performed a function of specific interest articulation for Japanese trading companies, especially small and medium-sized ones, but also demonstrated an international influence that the Japanese government lacked. The JSP also used the trade issue to show how faithfully the Japanese government had followed the U.S. policy of diplomatic containment and strategic embargo against the PRC.

Yet the fact that some LDP dietmen played an increasingly visible role in promoting both memorandum trade and friendship trade with China deprived the JSP of an effective weapon with which they wished to attack the LDP government's anti-China policy. Their dilemma was further compounded by the lingering tensions and misunderstandings between the JSP and the PRC; in spite of all the formal cooperation, some wounds were too deep, and the JSP and China were still uneasy with one another. This situation required the JSP to send its fourth official mission to China in October 1964. In the joint statement signed by Secretary-General Narita Tomomi and President Chang Hsi-jo of the Chinese People's Institute of Foreign Affairs, they emphasized that the trade should be expanded on the basis of Chou's three political principles.[70] The subsequent JSP Action Programs adopted each year at its national congress invariably included the normalization of Sino-Japanese diplomatic and economic relations among the top three "pillars" of its foreign policy, along with the unconditional Okinawa reversion and the abrogation of the U.S.-Japan security treaty. More specifically, it called for the removal of COCOM regulations, the formal nullification of the Yoshida letter, and the unrestricted exchange of economic and technical missions between Japan and China. It also proposed that the Export-Import Bank's funds as well as the Kennedy Round tariff reductions be applied to the China trade.[71] No sooner had the government investigated the JAPIT and the JCFA (Orthodox Headquarters) in November 1967 in connection with their involvement in demonstrations against Chiang Ching-kuo's Japan visit, than the JSP attacked the investigation as a "grave escalation of Satō's anti-China activities," which would only put trade with China in jeopardy.[72] And, to extend memorandum trade beyond 1968, it requested in October 1968 that the government lift its ban on imports of Chinese livestock products.[73] (This request was also intended to stop the soaring meat prices for Japanese consumers.)

In an effort to influence factional dynamics among Japanese Socialists, the Chinese deliberately favored those trading companies that maintained close economic ties with the left-wing Sasaki faction and the extremist *Heiwa Dōshikai*. For example, the Wasui Trading Company, which was established in 1966 by some leaders (and their wives) of the Sasaki faction, was given special privileges in trade contracts with China.[74] In return such outspoken *Heiwa Dōshikai* dietmen as Kuroda Hisao (president of the "Orthodox Headquarters"), Okada Haruo (ex-member of the JSP Central Executive Committee), and Ishino Hisao articulated an unmistakable pro-Peking position in Japan and strongly influenced the direction of Sino-Japanese trade. They suggested, among other things, that only a correct and favorable appreciation of the Cultural Revolution would promote trade with China, and that the JSP should repudiate any cooperation with the JCP revisionists in domestic politics.[75] As a result of such activities, the *Heiwa Dōshikai* was even accused by its opponents as a Japanese branch of the Chinese Communist Party.

Some moderate Socialists, however, became increasingly critical of China's discriminating trade policy toward Japan. Both the right-wing ex-Kawakami faction and the structural reformist Eda faction complained in their respective publications that the joint statements signed by Chinese and Japanese trade representatives in 1967 and 1968 had attacked Soviet "revisionism," praised the Cultural Revolution, and idolized Mao Tse-tung's doctrines. They also charged that, during his tenure as JSP chairman, Sasaki Kōzō had compromised the party line for Wasui's special commercial interest.[76] Moreover, the centrist Katsumata faction contended that a series of controversies surrounding Sino-Japanese trade, including the Wasui case and the JCP, had damaged the JSP's autonomous image and had ushered an undesirable aspect of international Communist conflicts into the party.[77] All these arguments about trade added a new dimension to the JSP's already complicated inter- and intra-factional rivalries. When the Chinese grew disillusioned with members of the Sasaki faction, such as Yamamoto Kōichi, Ōshiba Shigeo, Nonoyama Ichizō, and Ioka Daiji, who had organized the Wasui Trading Company and had joined Chairman Katsumata Seiichi's new party leadership in August 1967, they initiated a drastic decline in trade arrangements with the Wasui in late 1967. The action prompted Yamamoto and his associates to espouse a general foreign policy outlook that supported Soviet policies and opposed those of China.[78]

The JSP emphasized its unique position to represent a strong Japanese public opinion desiring normalization and expansion of Sino-Japanese economic relations. It also used the trade issue to strengthen a bridge of communications with Peking. But it was not easy for the JSP's heterogeneous factional leaders to reach a policy consensus on the China trade issue or to give a favorable appraisal to the Cultural Revolution as Peking so stubbornly expected. Hence the Sasaki faction and the *Heiwa Dōshikai* enjoyed an important role in promoting Japan's trade with the PRC, sometimes at the cost of the JSP's official party line, and the LDP remained critical of the JSP's confused trade policy toward China.

Economic Effects of the Cultural Revolution   It is unclear to what extent the Cultural Revolution had directly influenced the direction and volume of Sino-Japanese trade through its impact on China's ability to produce and export marketable commodities. In early 1967 the Chinese first asserted that the "excellent situation" that had emerged in China's industrial and agricultural production during the Cultural Revolution had laid "an even sounder material basis for the nation's foreign trade." They also boasted that the third Five-Year Economic Plan (1966-70) had been overfulfilled under the slogan "grasp revolution and promote production."[79] As the violent mass movement further developed, however, even Premier Chou En-lai admitted that the Cultural Revolution had forced China to pay a "great price" in the economic field. In early 1968 he observed: "A summing up of last year's results shows that the planned targets had not been realized and output figures for many products were lower than those of 1966. . . . Armed fights occured, factory and mining equipment was damaged and stoppages of work or slowdowns were reported."[80] Indeed, the setback to industrial production, the confusion of transport networks, the disintegration of economic and labor organizations, the disturbances at port cities, and the pervasive breakdown of central bureaucratic authority could not but hinder efficient commercial intercourse with foreign countries. In fact, the Chinese Ministries in charge of economic affairs were the first central governmental targets of the Red Guards' and other rebels' concerted attacks.[81]

The opening of the Canton fair was postponed for one month in the fall of 1967 as that city was caught in the middle of violent Red Guard clashes. The shipping procedures for Japanese commodities were long held up or harassed at Chinese ports. The number of Japanese trade representatives stationed in China decreased from 100 to 20 by mid-1968. Some of them were harassed by the rampaging Red Guards, and 12 persons, and a correspondent, were arrested in Peking on seven different spy charges. And as the CCP-JCP conflict further deteriorated in the course of the Cultural Revolution,

Japan's trading companies and organizations that had anything to do with
the JCP were in a state of utter confusion. The daily avalanche of highly
unfavorable press reports about the extreme Red Guard activities increased
a sense of uncertainty among Japanese trading circles. After reaching the
postwar peak in 1966, the volume of Sino-Japanese trade dropped for two
years in a row. The Japanese Ministry of International Trade and Industry
attributed this decline at least in part to the Cultural Revolution.[82]

The revolutionary turmoil also weakened the political stand of those
Chinese leaders who had been responsible for the promotion of Sino-
Japanese trade. Notably Liao Cheng-chih (a primary negotiator for memorandum trade and president of the China-Japan Friendship Association)
and Nan Han-chen (a chief architect of friendship trade and chairman of
the Chinese Association for Promotion of International Trade) were profusely assailed by the Red Guards and thus were deprived of the freedom
to make any systematic approach toward Japan. Nan was irrevocably
purged, and Liao, who was attacked for his "erroneous" policy toward Japan
and Overseas Chinese problems and for his "bourgeois" life style, suffered
political disgrace until 1971 when Chou En-lai brought him back to public
life. The Ministries of Foreign Affairs and Foreign Trade, too, were
thoroughly disrupted or were dominated by the radical rebels for a while;
therefore, neither agency was capable of initiating or executing a consistent,
imaginative policy toward Japan.[83] Furthermore, as discussed earlier,
Chinese negotiators adopted an extremely rigid and doctrinaire attitude
about trade with Japan. They frequently raised political issues prior to trade
negotiations, linked economic problems to Mao's political dogmas and
revealed an awkward and inefficient negotiating procedure by engaging in
prolonged consultations with their own subordinates—a new negotiating
procedure that was consistent with a functional requirement of the Cultural
Revolution that inspired a more democratic or participatory decision-
making style in China's bureaucratic structures. Furui, for instance, missed
the "good old days," when Liao Cheng-chih had made a quick, efficient
decision on trade issues in direct consultation with Chou En-lai.[84]

No doubt the Cultural Revolution was at least a contributing factor to the
two-year decline in Sino-Japanese trade, but there were other important
reasons accounting for that decline. First, Japan was unwilling to purchase
China's exportable items such as rice, livestock, tobacco, and iron ores
during this period, while China was unable to meet Japan's demands for coal
and corn. The LDP government's refusal to import China's meat and rice
stemmed from its policy to protect domestic farmers and meat producers.
The principle of balanced trade under these circumstances led to a vicious
circle in Sino-Japanese economic relations. Second, since Japan restricted
the use of Export-Import Bank funds and adopted the application of
stringent COCOM regulations, the Chinese were forced to turn more to

Western European countries, which offered much-needed industrial plants (aircraft, shipbuilding, textiles, chemicals, etc.), high-quality machinery, steel, and fertilizers with easy terms of payment. Hence, in contrast to the decline in Sino-Japanese trade, the volume of China's trade with some Western European countries, West Germany, Italy, the Netherlands, and Austria, increased even during the Cultural Revolution.

In order to arrest the declining trade with China, Furui directly suggested to Prime Minister Satō in early 1968 that the government should formally nullify the controversial Yoshida letter and permit Japan's imports of Chinese meat and rice. Unless these political decisions were taken, he warned, memorandum trade might totally be suspended in the near future.[85] A similar observation was made by Sōma Tsunetoshi, chief representative of the Japan-China Memorandum Trade Office in Peking, who returned to Japan in July 1968.[86] Yet Minister of Agriculture Nishimura Naomi replied that Japan would not import Chinese livestock products without meeting satisfactory hygienic standards; Furui, however, attacked Nishimura's politically-motivated statement against China, suggesting that Japanese experts' careful investigation showed no health risks in Chinese meat.[87]

When Satō, pressed by pro-Peking business interest groups and their LDP supporters, suggested that the Yoshida letter might as well be considered "dead" in 1968, he encountered a strong reaction from Taipei, including Nationalist Chinese Ambassador Chen Chih-mai's personal protest to the Japanese Foreign Ministry in April and Foreign Minister Wei Tao-ming's protest to Japanese Ambassador Shimizu Hisanaga in May. More important, President Chiang Kai-shek warned in June that he would regard the nullification of the Yoshida letter as a step toward abrogation of the Japan-Taiwan peace treaty.[88] On the other hand, when some Japanese companies were encouraged by Satō's remarks to explore possible exports of complete plants to the PRC, the latter requested the Japanese government's formal renunciation of the Yoshida letter as a precondition for such exports. The Satō government had no intention of giving up a profitable trade relationship with Taiwan; Japan, during 1967, bought $126 million worth of Nationalist Chinese goods (nearly half of which were bananas), but sold $314 million worth. Exports to Japan constituted 19.5% of Taiwan's total foreign sales, and the imports made up 37.2% of its purchases from abroad.[89]

So the Japanese government refused to declare a formal nullification of Yoshida's "private" letter, and the Chinese stepped up their political and economic pressures against Satō. The *People's Daily* (October 23, 1968), for instance, accused Satō of being the "No. 1 lackey of U.S. imperialism in Asia" for adopting a "revamped version of the Greater East Asia Coprosperity Sphere" and for isolating China in the diplomatic and economic fields. Their antagonism was so intense that the Chinese were willing to suffer economic sacrifices, if necessary, rather than to condone Satō's "high-posture." They rendered the semiofficial memorandum trade precarious and unpredictable in the eyes of Japanese beholders, and then attributed this situation to Satō's anti-China policy. Even during the most difficult time in Tokyo-Peking relations, however, there was no indication that the Chinese intended to suspend memorandum trade altogether as they had done in 1958. It was true that their original expectations for the cumulative political effect of memorandum trade as envisaged in the Chou-Matsumura accord of 1962 were far from realized, but they seemed to appreciate its continuing usefulness, including the politically meaningful presence of their trade mission in Japan and the declaratory value of trade-related joint statements. Trade relations still provided them with a crucial tool to influence factional dynamics within the LDP and the JSP and to fight the recalcitrant JCP. They attempted to maximize the semidiplomatic operations of their trade office in Japan and to manipulate the competitive relationship between friendship and memorandum trades for political mobilization. Trade was the concrete manifestation of their ideologically-inspired international behavior during the Cultural Revolution.

Linkage of Economic and Political Relations

After the Cultural Revolution   Upon the gradual passing of the Cultural Revolution, the Chinese began to reduce the political requirements of foreign trade policy. Although they still continued to criticize the practice of "economism" at home and abroad, the slogan "politics in command" was somewhat softened, at least in economic areas. Mass movements designed to emphasize productivity spread the revitalized economic catch-phrases, "In agriculture, learn from Tachai" and "In industry, learn from Taching." The logic of economic rationalism was thus being stressed in the conduct of Sino-Japanese trade.

The combination of China's political stabilization, diplomatic fence-mending, and economic priority was reflected in a renewed optimism among Japanese businessmen engaged in trade with China. Departing from their ideologically-inspired negotiating style of the Cultural Revolution, the Chinese delegates at Canton trade fairs in 1969 displayed a speedy, efficient, and business-like behavior. Political discussions were de-emphasized in trade negotiations; gone were the sessions of studying Mao's "Quotations," the street demonstrations, and the Red Guards.[90] An additonal incentive to trade with Japan was provided by the closing of the Suez Canal, which pushed up the prices of Western European goods, and thus made Japanese products more attractive to China. At Canton, in the fall of 1969, Japanese trading firms concluded the largest amount of contracts ($210 million, about 60% increase over the previous fair) with China since the beginning of the fair; the Chinese bought a large quantity of steel, machinery, and chemicals, which were needed for their immediate economic development. Under these new conditions, the volume of total trade ($625 million) during 1969 reached the highest level in history, representing 13.6% increase over the previous year. Japan's exports grew by 20.2%, though her imports showed only a moderate increase of 4.6%, perhaps due to China's limited export capability following the Cultural Revolution, and its preservation of raw materials for war preparations, especially in the light of Sino-Soviet border clashes.[91]

In spite of the generally improved trade picture, the share of memorandum trade in total Sino-Japanese transactions further declined from 20.8% in 1968 to 10.1% in 1969, and Japanese business pressure against Prime Minister Satō's China policy also increased. Trading firms, steelmakers, and fertilizer-producers were eager to improve their profits in the China market, but the mainstream business circles, especially the *Keidanren* leadership, remained skeptical about the immediate prospect of Sino-Japanese trade expansion. At the House of Representatives Committee on the Budget meeting in March 1969, Satō said that while the Japanese government could not nullify, revise, or relax Yoshida's "private" letter, he would carefully consider each company's application for the use of Export-Import Bank funds in its trade with China.[92] After the Tokyo District Court ruled in July 1969 that the COCOM regulations had no legal basis for limiting Japanese exports to China, the government in October removed seventy-nine items from the COCOM list, but added twenty-three new items to it.[93] (In the winter of 1969 the Chinese released five representatives of the Daiichi Trading Company and one correspondent from captivity at Peking; they still kept six other trade representatives and one interpreter in prison.)

The moderation of China's trade policy toward Japan contrasted sharply with its continuing political friction with the Satō government. As discussed in Chapter III, in the joint communique on memorandum trade signed by LDP Dietman Furui Yoshimi and Liu Hsi-wen in April 1969, the Chinese condemned the Satō government's anti-China policy, and Furui promised to wage a determined struggle against such a policy. The JSP promptly urged the government to implement the memorandum trade agreement, especially in regard to lifting the restrictions imposed on imports of Chinese meat and on Japanese scientific and industrial exhibitions to be held in China. Yet it was quite evident in 1969 that both the Satō government and the top LDP leadership decided to tolerate the harsh rhetoric of the communique in an attempt not to aggravate the already crippled memorandum trade with China. This benign attitude was indicative of their wish to sustain memorandum trade as a potentially useful, semiofficial pipeline between Tokyo and Peking.

At the end of 1969, however, another political event threatened to mar the renewed expansion of trade between Japan and China. Along the lines

Figure 4. Memorandum Trade and Friendship Trade: 1963–72
(in million dollars)

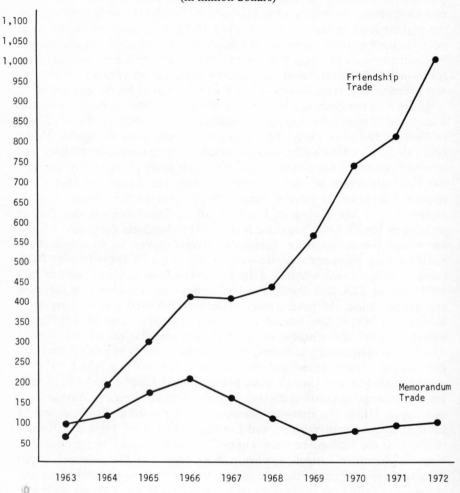

of the Nixon Doctrine, and perhaps as a quid pro quo for the Okinawa reversion, Satō, in the joint statement signed with President Nixon, declared that the maintenance of peace and security in the Taiwan area (as well as South Korea) was an important factor for Japan's own security. This identification of Japanese and Taiwanese security interests provoked China's angry attack against Satō's "militarist" foreign policy. The issue of Japanese militarism was the most salient political point in China's trade policy toward Japan during the following year; this was most seriously reflected in the Furui-Liu joint communique of April 1970 and in the LDP's reaction thereto.

As examined in Chapter III, the Furui-Liu joint communique and attendant political controversies, which were prominently reported in the mass media, aroused some public interest in Japan, and both the LDP and the JSP attempted to gain a partisan political dividend out of the episode. How did the Japanese public react to this controversial development? Asked how they felt about the Chinese arguments contained in the joint communique, about a half of Japanese interviewees (51.0%), according to a nationwide sample survey conducted by *Yomiuri Shimbun* in May 1970, chose either "Do Not Know" or "No Answer" categories (see table 25).[94] It was readily apparent that a considerable number of Japanese people were either unaware of the development or unwilling to express a definite response thereto. Even if the result was by no means surprising, it demonstrated relatively low public interest in memorandum trade itself. While only 5.2% took a sympathetic attitude toward the Chinese complaints, which they regarded as legitimate, 22.7% said that the Chinese had no other alternative but to register their complaints as they did. On the other hand, 10.8% answered that the Chinese arguments stemmed from their distorted view of Japan, and 9.7% flatly called them a political slander. Those who regularly supported the LDP in general elections were far more critical of the Chinese position than were the JCP supporters, while voters for the JSP were somewhere in between these two parties. The pattern of Japanese public responses on the communique issue was markedly associated with their partisan preferences. However, when they were asked whether or not they

Table 25—Japanese Public Opinion on Memorandum Trade, May 1970

"How did you feel about the Chinese position expressed in the recent joint statement on memorandum trade?"

(percentage)

Sample	Correct Position	No Other Alternative	Distorted Views	Political Slander	Other Answers	Do Not Know or No Answer
National	5.2	22.7	10.8	9.7	0.6	51.0
LDP	3.0	19.9	15.2	12.2	0.4	49.2
JSP	6.8	31.9	8.6	6.8	1.3	44.5
JCP	23.2	28.6	3.6	5.4	1.8	37.5
CGP	12.8	25.6	6.4	7.7	1.3	46.2
DSP	3.0	28.7	11.9	21.8	0.0	34.7

SOURCE: Opinion Research Section of *Yomiuri Shimbun.*

favored the continuation of memorandum trade, there was no appreciable partisan division in their answers. One third of them favored it, and one out of ten Japanese interviewees was opposed; again, a little more than a half of them said "Do Not Know" or "No Answer." And, as table 26 shows, these answers were almost equally distributed among all five partisan groups.

Meanwhile, the determined application of China's new trade policy, commonly called "Chou's four conditions," exerted a profoundly destabilizing effect on the whole business community in Japan—particularly those industries that had long enjoyed comfortable and profitable commercial transactions with China and Taiwan. Upon the release of the two memorandum and friendship trade communiques on April 15 and 19, Chou explained his new trade guidelines to Japanese trade delegates and their political sponsors (including Matsumura Kenzō) and stressed the need to make a clear distinction between "friends" and "enemies" in Sino-Japanese relations. As related by Hagiwara Teiji (ex-member of the JCP), managing director of the Japanese Association for Promotion of International Trade, on April 28, Chou decided to have no more commerical exchanges with any of the following Japanese companies: (1) factories and firms helping South Korea's intrusion into North Korea or Taiwan's "come back to the mainland" attempt; (2) factories and firms with large investments in South Korea or Taiwan; (3) enterprises supplying arms and ammunition to U.S. war efforts in Vietnam, Laos, or Cambodia; and (4) U.S.-Japanese joint ventures or subsidiaries of U.S. companies in Japan.[95]

A few days later Wu Shu-tung, deputy secretary-general of the Canton fair, elaborated on these four conditions to Japanese participants in the fair. As specific examples of "unfriendly" firms, he singled out Sumitomo Chemical Co., Mitsui Heavy Industry, Teijin Co., and Asahi-Dow Chemical Company.[96] He also told the representatives of major "dummy companies,"

Table 26—Japanese Public Opinion on Memorandum Trade, May 1970

"Do you favor or disfavor the continuation of memorandum trade between Japan and China?"

(percentage)

Sample	Favor	Disfavor	Do Not Know or No Answer
National	33.1	12.9	54.0
LDP	33.3	14.2	52.5
JSP	36.9	14.1	49.0
JCP	37.5	12.5	50.0
CGP	38.5	14.1	47.4
DSP	45.5	14.9	39.6

SOURCE: Opinion Research Section of *Yomiuri Shimbun*.

such as Meiwa Sangyō (Mitsubishi), Keimei Koeki (Mitsui), Wako Koeki (Marubeni-Iida), Shinnihon Tsūshō (Itōchū), and Daihō Co. (Nisshō Iwai), that they would be ignored in trade negotiations until their parent companies accept Chou's four conditons.[97] Some Japanese companies entertained a hope that these conditions were merely the rhetoric of another ideologically inspired proclamation that would soon wither away. Yet the Chinese were firmly determined to enforce them to the end; they not only eliminated from new trade negotiations those Japanese companies that violated any one of the conditions but also cancelled existing trade agreements with them. The form of every trade contract was prefaced by the statement that both parties agreed to conclude the contract through friendly negotiations and on the basis of the three political principles, the three trade principles, the principle of inseparability of economic and political matters, and the Chinese government's four conditions. As a result of China's rigid discriminatory trade policy, the volume of contracts made at Canton in the spring of 1970 drastically declined, showing almost a 50% drop from the previous fair (see table 27). The immediate prospect for Sino-Japanese trade appeared bleak.

Why did Chou En-lai adopt these four conditions toward Japan? One obvious external factor was the 1969 Nixon-Satō joint statement, which he interpreted as a formal declaration of Japan's security identification with Taiwan and South Korea. Especially disturbing to him was Kishi Nobusuke's (and Japan's) escalating economic and political collusion with Chiang Kai-shek and Park Chung-hi. On the very day that Satō issued the controversial joint statement in Washington, D.C., his brother and other influential LDP leaders (including Ishii Mitsujirō) and businessmen signed another joint statement with their Nationalist Chinese hosts in Taipei. This statement adopted by the fourteenth session of the Committee on Japan-(Nationalist) China Cooperation supported Chiang's policy of "mainland recovery" and sought to create the international environment that would expedite the collapse of the Communist regime.[98] Emphasizing Japan's "active political responsibility" for maintaining freedom and security in Asia, it asked for the restructuring of the Asian "free world," embracing Japan, Taiwan, and South Korea. This followed Kishi's organization, in 1969, of the Committee on Japan-(South) Korea Cooperation (*Nikkan kyōryoku iinkai*) as an identical twin of the Japan-(Nationalist) China Committee.

From their own perspective, the Chinese suspected a coordinated duet between Satō and his brother, and used it as further demonstrable evidence to buttress their favorite argument that Japan's deepening economic penetration into Taiwan was directly linked to its plot to annex Taiwan.[99] In 1969 the total volume of Japanese-Taiwanese trade was $780 million, $160 million more than Japan's trade with the mainland; Japan had $63 million of cumulative direct capital investment in Taiwan; the number of Japanese companies engaged in economic cooperation with Taiwan surpassed that of

Table 27—Canton Fairs, 1961-72

Year	Season	Total Participants	Japanese Participants	Japanese Companies	Japanese Contracts ($ million)
1961	Spring	3,000	40	38	11
	Autumn	2,500	51	37	18
1962	Spring	2,500	110	64	12
	Autumn	2,600	160	80	25
1963	Spring	2,800	182	100	14
	Autumn	3,300	228	101	39
1964	Spring	3,700	296	140	34
	Autumn	4,400	433	154	47
1965	Spring	5,000	470	190	74
	Autumn	5,600	602	202	131
1966	Spring	6,000	688	206	92
	Autumn	6,000	750	230	127
1967	Spring	7,800	850	250	130
	Autumn	9,000	928	280	130
1968	Spring	6,000	900	280	113
	Autumn	10,000	911	260	139
1969	Spring	7,000	957	268	128
	Autumn	6,000	900	260	210
1970	Spring	6,000	1,006	221	121
	Autumn	6,000	1,140	618	147
1971	Spring	16,000	1,451	815	176
	Autumn	20,000	2,200	1,365	221
1972	Spring	21,000	2,272	1,550	210
	Autumn	23,000	2,648	1,650	234

SOURCE: *Tōzaibōeki Repōto* [East-West trade report] (Spring 1973).

U.S. companies. The Japanese government had started in 1965 to provide Taiwan with the first loan in *yen* currency ($150 million), which was initiated by the Committee on Japan-(Nationalist) China Cooperation. This economic expansion, according to Peking's arguments, was inevitably accompanied by Japan's growing political and military involvement in Taiwan. As proof of this trend, the Chinese cited the *Nikka* statement, Nationalist Chinese leaders' frequent visits to Japan, and Japan's leading role in the Asian and Pacific Council (ASPAC) and in the alleged Northeast Asia Treaty Organization (NEATO).

The same Chinese logic was applied to Japan's growing economic domination of South Korea, which they considered a "puppet" and a "colony" of the U.S. and Japan.[100] While Japan was in the process of replacing the United States as a principal economic patron, trading partner, and diplomatic sponsor of South Korea at the United Nations, the PRC countered by diligently seeking to improve its once strained relations with

North Korea. For this purpose it shrewdly took advantage of Pyongyang's less than enthusiastic attitude toward the Soviet Union following the EC-121 reconnaissance plane incident. It should be recalled that during the height of the Cultural Revolution, an atmosphere of mutual suspicion and hostility had prevailed between Peking and Pyongyang. There had been various reports of intermittent Sino-North Korean conflicts, such as scattered armed clashes along the Yalu River, territorial disputes, and the Red Guards' condemnation of Kim Il-song's "revisionism." Kim had failed to praise the universal importance of the Cultural Revolution and Mao Tse-tung's political thought, and to send a fraternal greeting to the ninth National Congress of the Chinese Communist Party.

At the end of September 1969, Choe Yong-kon, chairman of the Presidium of North Korea's Supreme People's Assembly, led a delegation to attend the twentieth anniversary of China's founding. He held long discussions with Chou En-lai, who stressed the "continuous growth and consolidation of the militant friendship between the peoples of China and Korea."[101] This new development marked China's major fence-mending gesture toward North Korea in the aftermath of the Cultural Revolution. In the following spring both countries exchanged ambassadors for the first time in three years.

The most decisive turning point was Chou's three-day visit to North Korea in April 1970. He pledged to support North Korea's struggle against U.S. imperialism and Japanese militarism. The fact that Chou presented his four conditions less than two weeks after his return from Pyongyang (and that his statement, as relayed by Hagiwara, mentioned South Korea prior to Taiwan) suggests that these conditions were intended to demonstrate his "militant solidarity" with North Korea in checking Japan's economic assistance to South Korea, at least as much as to reflect his own concern with Japanese-Taiwanese relations. It is conceivable that Kim requested Chou's cooperation in trying to prevent Japan from increasing its role in South Korea's economic development. At the same time Chou was conscious of Moscow's relations with North Korea and Japan.

In addition to his assessment of Japanese economic penetration into Taiwan and South Korea, Chou apparently felt that the year 1970 was a right time to impose on the Japanese business community a clear-cut choice between China and Taiwan as their economic partner. He was probably confident that, since Japanese businessmen were wary of West European countries' aggressive pursuit of contacts with the China market and were hopeful for a substantial expansion of Sino-Japanese trade in the 1970s as part of their market diversification plans, they, or at least a significant number of them, would decide that they could not afford to lose their existing foothold in China altogether. At the least, his insistence on observation of his four conditions provided a decisive test case for him to see whether or not he could ultimately rely upon Japan's business circles as an effective weapon for changing the LDP government's China policy.

How did Japan respond to Chou's four conditions during 1970? Or, how did this response affect the nature and direction of Sino-Japanese relations in the years that followed? The entire Japanese business community was thrown into disarray. The general pattern of Japanese businessmen's reaction depended upon three main considerations: (1) the degree of their present economic dependence on China and Taiwan, (2) the projection of their future share in the China market, and (3) the extent of their assessment of China's policy consistency and seriousness. The most sensitive and positive response came from chemical fertilizer industries, which heavily relied on China for their foreign sales. Half of the chemical fertilizer produced in Japan was for foreign consumption, and 61.7% of the foreign sale went to China in 1970. Since Taiwan and South Korea had both become almost self-sufficient in chemical fertilizer and Western European producers were highly competitive in China, all major Japanese fertilizer industries had no realistic choice but to accept the four conditions, which they did in May.

The next group of Japanese industries to accept Chou's ultimatum was the major steelmakers. Although Japanese steel industries did not depend on China as much as fertilizer producers did, steel was Japan's top export item to China. As table 28 shows, in 1970 it represented 41.7% of total Japanese sales to China, and constituted 8.3% of Japan's total steel export. This amount made China the second largest purchaser of Japanese steel—after the U.S. (31.6%). Japanese steelmakers had been forced to exercise self-restraint on their inroads into the United States and West Europe, but had expected to increase their sales to China, which needed steel for its fourth Five-Year Economic Plan starting in 1971, and which imported more than 10% of its domestic steel demand. Hence four of the five major steelmakers, Kawasaki Steel, Sumitomo Metal Industry, Kobe Steel, and Japan Steel Pipe, gave in. However, New Japan Steel, whose board chairman Nagano Shigeo (chairman of the Nisshō-Japan Chamber of Commerce and Industry) took part in the fifteenth session of the Committee on Japan-(Nationalist) China Cooperation in July 1970, was completely eliminated in trade negotiations with China.

Large industrial or commercial firms such as Sumitomo Shōji, Chōri Co., Nichimen Jitsugyō, Nisshō Iwai, and Ataka Sangyō, which had enjoyed a lion's share of China trade, readily subscribed to the Chinese demand. Unlike these other companies, Japan's "big four" trading firms—Mitsubishi Shōji, Mitsui Bussan, Itōchū Shōji, and Marubeni-Iida, whose subsidiaries conducted 40% of the total Sino-Japanese trade—refused to terminate their equally profitable economic ties with Taiwan and South Korea, and continued to attend meetings of the Committees on Japan-(Nationalist) China Cooperation and on Japan-(South) Korea Cooperation for the time

Table 28—Composition of Sino-Japanese Trade, 1968–72
(percentage)

Japanese Exports

Category of Item	1968	1969	1970	1971	1972
Steel and Iron	41.9	41.8	41.7	46.7	40.2
Chemicals	34.3	31.3	24.3	28.5	32.7
(Chemical Fertilizer	22.7	20.7	15.5	17.5	19.4)
Machinery	10.1	12.4	20.9	15.8	12.9
Synthetic Textiles	5.6	4.5	3.7	3.8	7.5
Others	8.2	10.0	9.3	5.5	6.7

Japanese Imports

Foodstuff	32.3	22.9	26.3	27.5	24.8
Oils and Fats	24.3	21.5	16.5	13.8	9.4
(Soybean	20.6	18.1	14.2	11.7	7.7)
Textiles	10.6	13.7	14.0	19.7	27.1
Chemicals	4.4	6.9	9.1	8.1	5.5
Minerals	7.1	8.6	8.7	7.3	4.8
Silk Fabrics	2.8	3.4	3.2	2.3	3.2
Others	18.5	23.0	22.2	21.4	25.2

SOURCES: *Nitchū kankei shiryōshū, 1945-1971* [Collected documents on Japan-China relations, 1945-1971] (Tokyo, 1971), and *Shin Chūgoku Nenkan* [New China yearbook] (Tokyo: 1973).

being. Some of their subsidiaries, such as Wako Koeki and Shinnihon Tsūshō, subsequently decided to dissociate themselves from their parent organizations (Marubeni-Iida and Itōchū, respectively), and returned to trade negotiations with China in September. By the end of 1970 about 700 Japanese industries and trading firms had accepted the Chinese ultimatum.[102] (Conversely, as Taiwan, too, took an "all-or-nothing" trade policy, some Japanese trading firms like Beisei Shōji, which were deeply involved in the Taiwan market, were forced to announce their departure from their parent companies (Nisshō Iwai in this case) that had accepted Chou's conditions.)

While the JSP, as usual, endorsed the correctness of Chou's four conditions, the LDP's Committee on Foreign Affairs held a discussion session with Japanese government officials and instructed them to "direct and guide" businessmen regarding the conditions.[103] Confronted with the widespread bandwagon effects of Chou's four conditions, however, pro-Taiwan political and economic leaders organized a countermove. The "Prime Minister of business circles" (*Zaikai Sōri*), Uemura Kogorō, who as chairman of the *Keidanren* and adviser to the Foreign Ministry had been active in the Committees on Japan-(Nationalist) China Cooperation and on Japan-(South) Korea Cooperation, expressed his intention to "ignore"

Chou's conditions.[104] Prime Minister Satō concurred with advice given by Ishii Mitsujirō to follow a similar course, and Minister of International Trade and Industry Miyazawa Kiichi expressed at the House of Representatives his opposition to attaching a political condition to foreign trade.[105] The Japanese leaders of both Committees on Japan-(Nationalist) China and Japan-(South) Korea Cooperation, including Kishi, Ishii, Shiina Etsusaburō (ex-foreign minister), Nadao Hirokichi, Uemura Kogorō, and Yatsuki Kazuo (a leading architect of both committees), held a strategy session with Finance Minister Fukuda Takeo and other government officials.[106] At the fifteenth session of the Committee on Japan-(Nationalist) China Cooperation, which was held at the *Keidanren* Hall in July 1970 with three South Korean observers, Chou's four conditions were discussed and denounced.[107] However, the participants adopted a more moderate statement, which, unlike their previous communique, was without a specific endorsement of Chiang's "mainland recovery" policy, but which still pointed out the urgency of anti-Communist solidarity among Japan, Taiwan, and South Korea.[108] They decided to form a "three-nation liaison committee" of both committees; and the liaison committee, inaugurated at Seoul in November, organized a committee for joint research and development of seabed oil resources. The Chinese vehemently opposed the liaison committee's activities, which the *People's Daily* (December 29, 1970) called a "flagrant encroachment" on the sovereignty of China and North Korea. The political turmoil over Chou's conditions did not stop the rapid expansion of Sino-Japanese trade during 1970; it reached a new peak of $823 million, a whopping 31.6% rise over the previous year, but China's trade deficit was substantial. This deficit itself indicated how badly China wanted to expand economic cooperation with Japan.

Attitudes of the Japanese Zaikai   In the latter half of 1970 a number of new events took place in Japan's domestic political scene and in China's external relations, which together favorably influenced the pace of Sino-Japanese trade. These events included the inauguration of the Japanese Dietmen's League for Promoting Restoration of Japan-China Diplomatic Relations and China's diplomatic offensive toward the NATO member-states. The fact that Canada and Italy established diplomatic relations with China in October and November further stimulated the restless mood among Japan's political and economic leaders, who were afraid of being left out in diplomatic approaches toward China. Even though Uemura Kogorō flatly denied any impact of these external developments upon Japan's China policy, the Canadian-Chinese diplomatic rapprochement had a considerable effect on Japanese automakers, especially Toyota and Nissan, who suspected that the U.S. car industries would move into the China market through their Canadian partners.[109] The situation was further compounded in November by a development in the twenty-fifth U.N. General Assembly:

for the first time in U.N. history, the Albanian resolution for China's representation attained a plurality by 51 to 49 votes with 27 absent or abstaining. The U.N. resolution failed to achieve a two-third majority vote required (under the "important question" rule) for China's representation, but it marked a turning point in the Satō government's and Japanese business community's thinking about the Chinese question.

The *Keizai Dōyūkai* (Japan Committee for Economic Development), one of Japan's four mainstream economic organizations, and the *Kansai Keizai Dōyūkai* spearheaded a new, positive orientation toward China. In January 1971, the *Keizai Dōyūkai's* Chairman Kikawada Kazutaka (chairman of Tokyo Electrical Power Co., adviser to the Foreign Ministry, head of the exclusive *Sangyō mondai kenkyūkai*, and Miki Takeo's financial supporter) argued that, on the basis of peaceful coexistence, Japan must invite China to join the international community, and it held a number of discussion sessions with other business leaders and Foreign Ministry officials.[110] At the request of LDP Dietman Fujiyama Aiichirō (chairman of the new Dietmen's League), Kikawada promised to provide financial support for the league's activities.[111] He also asked Fujiyama, who was about to visit China, to ascertain whether or not Chou En-lai would accept a high-level economic delegation from Japan. Fujiyama received the same inquiry from the *Kansai Keizai Dōyūkai*, which represented a traditional stronghold of Japan's commercial transactions with China. (The Kansai region, especially Osaka, had been a center for Sino-Japanese trade.) Unlike the more powerful *Keidanren* dominated by Uemura and other pro-Taiwan businessmen, the *Keizai Dōyūkai* was known to be a group of relatively young, liberal, and independent-minded entrepreneurs, who tended to take bold initiatives in economic and political matters.[112] The *Dōyūkai's* "forward-looking" approach toward China opened the possibility of China's direct relations with Japan's mainstream business circles.

At the same time Chou En-lai was beginning to moderate his trade policy toward Japan. Having already witnessed an encouraging situation in Japan—the emerging configuration of interparty coalition about China, the businessmen's favorable reaction to his four conditions, and the growth of public opinion in favor of diplomatic normalization between Japan and China, Chou adopted a strategy of helping to mobilize and direct a "grand alliance" among all Japanese forces that could be united for the goal of Sino-Japanese cooperation in economic and diplomatic matters. The term "grand alliance" was first used in the talks between Chou and Sasaki Kōzō (ex-JSP chairman) in August 1970, but Chou repeated the same idea to many Japanese visitors to China in early 1971.[113] In particular, he welcomed Japanese economic leaders to visit China; "If Japanese business leaders desire diplomatic normalization between Japan and China and consider termination of their ties with Taiwan," said he, "they can be called 'leftists.' "

It was a convenient political justification for China's willingness to cooperate with these "leftists". He expressed a special interest in Kikawada's conciliatory overtures and told Fujiyama that once diplomatic relations were restored, trade would be substantially expanded.[114]

The "grand alliance" strategy was derived from Chou's apparent assumption that the beginning of the post-Satō era in Japan would be a crucial moment in Sino-Japanese relations, and that the diligent cultivation of friendly channels with as many Japanese leaders as possible, particularly those in the LDP and in the *zaikai*, would assist Chinese policy at that moment.[115] While Chou was reassured of the political efficacy of his manipulative (and penetrative) capabilities over Japanese businessmen, which had been tested in the case of his four conditions, he was also inspired to employ the "grand alliance" strategy due to the need for Japanese industrial products and technical know-how for China's fourth Five-Year Economic Plan. Further, his softened trade policy toward Japan may also be related to his attempt to obstruct or limit the joint Soviet-Japanese economic development of Siberia. After V. N. Novikov, vice-chairman of the Soviet Council of Ministers, conferred with Japanese leaders at the World Exposition in Osaka in April 1970, the Chinese had become increasingly sensitive to the accelerated move for Soviet-Japanese economic cooperation. While they attacked the Siberian joint development program as a betrayal of the best interests of the Japanese and Soviet peoples and as a source of Japan's militarist expansionism, they were obviously concerned primarily with their own security problem facing the vast, well-developed Siberian border areas.[116] Another factor encouraging a position more open to economic interdependence with the Japanese was the potentially serious economic friction between Japan and the United States, both in their bilateral issues (such as trade imbalance, exchange rate, liberalization of capital investment, and development of energy resources) and in their approaches toward the China market. It is also conceivable that by establishing a tangible link with Japan's mainstream business leaders, they hoped to be an influence in restraining major Japanese industries' active participation in Japan's domestic arms production.

The Chinese attitude of conciliation was best demonstrated in memorandum trade negotiations in the spring of 1971. Furui, Tagawa, and Okazaki were surprised by the speed and harmony with which they could conclude political talks with their Chinese hosts.[117] However, this speed was not purely the result of the Chinese attitude; the Japanese negotiators also showed an accommodating attitude when they joined Liu Hsi-wen in condemning "the Japanese reactionaries for intensifying collusion with U.S. imperialism in reviving Japanese militarism and joining U.S. imperialism's aggression and expansion in Asia."[118] Their opposition to the "three-nation liaison committee" was duly registered. Compared with their tough experience with Chinese negotiators in 1968-70, Furui and Tagawa had an easier, more comfortable discussion with Liu Hsi-wen in Peking.

As usual, the JSP welcomed the "correctness" of the memorandum trade statement that criticized Satō's policy of militarism and containment against China. But the Satō cabinet and the LDP decided not to repeat their formal rebuttals to the statement, in part because of the growing division of opinions between "hawks" and "doves" within the LDP itself.[119] Rather they satisfied themselves with a perfunctory statement issued by Kosaka Zentarō (chairman of the LDP's Committee on Foreign Affairs), which regretted China's criticism against Japan, emphasized the defensive purpose of the U.S.-Japan security treaty, and asked China not to interfere in Japan's affairs.[120]

According to a *Sankei Shimbun* survey conducted in March 1971, 68.2% of Japanese interviewees knew something about the Furui-Liu joint statement on memorandum trade, and the Japanese people appeared to be more sympathetic to the Chinese position in 1971 than they had been in 1970: 11.8% said that the Chinese held a legitimate position, and 44.8% understood that they had no other choice.[121] As to the key Chinese contention that Japanese militarism had already revived, 10.3% agreed with it, and 15.9% answered "probably so"; 41.3% admitted the future possibility of Japanese militarism, 24.0% flatly denied it, with 8.6% "Do Not Know" responses. The following month a Jiji News Agency survey reported that an overwhelming majority of Japanese people (71.7%) wanted Japan to positively pursue trade with China, with 5.0% negative answers and 23.2% in the "Do Not Know" category.[122]

Meanwhile, China's direct contacts with Japan's mainstream business leaders were already underway. As deputy head of the Chinese team at the thirty-first World Table Tennis Championship contest in Nagoya, Wang Hsiao-yün (deputy secretary-general of the China-Japan Friendship Association and director of the Chinese People's Association for Friendship with Foreign Countries) conducted a wide range of political and economic activities in March and April 1971. He held a series of meetings with the LDP's anti-Satō leaders such as Miki Takeo, and with opposition party chiefs (the CGP's Chairman Takeiri Yoshikatsu in Fukuoka and the JSP's Chairman Narita Tomomi in Tokyo).[123] He visited the Toyota Motor Company in Nagoya and a Hitachi shipbuilding yard in Osaka; and he met with the president of Hitachi Shipbuilding and Engineering Company, from which China wished to buy a large freighter. In talks with representatives of Japanese textile industries, he showed a keen interest in their disputes with the United States.[124] More important, he conferred with the principal leaders of Kansai-based Sumitomo industrial complexes, such as President Hiuga Hōsai of Sumitomo Metal Industry and President Yamamoto Hiromu of Sumitomo Bank, in Osaka and invited them to visit China. The most important occasion was his meeting with top business leaders in Tokyo; they were Kikawada Kazutaka, Iwasa Yoshizani (president of Fuji Bank and vice-chairman of the *Keizai Dōyūkai*), Imasato Hiroki (president of Nippon Seikō and director of the *Nikkeiren*-Japan Federation of Employers' Organizations), Kawai Ryōichi (president of Komatsu Manufacturing Co. and vice-chairman of the *Dōyūkai*), Suzuki Haruo (president of Shōwa Electrical Engineering Company and vice-chairman of the *Dōyūkai*), Nakayama Sōhei (adviser to Japan Industrial Bank and permanent director of the *Dōyūkai*), and Yamashita Seiichi (managing director of the *Dōyūkai*). At this meeting Wang reiterated China's various principles for trade with Japan, while Japanese participants requested a further increase in exchange programs between China and Japan, including their own visit to China.[125]

The LDP Executive Council was initially critical of the table tennis program that excluded Taiwan, but China's skillful utilization of "ping-pong diplomacy," ranging from Wang's versatile activities to an invitation of the U.S. team to China, demonstrated its calculated overtures toward the United States and Japan.

The announcement of President Nixon's planned visit to China, combined with his earlier decision easing restrictions on U.S. trade with China, prompted genuine fear and panic among Japanese business leaders that the United States had not only bypassed Japan in its rapprochement with China, but also intended to penetrate into the China market.[126] The situation grew worse with Nixon's subsequent imposition of a 10% surcharge on foreign imports because the Japanese had long been dependent on U.S. markets. The Japanese businessmen were increasingly impatient with their own government's inability to reach a reconciliation with China, as the impetus for diversification of their export markets was stronger than ever before. They feared that the United States would in the long run establish a preeminent foreign economic base in the China market, but believed that if they moved quickly, Japan would be able to gain much economic benefit from China. All these events, coupled with their emotional desire to settle the China dilemma, prompted the Japanese business leaders' most positive approach toward China, which they initiated a step ahead of the Satō government. If they had been apprehensive that the United States might take retaliatory measures in the event of their extensive economic cooperation with China, Nixon's own reconciliation reassured them.

On the very day the Nixon visit was announced, Chairman Nagano Shigeo and President Inayama Yoshirō (also vice-chairman of the *Keidanren*) of New Japan Steel made it clear at a press conference that both would be absent in the forthcoming meetings of the Committees on Japan-(South) Korea Cooperation and on Japan-(Nationalist) China Cooperation.[127] This meant a serious setback to those LDP leaders who had sponsored both Committees. Furthermore, the fact that Nagano, who was known to be a principal "right-wing" business leader, and Inayama, who aspired to succeed Uemura Kogorō as the *Keidanren*'s chairman, were favorably inclined toward China was bound to have a far-reaching effect upon the entire Japanese *zaikai*. Indeed, their position was soon followed by Itōchū Shōji, Marubeni-Iida, and Nisshō Iwai. Only eleven Japanese companies were represented at the sixteenth session of the Committee on Japan–(Nationalist) China Cooperation, which was held in Taipei in October 1971, and contrary to their established pattern, the participants failed to issue a joint statement.[128] In the same month the second largest bank in Japan—Fuji Bank, which had earlier lost its contacts with the Bank of China—became the first Japanese financial institution to accept Chou's four conditions; other commercial banks were to follow suit in subsequent months.

The direct contacts between China and Japanese business circles were further solidified in August 1971, when Wang Kuo-chuan (vice-president of the China-Japan Friendship Association) visited Japan to attend the funeral of Matsumura Kenzō. As a follow-up of Wang Hsiao-yün's talks with the Japanese *zaikai*, Wang Kuo-chuan met Kikawada Kazutaka, Iwasa Yoshizani, Imasato Hiroki, Kawai Ryoichi, Yamashita Seiichi, and Nagano Shigeo (who had not met Wang Hsiao-yün in April). During these meetings Kikawada accepted the five principles of peaceful coexistence as a basis for Sino-Japanese economic cooperation. A few days later New Japan Steel formally accepted Chou's four conditions and terminated its membership in both committees on cooperation with Taiwan and South Korea.

As a result of its contacts with the Japanese business community, the PRC invited in September 1971 the Kansai businessmen's delegation, which was led by Saeki Isamu (president of the Kinki Railroad Company and chairman of the Osaka Chamber of Commerce) and was composed of all major figures in the Kansai business circles. They included Hiuga Hōsai (president of Sumitomo Metal Industry), Nagata Takao (president of Hitachi Shipbuilding and Engineering Company and chairman of the Kansai Federation of Employers' Organizations), Yamamoto Hiromu (president of Sumitomo Bank and cochairman of the *Kansai Keizai Dōyūkai*), Nakatsukasa Kiyoshi (chairman of Shoen Chemical Company and vice-chairman of the Kansai Federation of Economic Organizations), and Muroga Kunitake (president of Shikijima Textile Company and chairman of the Osaka Industrial Association). Saeki told Chou En-lai at Peking that before its departure from Japan, the Kansai group had reached a "unified view" that the PRC represented China, that Taiwan was China's territory, and that the resolution of the Taiwan question was an internal matter of China.[129]

The Kansai mission was soon followed by a similar delegation from Tokyo in November. Led by Shōji Takeo (ex-president of Nihon Aeroplane Manufacturing Company and permanent director of the *Keizai Dōyūkai*), the Tokyo businessmen's delegation consisted of Kikawada Kazutaka, Nagano Shigeo, Iwasa Yoshizani, Imasato Hiroki, Kawai Ryōichi, Yamashita Seiichi, Nakajima Masaki (president of Mitsubishi Steel Manufacturing Company), and Minato Moriatsu (president of Nikkō Research Center). The visit of these two powerful mainstream business teams to China indicated the extent to which Japanese business leaders were prepared to help increase their economic cooperation with China. Given their close financial and political ties with Japan's ruling political elite, they were expected to exert an effective pressure on the Japanese government's policy-making process. At Peking, Chou En-lai, Kuo Mo-jo (honorary president of the China-Japan Friendship Association), Vice-Premier Li Hsien-nien, Minister of Foreign Trade Pai Hsiang-kuo, and other Chinese officials warmly welcomed and entertained Japan's "monopoly capitalists."[130] Emphasizing the possibility of peaceful coexistence between socialism and capitalism, Chou hinted that diplomatic normalization would be accompanied by a substantial expansion of Sino-Japanese economic cooperation.[131] Yet Chou was quick to suggest to his guests the importance of such expansion in light of what he called the three aspects of Japan's "abnormal" economic conditions—lack of natural resources, urban-rural imbalance, and problems of pollution and ecology. When Sumitomo's Hiuga proposed that Japan would invest $400 million in the development of Chinese coal mines and then buy 5 million tons of coal each year, Chou replied that diplomatic normalization was a prerequisite for considering the proposal.[132]

Trade and Diplomacy   The lure of material benefits was intended to solicit and mobilize Japanese businessmen's active role in promoting diplomatic normalization and economic cooperation between Japan and China. However, Chou did not forget to warn them against the danger of connections between Japan's foreign economic expansionism and revived militarism. Trade increased smoothly in 1971, up 9.4% over the previous year, and Furui and Tagawa found it easy to negotiate on memorandum trade in December 1971.[133] The joint communique signed by Furui and Liu Hsi-wen on December 21 reiterated the previous charges against the Satō government, but Foreign Minister Fukuda Takeo, while voicing his hope for intergovernmental talks with the PRC, refused to offer a comment on the communique. So did the LDP.[134] The JSP wholeheartedly supported Furui's and Liu's attack against Satō's China policy, which it said was ignorant of Japanese public opinion.[135] The fact that the twenty-sixth U.N. General Assembly passed the Albanian resolution in October 1971 changed the manner in which the LDP and the Satō cabinet approached the Chinese question; compared with their earlier reactions to the memorandum trade communiques, Satō and his associates became more careful and conciliatory in their remarks on China.

After their journey to China (and especially in the aftermath of the Nixon-Chou joint communique), members of the Tokyo businessmen's delegation pressed upon the LDP a "foward-looking posture" (*maemuki shisei*) toward China, coordinated their activities with the Kansai group, and sponsored various seminars on China. Some of them asked the Japanese government to take a number of specific measures, for example, to normalize diplomatic relations with China under the five principles of peaceful coexistence, to nullify the Yoshida letter, to abrogate the Japan-Taiwan peace treaty, and to invite a Chinese economic delegation to Japan.[136] Even Uemura Kogorō himself admitted at the thirty-third *Keidanren* Congress, with Prime Minister Satō and Minister of International Trade and Industry Tanaka Kakuei present, that it was an unavoidable historical trend for many Japanese businessmen to visit China; and he expressed a hope that the increase in exchange of visitors would eventually lead to diplomatic normalization between China and Japan.[137] Undoubtedly pro-Taiwan LDP dietmen were unhappy with the unrestrained rush of Japanese business leaders toward China, but it was difficult for anyone to stop the rapidly changing mood in Japan. The radical transformation of the *zaikai's* attitude toward China in a matter of less than two years was remarkable evidence of Japanese businessmen's flexibility and adaptability in the pursuit of pragmatic interests. In this respect both major political parties lagged behind the business community; while the LDP was unable to initiate a radical policy change in regard to China, the JSP was bewildered by a suddenly blossoming cooperation between China and Japanese "monopoly capitalists."

Under strong business pressures, the Japanese government took several steps to help improve trade with China during the first half of 1972. It decided to strike out sixty items from the list of COCOM regulations, to allow the use of Export-Import Bank funds in plant exports to China, and to abolish the advance approval system for imports from China.[138] The Ministry of International Trade and Industry set up a new section entrusted with China trade, and considered the elimination of all discriminatory tariffs imposed on imports from China. Compared with the MITI headed by Tanaka Kakuei, however, the Foreign Ministry under Fukuda Takeo appeared to be less willing to improve the circumstances of Sino-Japanese trade.

As far as the general orientation of Japan's major industrial and commercial complexes toward China was concerned, the most critical turning point, perhaps after the Tokyo businessmen's mission to China, took place in 1972, when Mitsubishi Shōji and Mitsui Bussan consulted each other and simultaneously decided to accept Chou's four conditions and to assume direct commercial transactions with China as "friendly companies."[139] Thus by mid-1972 almost all major industries and trading firms, with the notable exceptions of Matsushita Electric, Nihon Electric, Kawasaki Heavy Industry, and Teijin, had succumbed to Chou's trade policy in hopes that they could start or continue to profit from the attractive China market.

In order to expand and solidify their connections with Japanese business circles, the Chinese gradually softened the application of Chou's original four conditions; if a Japanese company announced its formal acceptance of Chou's conditions and pledged to leave the two committees on cooperation and to make no new contracts with Taiwan or South Korea, they were willing to resume trade with it. In defense, on the other hand, both committees, in view of their declining corporate memberships, decided in May 1972 to be exclusively concerned with political matters, leaving economic matters to be dealt with by separate organizations led by *Keidanren* Chairman Uemura Kogorō for South Korea and by *Keidanren* Vice-Chairman Horikoshi Teizō for Taiwan. Moreover, the Chinese concluded a cash deal for purchasing a synthetic textile plant from the Kurashiki Rayon Company; it was the first plant exported to China since 1963. From Hitachi Shipbuilding and Engineering Company with which they had had an abortive contract in 1965, they bought two heavy cargo transport freighters (20,000-ton class), which were expected to ship railroad locomotives, tractor equipment, and mineral ores. Negotiations were underway in June to buy an ethylene plant from Tōyō Engineering Company with the use of Export-Import Bank funds.

At the invitation of the Japanese Association for Promotion of International Trade and the Kurashiki Rayon Company, a ten-member Chinese synthetic textile industrial mission came to Japan in March 1972. It was the first large-scale technical exchange mission since the Cultural Revolution and was to be followed by other Chinese technical delegations in the fields of shipbuilding, automobiles, steel, hydro-electrical power, machinery, and color television. And when Hsiao Hsiang-chien (as chief representative of the Tokyo Liaison Office of the China-Japan Memorandum Trade Office) and Sun Ping-hua (as head of the Shanghai Dance-Drama Troupe) arrived at Tokyo during the Satō-Tanaka transition, they were given a very cordial reception. Hsiao and Sun not only strengthened their old ties with those business leaders (such as Kikawada, Nagano, and Iwasa) who had already visited China, but also cultivated new links with Uemura, Mitsubishi and Mitsui leaders, and other leading Japanese businessmen. In the process China's tangible (and material) ties with Japan's mainstream business community were firmly cemented.

Following President Nixon's announcement of his China trip, more than fifty Japanese business delegations had visited China by August 1972 (see table 29 for the representative examples of these delegations, notable among whom were leaders of the Mitsubishi group.) Although the Mitsubishi and Mitsui groups accepted Chou's four conditions at the same time, the Chinese hurriedly invited the former to Peking first in August, and then the latter in October. Since Mitsubishi's economic involvement in Taiwan and South Korea was deeper than Mitsui's, the Chinese apparently wished to woo the Mitsubishi group prior to Tanaka's China visit so that it would not torpedo his expected concessions on Taiwan.[140] In a three-hour midnight talk with Mitsubishi leaders, Chairman Tajitsu Wataru of the Mitsubishi Bank, President Fujino Chūjirō of Mitsubishi Shōji, and President Koga Shigeichi of Mitsubishi Heavy Industry (and amidst the report that Chairman Kōno Fumihiko of Mitsubishi Heavy Industry was in Taipei to complete a sale of nuclear power plant to Taiwan), Chou En-lai did not even refer to the Taiwan issue, monopoly capitalism, or military procurement.[141] It was a delightful surprise to the Mitsubishi leaders, and Tajitsu Wataru was so impressed by Chou that he later composed a poem praising the Chinese premier's wisdom and achievement.[142]

Thus, even before diplomatic relations were established, China and Japan consolidated a mutually satisfying economic link that had an unmistakable influence over the direction of political relations between their governments. The systematic Chinese cultivation and mobilization of Japanese business leaders, and the latter's willing susceptibility, produced a set of economic and psychological conditions in Japan that no serious political leader could easily afford to ignore. Given its heavy reliance on business circles for campaign funds and political support, the LDP, and its government, had no alternative but to accommodate quickly an irresistible pressure from business circles for diplomatic normalization with the PRC. Hence the politics of "economic diplomacy," coupled with party politics and external stimuli, constituted a firm basis for Tanaka's historic journey to Peking in September 1972.

Upon establishment of diplomatic relations, there emerged a new three-way pattern in Japan's trade policy toward China. According to the Chou-Tanaka joint statement, the Japanese government assumed a central responsibility for arranging intergovernmental economic accords ranging from trade and fishery to aviation and navigation. These proposed governmental agreements were expected to replace the memorandum trade formula, which Okazaki Kaheita and Matsumoto Shunichi, in cooperation with a MITI official but without Furui's or Tagawa's participation, subsequently negotiated in October 1972 to extend for one more year.[143] The memorandum trade liaison missions stationed in Peking and Tokyo were to be replaced by respective government agencies by the end of 1973. The Chinese Embassy in Tokyo absorbed the functions and personnel of the Tokyo Liaison Office of the China-Japan Memorandum Trade Office with Hsiao Hsiang-chien being appointed a counselor at the embassy, the second most important official next to the ambassador. Since the ambassador (Chen Chu) was relatively inexperienced in Japanese affairs, Hsiao assumed a broad range of responsi-

Table 29—Major Japanese Economic Delegations to China
from September 1971 to August 1972

Name of Delegation	Number of Members	Status of Leader(s)	Month of Depature
1971			
Kansai Businessmen's Delegation	20	Saeki[1]	September
Participants at Canton Fair	2,200	—	October
New Japan Steel	8	Vice-president	November
Tokyo Businessmen's Delegation	15	Shōji[2]	November
1972			
Itōchū Shōji	7	President	March
Nippon Yūsen Kaisha	3	President	March
Fertilizer Manufacturers' Group	11	Suzuki[3]	April
Sumitomo Shōji	7	Board chairman	April
Participants at Canton Fair	2,272	—	April
Sumitomo Bank	5	President	June
Dōmen Co.	7	President	June
Sanwa Bank	5	President	June
Marine Transportation Group	25	Sanwa[4]	June
Marubeni-Iida	8	President	June
Nichiro Fisheries Co.	14	President	July
Hitachi Shipbuilding and Eng. Co.	6	Board chairman	July
Taisei Construction Co.	10	President	July
Nagoya Businessmen's Delegation	16	Ishii[5]	July
Bank of Tokyo	6	President	August
Mitsubishi Group	7	Tajitsu[6]	August
Japan Air Lines/All-Nippon Air Line	12	President	August
Japan Economists' Delegation	13	Inayama[7]	August

SOURCE: *Shūkan Asahi*, September 22, 1972, p. 130.
NOTES: 1. Chairman of Osaka Chamber of Commerce
2. Ex-president of Nihon Aeroplane Manufacturing Co.
3. President of Shōwa Electrical Engineering Co.
4. President of Shinwa Marine Transportation Co.
5. Vice-chairman of Nagoya Chamber of Commerce
6. Board chairman of Mitsubishi Bank
7. President of New Japan Steel

bilities in both economic and diplomatic fields. And, performing groundwork for intergovernmental trade negotiations, Minister of International Trade and Industry Nakasone Yasuhiro himself paid a visit to China in January 1973.

The Japanese *zaikai*, particularly Uemura (*Keidanren* chairman), Kikawada (*Dōyūkai* chairman), and Nagano (*Nisshō* chairman), set up in November a Japan-China Economic Association (*Nitchū keizai kyōkai*) to negotiate large-scale contracts with China and to regulate excessive competition among Japanese industries. Akin to the Japan-Soviet Economic

Committee, the association was supported by the Japanese government, which assumed half of its operating costs. It was headed by Inayama Yoshirō (vice-chairman of the *Keidanren*, president of New Japan Steel, and member of Kikawada's *Sangyō mondai kenkyūkai*), who had led an economic delegation to China in August; its vice-chairmanships were allocated to the Kansai region (Nakatsukasa Kiyoshi) and the Chubu region (Tsuchikawa Motoo, chairman of the Nagoya Chamber of Commerce and of the Nagoya Railroad Company). Okazaki Kaheita, head of the Japan-China Memorandum Trade Office, was named its adviser, and Kawai Ryōichi, who had taken part in several memorandum trade negotiations, was its board chairman.[144]

On the other hand, Horikoshi Teizō (*Keidanren* vice-chairman and Kikawada's arch-rival) headed a new pro-Taiwan Interchange Association (*Kōryu kyōkai*) in December 1972. In order to continue the profitable trade relation with Taiwan, the Japanese government adopted a reverse application of the separation of economic and political matters in regard to Taiwan and sponsored the semidiplomatic mission for consular and commercial functions with Taiwan, probably with Peking's prior understanding.

Overshadowed by the direct trade functions of the government and of the *zaikai* were the activities of those several hundred small and medium-sized industries and trading firms that had traded with China through the friendship trade formula. Ironically, they were fearful of being squeezed out of the China market as a direct casualty of diplomatic normalization to which they had made no small contribution. When Sasaki, during his China visit in July 1972, expressed the fear of these companies, which he called the JSP's "allies," Chou En-lai replied that China would never abandon Japan's old, helpful friends.[145] The same assurance was repeated to Furui, Tagawa, Fujiyama, and Hagiwara during 1972; "when one drinks water," said Chou, "he should never forget those who sank the well."[146] He expressed his intentions to respect "old friends," but to welcome "new friends" (big business), provided they promise to support and follow the Chou-Tanaka joint statement that superseded Chou's four conditions and other principles China had imposed on trade with Japan. Yet, as the Japanese government, in cooperation with the Japan-China Economic Association, intended to provide an orderly guidance over the friendship trade method, and China, too, planned to expand direct economic transactions with Japanese industrial groups, the Japanese Association for Promotion of International Trade, which had organized and controlled friendship trade almost exclusively since 1966, was likely to lose its hitherto dominant role in Sino-Japanese trade. Later, in March 1973, China notified the JAPIT that Chou's four conditions are to be removed and that the system for recognizing Japan's "friendship companies" will be abolished. The Chinese quickly learned to their chagrin that the Japanese government was a tougher, but more resourceful trade negotiator than representatives of the friendship and memorandum trade organizations.

As a part of the intergovernmental trade agreements, some of Japan's remaining restrictions (such as COCOM regulations, discriminatory tariffs, ban on imports of meat and silk, and absence of the most-favored-nation status) were expected to be resolved or at least eased. The United States, the leading proponent of the COCOM policy, started negotiations in 1972 to sell to China COCOM-regulated items—the communication facilities in Shanghai installed for Nixon's visit ($2.5 million) and ten Boeing 707s ($150 million), which contained sensitive radar, a jet engine, and other restricted equipment. The U.S. policy was likely to facilitate or require Japan's further relaxation of the COCOM regulations. Moreover, Japanese trade representatives at the Canton fair started to use in October 1972 the *yuan-yen* direct exchange system (1 *yuan* = 135 *yen*) as arranged by the Bank of Tokyo and the Sanwa Bank two months earlier; it helped stabilize Sino-Japanese trade irrespective of the changing value of third-nation currencies. Hence the normalization of diplomatic relations and resultant development in Sino-Japanese rapprochement were to set a favorable stage for further expansion of economic cooperation between Japan and China.

Prospects and Problems   The Chinese expected to utilize Japan's industrial products, advanced technology, and long-term credits for their programs of economic modernization, and Japan was hopeful for a bigger share in the reinvigorated China market and, perhaps, for a direct capital investment in joint development of Chinese natural resources, especially oil and coal. The sheer size of Chinese territory and its more than 800 million people were tremendously attractive to Japanese businessmen. Further, the fact of geographic proximity meant low transportation and communications costs, and facilitated exchanges of goods and persons. Cultural affinity, frequently referred to as *dōbun dōshu* (common script and common race), reduced, though it did not eliminate, cultural and social barriers. Moreover, the Japanese leaders were recently disillusioned with the United States and European Economic Community member-states in economic areas; this disillusionment, coupled with a rising nationalist sentiment, had already prompted them to seek autonomous diplomacy and Asian "consciousness" or "self-identity." Even though they had outgrown their prewar Asian orientations, they appeared to be enormously satisfied with the normalization of their close traditional ties with China.

Nevertheless, the expansion of economic cooperation contained some potential elements of constraint. Whereas Japan was fully integrated within the world economy, the Chinese espoused a basic bias for economic autarky and had a narrow concept of foreign trade, which was considered "a temporary expedient rather than a healthy economic activity."[147] The Maoist notion of economic self-reliance and self-sufficiency, though consid-

Table 30—Comparative Economic Capabilities, 1960-80

Gross National Product
(in billion dollars)

Countries	GNP			Annual Growth Rate (percentage)		Share in Total World GNP (percentage)		
	1960	1970	1980	1960-70	1970-80	1960	1970	1980
Japan	14.9	196.2	956.9	15.9	17.2	3.2	6.4	12.5
China	60.3	79.8	230.1	2.8	11.2	4.3	2.6	3.0
USA	511.4	976.5	1,932.8	6.7	7.1	36.4	32.1	25.3
USSR	159.5	405.9	1,155.4	9.8	11.0	11.4	13.3	15.1
World	1,404.6	3,048.9	7,642.6	8.1	9.6	100.0	100.0	100.0

Foreign Exports
(in billion dollars)

Countries	Volume of Exports			Annual Growth Rate (percentage)		Share in Total World Exports (percentage)		
	1960	1970	1980	1960-70	1970-80	1960	1970	1980
Japan	4.1	19.3	92.2	16.9	16.9	3.2	6.2	10.8
China	1.9	2.1	5.6	1.3	10.2	1.5	0.7	0.5
USA	20.4	42.6	116.6	7.6	10.6	15.9	13.7	13.7
USSR	5.6	12.8	40.0	8.7	12.1	4.3	4.1	4.7
World	128.1	311.3	850.0	9.3	10.6	100.0	100.0	100.0

SOURCE: *Japan Report*, July 16, 1972.

erably relaxed in the early 1970s, ran counter to the radical expansion of foreign economic ties by means of aid, loans, large capital investment, and joint ventures. In general, the Chinese opposed the international division of labor and trade specialization; just as Chou En-lai attacked Moscow's policy of international division of labor toward East European countries, he criticized Nosaka Sanzō's "colonialist" and "imperialist" suggestions that China should supply raw materials to, but buy finished products from, Japan. He stressed the principles of equality, reciprocity, and mutual benefits in international trade.[148] The priority of domestic industries in China was jealously protected by stiff tariff barriers, which resulted in as high as 400% in import taxes.[149] Exports were regarded as a principal means of importing goods needed for the domestic socialist economy, not as a foreign sale qua sale. Only when import requirements were known, the quotas for exports were determined.[150] Sino-Japanese trade was more important to China than to Japan, but the function of foreign trade in the total national economy was less vital for China than for Japan. While Japan depended on foreign trade for 18-20% of its Gross National Product (GNP), Chinese dependency was only about 4-5% in the early 1970s. As table 30 shows, Japan's share in total world exports was expected to grow from 6.2% in 1970 to 10.8% in 1980, while China was to suffer a relative decline in its share, from 0.7% to 0.5%.

These projected differences in their trade performance were closely associated with their comparative economic capabilities. The Japanese economic power, measured only by GNP figures, was about 2.5 times greater than China's in 1970, and, as shown in table 30, this was expected to grow to a 4-to-1 gap by 1980. Further, the operation of China's decentralized regional economic centers, whose national integration was deterred by both underdevelopment of the economic infrastructure and consideration of strategic dispersion, was less than conducive to effective foreign trade.[151] Most important, China's policy of a balanced foreign trade was likely to constrain the pace of trade with Japan. The L-T trade was conceived as a balanced barter system, but table 31 shows that China's deficits increased from 1968 ($100 million) to 1970 ($315 million) and then tapered off somewhat in 1971 ($255 million) and 1972 ($117 million). The improvement of this situation depended on Japan's willingness to buy more Chinese raw materials and on China's ability to produce more exportable goods, such as oil and coal.[152] The Japanese Ministry of International Trade and Industry estimated in 1972 that by 1980 China's total foreign trade would at least reach $15 billion, thus pushing Japan's share up to $3.7 billion (a four-fold increase over 1971).[153] Tomiyama Eikichi, an expert on Sino-Japanese trade relations, made a little more conservative projection; by 1980 the two-way trade turnover would reach only $3.3 billion. He also estimated that while the commodity composition of Japanese exports in 1980 would include steel and other metals (34.5%), machinery (30.0%), and chemicals

Table 31—Trends in Sino-Japanese Trade, 1967-72
(in million dollars)

Year	Japanese Exports	Japanese Imports	Total Volume	Annual Change (percentage)	Percentage of China's Total Foreign Trade
1967	288.3	269.4	557.7	-10.2	14.4
1968	325.4	224.2	549.6	-1.5	15.5
1969	390.8	234.5	625.3	13.8	16.2
1970	568.9	253.8	822.7	31.6	20.1
1971	578.2	323.2	901.4	9.5	19.3
1972	608.9	491.1	1,100.0	22.0	—

SOURCE: *Chūgoku Yoran* [China almanac] (Tokyo: Jiji tsūshinsha, 1973).

(26.1%), Japanese imports would mainly consist of oil, fats, and vegetable matter (32.7%), minerals (12.7%), coal and petroleum (12.2%), and foodstuff (12.1%).[154] There were, however, many Japanese businessmen who cherished a far more optimistic outlook on the China market than these two estimates; for example, the Mitsui Bussan projected in August 1972 that the Chinese were expected to achieve an average annual economic growth rate of 10% for their fourth Five-Year Economic Plan (1971–75) and that if the method of deferred payment were stimulated, the volume of Sino-Japanese trade would reach $5 billion by 1977 and $10 billion by 1980.[155]

The normalization of diplomatic and economic relations between Tokyo and Peking eliminated the overt political role of trade and reduced the intense inter- and intraparty cleavage on China in Japanese politics. The JSP, in general, was proud of its past contributions to the promotion of Sino-Japanese trade, and the LDP wished to continue the smooth growth of Japan's economic transactions with both China and Taiwan. Yet the possible continued political manipulation of Sino-Japanese trade relations still remained. The Chinese never abandoned their conception of foreign trade as an important and effective instrument of their external political strategies; this was amply demonstrated in the Nagasaki flag incident, during the Cultural Revolution, and in the case of Chou's four conditions. If, however, the Chinese, as political and economic realists, were to achieve a conceptual breakthrough in their trade policy toward Japan and to seek Japan's massive economic and technological assisstance in exchange for China's abundant natural resources, the immediate prospect for substantial Sino-Japanese economic cooperation looked brighter than ever before. The expansion of mutually beneficial economic ties was also expected to mitigate other potential sources of tensions and suspicious between Japan and China. In the long run, the extent and direction of their economic cooperation were inevitably contingent upon how much they would need each other for their respective economic interests, and what priorities they would assign to their economic relations among all conceivable policy considerations. Another important determinant of their economic relations would continue to be the changing roles of the United States and the Soviet Union in Japan's and China's domestic and foreign policies.

5
Summary and Conclusions

The preceding discussions suggest that Japan and the People's Republic of China developed a highly unstable, paradoxical relationship from 1949 through 1972. Overshadowed by an unfortunate historical legacy and a profound cold-war cleavage, both equally failed to understand each other's complex domestic and external circumstances and to initiate a bold, innovative, and constructive foreign policy for their mutual benefit. Neither common cultural background nor geographic proximity had any appreciable beneficial effect upon their conceptual deficiencies, political estrangement, or diplomatic confrontation. The Japanese people's sense of guilt toward China diminished as a determinant of Sino-Japanese relations. Even though Japan was never subjected to a direct military threat from China, the ruling Liberal-Democratic Party, and its predecessor, supported until recently the U.S. policy of peripheral military containment against China.

The only tangible contacts Japan and China sustained since 1949 consisted of limited economic cooperation and "people's diplomacy." Various organizations and campaigns for people-to-people diplomacy were extensively utilized to facilitate the exchange of persons, cultural programs, and political messages. Usually spearheaded by opposition political parties —especially the Japan Socialist Party and the Japan Communist Party —these activities challenged the Japanese government's China policy and performed a function for China's unilateral penetrative process into Japan's domestic scene. Economic intercourse often suffered from the disturbing role of political and diplomatic considerations, but it constituted the most substantive aspect of Sino-Japanese relations. The establishment of a nongovernmental trade liaison office provided a semblance of de facto diplomatic exchange between Tokyo and Peking, but this arrangement was not an effective substitute for intergovernmental relations. Ultimately the concerted pro-Peking pressure from Japan's powerful economic circles exerted a decisive impact upon the LDP government's diplomatic normalization with China.

It is also suggested that the predominant pattern of Japanese relations with China moved in a cyclical way, typically starting with a period of intense political friction followed by a period of relative relaxation. Accordingly, the entire twenty-three-year span under consideration can be divided into six major periods: (1) formal estrangement, 1949-52; (2) gradual relaxation, 1953-57; (3) total collapse 1958-62; (4) limited adjustment, 1963-65; (5) extreme hostility, 1966-70; and (6) comprehensive reconciliation, 1971-72. Although these labels for the various periods are not completely descriptive of the details of Sino-Japanese relations and the chronological boundaries of these periods are often overlapped, each tended to characterize a distinct phase in the evolving cycle of Japanese-Chinese relations and to demonstrate a particular impact of Japan's domestic and external conditions upon its China policy.

In the immediate postwar period (1949-52), Japan became a completely docile, inward-oriented, and peace-minded nation under the U.S. military occupation. Japan's conservative political leaders led by Prime Minister Yoshida had no identifiable foreign policy except as an integral adjunct of the U.S. policy and as a limited extension of Japan's moderate economic reconstruction efforts. The PRC, similarly guided by a rigid two-camp international perspective, formed a military alliance with the Soviet Union and fought against the U.S. forces in the Korean War. The resultant international tensions effectively smashed the initial opening of Sino-Japanese economic relations. Moreover, the Americanization of Japanese policy toward China was consummated by the San Francisco peace treaty, U.S.-Japan security treaty, and Japan-Taiwan peace treaty. All these agreements codified a deep political, diplomatic, and strategic estrangement between Japan and China and severely limited the range of Japan's options in dealing with the Chinese questions. And the resumption of Japan's political independence in 1952 did not do much to change this situation immediately because it depended heavily on the U.S. for military protection, diplomatic guidance, and economic assistance. The U.S. policy was therefore a principal determinant of Japanese relations with China during this period.

When conditions in Japan's external environments improved in the mid-1950s with the conclusion of the Korean War, China's adoption of peaceful coexistence, and the initiation of Sino-American diplomatic talks, the Japanese government, particularly under the aegis of Prime Ministers Hatoyama and Ishibashi, helped achieve a gradual relaxation of tensions and suspicions between Japan and China. Economic cooperation expanded with a series of private trade agreements, and both labor unions and business groups maintained an intimate relationship with China. Much progress was made in the area of "people's diplomacy" as Japanese Socialists and Communists encouraged a proliferation of organizations friendly toward China and arranged a variety of activities and programs aimed at promoting Sino-Japanese cooperation and friendship. Still inhibited by external pressure from Washington and Taipei and intraconservative differences, however, the Hatoyama government failed to accept China's secret proposals for bilateral diplomatic negotiations in 1955 and 1956. Newly admitted to the United Nations, Japan remained a reluctant and timid nation, lacking a will to assert itself externally. And the U.S. policy preference continued to be a deterrent against any radical restructuring of Japan's diplomatic relations with China.

The ascendancy of Prime Minister Kishi's staunch anti-Communist policy, which was symbolized by his state visit to Taipei in 1957, coincided with China's leftist swing in its domestic and foreign policies. This coincidence culminated in the Nagasaki flag dispute, which led to a total collapse of all relations between Japan and China in 1958. The Tokyo-Peking conflict was further aggravated by the crisis over the U.S.-Japan security treaty revision. While the PRC assailed the treaty as a militaristic and aggressive collusion between Japan and the United States, the LDP government was determined to carry through the National Diet's ratification of the revised security treaty. At the same time, however, some antimainstream leaders of the LDP, in particular Matsumura Kenzō, cultivated an informal bridge of communications with the PRC. The JSP, too, maintained close links with China during this period, but Eda's jealously autonomous international posture prevented the JSP's drift into China's embrace.

With Prime Minister Ikeda's explicit blessings in the early 1960s, LDP Dietman Matsumura began memorandum trade with China, which required Japanese goods and technology for her economic programs in the aftermath of the unsuccessful Great Leap Forward Movement and because of the Sino-Soviet conflict. The tensions that Kishi had developed with China tapered off somewhat. Trade reached a postwar peak in 1965, and Japan became China's number one trading partner. Exchange of trade liaison offices and resident correspondents was realized, and "people's diplomacy" was greatly revitalized. While the LDP's antimainstream factional leaders enjoyed friendly and cooperative contacts with China during the 1963-65 period, the JSP, due to its factional disagreements and ambivalent external stand, had a less than harmonious relationship with China.

However, the process of Japan's cautious accommodation with China came to an abrupt end in 1966 when the Great Proletarian Cultural Revolution had its adverse spillover effects on Sino-Japanese relations. The escalation of the Vietnam War and of the Sino-Soviet disputes also poisoned the atmosphere of Japan's international environments. The Chinese assumed an increasingly radical foreign policy and imposed a rigid political requirement on their relations with Japan—the requirement that the universal significance of the Cultural Revolution and of Mao Tse-tung's political thought be openly recognized and emulated. A great deal of confusion and division took place in the conduct of "people's diplomacy"; many Japanese organizations, including the JCP, were alienated from China, and others, such as the Japan-China Friendship Association, were split into rival groups. The JSP under Sasaki's leftist leadership initially showed a sympathetic reaction to the Cultural Revolution, but Chairman Katsumata attempted to reorient the party's international position along an autonomous line. The party's inability to achieve interfactional policy consensus on the Cultural Revolution became one of its major domestic political liabilities. Nor was the situation always better for the governing LDP, which manifested a growing policy cleavage on the Chinese questions—especially, between the pro-Taipei Asian Problems Study Group and the pro-Peking Asian-African Problems Study Group. This intraconservative disarray undermined the effectiveness and stability of Prime Minister Satō's foreign policy, but he steadfastly refused to deviate from his pro-Taipei policy as demonstrated in his state visit to Taiwan in 1967.

Although Japan had regained its national self-confidence in economic areas and had achieved a measure of external self-assertion in the 1960s, Satō and his LDP associates envisaged no new foreign policy option, but simply continued to support the U.S. policy of military containment and diplomatic discrimination against the PRC. They also increased Japan's defense expenditure, extended the U.S.-Japan security treaty indefinitely, and expedited the return of the Ryūkyū Islands to Japan's control. Further, Satō publicly identified Japan's security interest with that of Taiwan and South Korea and accelerated Japan's regional political and economic competition with China. Even after the Cultural Revolution, the Chinese stepped up their vehement attack against Satō's alleged revival of Japanese militarism. Hence this period (1966-70) represented the most hostile political confrontation between Tokyo and Peking since the end of World War II. Yet, despite China's stringent political preconditions attached to economic transactions with Japan, trade expanded substantially. An increasing number of Japan's mainstream business leaders and their political sponsors were well prepared to jump on the forthcoming pro-Peking bandwagon, and in the process they exercised a moderating influence on the LDP government's China policy.

The rapid emergence of a pro-Peking mood in Japan during the early 1970s reflected the nearly universal acceptance of China's great-power status and the demonstrable erosion of the U.S. containment policy toward China. Confronted with a serious military threat from the Soviet Union and with the need for economic and diplomatic expansion, the Chinese sought to improve their relations with the United States and Japan. The announcement of President Nixon's visit to Peking, China's representation at the United Nations, and the Kissinger-Le Duc Tho negotiations on the Vietnam War constituted factors in Japan's regional environment favoring détente. This external stimulus directly challenged the LDP government's outdated policy toward China and provoked a dynamic reactive process in Japan's

SUMMARY AND CONCLUSIONS   189

political and economic circles. The JSP and other opposition political parties joined some liberal members of the LDP and major business groups in demanding Japan's diplomatic normalization with China. This demand was buttressed by Japan's manifest public opinion and mass movements. In order to accommodate these irresistible domestic pressures and to readjust Japan's foreign policy to the changing global and regional reality, Prime Minister Tanaka did not have any other viable policy option but to establish diplomatic relations with the PRC.

Much of this tortuous evolution of Japanese-Chinese relations took place in the context of Japanese party politics, especially the LDP-JSP competition. The way in which both major political parties pursued their respective approaches toward China was determined by the combined effects of Japan's external environments, domestic situations, and each party's internal conditions. The relative importance of these determinants varied from the LDP to the JSP and from one issue to another. The LDP's (and therefore the Japanese government's) policy toward China was most strongly and directly influenced by Japan's external environments, notably the shifting U.S. position on Asia; the party's internal conditions were more important than its consideration of Japan's domestic factors. As to the JSP's China policy, however, its internal conditions had a greater influence than Japan's foreign setting, but, as with the LDP, Japan's domestic conditions were the least important determinant of the JSP's China policy.

In general, therefore, both major political parties were more concerned with and more responsive to Japan's external stimuli than to such domestic inputs as public opinion, interest articulation, electoral processes, parliamentary maneuvers, and intrabureaucratic dynamics. When, however, the shift in Japan's external environments dramatically changed the attitudes and aspirations of Japanese political and economic forces to a degree intolerable to each party, it was compelled to heed and accommodate domestic inputs. The dominant influence on Japan of external factors was more evident in ideological, political, strategic, and diplomatic aspects of each party's China policy than in economic and cultural aspects. The degree of the LDP's internal policy cohesion vis-a-vis China was strong on ideological and political issues, less so on strategic and economic matters, and weak on diplomatic problems. The exact reverse of this relationship was found in the JSP's policy toward China. Yet the LDP considered it easier than did the JSP to transcend the ideological aspect of its China policy, despite a definite decline in ideological determination of the JSP's policy toward China in recent years.

There appeared no substantive difference between the LDP and the JSP in their usual preferences for a consensual and collectivist decision-making process on foreign affairs; this was particularly so in their high-level policy-making organs—such as the cabinet, the LDP's Policy Affairs Research

Council and Executive Council, and the JSP's Central Executive Committee. The prevailing desire to avoid nonconsensual decisions, together with the established system of factional checks and balances, tended to perpetuate a routine organizational response to foreign stimuli by default, or to result in policy *immobilisme*. It does not necessarily follow that each decisional participant had veto power on all issues, for emphasis on the appearance of consensus easily stifled the dissenting voice and disguised reluctant acquiescence. All these tendencies rendered both major parties equally inefficient and ambiguous in dealing with the Chinese questions.

The principle of consensual decision was violated in some unusual circumstances, as exemplified by Prime Minister Satō's controversial decision to cosponsor the U.N. resolutions against China in 1971 and by JSP Secretary-General Asanuma's unilateral decision to identify U.S. imperialism as a common enemy of the Japanese and Chinese peoples in 1959. Furthermore, majority decisions on foreign affairs were sometimes made in the JSP's national congresses, though they were extremely rare in the LDP's national conferences. While the sources of decisions in both major parties were more pluralistic and competitive than in the JCP, the decision-making process in the LDP was far more elitist than in the JSP in terms of the number of persons who were involved in making decisions.

Just as the LDP and the JSP attempted to use the Chinese issues as a central instrument for their partisan political interests, these issues were also a convenient and effective vehicle for interfactional contests in both parties. Even though this factional infighting endangered the unity and discipline of both parties in their respective relations with China, the intensity and consequences of socialist disagreements on China seemed to be much more profound and enduring than in the conservative case.

However, each of the two major parties (and their factional and individual constituents) performed an important role in promoting Sino-Japanese relations in a manner appropriate to its political status and resources. Since the LDP, as a ruling party, virtually monopolized Japan's foreign-policy making authority in a way conducive to its partisan interests and used a variety of governmental institutions and resources for accommodating factional differences on China, it could afford to be more tolerant and flexible than the JSP in its approaches toward China. Indeed, the LDP and its government demonstrated a high degree of self-restraint in averting a tit-for-tat strategy against the excesses of China's public vituperation. Compared with the JSP, less emphasis on the LDP's ideological commitment than on its pragmatic pursuit enabled conservative political leaders to have a wider range of foreign-policy options. The peaceful coexistence between pro-Peking and pro-Taipei spokesmen within the LDP was a useful device for maintaining its linkages with both of China's rival governments. The availability of these disparate informal foreign linkages compensated for the rigidity of the LDP's formal policy and allowed the articulation of various Japanese interests and aspirations concerning China. This amounted to an effective division of responsibilities for the governing party's relations with foreign entities on both sides of the China question. Even when a number of influential pro-Peking LDP dietmen openly opposed and violated the party's official policy on China, their activities and utterances were not only tolerated, but also accorded a varying degree of the LDP government's tacit understanding. Under the surface of the LDP's stagnant and unimaginative policy toward China, some conservative factions and individual leaders embarked on a series of innovative programs toward China and assumed a catalytic or instrumental function in improving Tokyo-Peking relations. After all it was these forward-looking conservative leaders who sponsored the most tangible personal and economic ties with China and ultimately helped pave the way for diplomatic normalization. This "two China" option was even unthinkable for the JSP.

Nevertheless, it is incorrect to conclude that the JSP totally failed to affect the direction of Japanese relations with China. Although the immediate outcome of its official pronouncements and activities did not have an appreciable impact on Japan's foreign policy, the JSP advanced some proposals and recommendations aimed at normalizing Sino-Japanese diplomatic and economic relations. In the absence of diplomatic relations, it established an informal bridge of communications with China. It also constantly attacked the inadequacy of the LDP's China policy and kept this issue alive before the Japanese public until 1972. The fact that successive LDP governments were unable to improve Japan's relations with the PRC was often used by the JSP for its anti-LDP campaign. Since the late 1960s when both the LDP government and the JCP were almost irrevocably alienated from Peking, the JSP enjoyed the unique status of providing a mutually reinforcing organizational link with the PRC. In particular, the JSP or its members conducted various forms of "people's diplomacy"; for example, the official party missions signed five joint statements with their Chinese counterparts between April 1957 and November 1970. In spite of its internal disagreements, the JSP performed the role of functionally specific interest articulation and political representation for interest groups desiring better Sino-Japanese relations, and organized a nationwide mass movement to demand diplomatic rapprochement between Tokyo and Peking.

When the Tanaka-Chou statement was declared a common, basic guideline for Japanese-Chinese relations, the immediate political saliency of diplomatic conflict between Japan and China was reduced, if not eliminated. The Taiwan issue was at least temporarily defused, but it still contained an element of potential irritation to Tokyo-Peking relations. A variety of intergovernmental exchanges and agreements were promptly instituted or negotiated. Embassies, consulates, trade missions, and cultural delegations were sent by each side, and negotiations on trade, civil aviation, and maritime transportation were underway. Hence a new sense of shared accomplishments and commitments was prevalent both in Japan and in China. They tended to bend backward in their efforts not to hurt each other's feelings and interests. The joint statement also committed both governments to conclude a comprehensive treaty of peace and friendship. All these activities and promises were further expected not only to stimulate their cooperative relations, especially in the economic field, but also to lessen Japan's dependence on the postwar San Francisco system and to enhance its international posture commensurate with its economic capabilities.

The search for Japan's diplomatic self-identity as symbolized by its intergovernmental negotiations with China is a basically nationalistic imperative, but it is yet uncertain whether this consideration will aid or hinder the smooth expansion of Sino-Japanese cooperation in the long run. The recent record of Sino-Japanese relations suggests that diplomatic normalization may not be a sufficient, though perhaps necessary, condition for mutually acceptable solutions of all their substantive problems, actual and potential, for both Japan and China continue to have their bitter historical legacy, ambivalent attitudes, and irreconcilable systems. The relationship between a pluralistic and insular political system and an extremely authoritarian and continental political system is perhaps inherently asymmetrical and unstable. While the Chinese may still have a traditional sense of cultural superiority over Japan and a nightmarish memory of Japan's brutal aggression and exploitation, the Japanese espouse a confused and sometimes schizophrenic attitude toward China—a mixture of admiration for China's achievements, fear of its military power, and contempt for its economic underdevelopment. Further, a number of sensitive issues, such as Japan's de facto relations with Taiwan, disputes over the Senkaku Islands and over the continental shelf, and competition over Korea and Southeast Asia, constitute potential causes of Sino-Japanese conflict.

The prospects for Japanese relations with China also depend upon how much both countries value each other in the hierarchy of their respective foreign policy priorities, especially, in regard to the United States and the Soviet Union. Our study does not support the simplistic prediction that Japan and China are about to dominate East Asia's emerging regional political subsystem or to form a political or military united front against the United States or the Soviet Union. While China's preoccupation with the Soviet military threat may further precipitate its pursuit of political or military accords with Japan, this move may be constrained by Japan's own desire to preserve its close security ties with the United States and to pursue an equidistant policy toward Moscow and Peking. A series of recent global and regional developments, which range from the erosion of a loose bipolar international system and the intensification of Sino-Soviet disputes to

China's rapprochement with the United States and Japan, suggest that the immediate future of Sino-Japanese relations will be inevitably intertwined with the changing policies of the United States and the Soviet Union. The intervening influence of these two super-powers in Asia may be somewhat counterbalanced by the promise of substantial economic cooperation between Japan and China, but this would require China's conceptual breakthrough in accepting Japanese capital and technology for massive collaborative projects.

Of particular importance to the future of Sino-Japanese relations are potential security conflicts and traditional regional rivalries that may easily upset or undo the edifice of diplomatic and economic cooperation between Japan and China. In fact, the economic-military disparity is a principal source of Japan's foreign-policy dilemma. So long as Japan remains a weak military power and requires U.S. nuclear protection, it can hardly achieve a genuinely independent status of international political influence. If, however, it decides to undertake a full-scale military build-up, complete with nuclear development, correspondent to its economic power, the result would greatly arouse China's apprehension about Japanese militarism and would have a highly destabilizing effect on Japan's domestic and external environments. And if Japan and/or China are directly or indirectly drawn into a regional military conflict, such as another Korean War, both would be forced to reappraise their bilateral relations. Especially as Japan and China offer opposing models of political and economic development to their neighbors, their regional competition may be intensified. And still unclear is Japan's own orientation as to what role or status it wishes to achieve in relation to China and in regional and global political arenas.

Moreover, neither Japan nor China are completely devoid of some unsettling domestic and external problems. Whereas China may undergo a seriously disturbing process of succession struggles, factional alignments, policy cleavage, or armed conflicts with the Soviet Union, the LDP government is faced with such gnawing problems as interparty competition, intraparty bickering, energy crisis, consumer revolts, and national security. The LDP's parliamentary majority and voting cohesion are not to be taken for granted; not is the JSP's status as the largest opposition force in the National Diet preordained. Both parties are not intrinsically immune to the possibilities of internal disintegration or of erosive penetration by other domestic political forces. Any major change in the LDP's governmental responsibilities, policy commitments, or interfactional alliances may disrupt the fragile domestic political foundation of Japan's conciliatory policy toward China. If the LDP's hegemonic role is replaced by a coalition government, the JSP, irrespective of its own coalition participation, is likely to exert a greater influence over Japan's China policy than it does now. Added to this uncertainty of interparty dynamics is each political party's

diminishing freedom from Japan's domestic environments, which are growing more attuned to the trends of regional and global politics. The Japanese
people are continuously internationalized, and political and bureaucratic
institutions now tend to transcend organizational parochialism. Debates on
Japan's foreign and security policies are abundant, and electoral decisions
based on issues and policies loom larger, at least in urban districts. Most
important, economic, cultural, and other interest groups are extremely
sensitive and adaptive to their foreign opportunities and challenges. Hence
the pattern of domestic-foreign linkages in Japan is expected to be increasingly close and complex.

No doubt Japan and China are close in a cultural, racial, and geographic
sense, but they are still far apart in terms of their political preferences,
economic capabilities, and strategic preparedness. On the diplomatic level
both governments remain correct and cordial, but they are not always
intimate and harmonious either between themselves or in relation to other
countries. They also attempt to expand and strengthen their economic ties,
and this material interdependency is likely to constitute the most useful and
significant basis for Sino-Japanese cooperation. Much bilateral and regional
benefit can be attained from their cooperation rather than from their
conflict. However, there is no empirical evidence to propose that either
cooperation or conflict alone is inherent in the cumulative structure of
Japanese policy toward China; rather, the structure consists of both
cooperative and conflictive aspects. While the symbols of ideological and
diplomatic confrontations characterized much of Sino-Japanese relationships in the postwar period up until 1972, the balance of more pragmatic
considerations—such as economic benefits, strategic requirements, and
regional influence—is likely to dominate the future of Tokyo-Peking
relations. Yet, as the present cycle of Japan's friendly and cooperative policy
toward China is far from solidified and institutionalized, and is constantly
subject to the multiple pressures from Japan's and China's changing
domestic and external environments, the direction and substance of Japanese-Chinese relations still remain in a state of flux. If our study is any
indication, the Chinese question will continue to be a crucial element of
Japan's domestic politics and foreign policies.

Appendix 1

Letter from Prime Minister
Yoshida Shigeru to John Foster Dulles,
December 24, 1951*

Dear Ambassador Dulles:

While the Japanese Peace Treaty and the U.S.-Japan Security Treaty were being debated in the House of Representatives and the House of Councillors of the Diet, a number of questions were put and statements made relative to Japan's future policy toward China. Some of the statements, separated from their context and background, gave rise to misapprehensions which I should like to clear up.

The Japanese Government desires ultimately to have a full measure of political peace and commercial intercourse with China which is Japan's close neighbor.

At the present time it is, we hope, possible to develop that kind of relationship with the National Government of the Republic of China, which has the seat, voice and vote of China in the United Nations, which exercises actual governmental authority over certain territory, and which maintains diplomatic relations with most of the members of the United Nations. To that end my Government on November 17, 1951, established a Japanese Government Overseas Agency in Formosa, with the consent of the National Government of China. This is the highest form of relationship with other countries which is now permitted to Japan, pending the coming into force of the multilateral Treaty of Peace. The Japanese Government Overseas Agency in Formosa is important in its personnel, reflecting the importance which my Government attaches to relations with the National Government of the Republic of China. My Government is prepared as soon as legally possible to conclude with the National Government of China, if that

*Department of State Bulletin, January 28, 1952, p. 120.

195

Government so desires, a Treaty which will reestablish normal relations between the two Governments in conformity with the principles set out in the multilateral Treaty of Peace. The terms of such bilateral treaty shall, in respect of the Republic of China, be applicable to all territories which are now, or which may hereafter be, under the control of the National Government of the Republic of China. We will promptly explore this subject with the National Government of China.

As regards the Chinese Communist regime, that regime stands actually condemned by the United Nations of being an aggressor and in consequence, the United Nations has recommended certain measures against that regime, in which Japan is now concurring and expects to continue to concur when the multilateral Treaty of Peace comes into force pursuant to the provisions of Article 5 (a) (iii), whereby Japan has undertaken "to give the United Nations every assistance in any action it takes in accordance with the Charter and to refrain from giving assistance to any State against which the United Nations may take preventive or enforcement action." Furthermore, the Sino-Soviet Treaty of Friendship, Alliance and Mutual Assistance concluded in Moscow in 1950 is virtually a military alliance aimed against Japan. In fact there are many reasons to believe that the Communist regime in China is backing the Japan Communist Party in its program of seeking violently to overthrow the constitutional system and the present Government of Japan. In view of these considerations, I can assure you that the Japanese Government has no intention to conclude a bilateral Treaty with the Communist regime of China.

Yours sincerely,
Yoshida Shigeru

Appendix 2

Minutes on Talks Between
Dietman Matsumura Kenzō and Premier Chou En-lai,
September 19, 1962*

Premier Chou En-lai and Vice-Premier Chen Yi held friendly and frank discussions with Matsumura Kenzō, adviser to the Liberal-Democratic Party, for three days on September 16, 17, and 19, 1962. The Chinese side reiterated its determination to uphold the three political principles, the three principles for trade, and the principle of inseparability of political and economic matters, and declared that these principles would continue to be effective.

Both sides expressed their desire to further promote and expand trade between Japan and China. Both sides also agreed that by adopting a gradual and cumulative method, they should attempt to normalize political and economic relations between the two countries.

---

*My translation from *Jih-pen wen-ti wen-chien-hui-pien* [Collected documents on problems of Japan], vol. 4, p. 16.

Appendix 3

Communique on Talks Between Chinese and Japanese Representatives of Memorandum Trade Offices, April 4, 1969*

The Chinese representatives of the China-Japan Memorandum Trade Office and the Japanese representatives of the Japan-China Memorandum Trade Office held talks in Peking between February 22 and April 4, 1969. Both sides exchanged frank views on the present relations between China and Japan and other questions of common interest.

Both sides reviewed Sino-Japanese relations since the issuing of the communique on the talks between the two sides held in 1968.

The Chinese side points out: U.S. imperialism and the Satō government of Japan which tails after it have stubbornly pursued a policy of hostility towards China and have placed obstacles in the relations between China and Japan, including the relations between us.

The Japanese side frankly admits that the causes for the worsening of the relations between Japan and China lie with the Japanese Government. In view of its anxiety about the present situation and from the angle of serious self-examination, the Japanese side expresses its determination to make positive efforts to remove these obstacles and promote the normal development of relations between Japan and China.

Both sides reaffirm that the three political principles confirmed by both sides in 1968, (One, not to pursue a policy of hostility towards China; two, not to participate in any conspiracy to create "two Chinas"; and three, not to obstruct the restoration of normal relations between China and Japan) and the principle that politics and economics are inseparable must be abided by in the relations between China and Japan, and are also the political basis for our relations. Both sides express the determination to continue to make

*Peking Review, April 11, 1969, pp. 38–39.

efforts to abide by the above-mentioned principles and safeguard this political basis.

The Chinese side sternly condemns the policy of "separating politics from economics" which the Satō government stubbornly clings to in Sino-Japanese relations. That is a policy of hostility towards China and the Chinese people resolutely oppose it.

The Japanese side holds that the policy of "separating politics from economics" adopted by the Japanese Government in relations between Japan and China runs counter to the three political principles and the principle that politics and economics are inseparable. This policy constitutes a great obstacle hampering the development of relations between the two countries. It is therefore imperative to urge the Japanese Government to immediately change this policy.

The Chinese side strongly denounces the Satō government for stepping up its efforts to follow U.S. imperialism, for participating in the conspiracy to create "two Chinas" and for barefacedly adopting a policy of hostility towards China.

The Chinese side reiterates that to liberate Taiwan is China's internal affair and that the Chinese people will definitely liberate Taiwan. The so-called peace treaty concluded by the Japanese Government with the Chiang Kai-shek gang, which has long been rejected by the Chinese people, is hostile to the Chinese people and is illegal and is resolutely opposed by the Chinese people.

The Japanese side agrees with the just stand of the Chinese side. It explicitly states that the Government of the People's Republic of China is the only legitimate government representing the Chinese people, that Taiwan Province is an inseparable part of China's territory, that this must be the basis for understanding the promotion of the normalization of diplomatic relations between Japan and China, and that it opposes the conspiracy of creating "two Chinas" in any form.

The Chinese side sternly condemns the Satō government for redoubling its efforts in following the U.S. imperialist policy of aggression in Asia and for perpetuating the Japan-U.S. "security treaty" against the wishes of the Japanese people.

The Chinese side also points out that this treaty is for oppressing the Japanese people and is an aggressive military alliance hostile to China and the Asian people. It not only gravely threatens peace in Asia and throughout the world, but will inevitably bring grave calamities to the Japanese people. The Chinese people resolutely oppose the Japan-U.S. military alliance treaty.

The Japanese side expresses its understanding of the stand of the Chinese side and duly takes cognizance of the fact that the Japan-U.S. "security treaty" is a threat to China and to the people of the Asian countries, and that it constitutes a serious obstacle to relations between Japan and China. The Japanese side also expresses the determination to take an independent stand and work actively to prevent Japan from getting involved in a war of aggression and to remove this great restriction on its sovereignty.

Both sides hold that China and Japan are close neighbors and that a traditional friendship exists between the two peoples. The promotion of friendly relations between the two peoples and normalization of the relations between the two countries not only conforms to the common aspirations of the people of China and Japan, but is beneficial to preserving peace in Asia and the whole world.

Both sides reached agreement on memorandum trade matters for 1969.

Appendix 4

Joint Statement of the Delegation of the Japan Socialist Party and the China-Japan Friendship Association, November 1, 1970*

The Fifth Delegation of the Japan Socialist Party to China with Narita Tomomi, Chairman of the Central Executive Committee of the Japan Socialist Party, as its leader and Ishibashi Masashi, Member of the Central Executive Committee and Director of the International Affairs Bureau of the Japan Socialist Party, as its deputy leader, is paying a friendly visit to the People's Republic of China from October 22 to November 3, 1970.

The Delegation of the Japan Socialist Party is composed of the above-mentioned leader and deputy leader of the delegation; and Sōga Yūji, Member of the Central Executive Committee and Director of the Organization Bureau; Takazawa Torao, Member of the Central Executive Committee and Director of the Education and Publicity Bureau; Itō Shigeru, Member of the Central Executive Committee and Director of the Bureau of National Movement; and Tatebayashi Chisatō, Secretary of the International Affairs Bureau.

During the stay of the Delegation of the Japan Socialist Party in China, Chou En-lai, Premier of the State Council of the People's Republic of China, and Kuo Mo-jo, Vice-Chairman of the Standing Committee of the National People's Congress, met all the members of the delegation and had a long and friendly talk with them in an atmosphere of amity. The delegation visited a factory, a people's commune, schools and other places and was given a warm welcome by the Chinese people.

During its visit, the Delegation of the Japan Socialist Party held talks with the Delegation of the China-Japan Friendship Association with Kuo Mo-jo as its leader and Wang Kuo-chuan as its deputy leader. Both sides

Peking Review, November 6, 1970, pp. 14–16.

explained their respective stands and viewpoints and exchanged views in the spirit of seeking major common ground while reserving minor differences and deepened their mutual understanding.

Also taking part in the talks on the Chinese side were: members of the Delegation of the China-Japan Friendship Association Hsü Ming, Yen Fu, Wang Hsiao-yün, Lin Po and Ting Min.

During the talks, the Delegation of the Japan Socialist Party expressed its deep respect for the Chinese people for victoriously carrying out the Great Proletarian Cultural Revolution, deciding to convene the Fourth National People's Congress at an appropriate time and, rallying closely around the Central Committee of the Communist Party of China with Chairman Mao Tse-tung as its leader and Vice-Chairman Lin Piao as its deputy leader, struggling to fulfill all the fighting tasks set by the Ninth National Congress of the Communist Party of China and to score still greater victories in the socialist revolution and socialist construction; and for China for supporting the people of various countries of the world in their national liberation movements and revolutionary struggles, powerfully opposing U.S. imperialism and old and new colonialism and carrying out diplomatic activities in line with Five Principles of Peaceful Coexistence.

The Chinese side firmly supports the broad masses of the Japanese people in their heroic struggle against U.S. imperialism and the revival of Japanese militarism by the U.S. and Japanese reactionaries. It expresses heartfelt respect to the great Japanese people for waging struggles for the nullification of the Japan-U.S. "security treaty," the dismantlement of U.S. military bases, and the immediate, unconditional and complete recovery of Okinawa, for opposing nuclear armament of Japan and smashing the new Japan-U.S. military alliance and for winning independence, democracy, peace, and neutrality for Japan. It sincerely wishes them constant new victories.

The Chinese side admires the contributions which the Japan Socialist Party, following and carrying forward the "Asanuma spirit," has made together with the masses of the Japanese people, in opposing U.S. imperialism and the revival of Japanese militarism by the U.S. and Japanese reactionaries, in upholding a peaceful constitution and in striving for complete national independence and neutrality. It expresses thanks to the Japan Socialist Party for its just stand in consistently opposing the varied machinations engineered by the U.S. and Japanese reactionaries to create "two Chinas." The Chinese people are determined to liberate Taiwan!

The two sides exchanged views on the world situation, particularly the situation in Asia and the corresponding fighting tasks of the people of Asian countries, and on the relations of friendship and unity between the Chinese and Japanese people.

Both sides unanimously hold: In the twenty-five years since the Second World War, U.S. imperialism has ceaselessly pushed its policies of aggression and war in the world while the people of various countries have ceaselessly used revolutionary wars and revolutionary struggles to defeat the U.S. aggressors. The situation is turning ever more favorable for the revolutionary people to the disadvantage of U.S. imperialism and all its running dogs. A new upsurge in the struggle against U.S. imperialism is now emerging throughout the world. Superpowers, which are pushing power politics, bullying the weak, throwing their weight about and trying to dominate the destiny of the world, are meeting with opposition by more and more countries and becoming ever more isolated before the people of the world.

To save itself from its doom, U.S. imperialism has even more obstinately stuck to its policies of aggression and war. In Asia in particular, it has extended the war of aggression against Viet Nam to Laos and Cambodia, continued its forcible occupation of China's sacred territory Taiwan Province, continued its occupation of south Korea and unceasingly carried out military provocations against the People's Republic of China and the Democratic People's Republic of Korea. Moreover, it has dished up the cunning, treacherous "Nixon doctrine" in a vain attempt to use Asians to fight Asians.

The Japanese reactionary forces, in active collaboration with the "Nixon doctrine," have stood in the van of the puppet cliques of U.S. imperialism such as the Pak Jung Hi, Chiang Kai-shek, Nguyen Van Thieu and Lon Nol puppet cliques in suppressing the forces of socialism, national independence and peace in Asia. They are trying to act as an advance force in the aggression against the people of Asian countries and thereby seize a Japanese sphere of influence in Asia. The communique on the talks between Satō and Nixon released in November of last year and the "automatic extension" of the Japan-U.S. "security treaty" are a naked exposure of this wild ambition. Ignoring the revival of Japanese militarism and the danger it entails and befriending the Japanese reactionaries, mean encouraging Japanese militarism to carry out expansionist activities abroad and serving the U.S. imperialist policies of aggression and war.

Both sides hold: The famous and penetrating statement that "U.S. imperialism is the common enemy of the Japanese and Chinese people" made by Asanuma Inejirō, leader of the Second Delegation of the Japan Socialist Party to China, has become increasingly important as the situation develops. U.S. imperialism is the most ferocious common enemy of the people all over the world. The collusion of U.S. imperialism with Japanese militarism has brought an imminent danger before the people of Asian countries. The Delegation of the Japan Socialist Party agrees with and supports Chairman Mao Tse-tung's solemn statement "People of the World, Unite and Defeat the U.S. Aggressors and All Their Running Dogs!" published on May 20, and expresses its determination to carry out independently the most effective struggle in Japan in accordance with its own stand and conditions. Both sides hold: The people throughout the world must unite and defeat the U.S. aggressors and all their running dogs. The people of Asian countries, particularly the people of Japan, China, Korea and the three countries of Indo-China, must unite and defeat U.S. imperialism and Japanese militarism. Both sides express resolute solidarity with the all-round support for the Korean people in their just struggle against U.S. imperialist aggression and for the peaceful unification of the fatherland, the Vietnamese, Cambodian and Laotian people in their heroic struggle against U.S. aggression and for national salvation, and the National United Front of Kampuchea and the Royal Government of the National Union of Cambodia led by Samdech Norodom Sihanouk, Head of State of Cambodia. U.S. imperialism must get out of all the places it has invaded!

Both sides unanimously express the determination to struggle against nuclear war and for complete prohibition and thorough destruction of nuclear weapons. The Delegation of the Japan Socialist Party supports the stand of China that at no time and in no circumstances shall China be the first to use nuclear weapons and China's proposal that a summit conference of all the countries of the world, big and small, be convened to sign an agreement on not using nuclear weapons. The Chinese side expresses thanks for this.

Both sides point out: The movement for Japan-China friendship and restoration of diplomatic relations between Japan and China is a component of the Japanese people's struggle against U.S. imperialism and the revival of Japanese militarism by the U.S. and Japanese reactionaries. The Delegation of the Japan Socialist Party expresses willingness to make effort to unite on a broad scale with all the forces in Japan that are truly for Japan-China friendship and the restoration of diplomatic relations between Japan and China and determination to strengthen this movement, and at the same time raises the following four principles for carrying out the movement:

1. Unite with the anti-imperialist forces of the people of Asian countries to oppose U.S. imperialism and the revival of Japanese militarism and strive for the nullification of the Japan-U.S. "security treaty";

2. Fight against all policies of hostility towards China, adhere to the stand of one China and demand the nullification of "Japan-Chiang Kai-shek treaty," and, in accordance with the Five Principles of Peaceful Coexistence and the three political principles, struggle for the restoration of diplomatic relations between Japan and China;

3. In adherence to the stand of true friendship between Japan and China and that politics and economy are inseparable, develop exchanges in trade, culture, friendly relations and other fields between the people of Japan and China;

4. Rally on a broad scale forces in Japan which genuinely desire friendship between Japan and China and the restoration of diplomatic relations between Japan and China and organize a united front.

The Chinese side expresses its appreciation of the abovementioned stand of the Delegation of the Japan Socialist Party and reaffirms that the Chinese side will, as always, warmly support all efforts beneficial to opposing the U.S.-Japanese reactionaries and their followers, to the development of friendship between China and Japan and the restoration of diplomatic relations between China and Japan, and to the promotion of the unity and alliance of forces genuinely and earnestly for friendship between China and Japan.

Both sides unanimously express the conviction: Utterly unlike in the thirties, the people of Japan, China and other Asian countries, who have been tempered in the struggle against imperialism and have awakened, struggling in unity, can surely defeat U.S. imperialism and all its running dogs. The struggle of the people of various countries for independence, peace, democracy and socialism will certainly triumph.

Both sides express satisfaction at the result of the visit to China of the Delegation of the Japan Socialist Party. They hold that this visit is greatly beneficial to the strengthening of the struggle of the people of China and Japan against U.S. imperialism and its collaborator, running dogs and accomplices. Both sides will make further efforts to promote the militant friendship between the people of China and Japan.

(signed), Kuo Mo-jo, leader
(signed) Wang Kuo-chuan, deputy leader
of the Delegation of the China-Japan Friendship Association

(signed) Narita Tomomi, leader
(signed) Ishibashi Masashi, deputy leader
of the Fifth Delegation of the Japan Socialist Party to China

Appendix 5

Joint Statement of the Delegation of the Japanese Dietmen's League for Promoting Restoration of Japan-China Diplomatic Relations and the China-Japan Friendship Association, October 2, 1971*

At the invitation of the China-Japan Friendship Association of China, the Delegation to China of the Japanese Dietmen's League for Promoting Restoration of Japan-China Diplomatic Relations ("Dietmen's League for Japan-China Relations," for short) paid a friendly visit to the People's Republic of China from September 17 to October 4, 1971. The delegation attended the celebrations of the twenty-second anniversary of the founding of the People's Republic of China and visited factories, people's communes, schools and hospitals. It was accorded a warm welcome and cordial hospitality by the Chinese people.

Chou En-lai, Premier of the State Council, and Kuo Mo-jo, Vice-Chairman of the Standing Committee of the National People's Congress, of the People's Republic of China, met all the members of the delegation and had a friendly conversation with them.

The Delegation of the "Dietmen's League for Japan-China Relations" and the Delegation of the China-Japan Friendship Association held friendly, earnest and frank talks on questions of common concern.

The two sides unanimously affirm that the basic principles for the restoration of Japan-China diplomatic relations are:

1. There is only one China, that is, the People's Republic of China. The Government of the People's Republic of China is the sole legal government representing the Chinese people. "Two Chinas," "one China, one Taiwan,"

*Peking Review, October 8, 1971, pp. 14–15.

"one China, two governments," and other such absurdities must be firmly opposed.

2. Taiwan Province is an inalienable part of the territory of the People's Republic of China. The assertion that "the title to Taiwan remains to be settled" and the scheme of creating "an independent Taiwan" hatched by the U.S. and Japanese reactionaries must be strongly opposed. The Taiwan question is China's internal affair and brooks no interference by any foreign country.

3. The so-called Japan-Chiang Treaty was signed after the founding of the People's Republic of China and therefore is illegal and invalid and should be abrogated.

4. It is imperative to restore all the lawful rights of the People's Republic of China in all the organs of the United Nations, including the seat in the Security Council as a permanent member, and expel the representatives of the Chiang Kai-shek clique from the United Nations.

The Japanese side expresses the view that the "Dietmen's League for Japan-China Relations" is a supraparty organization of Diet members aimed at restoring diplomatic relations between Japan and China. In order to restore diplomatic relations between Japan and China at the earliest possible date, it is determined to exert all efforts for the adoption of the abovementioned basic principles as resolutions of the Japanese Diet, and urge the Japanese Government to accept these principles and, on this basis, to negotiate with the Government of the People's Republic of China so as to end the state of war between Japan and China, restore diplomatic relations and conclude a peace treaty.

The Chinese side holds that the abovestated stand of the "Detmen's League for Japan-China Relations" and the positive efforts it has made to promote Japanese-Chinese friendship and restore diplomatic relations between Japan and China correspond to the aspirations and interests of the people of China and Japan, and expresses its appreciation and support for them.

Both sides are of the opinion that all countries, big or small, should be equal. The internal affairs of each country should be settled by the people of that country themselves. The power politics pushed by the two superpowers with armed force at their back and their policy of armed intervention are bound to fail. They must withdraw their troops stationed in foreign countries and dismantle their military bases abroad. The United States must withdraw all its armed forces and military installations from Indochina and other areas in the Far East.

The Chinese side points out that the revival of Japanese militarism has already become an actual threat to the people of the various countries in Asia. However, the Japanese people and the people of other Asian countries will absolutely not allow Japanese militarism to take the road of aggression again. It is the Japanese people who determine the destiny of Japan. The Japanese people will certainly realize their aspirations to establish an independent, democratic, peaceful, neutral and prosperous new Japan.

The Japanese side holds that the promotion of Japanese-Chinese friendship and the restoration of Japanese-Chinese diplomatic relations are inseparable from opposition to the revival of Japanese militarism. The people of China and other Asian countries suffered from Japanese militarist aggression and this is still fresh in their memory. It is natural for them to maintain a high vigilance against and strongly oppose the revival of Japanese militarism. The Japanese side stresses that it is absolutely impermissible to let Japan replace the United States in pursuing its already defeated military policy, to lead Japan once again on to the erroneous road of militarism and to bring new disasters to the people of Japan and the rest of Asia. It pledges to struggle against the revival of Japanese militarism.

The Japanese side deeply regrets that the Satō cabinet, in disregard of opposition by public opinion, has acted as a cosponsor for the "reverse important question" and "complex dual representation" draft resolutions.

The Chinese side points out that the Satō government, which follows its own bigoted course and stubbornly pursues the policies of following the U.S. and of hostility towards China, is becoming more and more isolated and it will surely meet with irretrievable defeat.

The two sides are unanimous that China and Japan are close neighbors just across the sea and there is a long-standing friendship between the two peoples. China-Japan friendship represents the fundamental interests of the people of the two countries and is an irresistible trend of history. The two sides are determined to fight to smash the numerous obstacles placed by the U.S. and Japanese reactionary forces.

Taking part in the talks on the Chinese side were Wang Kuo-chuan leader of the delegation, and members of the delegation Hsü Ming, Wang Hsiao-yün, Hsiao Hsiang-chien, Lin Po, Chin Su-cheng, Ting Min, Hsü Tsung-mao, Wang Hsiao-hsien, Chiang Pei-chu and Chou Pin.

Taking part in the talks on the Japanese side were Fujiyama Aiichirō, Member of the House of Representatives, leader of the delegation, and members of the delegation: Members of the House of Representatives of the Liberal-Democratic Party Utsunomiya Tokuma, Shibuya Naozō, Urano Sachio, Shionoya Kazuo and Yamaguchi Toshio; Members of the House of Representatives of the Socialist Party Matsudaira Tadahisa, Kobayashi Susumu, Narazaki Yanosuke and Ino Masaki; and Members of the House of Councillors of the Socialist Party Naruse Banji and Agune Noboru; Members of the House of Representatives of the Kōmeitō (Kōmei Party) Fushiki Kazuo, Suzukiri Yasuo and Kuwana Yoshiharu; and Member of the House of Councillors of the Kōmei Party Shibuya Kunihiko; Members of the House of Representatives of the Democratic Socialist Party Imazumi

Isamu and Kawamura Katsu; and Members of the House of Councillors of the Democratic Socialist Party Mukai Nagatoshi; and assistants Uemura Sachio, Yamamoto Tamotsu and Murakami Yasushi.

The two sides express satisfaction at the result of the visit to China by the Delegation of the "Dietmen's League for Japan-China Relations" and are of the opinion that the talks between the two sides have deepened mutual understanding and are very helpful.

Appendix 6

Joint Statement of the Government of Japan and the Government of the People's Republic of China, September 29, 1972*

At the invitation of Premier Chou En-lai of the State Council of the People's Republic of China, Prime Minister Tanaka Kakuei of Japan visited the People's Republic of China from September 25 to 30, 1972. Accompanying Prime Minister Tanaka Kakuei were Foreign Minister Ōhira Masayoshi, Chief Cabinet Secretary Nikaidō Susumu and other government officials.

Chairman Mao Tse-tung met Prime Minister Tanaka Kakuei on September 27. The two sides had an earnest and friendly conversation.

Premier Chou En-lai and Foreign Minister Chi Peng-fei had an earnest and frank exchange of views with Prime Minister Tanaka Kakuei and Foreign Minister Ōhira Masayoshi, all along in a friendly atmosphere, on various matters between the two countries and other matters of interest to both sides, with the normalization of relations between China and Japan as the focal point, and the two sides agreed to issue the following joint statement of the two Governments:

China and Japan are neighboring countries separated only by a strip of water, and there was a long history of traditional friendship between them. The two peoples ardently wish to end the abnormal state of affairs that has hitherto existed between the two countries. The termination of the state of war and the normalization of relations between China and Japan—the realization of such wishes of the two peoples will open a new page in the annals of relations between the two countries.

The Japanese side is keenly aware of Japan's responsibility for causing enormous damages in the past to the Chinese people through war and deeply reproaches itself. The Japanese side reaffirms its position that in seeking to

*Peking Review, October 6, 1972, pp. 12–13.

realize the normalization of relations between Japan and China, it proceeds from the stand of fully understanding the three principles for the restoration of diplomatic relations put forward by the Government of the People's Republic of China. The Chinese side expresses its welcome for this.

Although the social systems of China and Japan are different, the two countries should and can establish peaceful and friendly relations. The normalization of relations and the development of good neighborly and friendly relations between the two countries are in the interests of the two peoples, and will also contribute to the relaxation of tension in Asia and the safeguard of world peace.

(1) The abnormal state of affairs which has hitherto existed between the People's Republic of China and Japan is declared terminated on the date of publication of this statement.

(2) The Government of Japan recognizes the Government of the People's Republic of China as the sole legal government of China.

(3) The Government of the People's Republic of China reaffirms that Taiwan is an inalienable part of the territory of the People's Republic of China. The Government of Japan fully understands and respects this stand of the Government of China and adheres to its stand of complying with Article 8 of the Potsdam Proclamation.

(4) The Government of the People's Republic of China and the Government of Japan have decided upon the establishment of diplomatic relations as from September 29, 1972. The two Governments have decided to adopt all necessary measures for the establishment and the performance of functions of embassies in each other's capitals in accordance with international law and practice and exchange ambassadors as speedily as possible.

(5) The Government of the People's Republic of China declares that in the interest of the friendship between the peoples of China and Japan, it renounces its demand for war indemnities from Japan.

(6) The Government of the People's Republic of China and the Government of Japan agree to establish durable relations of peace and friendship between the two countries on the basis of the principles of mutual respect for sovereignty and territorial integrity, mutual nonaggression, noninterference in each other's internal affairs, equality and mutual benefit and peaceful coexistence.

In keeping with the foregoing principles and the principles of the United Nations Charter, the Governments of the two countries affirm that in their mutual relations, all disputes shall be settled by peaceful means without resorting to the use or threat of force.

(7) The normalization of relations between China and Japan is not directed against third countries. Neither of the two countries should seek hegemony in the Asia-Pacific region and each country is opposed to efforts by any country or group of countries to establish such hegemony.

(8) To consolidate and develop the peaceful and friendly relations between the two countries, the Government of the People's Republic of China and the Government of Japan agree to hold negotiations aimed at the conclusion of a treaty of peace and friendship.

(9) In order to further develop the relations between the two countries and broaden the exchange of visits, the Government of the People's Republic of China and the Government of Japan agree to hold negotiations aimed at the conclusion of agreements on trade, navigation, aviation, fishery, etc., in accordance with the needs and taking into consideration the existing nongovernmental agreements.

(Signed) Chou En-lai
Premier of the State Council of
the People's Republic of China

(Signed) Tanaka Kakuei
Prime Minister of Japan

(Signed) Chi Peng-fei
Minister of Foreign Affairs of the
People's Republic of China

(Signed) Ōhira Masayoshi
Minister for Foreign Affairs of
Japan

Notes

Chapter 1

1. C. Martin Wilbur, "Japan and the Rise of Communist China," in *Japan between East and West*, Hugh Borton, et. al. (New York: Harper and Brothers, 1957), p. 224.

2. For a succinct historical survey of contemporary Sino-Japanese relations, see Nozawa Yutaka, *Nitchū kankei shōshi* [Brief history of Japan-China relations] (Tokyo: Jitsugyō shuppan kabushiki kaisha, 1972); Ueno Hideo, *Gendai nitchū kankei no tenkai* [Development of modern Japan-China relations] (Osaka: Futaba shoten, 1972); Usui Katsumi, *Nitchū sensō* [Sino-Japanese war] (Tokyo: Chūōkoronsha, 1967); and Etō Shinkichi, *Higashi ajiya seijishi kenkyū* [Study on political history of East Asia] (Tokyo: Tokyo daigaku shuppankai, 1968). See also John H. Boyle, *China and Japan at War, 1937-1945: The Politics of Collaboration* (Stanford: Stanford University Press, 1972); Sadako N. Ogata, *Defiance in Manchuria: The Making of Japanese Foreign Policy, 1931-32* (Berkeley: University of California Press, 1964); Takehiko Yoshihashi, *Conspiracy at Mukden: The Rise of the Japanese Military* (New Haven: Yale University Press, 1963); Akira Iriye, *After Imperialism: The Search for a New Order in the Far East, 1921-1931* (Cambridge: Harvard University Press, 1965); F. C. Jones, *Japan's New Order in East Asia: Its Rise and Fall, 1937-1945* (London: Oxford University Press, 1954); and Nobuya Bamba, *Japanese Diplomacy in a Dilemma: New Light on Japan's China Policy, 1924-1929* (Vancouver: University of British Columbia Press, 1973).

3. For the U.S. occupation policy, see Kazuo Iwai, *Japan's American Interlude* (Chicago: University of Chicago Press, 1960); Edwin O. Reischauer, *The United States and Japan* (New York: Viking Press, 1957); and Robert E. Ward, "Reflections on the Allied Occupation and Planned Political Change in Japan," in *Political Development in Modern Japan*, Robert E. Ward, ed. (Princeton: Princeton University Press, 1968), pp. 477-535.

4. Chalmers Johnson, "How China and Japan See Each Other," *Foreign Affairs*, July 1972, pp. 711-21.

5. For Marius B. Jansen's comments, see Tang Tsou, ed., *China in Crisis: China's Policies in Asia and America's Alternatives* (Chicago: University of Chicago Press, 1968), pp. 458-63.

6. Johnson, "China and Japan," p. 721; Robert A. Scalapino, *American-Japanese Relations in A Changing Era* (New York: Library Press, 1972), p. 94.

7. For the concepts of bimodal and unimodal patterns, see Robert A. Dahl, ed., *Political Oppositions in Western Democracies* (New Haven: Yale University Press, 1966), pp. 372-77.

8. The framework used in this study is much influenced by Easton's model of a political system. For his model, see David Easton, *A Framework for Political Analysis* (Englewood Cliffs: Prentice-Hall, 1965).

9. See Donald C. Hellmann, *Japan and East Asia: The New International Order* (New York: Praeger Publishers, 1972), pp. 18-43.

10. For four-power multipolarity, see A. Doak Barnett, "The New Multipolar Balance in East Asia: Implications for United States Policy," *Annals of the American Academy of Political and Social Science*, July 1970, pp. 73-86; for quadrilateral structure, see Robert E. Osgood, *The Weary and the Wary: U.S. and Japanese Security Policies in Transition* (Baltimore: Johns Hopkins University Press, 1972), pp. 63-71.

11. David O. Wilkinson, *Comparative Foreign Relations: Framework and Methods* (Belmont: Dickenson Publishing Co., 1969), p. 59.

12. See Richard C. Snyder, H. W. Bruck, and Burton Sapin, eds., *Foreign Policy Decision-Making* (New York: Free Press, 1962), p. 212.

13. Robert T. Holt and John E. Turner, "Insular Politics," in *Linkage Politics: Essays on the Convergence of National and International Systems*, James N. Rosenau, ed. (New York: Free Press, 1969), pp. 207, 211.

14. For a list of these Japanese groups, which the PRC appreciated for their contributions to Sino-Japanese diplomatic normalization, see *Peking Review*, October 13, 1972, pp. 16–18.

15. Donald C. Hellmann has explained the domestic political sources of Japan's foreign policy in *Japanese Foreign Policy and Domestic Politics: The Peace Agreement with the Soviet Union* (Berkeley: University of California Press, 1969); also, see F. C. Langdon, *Japan's Foreign Policy* (Vancouver: University of British Columbia Press, 1973).

16. Sigmund Neumann, "Toward a Comparative Study of Political Parties," in *Modern Political Parties: Approaches to Comparative Politics,* Sigmund Neumann, ed. (Chicago: University of Chicago Press, 1956), p. 396.

17. The survey that was conducted by the Kyōdō News Agency in June 1967 was reproduced in *Ajiyakeizai Jumpō* [Asian economic review], August 1967, pp. 22–28.

18. David W. Abbott and Edward T. Rogowsky, *Political Parties: Leadership, Organization, Linkage* (Chicago: Rand McNally, 1971), p. 516.

19. As reported in *Shūgiin giin sōsenkyo kekkashirabe* [Survey of the general election results for the House of Representatives] (Tokyo: Jijishō, 1967), pp. 266–67.

20. *Seron Chōsa Nenkan* [Public Opinion Survey Yearbook] (Tokyo: Ōkurashō, 1970), p. 142.

21. See Rosenau, ed., *Linkage Politics*, p. 46.

22. Robert E. Ward, *Japan's Political System* (Englewood Cliffs: Prentice-Hall, 1967), p. 49.

23. Rosenau, *Linkage Politics*, pp. 46–47.

24. Harry Eckstein, "The Determinants of Pressure Group Politics," in *Comparative Politics: A Reader,* Harry Eckstein and David E. Apter, eds. (New York: Free Press, 1963), p. 409.

25. William D. Coplin and Charles W. Kegley, Jr., eds., *A Multi-Method Introduction to International Politics: Observation, Explanation, and Prescription* (Chicago: Markham Publishing Co., 1971), p. 79.

26. Frank Langdon, *Politics in Japan* (Boston: Little, Brown and Co., 1967), p. 138.

27. Coplin and Kegley, Jr., *Multi-Method Introduction,* p. 79.

28. For the notion of "veto group," see Karl W. Deutsch, *The Analysis of International Relations* (Englewood Cliffs: Prentice-Hall, 1968), p. 26.

29. Langdon, *Politics in Japan*, p. 137.

30. Allan B. Cole, George O. Totten, and Cecil H. Uyehara, *Socialist Parties in Postwar Japan* (New Haven: Yale University Press, 1966), p. 227.

31. For a discussion of the LDP's policy-making organizations, see Haruhiro Fukui, *Party in Power: The Japanese Liberal-Democrats and Policy-making* (Berkeley: University of California Press, 1970), pp. 81-106; and Nathaniel B. Thayer, *How the Conservatives Rule Japan* (Princeton: Princeton University Press, 1969), pp. 207–67.

32. The six-man conference consisted of the prime minister, chief cabinet secretary, the LDP's secretary-general, vice-president, chairman of the Executive Council, and chairman of the PARC. The four party officials' conference was composed of the above leaders, except the prime minister and his chief cabinet secretary.

33. For the JSP's organizational structure, see Cole, Totten, and Uyehara, *Socialist Parties*, pp. 241–72.

Chapter 2

1. U.S., Department of State, *United States Relations with China* (Washington, D.C.: Government Printing Office, 1949), p. xvi.

2. For President Truman's statement of January 5, 1950, see *Department of State Bulletin*, January 16, 1950, p. 79.

3. See, for example, Liu Shao-chi's speech delivered at the meeting of Asian and Australasian trade unions on November 16, 1949, in *Jen-min jih-pao* (hereinafter referred to as the *People's Daily*), November 22, 1949. The PRC captured an increasing number of Japanese fishermen in the East China Sea and the Yellow Sea. The figures were: 1950, 5 ships and 54 fishermen; 1951, 55 ships and 671 fishermen; 1952, 46 ships and 544 fishermen.

4. For the English text of the treaty, see *Oppose the Revival of Japanese Militarism: A Selection of Important Documents and Commentaries* (Peking: Foreign Languages Press, 1960), pp. 1-4.

5. See the discussion by Sebald (Gen. MacArthur's political adviser) in William J. Sebald, *With MacArthur in Japan: A Personal History of the Occupation* (New York: W. W. Norton, 1965), pp. 247-56.

6. *People's Daily*, May 25, 1951. For a collection of China's policy statements on Japan, see *Tui-jih-ho-yueh wen-ti-shih-liao* [Historical documents on the problems of the peace treaty with Japan] (Peking: Jen-min-chu-pan-she, 1951).

7. See Dean Acheson, *Present at the Creation: My Years in the State Department* (New York: W. W. Norton, 1969), p. 770.

8. Ibid., p. 700.

9. For the texts of the San Francisco treaties, see Edwin O. Reischauer, *The United States and Japan* (New York: Viking Press, 1957), pp. 363-80.

10. *Oppose the Revival of Japanese Militarism*, pp. 5-17; or *People's Daily*, August 16, 1951.

11. For a discussion of these demands, see Shao Chuan Leng, *Japan and Communist China* (Kyoto: Dōshisha University Press, 1958), pp. 4-5.

12. *People's Daily*, September 19, 1951.

13. See Yoshida Shigeru, *The Yoshida Memoirs: The Story of Japan in Crisis* (London: William Heinemann, 1961), pp. 265-66, and Martin E. Weinstein, *Japan's Postwar Defense Policy, 1947-1968* (New York: Columbia University Press, 1971), pp. 46-49.

14. See the Yoshida-Acheson notes of September 8, 1951, in *Nihon no anzen hoshō* [Japan's security] (Tokyo: Anzen hoshō chōsakai, 1969), pp. 484-90.

15. See Koyama Kōken and Shimizu Shinzō, *Nihon Shakaitōshi* [History of the Japan Socialist Party] (Tokyo: Haga shoten, 1965), pp. 94-104.

16. See Sebald, *With MacArthur in Japan*, pp. 261-62. Suzuki and Asanuma were the Socialist Party's chairman and secretary-general, respectively.

17. For example, see Yoshida's statement made at the House of Councillors Special Committee on Ratification of the Peace and Security Treaties on October 29, 1951, *Shiryō: Nihon to chūgoku, 1945-1971* [Documents: Japan and China, 1945-1971], hereinafter referred to as *Nihon to chūgoku* (Tokyo: Asahi shimbunsha, 1972), pp. 2-4.

18. For the text of Yoshida's letter, see *Nitchū kankei kihon shiryōshū* [Collected basic documents on Japan-China relations], hereinafter referred to as *kihon shiryōshū* (Tokyo: Kasumiyamakai, 1970), pp. 27-28. William J. Sebald told Usami Shigeru in 1972 that Dulles himself had drafted the letter and that Sebald's office had refined the draft. See *Ajiya Keizai* [Asian economy], July 1972, pp. 61-62.

19. A decade later, Yoshida recalled that he had not wanted to spell out his rejection of the PRC, but that he had found no choice because of the U.S. senators' apprehension. As quoted in Takaichi Keinosuke and Tomiyama Eikichi, *Nitchū mondai nyūmon* [Introduction to Japan-China problems] (Tokyo: Iwanami shoten, 1962), p. 42.

20. *People's Daily*, January 23, 1952.

21. The text of the treaty signed by Kawada Isao and Yeh Kung-chao appears in *kihon shiryōshū*, pp. 32-38.

22. See Sebald, *With MacArthur in Japan*, pp. 284-87.

23. For Okazaki's testimony given at the House of Representatives Committee on Foreign Affairs on May 1, 1952, see *Nihon to chūgoku*, pp. 7-11. He also stated that the Yoshida letter had no legally binding effect on future Japanese governments.

24. See Yoshida's testimony on June 26, 1952, in ibid., pp. 20-21.

25. Takaichi and Tomiyama, *Nitchū mondai nyūmon*, p. 37.

26. See Chou En-lai's statement of May 5, 1952, in *Oppose the Revival of Japanese Militarism*, pp. 18–25.

27. For a discussion of China's peaceful offensive, see Leng, *Japan and Communist China*, p. 6.

28. For Chou-Ōyama meeting, see *Jih-pen wen-ti wen-chien hui-pien*[Collected documents on problems of Japan], vol. 1, hereinafter referred to as *Jih-pen wen-ti* (Peking: Shih-chieh-chih-shih chu-pan-she, 1955), p. 116, or *kihon shiryōshū*, pp. 50–52.

29. On October 28, 1953, Kuo talked with a nonpartisan delegation of the Japanese National Diet led by Ikeda Masanosuke. See *kihon shiryōshū*, pp. 52–57, or *Jih-pen wen-ti*, vol. 1, p. 119.

30. The five principles were first promulgated in the Sino-Indian trade agreement of April 1954, and they were reaffirmed in Chou's joint statements with Nehru and U Nu. The principles are: (1) mutual respect for each other's territorial integrity and sovereignty; (2) mutual nonaggression; (3) noninterference in each other's internal affairs; (4) equality and mutual benefit; and (5) peaceful coexistence. See *Chung-hua-jen-min-kung-ho-kuo tui-wai-kuan-hsi wen-chien-chi*, [Documents on foreign relations of the People's Republic of China], vol. 3 (Peking: Shih-chieh-chih-shih chu-pan-she, 1958), pp. 10–14, 314–17.

31. For the Sino-Soviet joint declaration of October 12, 1954, see *Oppose the Revival of Japanese Militarism*, pp. 26–28. Morley discusses a difference in Chinese and Soviet approaches toward Japan. See James W. Morley, *Soviet and Chinese Communist Policies toward Japan, 1950–1957: A Comparison* (New York: Institute of Pacific Relations, 1958).

32. For an excerpt of Hatoyama's press conference on December 10, 1954, see Ishikawa Tadao, Nakajima Mineo, and Ikei Masaru, comps., *Sengo Shiryō: Nitchū kankei* [Postwar documents: Japan-China relations] (Tokyo: Nippon hyōronsha, 1970), p. 46. It must be noted that Suzuki Mosaburō's left-wing Socialists joined the Democratic Party in electing Hatoyama prime minister over Ogata Taketora of the Liberal Party. See Hugh Borton, "Politics and the Future of Democracy in Japan," in *Japan between East and West*, Hugh Borton, et al. (New York: Harper and Brothers, 1957), p. 18.

33. As quoted in *Shiryō: Sengo no nitchū kankei* (Documents: postwar Japan-China relations) (Tokyo: Sokibo jigyō shuppanbu, 1971), p. 35.

34. For Chou's report of December 21, 1954, see Ishikawa, Nakajima, and Ikei, *Sengo Shiryō*, p. 46. According to a Japanese government study completed in the spring of 1955, China's general policy toward Japan in the early 1950s was directed by the "Japan Problem Committee." It consisted of: Liu Shao-chi (Chairman), Chi Hu-ting (financial secretary), Kuo Mo-jo (political secretary), Liao Cheng-chih (liaison secretary), Liu Ning-yi (mass movement secretary), and Chang Han-fu (diplomatic secretary). See C. Martin Wilbur, "Japan and the Rise of Communist China," in *Japan between East and West*, Hugh Borton, et. al., pp. 205–6.

35. John Foster Dulles, "Policy for Security and Peace," *Foreign Affairs*, April 1954, p. 156.

36. For Chou's speeches and activities at Bandung, see *China and the Asian-African Conference: Documents* (Peking: Foreign Languages Press, 1955), or George McT. Kahin, *The Asian-African Conference: Bandung, Indonesia, April 1955* (Ithaca: Cornell University Press, 1956).

37. See Kenneth T. Young, *Negotiating with the Chinese Communists: The United States Experience, 1953–1967* (New York: McGraw-Hill, 1968), pp. 44–52.

38. For Tatsuke's note of July 15, the Japanese Foreign Ministry's public statement of July 16, the Chinese Foreign Ministry's public statement of August 16, and Shen's note of August 17, see *kihon shiryōshū*, pp. 87–92. (Later, in the 1970s, Shen was named China's ambassador to Italy.) For the Chinese texts, see *Jih-pen wen-ti*, vol. 2 (1958), pp. 37–39.

39. *Jih-pen wen-ti*, vol. 2, pp. 10–16.

40. Ibid., pp. 39–43. The joint statement signed by Peng Chen (secretary-general of the Standing Committee of the National People's Congress) and Kanbayashiyama Eikichi (head of the twenty-five-member nonpartisan delegation of the Japanese National Diet) on October 17, 1955 asked their respective governments to make "positive efforts" for diplomatic normalization. See *Nitchū kankei shiryōshū*, 1945–1972 [Collected documents on Japan-China relations, 1945–1972], hereinafter referred to as *shiryōshū* (Tokyo: Nitchū kokkō kaifuku sokushin giinrenmei, 1971), pp. 110–111.

41. *People's Daily*, January 31, 1956.

42. See Shigemitsu's statements of February 3 and 16, 1956, in *Nihon to chūgoku*, pp. 25–26. For China's rebuttal of Shigemitsu's denial, see *Jih-pen wen-ti*, vol. 2, pp. 43–45.

43. The Hatoyama-Suzuki conversation took place just prior to Hatoyama's resignation as prime minister in 1956, but it was revealed in 1962 upon Suzuki's return from China. The late Hatoyama was unable to comment on the story. For Suzuki's recollection, see *Nitchū no kake-hashi* [Japan-China viaduct] (Tokyo: Nihon Shakaitō, 1962), pp. 3–4. For a Nationalist Chinese position, see Chang Chün, *Chung-jih-kuan-hsi yü mei-kuo* [China-Japan relations and the U.S.] (Taipei: Chung-kuo shin-wen-chu-pan-kung-she, 1956).

44. See Robert C. North, *The Foreign Relations of China* (Belmont: Dickenson Publishing Co., 1969), p. 98. Examples of China's continuous peaceful overtures toward the Hatoyama government were: Kuo Mo-jo's special broadcast to the Japanese people, March 16, 1956, the *People's Daily* comment (April 1) welcoming Hatoyama's willingness to meet with Chou En-lai, Chou's talks with JSP Dietman Katsumata Seiichi, October 9, Mao Tse-tung's talk with an Okayama cultural mission on November 18, and the *People's Daily* editorial (December 14, 1956).

45. Notable examples of visiting Chinese delegates were: the Chinese Academy of Sciences led by President Kuo Mo-jo in December 1955, the Peking Opera led by Mei Lan-fang in May 1956, the All-China Federation of Trade Unions led by Tung Hsin in November 1956, the trade delegation led by Lei Jen-min in March 1955, the fisheries delegation headed by Yang Yu in December 1956, and the Chinese delegation to the first World Conference against Atomic and Hydrogen Bombs led by Liu Ning-yi in August 1955.

46. See *Shiryō: Sengo no nitchū kankei*, p. 36.

47. *Asahi Shimbun*, June 4, 1957. See the joint communique issued by Japanese and Nationalist Chinese prime ministers on June 4, 1957, in Ishikawa et al., *Sengo Shiryō*, p. 84.

48. *People's Daily*, July 26, 1957, or *Jih-pen wen-ti*, vol. 2, pp. 54–58.

49. *People's Daily* editorial, July 30, 1957.

50. For a discussion of both Socialist parties' positions on China before their merger, see Allan B. Cole, George O. Totten, and Cecil H. Uyehara, *Socialist Parties in Postwar Japan* (New Haven: Yale University Press, 1966), pp. 227–30. See the foreign policy outline of 1955, in *Nitchū no kokkō kaifuku e* [Toward restoration of Japan-China diplomatic relations] (Tokyo: Nihon Shakaitō, 1957), pp. 3–4.

51. See *Asahi Shimbun*, December 27, 1955 for the left-wing pressure, and the CEC decision in *Nitchū no kokkō kaifuku e*, pp. 4–5.

52. Ibid., pp. 6–8. For the changing JSP policy on China, see Sone Eki, "Foreign Policy of the Japan Socialist Party," in *Japan's Foreign Policy: Conservative and Socialist Views*, Ashida Hitoshi and Sone Eki (Tokyo: Japanese Institute of Pacific Relations, 1958), pp. 18–33. For COCOM and other economic issues, see Chapter 4.

53. Vice-chairmen were Kodaira Tadashi, Yamahana Hideo, and Yoshida Hosei; secretary-general was Sasaki Ryōsaku.

54. *Yomiuri Shimbun*, October 23, 1956.

55. Sone Eki, "Foreign Policy" in *Japan's Foreign Policy*, pp. 24–25.

56. *Asahi Shimbun*, March 29, 1957.

57. For the text, see *Jih-pen wen-ti*, vol. 2, pp. 46–49, or *Nitchū no kokkō kaifuku e*, pp. 143–47.

58. See Mao Tse-tung's meeting with the JSP delegation on April 21, 1957, in ibid., pp. 120–39.

59. See Chou's talks with Japanese correspondents on July 25, 1957, in *Jih-pen wen-ti*, vol. 2, pp. 54–58, or *Oppose the Revival of Japanese Militarism*, p. 129.

60. *Asahi Shimbun*, April 24, 1957. JCP First Secretary Nosaka Sanzō welcomed the joint communique (*Akahata*, April 24, 1957), while a spokesman of the Nationalist Chinese Embassy in Tokyo denounced the joint communique as a conspiracy to create "two Japans"—namely, to bipolarize Japanese public on China (*Mainichi Shimbun*, April 27, 1957).

61. *Dokyumento: Nitchū fukkō* [Documents: Japan-China diplomatic restoration] hereinafter referred to as *Dokyumento* (Tokyo: Jiji tsūshinsha, 1972), p. 284.

62. See *Nitchū yūkōundō no rekishi* [History of Japan-China friendship movement] (Tokyo: Nihon chūgoku yūkō kyōkai, 1966), pp. 43–44.

63. *Jih-pen wen-ti,* vol. 2, pp. 87-89, or *shiryoshu,* pp. 214–16.

64. See the Foreign Ministry statement of May 10, 1958, and the LDP's statement of May 12, 1958, in Ishikawa, Nakajima, and Ikei, *Sengo Shiryō,* pp. 93–94. For a critical review of Sino-Japanese relations during this time, see Edward Friedman, "Limits on Chinese-Japanese Relations in the Era of the Dominant American Cold War: 1947–1958" (unpublished paper, 1973).

65. For his address delivered at the auditorium of Moscow University on November 17, 1957, see *People's China,* December 16, 1957, p. 44.

66. For Nan's earlier telegram to LDP Dietman Ikeda Masanosuke, April 13, 1958, see *shiryoshu,* pp. 210–14. Nan was chairman of the Chinese Association for Promotion of International Trade.

67. See Chen Yi's statement of November 19, 1958 in *Oppose the Revival of Japanese Militarism,* pp. 46–50.

68. See the Japanese Foreign Ministry's response to Chen's statement on November 20, 1958, in *kihon shiryōshū,* pp. 156–57.

69. *Asahi Shimbun,* September 21, 1958.

70. Ibid., September 12, 1958.

71. See the Teng Hsiao-ping-Miyamoto Kenji joint communique of March 3, 1959, in *kihon shiryōshū,* pp. 157–60.

72. Asanuma, in fact, used the same expression three days before in his talk with Chang Hsi-jo. For the text of his speech, see *Gekkan Shakaitō,* May 1959, pp. 23–29.

73. *Mainichi Shimbun,* March 14, 1959. Eda Saburō (then member of the JSP CEC and chief of its Organization Bureau) recalls that the CEC members were dumbfounded by Asanuma's statement because they were not informed of it. Interview with Eda in Tokyo, October 24, 1973.

74. For the Japanese and Chinese texts of the joint statement, see *Gekkan Shakaitō,* May 1959, pp. 43–46, and *Jih-pen wen-ti,* vol. 3 (1961), pp. 52–55.

75. The principles are: (1) not to adopt a policy hostile to China, (2) not to join a plot to recognize two Chinas, and (3) not to hamper attempts to normalize Sino-Japanese relations.

76. See *Jih-pen wen-ti,* vol. 3, pp. 15–16, or *Report on the Work of the Government* (Peking: Foreign Languages Press, 1959), pp. 68–69.

77. Foreign Minister Fujiyama admitted that 70% of his proposal was a campaign tactic, but the Nationalist Chinese ambassador registered his protest to the Japanese Ministry of Foreign Affairs. *Asahi Shimbun,* February 3, 1959.

78. For example, see *People's Daily* editorial, July 7, 1958.

79. See the Chou-Ishibashi joint communique of September 20, 1959, in *Jih-pen wen-ti,* vol. 3, pp. 71–72, or *kihon shiryōshū,* pp. 165–66.

80. For these points, see Tagawa Seiichi, *Nitchū kōshō hiroku* [Secret record of Japan-China negotiations] (Tokyo: Mainichi shimbunsha, 1973), pp. 11–30.

81. For China's role in the security treaty crisis, see George R. Packard, III, *Protest in Tokyo: The Security Treaty Crisis of 1960* (Princeton: Princeton University Press, 1966).

82. See Ikeda's first press conference on July 19, 1960, in Ishikawa, Nakajima, and Ikei, *Sengo Shiryō,* p. 183.

83. As revealed by Chou in his talk with a Japanese author in June 1961. See Takaichi and Tomiyama, *Nitchū mondai nyūmon,* p. 97.

84. See Hanyū Sanshichi (JSP member of the House of Councillors), *Sengo Nihon no gaikō: Ichi yatō giin no kiroku* [Postwar Japanese diplomacy: record of an opposition dietman] (Tokyo: Sanichi shobō, 1971), pp. 85–88.

85. For these comments, see *People's Daily,* July 25, July 26, and August 17, 1961; and the *Bulletin of Activities,* August 1, 1961, as translated in *The Politics of the Chinese Red Army,* ed. J. Chester Cheng (Stanford: Hoover Institution Press, 1966), pp. 738–40.

86. The report also pointed out that there was no guarantee that China would not pose a military threat to Japan and stressed the need to pay special attention to Japan's national security and to rearrange domestic political conditions for this purpose. Ishikawa, Nakajima, and Ikei, *Sengo Shiryō,* pp. 199–201.

87. On November 18, 1949, Foreign Minister Chou En-lai requested the U.N. General Assembly to reject the credentials of the Nationalist Chinese government delegation and to seat

the representatives of his new government. No action was taken on the request. In 1950 the General Assembly, by a vote of 16 for to 33 against, with 10 abstentions, defeated the Indian proposal to seat the PRC. For the following ten years the U.S. successfully imposed a moratorium on the question of Chinese representation at every General Assembly session. For the reasons given to justify Japan's cosponsorship, see *Waga gaikō no kinkyō* [Recent state of our diplomacy] (Tokyo: Gaimushō, 1962), pp. 17–21. It was later claimed by the JCP that the "important question" resolution was a Japanese diplomat's (Tsuruoka Senjin, director of the U.N. Bureau of the Japanese Foreign Ministry) idea. See *Zenei* [Vanguard] (Tokyo: Nihon Kyōsantō), December 1971, p. 121.

88. See *Official Records of the General Assembly, Sixteenth Session, Plenary Meetings, 1,072nd meeting*, paragraphs 99–129.

89. See his speech of December 1, 1961, and other related documents, including the "important question" resolution, in *Department of State Bulletin*, January 15, 1962, pp. 108–117.

90. For the U.N. debates and votes on the Tibetan question, see *Official Records of the General Assembly, Sixteenth Session, Plenary Meetings, 1,084th meeting and 1,085th meeting*.

91. For the JSP's criticism, see Ishikawa, Nakajima, and Ikei, *Sengo Shiryō*, p. 212. Douglas H. Mendel, Jr. discusses the development of Japanese-Taiwanese relations in, "Japan's Taiwan Tangle," *Asian Survey*, October 1964, pp. 1073–84.

92. Chou's expectation and disappointment were explained to Matsumura Kenzō in 1962. See Tagawa, *Nitchū kōshō hiroku*, p. 47.

93. For the Chinese Foreign Ministry's statement of December 21, 1961, see *Oppose the New U.S. Plots to Create "Two Chinas"* (Peking: Foreign Languages Press, 1962), pp. 11–16. For a detailed legalistic argument, see Chou Keng-sheng's thesis in ibid., pp. 55–75.

94. For the contents of Mao-Kuroda talk on January 24, 1961, see *kihon shiryōshū*, pp. 186–91.

95. See Haruhiro Fukui, *Party in Power: The Japanese Liberal-Democrats and Policy-making* (Berkeley: University of California Press, 1970), p. 250.

96. See Chou En-lai's and Chen Yi's speeches welcoming Takasaki's China visit, in *Jih-pen wen-ti*, vol. 3, pp. 150–55.

97. *Kihon shiryōshū*, p. 214.

98. For the process of Chou-Matsumura negotiations, including the original Chinese draft, see Tagawa, *Nitchū kōshō hiroku*, pp. 32–51.

99. For the Takasaki-Liao agreement, see *Jih-pen wen-ti*, vol. 4 (1963), pp. 90–91, or *kihon shiryōshū*, pp. 215–16.

100. See the text of Ikeda's letter of November 3, 1962, in *Waga gaikō no kinkyō* (1963), appendix, pp. 21–22.

101. See Chapter IV.

102. Fukui, *Party in Power*, p. 244.

103. In October 1963, Chou Hung-ching, Japanese-educated interpreter of a Chinese trade delegation to Tokyo, first went to the Soviet Embassy seeking political asylum in Japan or in Taiwan, but then changed his mind and decided to return to China. Subsequently, the Ikeda government sent him back to the PRC. See Mendel, "Japan's Taiwan Tangle."

104. For the Japanese Foreign Ministry's statement of March 5 and the LDP's statement of March 26, 1964, see *kihon shiryōshū*, pp. 231–32, and *Mainichi Shimbun*, April 2, 1964, respectively. For the Foreign Ministry's reaction to the French recognition of China, see *Asahi Shimbun*, January 28, 1964.

105. See the appeal of February 13, 1964, in *shiryōshū*, pp. 19–20.

106. *Kihon shiryōshū*, p. 239.

107. As reported in *Ushino*, July 1968, p. 199.

108. Takaichi and Tomiyama, *Nitchū mondai nyūmon*, p. 203, and *Ushino*, July 1968, pp. 199–200.

109. Later, Nan Han-chen was reportedly blamed for his misjudgment of Satō's intentions and thus was held politically responsible for it. *Asahi Shimbun*, March 29, 1972.

110. For these complaints, see *People's Daily*, November 25 and December 12, 1964, *Peking Review*, January 22, 1965, Chou En-lai's report of December 21 and 22, 1964, in *Main*

Documents of the First Session of the Third National People's Congress of the People's Republic of China (Peking: Foreign Languages Press, 1965), p. 49, or *Hung-chi* [*Red flag*], January 6, 1965, pp. 4–19.

111. For the Satō-Johnson joint communique, see *Department of State Bulletin*, February 1, 1965, pp. 134–36. The LDP, too, adopted an Action Program in January 1965, in which it accused China of becoming arrogant in foreign affairs following its successful nuclear test. See *Wagatō no kihōn hoshin* [Basic programs of our party] (Tokyo: Jiyūminshutō, 1965), p. 41.

112. *People's Daily*, February 12, 1965.

113. See Tsukasa Matsueda and George Moore, "Japan's Shifting Attitudes toward the Military: *Mitsuya Kenkyū* and Self-Defense Force," *Asian Survey*, September 1967, pp. 612–25; for China's criticism, see *People's Daily commentary*, February 19, 1965, and *Peking Review*, February 26, 1965, p. 17.

114. See Sadako N. Ogata, "Japanese Attitude toward China," *Asian Survey*, August 1965, p. 395.

115. Fukui, *Party in Power*, pp. 251–54.

116. For these points, see ibid., pp. 247–51, Ogata, "Japanese Attitude toward China," pp. 389–98, and Donald C. Hellmann, "Japan's Relations with Communist China," *Asian Survey*, October 1964, pp. 1085–92.

117. *Asahi Shimbun*, February 17, 1968.

118. For Utsunomiya's outspoken views, see *Chūgoku mondai no bunseki* [Analysis of China problems] (Tokyo: Jiyūminshutō ajiya afurika mondai kenkyukai, 1966), a document on public hearings concerning China sponsored by the Asian African Problems Study Group, pp. 34–35, 307–8.

119. Kaya Okinori, *The Communist China Policy of the Government and the Liberal-Democratic Party* (Tokyo: Japan National Foreign Affairs Foundation, n.d.), p. 14.

120. For a discussion of reparation issues, see Ueno Hideo, *Gendai nitchū kankei no tenkai* [Development of modern Japan-China relations] (Osaka: Futaba shoten, 1972), pp. 213–15.

121. For a comparison of their positions on the state of war, see *Shinhyō*, July 1971, pp. 107–9.

122. Ibid., pp. 104–7.

123. In January 1968 Utsunomiya sent to 535 U.S. congressmen and many journalists and scholars a letter urging a change in the U.S. policy toward China. See *Shiryō Geppō* [Monthly Data] (Tokyo: Nitchū bōeki sokushin giinrenmei), March 1968, pp. 16–19.

124. Kosaka Zentarō, *Chūgoku mita mama* [As I saw China] (Tokyo: Kajima kenkyūsho, 1967), p. 108.

125. Kaya Okinori, *Communist China Policy*, pp. 7-8.

126. *Shinhyō*, July 1971, p. 105.

127. For these comments, see John Welfield, *Japan and Nuclear China* (Canberra: Australian National University Press, 1970), pp. 2–3.

128. Ibid., pp. 8–9.

129. Ibid., pp. 9–10.

130. For China's postdetonation statement and proposals, see *Hung-chi*, October 28, 1964, pp. 1–7.

131. As quoted in Welfield, *Japan and Nuclear China*, p. 12.

132. *Chūgoku mondai no bunseki*, pp. 220–21.

133. *Asahi Shimbun*, May 31 and September 26, 1968; also see *Ushino*, July 1968 (special summer edition on China), pp. 174–76.

134. *Shinhyō*, pp. 109–12.

135. Kaya Okinori, *Communist China Policy*, pp. 13–14.

136. *Asahi Shimbun*, January 28, 1966.

137. *Waga gaikō no kinkyō* (1966).

138. See the Japanese Foreign Ministry's memorandum dated January 11, 1967, in Ishikawa, Nakajima, and Ikei, *Sengo Shiryō*, p. 389.

139. For the full text of Matsui's speech of November 11, 1965, see *Official Records of the General Assembly, Twentieth Session, Plenary Meetings, 1,375th meeting*, paragraphs 38–50.

140. For Chen Yi's press conference on September 29, 1965, see *Vice-Premier Chen Yi Answers Qestions Put by Correspondents* (Peking: Foreign Languages Press, 1966), pp. 15-17.

141. *People's Daily* editorial, November 19, 1965, or *Peking Review*, November 26, 1965, pp. 15-18.

142. See *Official Records of the General Assembly, Twenty-First Session, Plenary Meetings, 1,414th meeting*, paragraphs 127-79.

143. For a summary of Matsui's arguments, see *Waga gaikō no kinkyō* (1967), pp. 62-63.

144. For a Chinese reaction, see *Peking Review*, December 2, 1966, pp. 30-31.

145. *Dokyumento*, p. 285.

146. *Waga gaikō no kinkyō* (1967), appendix, pp. 2-4.

147. For a summary of the Satō-Yen joint communique of September 9, 1967, see Ishikawa, Nakajima, and Ikei, *Sengo Shiryō*, p. 458.

148. For the Satō-Johnson joint communique, see *Department of State Bulletin*, December 4, 1967, pp. 744-47 or *Waga gaikō no kinkyō* (1968), appendix, pp. 22-26.

149. For the texts of both Satō's speeches, see *Japan Report*, November 20, 1967, pp. 6-11.

150. *Waga gaikō no kinkyō* (1967), appendix, pp. 4-8.

151. For the background of the ASPAC meeting, see *Waga gaikō no kinkyō* (1968), pp. 162-63.

152. For the text, see *Japan Report*, September 30, 1967, pp. 4-9.

153. For the background, see *Waga gaikō no kinkyō* (1968), pp. 87-88.

154. See Congressman Fountain's speech of November 21, 1967, the "important question" resolution, and the Albanian resolution, in *Department of State Bulletin*, December 18, 1967, pp. 829-33.

155. *Peking Review*, December 8, 1967, pp. 20-21.

156. See *A Review of World Problems* (Tokyo: Ministry of Foreign Affairs, 1968), pp. 10-11. For Tsuruoka's statement of November 11, 1968, see *Official Records of the General Assembly, Twenty-Third Session, Plenary Meetings, 1,712th meeting*, paragraphs 1-13.

157. *Waga gaikō no kinkyō* (1968), pp. 7-9.

158. *Asahi Shimbun*, January 27, 1969.

159. See Prime Minister Satō's response at the House of Councillors on January 30, 1969, in Hanyu, p. 43, and Foreign Minister Aichi's testimony made at the House of Councillors Committee on the Budget on March 6, 1969, in *Asahi Shimbun*, March 7, 1969.

160. For their statements made at the House of Councillors Committee on the Budget on March 13, 1969, see *Nihon to chūgoku*, pp. 69-71.

161. "Japan's Legacy and Destiny of Change," *Foreign Affairs*, October 1969, pp. 21-38.

162. See Chae-Jin Lee, "The Japan Socialist Party in World Politics: Problems and Prospects," *Asian Forum*, October-December 1971, pp. 185-92.

163. See Eda's positions in Eda Saburō, *Nihon no shakaishugi* [Japanese socialism] (Tokyo: Nippon hyōronsha, 1967).

164. *Tokyo Shimbun*, August 2, 1961.

165. *Nihonkeizai Shimbun*, December 1, 1961.

166. *Asahi Shimbun*, January 3, 1962.

167. *Nitchū no kakehashi*, pp. 64-65.

168. *Jih-pen wen-ti*, vol. 4, pp. 75-79, or *Nitchū no kakehashi*, pp. 51-57.

169. *Asahi Shimbun*, January 14, 1962.

170. Ibid., January 14, 1962. For the LDP's "unified view" on the issue dated January 28, 1962, see Ishikawa, Nakajima, and Ikei, *Sengo Shiryō*, pp. 219-20.

171. *Asahi Shimbun*, January 29 and February 14, 1962.

172. Ibid., August 3, 1962.

173. Ibid., August 4, 1962.

174. See the statement by Chao An-po (secretary-general of the Chinese delegation) on August 12, 1962, in *Jih-pen wen-ti*, vol. 4, pp. 246-48. For a discussion of the confused antibomb movement in Japan, see George O. Totten and Tamio Kawakami, "Gensuikyō and the Peace Movement in Japan," *Asian Survey*, May 1964, pp. 833-41.

175. Eda's article entitled "Japan-China Friendship and Chinese Line" appeared in *Shakai Shimpō*, September 9, 1962.

176. *Jih-pen wen-ti*, vol. 4, pp. 119–22.

177. Ibid., pp. 87–90, or *shiryōshū*, pp. 132–34.

178. *Jih-pen wen-ti*, vol. 4, pp. 302–8. Eda flatly denied Hsieh's allegation, and said that he had never met Reischauer. Interview with Eda in Tokyo, October 24, 1973.

179. For the anti-Eda resolution, see *Kokumin Seiji Nenkan* [People's political yearbook] (Tokyo: Nihon Shakaitō, 1963), pp. 659–60. Eda was elected a member of the CEC and chief of the Organization Bureau.

180. See, for example, an increase in JCP leaders' and members' visits to China from 1962 to 1964.

	1962		1963		1964	
	Leaders	Members	Leaders	Members	Leaders	Members
Visits to China	7	65	6	84	16	117
Visits to Russia	11	120	7	87	4	24

Source: *Nihon Kyōsantō no genjō* [Present situation of the Japanese Communist Party] (Tokyo: Kōan chōsachō, 1965), pp. 37, 40.

181. See Narita's report to the JSP Central Committee on January 24, 1963, in *Gekkan Shakaitō*, March 1963, pp. 133–34.

182. See Koyama and Shimizu, *Nihon Shakaitō*, p. 259.

183. *Asahi Shimbun*, March 3, 1964.

184. See "Toward True Friendship between Japan and China," *Shakai Shimpō*, March 7, 1964, or the CEC's statement, ibid., March 15, 1964.

185. See *Nihon no nakano chūkyō* [Communist China in Japan] (Tokyo: Kōan chōsachō, 1967), p. 41. For Moscow's rebuttal of Mao's statement, see *Pravda*, September 2, 1964.

186. See *Jih-pen wen-ti*, vol. 5 (1965), pp. 58–63, or *Nitchū yūkōno soseki* [Cornerstone of Japan-China friendship] (Tokyo: Nihon Shakaitō, 1964), pp. 70–78.

187. See Eda's factional journal, *Shakaishugi Undō* [Socialist movement] (Tokyo: Shakaishugi undō kenkyūkai, December 1965), pp. 2–10. For an examination of Sasaki's leadership, see J. A. A. Stockwin, "The Japanese Socialist Party Under New Leadership," *Asian Survey*, April 1966, pp. 187–200.

188. See Sasaki's factional journal, *Shakaishugi no Riron to Jissen* [Theory and practice of socialism] (Tokyo: Shakaishugi kenkyūkai, May 1966), pp. 20–21.

189. Ibid., May 1965, pp. 31–33, and March 1966, pp. 7–8.

190. *Shakaishugi Undō*, February 1967, pp. 6–15.

191. For this speech by Matsuba Jun (delegate from Miyazaki Prefecture), see *Hsinhua News Agency: Daily News Release*, December 12, 1966.

192. See the statements made by Kiyomiya Shirō (member of Tokyo Metropolitan Council) and by Sugiyama Atsuno (delegate from Yamaguchi Prefecture), ibid.

193. *Peking Review*, December 16, 1966, p. 38.

194. See *Shakaishugi no Riron to Jissen*, September 1966, p. 11.

195. *Shakaishugi Undō*, June 1967, p. 2.

196. See Kōno's factional journal, *Undō to Seisaku* [Movement and policy] (Tokyo: Nihon shakaishugi kenkyūkai), April 1967, pp. 4–5, and August 1967, pp. 7, 17–19.

197. *Shakaishugi Undō*, March 1967, pp. 2–3.

198. Ibid., August-September 1967, pp. 2–3.

199. See Kaya Okinori, *The Turmoil in Communist China over the "Cultural Revolution" and Red Guards* (Tokyo: Japan National Foreign Affairs Foundation, n.d.).

200. *Asahi Shimbun*, April 17 and 25, 1968.

201. Ibid., May 13, 1968.

202. For these JSP proposals, see ibid., July 4 and 5, 1968; for China's dissatisfaction with the JSP leadership, see *Japan Times*, March 3, 1968.

203. Narita was elected without contest, but Eda defeated Yaoita Tadashi, who was supported by a leftist coalition of the hard-core members of the Sasaki faction, the *Heiwa Dōshikai*, and the *Nōmin Dōshikai* [Farmers' comrades].

204. The group included Ōshiba Shigeo, Nonoyama Ichizō, Matsumoto Shichirō, Ioka Daiji, Morimoto Yasushi, and Narazaki Yanosuke. See *Asahi Shimbun,* December 12, 1968. For their foreign policy outlook, see J. A. A. Stockwin, "Foreign Policy Perspectives of the Japanese Left, Confrontation or Consensus?" (paper delivered at the Association for Asian Studies in March 1969), pp. 6-7.

205. *Gekkan Shakaitō*, November 1968, p. 10.

206. *China's Cultural Diplomacy* (New York: Frederick A. Praeger, 1963), p. 12.

207. Sadako N. Ogata, "Japanese attitude toward China," p. 390.

208. The *Mainichi Shimbun* survey was conducted in March 1970. See *Seron Chōsa Nenkan* [Public opinion survey yearbook] (Tokyo: Ōkurashō, 1971), p. 558.

209. See Chu Tu-nan's article in *Shih-chieh-chih-shih* [World knowledge], October 10, 1964, pp. 4-5.

210. Ross Terrill, *800,000,000: The Real China* (Boston: Little, Brown, 1972), pp. 193-96.

211. Other organizations were: All-China Students Federation, Chinese Writers' Union, All-China Federation of Literary and Artist Groups, All-China Federation of Newspaper Workers, All-China Athletic Association, Chinese Society of Politics and Law, Chinese Medical Association, Chinese Fisheries Association, and Chinese Buddhist Association. For the speeches made by Chu Tu-nan, Kuo Mo-jo, and Liao Cheng-chih, see *Jih-pen wen-ti*, vol. 5, pp. 72-76.

212. For the list of Chinese officials, see *Nitchū yūkōundō no rekishi,* pp. 83-84.

213. *Jih-pen wen-ti*, vol. 5, p. 76.

214. For example, see its support for Chinese nuclear test in *Nitchū yūkōundō no rekishi,* pp. 137-39.

215. The association's membership was: 11,040 in 1959; 16,558 in 1960; 16,561 in 1961; 21,181 in 1962; 27,031 in 1963; 30,743 in 1964. See ibid., p. 81.

216. The distribution of China's three major periodicals in Japan was as follows:

	Aug. 1963	Apr. 1964	Dec. 1965
Jinmin Chūgoku	20,000	25,000	30,000
Chūgoku Gahō	9,000	15,000	20,000
Pekin Shūhō	10,000	41,000	50,000

Source: *Nihon no nakano chūkyō*, p. 103.

217. *Shiryōshū*, pp. 21-22.

218. Ibid., pp. 80-81.

219. For the Peking rally, see *Peking Review*, October 14, 1966, pp. 33-34.

220. *Shiryōshū*, pp. 498-500.

221. See *Chūgokukenkyū Geppō* [Monthly research on China], November 1966, pp. 27-28.

222. *Shiryōshū*, pp. 81-82; the same support was reiterated in the joint statement signed by Liao Cheng-chih and Miyoshi Hajime at Peking in January 1967, ibid., pp. 501-2.

223. For the JCP's version, see *Akahata*, May 24, 1967.

224. See *Gaibuseiryoku ni yoru kanshō to bōkōwa yurusenai* [Interference and assault by foreign forces cannot be allowed] (Tokyo: Nihon chūgoku yūkō kyōkai, 1967).

225. See *Chūgokujin gakusei shūgekijiken o kyūdansuru* [Accuse the attack against Chinese students] (Tokyo: Nihon chūgoku yūkō kyōkai seitōhonbu, 1967).

226. See *Peking Review*, March 17, 1967, pp. 24-25, 30-31, and *Akahata*, March 19, 1967. The Japanese term *chankoro,* popularly used in Japan before the end of World War II, had a distinctly contemptuous and provocative implication; the Chinese attached a similar slur *wo-jen* [dwarfs] to the Japanese.

227. *Shakai Shimpō*, May 28, 1967.

228. See *Shakaitō no tsūtatsu o hihansuru* [Criticize the instruction of the Japan Socialist Party] (Tokyo: Nihon Kyōsantō, 1967).

229. See *Gekkan Shakaitō*, October 1967, pp. 19-37; for the JCP's criticism of the JSP decision, see *Akahata*, September 5 and 6, 1967.

230. *Asahi Shimbun*, April 8, 1969.

231. On August 29, 1971, they held a unity conference; Wang Kuo-chuan, who was in Japan to attend the funeral of Matsumura Kenzō, spoke at the conference. It elected Kuroda as president, Miyazaki as board chairman, and Miyoshi Hajime as secretary-general; the top leadership was therefore the same as before their split. The conference reiterated its promise to fight against "four enemies" and adopted the resolutions for Japanese-Chinese diplomatic normalization, against the Okinawa agreement, and for restoration of China's rights in the U.N. See *Shakai Shimpō*, September 5, 1971.

Chapter 3

1. *Waga gaikō no kinkyō* [Recent state of our diplomacy] (Tokyo: Gaimushō, 1969), pp. 8–13. The LDP, in its policy handbook published in December 1969, contended that China, in the immediate aftermath of the Cultural Revolution, had no room to initiate a moderate foreign policy or to hold a talk with the Japanese government. The proposal for immediate Sino-Japanese diplomatic normalization, it said, ran counter to Japan's respect for "international faith" toward the Republic of China. See *Shichijūnendai eno zenshin: Seisaku kaisetsu* [Progress toward the 1970s: policy discussions] (Tokyo: Jiyūminshutō, 1969), pp. 134–136.

2. See *Shakai Shimpō*, May 4, 1969.

3. Ibid., March 12, 1969, or *Nitchū kankei shiryōshū, 1945–1971* [Collected documents on Japan-China relations, 1945–1971], hereinafter referred to as *shiryōshū* (Tokyo: Nitchū kokkō kaifuku sokushin giinrenmei, 1971), p. 5.

4. For this communique, see ibid., pp. 306–8. For the bold policy recommendations articulated by other pro-Peking LDP dietmen, such as Utsunomiya Tokuma and Fujiyama Aiichirō, see Elaine H. Burnell, ed., *Asian Dilemma: United States, Japan and China* (Santa Barbara: The Center for the Study of Democratic Institutions, 1969). Unlike Furui, Utsunomiya refused to make a public denunciation of Satō's China policy in Peking. See Akioka Ieshige, *Pekin Tokuhain* [Special correspondent to Peking] (Tokyo: Asahi shimbunsha, 1973), pp. 162–63.

5. For a detailed description of Sino-Japanese trade negotiations, see Tagawa Seiichi, *Nitchū kōshō hiroku* [Secret record of Japan-China negotiations] (Tokyo: Mainichi shimbunsha, 1973), pp. 136–204.

6. *Shakai Shimpō*, April 13, 1969.

7. *Shiryō: Nihon to chūgoku, 1945–1971* [Documents: Japan and China, 1945–1971], hereinafter referred to as *Nihon to chūgoku* (Tokyo: Asahi shimbunsha, 1972), p. 115.

8. For the representative examples of these diverse views, see *Shiryō: Sengo no nitchū kankei* [Documents: postwar Japan-China relations] (Tokyo: Sokibo jigyō shuppanbu, 1971), pp. 58–59.

9. For the English text, see *Department of State Bulletin*, December 15, 1969, pp. 555–58.

10. See *Waga gaikō no kinkyō* (1970), pp. 369–76, or U.S., Congress, Senate, *United States Security Agreements and Commitments Abroad, Japan and Okinawa: Hearings before the Subcommittee on United States Security Agreements and Commitments Abroad of the Committee on Foreign Relations* (Washington, D.C.: Government Printing Office, 1970), pp. 1428–33. Osgood suggests that Satō overstated his case for the purpose of obtaining the U.S. Senate's approval of the forthcoming Okinawa reversion arrangements. See Robert E. Osgood, *The Weary and the Wary: U.S. and Japanese Security Policies in Transition* (Baltimore: Johns Hopkins University Press, 1972), pp. 27–28.

11. Under Secretary of State U. Alexis Johnson explained the Soviet Union's "private reaction" at the Senate hearings, see *U.S., Congress, Security Agreements and Commitments Abroad*, p. 1159.

12. *Peking Review*, November 28, 1969, pp. 28, 30; also see *People's Daily* editoral of November 28, 1969.

13. *Peking Review*, December 5, 1969, pp. 10–12. For a collection of China's documents critical of Satō's and Nixon's policies, see *Mei-jih fan-tung-pai chin-lueh-ya-chou-te shin-yin-mou* [A new scheme for American and Japanese reactionaries' aggression in Asia] (Hong Kong: San-lien-shu-tien, 1970).

14. *Peking Review*, April 10, 1970, p. 5.

15. For Chou's "four conditions," see Chapter 4. For an examination of Sino-Japanese relations during the 1968-70 period, see Walter LaFeber, "China and Japan: Different Beds, Different Dreams," *Current History*, September 1970, pp. 142-46, 178-79.

16. Okabe Tatsumi, *Gendai chūgoku no taigai seisaku* [Modern Chinese foreign policy] (Tokyo: Tokyo daigaku shuppankai, 1971), pp. 29-38.

17. Ibid., pp. 38-40.

18. See Kimura Kihachirō (JSP member of the House of Councillors), *Chūgoku Nihon o dō miteiruka* [How does China view Japan] (Tokyo: Zaiseikeizai kōshōsha, 1971), pp. 100-104.

19. See *shiryōshū*, pp. 313-15, or *Peking Review*, April 24, 1970, pp. 31-33.

20. Tagawa, *Nitchū kōshō hiroku*, pp. 219-64.

21. For the joint communique on friendship trade, see *Peking Review*, April 24, 1970, pp. 29-31.

22. Tilman Durdin, James Reston, and Seymour Topping, *Report from Red China* (New York: Avon Books, 1971), pp. 71-74.

23. *Nihon to chūgoku*, pp. 116-17.

24. *Asahi Shimbun*, April 20, 1970.

25. Ibid., April 27, 1970.

26. In protest over the LDP's expected statement, Furui and Tagawa walked out of the joint session of both committees.

27. *Asahi Shimbun,* April 29, 1970; and China's informal reaction to the LDP's statement was reported in ibid., April 28, 1970.

28. Interview with JSP Dietman Kawakami Tamio (son of the late Kawakami Jōtarō, member of the House of Representatives Committee on Foreign Affairs, and close associate of Eda Saburō) in Tokyo, October 19, 1973.

29. As reported by Kimura Kihachiro, who accompanied Sasaki to China. See Kimura, *Chūgoku Nihon*, p. 18.

30. See *Peking Review*, November 6, 1970, pp. 14-16, or *Shakai Shimpo*, November 8, 1970.

31. See *Akahata*, November 3 and 7, 1970; for the JSP's reaction, see *Shakai Shimpo*, November 25, 1970. Kawasaki Kanji (head of the JSP's Bureau of International Affairs) was aware of the plural expression in the English text, but he dissociated the party from that expression. Interview with Kawasaki in Tokyo, October 22, 1973.

32. *Asahi Shimbun*, December 1, 1970.

33. *Gekkan Shakaitō*, April 1971, pp. 189-98.

34. Vice-chairmen were: Kōno Kenzō (LDP), Katsumata Seiichi (JSP), Watanabe Ichirō (CGP), and Kasuga Ikkō (DSP).

35. See *shiryōshū*, pp. 629-30.

36. For the text of Satō's speech, see *Waga gaikō no kinkyō* (1971), pp. 390-96; for the JSP's criticism, see *Asahi Shimbun*, October 22, 1970.

37. Ibid., November 18, 1970.

38. The Japanese government did use the "PRC" in February 1970, but it was changed to the "Peking government" due to Taiwan's pressure. See *Asahi Shimbun*, February 13, 1970. For Satō's address, see *Waga gaikō no kinkyō* (1971), pp. 383-84.

39. *Dokyumento: Nitchū fukkō* [Documents: Japan-China diplomatic restoration], hereinafter referred to as *Dokyumento* (Tokyo: Jiji tsūshinsha, 1972), p. 288.

40. *Asahi Shimbun*, March 14, 1971.

41. See Chou's talks with Japanese trade representatives on March 1, 1971, in *Chūgokukenkyū Geppō*, March 1971, pp. 31-32.

42. The five-point demand was for acceptance of the position that: (1) there is only one China, and the PRC is the sole legitimate government of China; (2) the Taiwan question is China's internal matter; (3) the Japan-Taiwan peace treaty should be abrogated; (4) the U.S. must withdraw all its armed forces from Taiwan and the Taiwan Straits; and (5) the legitimate rights of the PRC must be restored in the U.N. See *Peking Review*, July 9, 1971, pp. 20-21.

43. See the LDP's reaction, in *Dokyumento*, p. 286.

44. The account was reported in *Sekai*, September 1971, pp. 125-28.

45. Morton H. Halperin, "America and Asia: The Impact of Nixon's China Policy," in *Sino-American Relations, 1949-71,* ed. Roderick MacFarquhar, (New York: Praeger Publishers, 1972), p. 12.

46. See William H. Overholt, "President Nixon's Trip to China and Its Consequences," *Asian Survey*, July 1973, p. 714.

47. Tang Tsou, "Statesmanship and Scholarship," *World Politics,* April 1974, p. 439. One day after Kissinger's secret departure from Peking, Chou En-lai met with one of his closest Japanese friends, Iwai Akira (former *Sōhyō* secretary-general and now secretary-general of the National Congress for the Restoration of Japan-China Diplomatic Relations), but he gave no hint of Sino-American contacts.

48. For the text of Satō's speech, see *Waga gaikō no kinkyō* (1972), pp. 401–3.

49. *Shakai Shimpō*, July 21, 1971.

50. *Shiryōshū*, p. 631.

51. See *Seron Chōsa* [Public opinion survey], September 1971, pp. 83–84.

52. Ibid., November 1971, pp. 77–84.

53. For this account, see Kawasaki Hideji, *Nitchū fukkō go no sekai* [The world after Japan-China diplomatic restoration] (Tokyo: Nyu saiensusha, 1972), pp. 15–16.

54. *Shakai Shimpō*, September 1, 1971.

55. The pro-Taiwan LDP dietmen, who set up *Gaikō mondai kondankai* [Consultative group on diplomatic problems] under the leadership of Kishi, Kaya, and Ishii, cautioned Satō against Japan-China rapprochement, *Asahi Shimbun*, September 3, 1971. For the Chinese Foreign Ministry's criticism of the U.S. and Japanese move at the U.N., see *Peking Review*, August 27, 1971, pp. 5–6.

56. The JCP was excluded at the request of Wang Kuo-chuan. For the delegation's activities, see Kawasaki, *Nitchu fukkō*, pp. 27–28.

57. See the joint statement, in *Peking Review*, October 8, 1971, pp. 14–15.

58. *Waga gaikō no kinkyō* (1972), pp. 404–7.

59. Ibid., pp. 407–12.

60. *Peking Review*, October 29, 1971, p. 21.

61. *Sankei Shimbun*, October 21, 1971.

62. For the texts of Aichi's speeches delivered on September 27 and on October 20, 1971, see *Waga gaikō no kinkyō* (1972), pp. 424–40; for the English texts, see *Official Records of the General Assembly, Twenty-Sixth Session, Plenary Meetings, 1,968th meeting*, paragraphs 85–111, and *1,941st meeting*, paragraphs 31–79.

63. For China's comments, see *People's Daily* editorial, October 28, 1971, *Peking Review*, October 29, 1971, pp. 6–8, and the Chinese government's statement of October 29, 1971, in ibid., November 5, 1971, p. 6.

64. Richard Moorsteen and Morton Abramowitz, *Remaking China Policy* (Cambridge: Harvard University Press, 1971), pp. 14–17.

65. *Dokyumento*, p. 287.

66. Satō was also willing to regard the U.N. decision as Japan's tacit recognition of the PRC. See *Nihon to chūgoku*, pp. 80–82.

67. Most of these legislators belonged to the Miki, Nakasone, and ex-Matsumura factions. The no-confidence resolution against the minister of International Trade and Industry was also defeated by a 171–280 vote, but without the LDP's disarray.

68. See Kawasaki, *Nitchū fukkō*, pp. 32–33.

69. The JCP asked the league to specify the five principles of peaceful coexistence in the resolution, but the league's Board of Directors rejected it. Consequently, the JCP did not cosponsor the resolution, but expressed its intention to vote for it. See *Asahi Shimbun*, October 16, 17, and 19, and November 8, 1971.

70. Ibid., October 14 and November 8, 1971.

71. Ibid., December 25, 1971.

72. For Fukuda's recollection, see *Dokyumento*, pp. 152–60.

73. Hori wrote this letter just prior to the U.N. decision on China. For Hori's revelation, see ibid., pp. 81–95.

74. At Peking, Minobe gave the Hori letter to Chen Kang, but he was not certain whether Chou himself read it or not. For Minobe's story, see ibid., pp. 75–80.

75. *Asahi Shimbun*, November 15, 1971.

76. *Peking Review*, December 3, 1971, p. 36.

77. Satō was not happy about the result of his talk with Nixon, but they agreed to consult closely in the future. For the Nixon-Satō joint statement of January 7, 1972, see *Waga gaikō no kinkyō* (1972), pp. 458–61, or *Department of State Bulletin*, January 31, 1972, pp. 118–19.

78. See Fukuda's statement of December 16, 1971, in *Nihon to chūgoku*, p. 84.

79. *Peking Review*, December 31, 1971, p. 4. The three principles were: (1) the PRC is the sole lawful government of China; (2) Taiwan is a part of China's territory; and (3) the Japan-Taiwan peace treaty be abrogated.

80. For Fukuda-Gromyko meeting, see *Dokyumento*, p. 159; see the Fukuda-Gromyko joint statement of January 27, 1972, in *Waga gaikō no kinkyō* (1972), pp. 461–63. For China's sensitive reaction to Gromyko's Japan visit, see *Peking Review*, February 11, 1972, pp. 19–20.

81. Ibid., January 7, 1972, p. 12.

82. For the Japanese Foreign Ministry's statement of March 3, 1972, see *Waga gaikō no kinkyō* (1972), pp. 507–8. The LDP, too, published a pamphlet for the same argument, *Senkaku shotō no rekishito ryōyūken* [History and sovereignty of the Senkaku Islands] (Tokyo: Jiyūminshutō, 1972). Also, see Jon Halliday and Gavan McCormack, *Japanese Imperialism Today* (New York: Monthly Review Press, 1973), pp. 62–67.

83. Shakai Shimpō, April 19, 1972. The JCP agreed with the JSP's view (*Asahi Shimbun*, March 31, 1972), but the Japan-China Friendship Association (Orthodox Headquarters) was one of a few Japanese groups supporting China's claims, ibid., July 8, 1972.

84. *Peking Review*, March 17, 1972, pp. 10–11.

85. For a detailed account, see Kawasaki Hideji, *Nitchū fukkō*, pp. 54–58.

86. *Shakai Shimpō*, August 22, 1971 and January 1, 1972.

87. Ibid., March 12, 1972.

88. Ibid., April 19, 1972.

89. For a discussion of the Japanese newspapers' capitulation to China's political pressure, see Miyoshi Osamu and Etō Shinkichi, *Chūgoku hōdō no henkō o tsuku* [Denounce the bias in reports on China] (Tokyo: Nisshin hōdō, 1972). When Professors Miyoshi of Kyoto Sangyō University and Etō of Tokyo University exposed the above information in the spring of 1972, 42 pro-Taiwan LDP dietmen led by Ishihara Shintarō organized a consultative group for the freedom of press and campaigned against the PRC in the National Diet.

90. *Asahi Shimbun*, March 19, 1972.

91. Ibid., June 10, July 2, and July 3, 1972.

92. Ibid., June 21, 1972.

93. See Tagawa, *Nitchū kōshō hiroku*, pp. 339–43.

94. The resolution was defeated by a 159–267 vote in the House of Representatives and by a 108–31 vote in the House of Councillors. *Asahi Shimbun*, June 16, 1972.

95. Ibid., July 6, 1972. At the first ballot Tanaka received 156 votes, Fukuda 150 votes, Ōhira 101 votes, and Miki 69 votes. In the run-off ballot Tanaka defeated Fukuda by a 282-190 vote with 4 invalid ballots.

96. Ibid., July 6, 1972, or *Peking Review*, July 14, 1972, pp. 22–23.

97. *Asahi Shimbun*, July 8, 1972.

98. *Peking Review*, July 14, 1972, p. 9, or *Asahi Shimbun*, July 10, 1972. In order to make sure that Japanese correspondents (who were invited to the banquet) make an accurate report on Chou's important message, they were given both Chinese and English texts of Chou's prepared speech. See Akioka, *Pekin Tokuhain*, p. 220.

99. For example, Chou En-lai, in his conversation with Matsumoto Shunichi (ex-ambassador to Great Britain and a principal architect of the Japanese-Soviet peace negotiations), expressed his concern about a possible Soviet initiative toward Japan. See Tagawa, *Nitchū kōshō hiroku*, p. 364.

100. The domestic political reason for Chou En-lai's policy toward Japan was suggested by Professor Ishikawa Tadao of Keiō University. Conversation with Ishikawa in Tokyo, October 15, 1973. For China's policy toward Japan, see Gene T. Hsiao, "The Sino-Japanese Rapprochement," *China Quarterly*, January-March 1974, pp. 101–23.

101. *Asahi Shimbun*, July 11, 1972.

102. Ibid., July 17, 1972.

103. Interview with Sasaki in Tokyo, October 18, 1973.

104. See *Dokyumento*, pp. 117–37, and *Shakai Shimpō*, July 30, 1972.

105. *Asahi Shimbun*, July 21, 1972.

106. When Japanese Ambassador Ushiba Nobuhiko, who had publicly rejected China's three principles, returned from the U.S. to Japan in July 1972, he was surprised by a drastic

change in the public mood on Sino-Japanese relations. He apologized about his earlier statement to Foreign Minister Ōhira. For this episode, see ibid., July 21, 1972.

107. Ibid., July 23, 1972.
108. Ibid., July 14, 1972.
109. Ibid., July 24, 1972.
110. See Kawasaki, *Nitchū fukkō*, pp. 75–76.
111. For the "basic positions," see *Asahi Shimbun*, August 3 and 4, 1972.
112. Ibid., August 8, 1972
113. *Peking Review*, August 18, 1972, p. 3.
114. *Asahi Shimbun*, August 16, 1972.
115. Ibid., September 8, 1972.
116. For the process of compromises in the council, see Kawasaki, *Nitchū fukkō*, pp. 91–93.
117. See Shimizu Minoru's commentary in *Japan Times*, July 27, 1972.
118. For Takeiri's reconstruction of his role, see *Dokyumento*, pp. 138–51, and "Imadakara hanasu" [Now I can talk], in *Shukan Asahi* [Weekly Asahi], October 13, 1972, pp. 137–39.
119. For Furui's role, see *Dokyumento*, pp. 57–74, and "Nitchū kokkō seijōka no hiwa" [Secret story of Japan-China diplomatic normalization], in *Chūō Kōron* (December 1972), pp. 136–49.
120. Ibid., pp. 146–49, and Tagawa, *Nitchū koshō hiroku*, pp. 358–59.
121. *Mainichi Shimbun*, September 5, 1972.
122. *Asahi Shimbun*, September 3, 1972.
123. According to Kawasaki, Chou En-lai told this story to him during their meeting in Peking on August 18, 1972. See Kawasaki, *Nitchū fukkō*, pp. 100–101.
124. For the Nixon-Tanaka joint statement, see *Asahi Shimbun*, September 2, 1972; or, *Department of State Bulletin*, September 25, 1972, pp. 331–32.
125. *Asahi Shimbun*, September 18, 1972.
126. They included Miki, Nakasone, LDP Secretary-General Hashimoto, Kosaka, Fujiyama, Sasaki, Takeiri, JSP Vice-Chairman Hino Yoshio, DSP Secretary-General Sasaki Ryōsaku, and Hsiao Hsiang-chien. JSP Chairman Narita had proposed that the Tanaka delegation be accompanied by representatives of opposition political parties as an expression of nonpartisan diplomacy, but it was rejected not only by Tanaka, but also by the CGP and the DSP.
127. Apparently Liao Cheng-chih and Chang Hsiang-shan were made advisers to the Foreign Ministry just for their official participation in the Chou-Tanaka summit meetings. Chang, who had studied at Tokyo's Higher Normal School, was standing director of the China-Japan Friendship Association. As a member of the CCP's Department of International Liaison, he appeared to be responsible for the CCP-JCP relations.
128. Wang Hsiao-yün, who was secretary-general of the China-Japan Friendship Association, was a recent appointee as deputy director; Chen Kang was director of the China-Japan Friendship Association and served as a member of the Tokyo Liaison Office.
129. The People's Liberation Army Band played local folk songs from Tanaka's, Ōhira's and Nikaidō's native prefectures. (At the airport 53 Chinese officials greeted Tanaka's arrival—43 for Nixon's arrival. No red carpet was used for Tanaka (contrary to Nixon) because he was not a head of state.)
130. *Peking Review*, September 29, 1972, pp. 7–8.
131. For the text of Tanaka's speech, see *Dokyumento*, pp. 181–82; for its English translation, see *Peking Review*, September 29, 1972, p. 8.
132. As reported in *Dokyumento*, p. 51, or *Asahi Shimbun*, September 28, 1972.
133. Mao Tse-tung gave Tanaka the six-volume annotated collection of *Chu-tzu-chi-chu* written by Chü Yuan, an ancient Chinese poet (340–278 B.C.). The political significance of this gift was interpreted in three ways: (1) Mao compared Chü Yuan's patriotism to Tanaka's "patriotic" decision to visit China; (2) Mao stressed the traditional cultural ties between China and Japan; and (3) Mao appreciated Tanaka's poem composed in Chinese characters at Peking. See *Asahi Shimbun*, September 28, 1972. Tanaka's poem was translated into English as follows:

"Japan and China broke their relations many years ago
But now the time has come to resume these links;
Autumn is approaching

Our neighbors welcome us with warmth in their eyes
The Peking sky is clear and the autumn air is deep."

(*Christian Science Monitor*, September 28, 1972.)

134. For the Japanese text, see *Dokyumento*, pp. 161–68; for the Chinese text, see *Hung-chi*, October 1, 1972, pp. 10–11; for its English translation, see *Peking Review*, October 6, 1972, pp. 12–13.

135. Article 8 of the Potsdam Proclamation states: "The terms of the Cairo Declaration shall be carried out and Japanese sovereignty shall be limited to the islands of Honshu, Hokkaido, Kyushu, Shikoku and such minor islands as we determine." The relevant portion of the Cairo Declaration (December 1, 1943) says "that all the territories Japan has stolen from the Chinese, such as Manchuria, Formosa, and the Pescadores, shall be restored to the Republic of China." On September 2, 1945, Japan, in its instrument of surrender, accepted "the provisions set forth in the Potsdam Proclamation.

136. For the Nixon-Chou joint communique, see *Peking Review*, March 3, 1972. pp. 4–5.

137. For a detailed legal background of the joint statement as explained by Kuriyama Takakazu (chief of the Treaties Section of the Japanese Ministry of Foreign Affairs and one of the aides for Tanaka's China visit), see *Dokyumento*, pp. 211–22.

138. *Peking Review*, October 6, 1972, p. 15.

139. *Asahi Shimbun*, September 30, 1972. The contents of the joint statement were conveyed to the Nationalist Chinese Foreign Ministry prior to its release in China.

140. The information about their prepared statement was obtained from a Japanese professor who was close to the Ministry of Foreign Affairs. At the joint session of the LDP dietmen on September 30, 1972, both Tanaka and Ohira stressed the facts of Japan-Taiwan relations. See *Dokyumento*, pp. 198–210.

141. The Chou-Tanaka conversation on the territorial issue was revealed by Tanaka during his informal discussion with journalists at a country club golf course on October 1, 1972. See *Asahi Shimbun*, October 2, 1972. Earlier, he said that Mao Tse-tung personally approved the joint statement and that the signing of the statement was delayed for some time because Chou En-lai needed time to obtain a prior approval from the armed forces, ibid., October 1, 1972.

142. At Peking some 70 foreign diplomats—including North Korean Ambassador Hyun Jun-gok—saw Tanaka off; present at Haneda Airport were Miki, Hashimoto, Shiina, Kōno Kenzō, Sasaki Kōzō, Hsiao Hsiang-chien, and other prominent Japanese and foreign persons.

143. For the English texts of their speeches, see *Peking Review*, October 6, 1972, pp. 19–21. For a perceptive report on those Japanese leaders who had visited the PRC for the purpose of Sino-Japanese cooperation, see Akioka, *Pekin Tokuhain*, pp. 196–24.

144. *Shakai Shimpō*, October 4, 1972.

145. Later, in April 1973, Liao Cheng-chih led a huge friendship delegation to Japan; it included Chang Hsiang-shan (now vice-president of the China-Japan Friendship Association) and Sun Ping-hua (now secretary-general of the association).

146. *Asahi Shimbun*, August 8, 1972.

147. For the JCP' assessment of Japanese-Chinese diplomatic normalization, see Ueda Kōichirō (chairman of the JCP's Policy Council), "Nitchū fukkō to Nihonkyōsantō" [Japan-China diplomatic restoration and the Japanese Communist Party], *Chūō Kōron* (December 1972), pp. 122-149.

148. *Asahi Shimbun*, September 30, 1972.

149. On September 30, just prior to Tanaka's return home, the pro-Taiwan LDP leaders convened their *Gaikō mondai kondankai* and discussed their strategy regarding the joint statement, ibid., September 30, 1972.

150. See *Dokyumento*, pp. 198-210. Tanaka also explained his China trip to a group of top *zaikai* leaders sponsored by *Keidanren* (Uemura) and by *Nisshō* (Nagano), ibid., October 13, 1972.

151. This view was shared by ex-Prime Minister Satō who subsequently criticized Tanaka's too prompt move toward China, ibid., May 1, 1973.

152. See Ohira's speech delivered at *Naigai jōsei chōsakai* [Research council on internal and external situations] on October 6, 1972, in *Dokyumento*, pp. 188–97. The public demand for immediate diplomatic establishment with the PRC increased upon Tanaka's assumption of the government leadership; it jumped from 57.8% in November 1971 to 62.1% in August 1972.

153. *Asahi Shimbun*, March 13 and 15, 1973.

154. They protested, for example, against Tanaka's decision to hand over Taiwan's diplomatic premises in Tokyo to the PRC and to conclude civil aviation agreements with China at the expense of Taiwan's interest.

155. As quoted in Y. N., "Nitchū kokkō seijōka o meguru roncho" [Comments on Japan-China diplomatic normalization], *Chōsa Geppō*, January 1973, p. 27.

156. Ishikawa Tadao, *Nitchū mondai shiken* [Personal views on Japan-China problems] (Tokyo: Sakai shoten, 1973), pp. 193-202.

157. For Tanaka-Narita meeting on October 4, 1972, see *Shakai Shimpō*, October 11, 1972. Narita rejected Tanaka's appeal, but requested that Tanaka should stop the fourth five-year defense build-up plan and dissolve the cold-war structure.

158. *Asahi Shimbun*, November 9, 1972.

159. The vice-chairmen of the league were Katsumata Seiichi (JSP), Watanabe Ichirō (CGP), and Utsumi Kiyoshi (DSP). Its membership was as follows: 144 from the LDP, 179 from the JSP, 52 from the CGP, 30 from the DSP, and 6 independent legislators. The inaugural meeting was attended by Ambassador Chen Chu and Liao Cheng-chih, ibid., April 24, 1973.

160. The Japanese gifts to China consisted of 1,000 cherry saplings and 1,000 larch saplings.

161. *Asahi Shimbun*, February 5, 1973. Wang Kuo-chuan became China's first ambassador to Australia.

162. Mei Kuo-chün was director of the China-Japan Friendship Association, Sung Wen came to Japan in the summer of 1972 as secretary-general of the Shanghai Dance-Drama Troupe, and Li Meng-ching was deputy section chief in the Department of Asian Affairs as well as director of the China-Japan Friendship Association. Third Secretary Chou Pin was a chief interpreter for the Chinese table tennis team at Nagoya in the spring of 1971. Mei visited Japan in 1962 and 1964, ibid., January 14, 1973.

163. Ibid., February 3, 1973. On his way to Japan, Chen Chu was accompanied by his wife, Hung Lan as first secretary of the embassy, and by Li Lien-ching as counselor in charge of economic affairs, ibid., March 28, 1973. Other embassy staff included Commercial Counselor Yeh Ching-hao, First Secretary Cheng Chih-mai, and Second Secretaries Kao Fu-chin, Pan Yi-feng (Mrs. Li Lien-ching), Kuan Tsung-chou, Sung Chin-ming, and Chang Shih-chang. Most of the Chinese staff were fluent in Japanese. Chinese diplomats I met in the embassy at Tokyo studied Japanese in China, but their Japanese was excellent. The embassy also hired some local overseas Chinese for clerical and other minor chores.

164. Ibid., January 26, 1973.

165. See his speech delivered at an extraordinary session of the National Diet, in ibid., October 28, 1972.

166. Ibid., December 2, 1972.

167. Ibid., December 2, 1972.

168. Ibid., December 27, 1972.

169. The Interchange Association's branch office in Taipei used the former Japanese embassy building and consisted of ex-Minister Itō Hironori and 14 other Japanese personnel; the ex-consul general and another person ran the Kaohsiung office at the former Japanese consulate general, ibid., December 27, 1972.

170. Aichi visited Thailand, Malaysia, Singapore, and Indonesia, while Aoki went to South Vietnam, Cambodia, and Laos; Kimura visited South Korea.

171. *Asahi Shimbun*, October 28, 1972.

Chapter 4

1. For a discussion of these economic questions, see Alexander Eckstein, *Communist China's Economic Growth and Foreign Trade* (New York: McGraw-Hill, 1966), pp. 200-201.

2. See Chae-Jin Lee, "The Politics of Sino-Japanese Trade Relations, 1963-1968," *Pacific Affairs*, Summer 1969, pp. 129-44.

3. Mao Tse-tung, "Report to the Second Plenary Session of the Seventh Central Committee

of the Communist Party of China," March 5, 1949, in *Selected Writings of Mao Tse-tung*, vol. 4 (Peking: Foreign Languages Press, 1961), pp. 361-75.

4. Mao-Tse-tung, "Address to the Preparatory Committee of the New Political Consultative Conference," June 15, 1949, ibid., pp. 405-9.

5. See Yashiki Hiroshi, *Nitchū bōeki annai* [A Guide to Japan-China trade] (Tokyo: Nihonkeizai shimbunsha, 1964), p. 151.

6. See *Nitchu kankei shiryoshu, 1945-1971* [Collected documents on Japan-China relations, 1945-1971], hereinafter referred to as *shiryōshū* (Tokyo: Nitchū kokkō kaifuku sokushin giinrenmei, 1971), pp. 155-57.

7. Ibid., pp. 1-2.

8. As reported in Takahashi Shōgoro and Tanaka Shūjirō, *Nitchū bōeki kyōshitsu* [A classroom for Japan-China trade] (Tokyo: Seinen shuppansha, 1968), p. 52.

9. The United States and Western European countries organized in November 1949 at Paris a consultative group for trade policy toward the Communist bloc, and set up a Coordinating Committee (COCOM) as its executive arm. After the United Nations adopted a recommendation for embargo against China, the COCOM established a special China Committee (CHINCOM) in 1952; it was abolished in 1957. See George P. Jan, "Japan's Trade with Communist China," *Asian Survey*, December 1969, p. 903.

10. See Bernhard Grossman, "International Economic Relations of the People's Republic of China," *Asian Survey*, September 1970, p. 797.

11. *Shiryōshū*, pp. 159-61.

12. Takahashi and Tanaka, *Nitchū bōeki kyōshitsu*, p. 53.

13. The three other trade agreements were concluded in October 1953, May 1955, and March 1958. See *shiryoshū*, pp. 174-77, 180-83, 202-6.

14. Yashiki, *Nitchū bōeki annai*, pp. 28-29.

15. See *Dokyumento: Nitchū fukkō* [Documents: Japan-China diplomatic restoration], hereinafter referred to as *Dokyumento* (Tokyo: Jiji tsūshinsha, 1972), p. 284.

16. The first unofficial agreement on fisheries was concluded in April 1955.

17. For the bitter recollection of China's arrogant and discourteous behavior, see Ikeda Masanosuke, *Nitchū bōeki kòshò hiroku* [Secret record of Japan-China trade negotiations] (Tokyo: Naigaijijō kenkyusho, 1968).

18. *Hsinhua News Agency: Daily News Release*, March 5, 1958 or *shiryōshū*, pp. 202-6.

19. Ibid., p. 199. The six leaders' meeting consisted of the secretary-general and the chairmen of the Executive Council, the Policy Affairs Research Council, and the Committees on Diet Policy, National Organization, and Party Discipline.

20. Takaichi Keinosuke and Tomiyama Eikichi, *Nitchū mondai nyūmon* [Introduction to Japan-China problems] (Tokyo: Iwanami shoten, 1962), p. 70. The U.S. under-secretary of Commerce advised Kishi to be careful in deciding policy toward Taipei.

21. See the statements made by Prime Minister Satō and Chief Cabinet Secretary Aichi Kiichi, in *shiryōshū*, p. 209.

22. Ibid., pp. 201-14.

23. For the exchange between Hozumi and Kishi, see *Shiryō: Nihon to chūgoku, 1945-1971* [Documents: Japan and China, 1945-1971], hereinafter referred to as *Nihon to chūgoku* (Tokyo: Asahi shimbunsha, 1972), pp. 100-102.

24. According to Ikeda, it was Chou En-lai himself who initiated in 1953 the notion of separation of economic and political matters. See Ikeda, *Nitchū bōeki kōshō hiroku*, p. 9.

25. For Ikeda's cable sent to Nan Han-chen on behalf of the Dietmen's League and the league's resolution of July 3, 1958, see *shiryōshū*, pp. 214, 217.

26. *Mainichi Shimbun*, May 21, 1958.

27. *Shiryōshū*, pp. 219-224.

28. *Yomiuri Shimbun*, August 31, 1958.

30. For the summary of *Sōhyō* Secretary-General Iwai Akira's discussion with Chou En-lai on February 12, 1959, see *shiryōshū*, p. 225. A month later the JSP's Secretary-General Asanuma visited China and signed a joint statement with Chang Hsi-jo, president of the Chinese People's Institute of Foreign Affairs, on March 17, 1959. See *Nitchū kankei kihon shiryōshū* [Collected basic documents on Japan-China relations], hereinafter referred to as *kihon shiryōshū*, (Tokyo: 1970), pp. 160-63.

31. *Shiryōshū*, pp. 225–27.
32. For a different interpretation, see David G. Brown, "Chinese Economic Leverage in Sino-Japanese Relations," *Asian Survey*, September 1972, pp. 753–71.
33. For the examination of Japanese disadvantages, see Yashiki, *Nitchū bōek: annai*, pp. 42–44, 94–96.
34. The text of the Chou-Matsumura minutes of September 19, 1962 appears in *shiryōshū*, p. 132, or in *Jih-pen-wen-ti wen-chien-hui-pien* [Collected documents on problems of Japan], vol. 4, hereinafter referred to as *Jih-pen wen-ti* (Peking: Shih-chieh-chih-shih chu-pan-she, 1963), p. 16.
35. For these agreements, see *shiryōshū*, pp. 228–30, or *Jih-pen-wen-ti*, pp. 90–91.
36. The first Chinese commodity exhibit was held in Tokyo and Osaka in 1955 (according to the third unofficial trade agreement); Takasaki, director-general of the Japanese Economic Planning Board, and 670,000 persons viewed it in Tokyo, and 1,240,000 persons in Osaka. The following year the Japanese exhibit took place in Peking and Shanghai; Mao Tse-tung led about three million attendants in both cities. See the following table for Japanese exhibits in China from 1956 to 1969. Again the Chinese exhibits were held in Tokyo and Osaka during 1964, and in Nagoya and Kitakyushu during 1966.

Japanese Exhibits in China: 1956–69

Year	Name	Place	Period	Attendance
1956	Commodity exhibit	Peking	Oct. 6-29	1,254,000
		Shanghai	Dec. 1-26	1,678,000
1958	Commodity exhibit	Canton	Feb. 1-24	760,000
		Wuhan	Apr. 1-24	700,000
1963	Industrial exhibit	Peking	Oct. 6-30	1,200,000
		Shanghai	Dec. 10-31	1,250,000
1965	Industrial exhibit	Peking	Oct. 4-25	Unknown
		Shanghai	Dec. 1-22	Unknown
1967	Scientific equipment exhibit	Tientsin	June 1-17	100,000
1969	Industrial exhibit	Peking	Mar. 22-Apr. 11	Unknown
		Shanghai	Cancelled	

Source: Hirai Hiroji, *Nitchū bōeki no jitsumu chishiki* [Practical knowledge of Japan-China trade] (Tokyo: Nihon jitsugyō shuppansha, 1972).

The first major Chinese technical delegation visited Japan in 1957; led by the vice-minister of Chemical Industry, the 14-member chemical industrial mission inspected 93 factories and held 61 technical conferences during 57 days. Other Chinese technical experts and trainees came to Japan in the following years, but many Japanese companies dispatched their technical experts and engineers to China, especially during Canton fairs and Japanese exhibits held in China. At the Japanese industrial exhibit in 1963, 1,600 sessions of technical consultations and discussions were held on 292 subject matters; in 1965, 1,650 sessions on 445 subject matters; in 1967, 590 sessions on 122 items with 116 Japanese experts representing 76 companies. See Hirai Hiroji, *Nitchū boeki no jitsumu chishiki* [Practical knowledge of Japan-China trade] (Tokyo: Nihon jitsugyō shuppansha, 1972), pp. 194–203.
37. Assistant Undersecretary of State Roger Hilsman made such a statement in his press conference on April 16, 1963. See Takahashi and Tanaka, *Nitchū bōeki kyōshitsū*, p. 179.
38. Ibid., pp. 180–81.
39. *Mainichi Shimbun*, August 5, 1965.
40. For the list of these cancelled trade contracts, see Hirai Hiroji, *Nitchū bōeki no kisochishiki* [Basic knowledge of Japan-China trade] (Tokyo: Tabata shoten, 1971), pp. 123–33.

41. *Far Eastern Economic Review*, April 15, 1964.

42. For example, see a speech delivered by Nan Han-chen at a reception in Tokyo on August 3, 1965, see *Nitchū kankei shiryōshū, 1945-1966* [Collected documents on Japan-China relations, 1954-1966] (Tokyo: Nitchū bōeki sokushin giinrenmei, 1967), pp. 221-22.

43. *Shiryōshū*, pp. 239-40.

44. Detailed biographical information of these Chinese personnel is given in *Nihon no nakano chūkyō* [Communist China in Japan] (Tokyo: Kōan chōsachō, 1967), pp. 108-110.

45. See *Ajiyakeizai Jumpō* [Asian economic review] (Tokyo: China Research Institute), March 1, 1967, pp. 8-9.

46. See Wu's full text in *People's Daily*, September 9, 1967, and the Japanese government's statement in *Asahi Shimbun*, September 12, 1967.

47. *People's Daily*, September 11, 1967.

48. *Asahi Shimbun*, September 14, 1967.

49. *Kokusai Bōeki* [International trade] (Tokyo: Japanese Association for Promotion of International Trade), April 1968, pp. 15-19.

50. *Shiryōshū*, pp. 252-53.

51. As reported by one of the three Japanese correspondents who were expelled from China in 1967. Egashira Kazuma, *Pekin o owarete* [Expelled out of Peking] (Tokyo: Mainichi shimbunsha, 1967), pp. 152-53.

52. For Chou-Ishino talk, see *Shiryō Geppō* [Monthly data] (Tokyo: Nitchū bōeki sokushin giinrenmei), February 1968, pp. 3-7.

53. *Asahi Shimbun*, March 7 and 14, 1968. See Tagawa Seiichi, *Nitchū kōshō hiroku* [Secret record of Japan-China negotiations] (Tokyo: Mainichi shimbunsha, 1973), pp. 71-108.

54. *Shiryōshū*, pp. 296-97.

55. Tagawa, *Nitchū kōshō hiroku*, p. 77.

56. *Asahi Shimbun*, March 7, 1968.

57. *Kokusai Bōeki*, April 1968, pp. 2-4.

58. The Chinese cancelled in October 1967 the right of *Yomiuri Shimbun* to send its correspondent to Peking on the grounds that it sponsored the Tibetan treasures exhibition in Tokyo and invited the Dalai Lama to Japan in September. See *Peking Review*, October 27, 1967, p. 37.

59. It was estimated that the JCP had received more than $100,000 a year from these three companies or almost $300,000 a year from many trading firms until 1966. See *Nihon no nakano chūkyō*, p. 18.

60. Examples of the most active anti-JCP trading companies were Gōdo Sangyō Co. (run by Nishizawa, ex-member of the JCP Central Committee and founder of the Research Institute on Mao Tse-tung Thought), Chōko Yūkōbōeki Co. (run by Fukuda Masayoshi, ex-member of the Standing Committee of the JCP's Yamaguchi Prefectural Committee and founder of a pro-Peking paper *Chōshu Shimbun*), Sekkōdō (run by Saionji Kinkazu, ex-JCP member, and his wife, Sekkō), and Western Japan Trading Co. (run by Yamada Koji).

61. For these protocols, joint statements, and minutes, see *Ajiyakeizai Jumpō*, March 1, 1967, pp. 22-25, and March 21, 1967, pp. 7-11, and *Tōzaibōeki Repōto* [East-West trade report] (Tokyo: Ajiya bōeki tsūshinsha, Spring 1968), pp. 106-9.

62. *Peking Review*, March 29, 1968, p. 9.

63. *Pravda*, March 31, 1967.

64. As reported in *Great Proletarian Cultural Revolution and Prospects of Japan-China Trade* (Tokyo: Japanese Association for Promotion of International Trade, 1967), pp. 58-59.

65. *Akahata*, March 10 and 25, 1967.

66. For a critique of some opportunistic Japanese trading firms, see Saionji Kinkazu, *Pekin jūninen* [Twelve years in Peking] (Tokyo: Asahi shimbunsha, 1970), pp. 51-52.

67. See Sakai Toyoichi's criticism in *Zenei* [Vanguard] (Tokyo: Nihon Kyōsantō), February 1968, pp. 56-77.

68. *Dokyumento*, p. 285.

69. In June 1967, 37 countries accepted the late President Kennedy's proposal for lowering tariffs by 50%, and this policy came into effect in 1968. However, Japan named 27 countries to which this policy did not apply, and they included China, North Korea, North Vietnam, Albania, Rumania, and East Germany.

70. *Kihon shiryōshū*, pp. 241-45.

71. For example, see the Action Program adopted by the JSP's 30th Party Congress in January 1968, in *Gekkan Shakaitō* [Socialist monthly] (Tokyo: Nihon Shakaitō), March 1968, pp. 70-71.

72. *Asahi Shimbun*, November 31, 1967.

73. *Gekkan Shakaitō*, December 1968, pp. 217-18.

74. The company was headed by ex-Dietman Ogasawara Fumio and was represented by wives and relatives of Yamamoto Kōichi (JSP's vice-chairman at that time), Nonoyama Ichizō (later, chief of Labor Bureau), Ōshiba Shigeo (later, chairman of Election Policy Committee), and Ioka Daiji (later, chief of National Movement Bureau.)

75. See, for example, Ishino Hisao's article in *Shakai Shimpō* [Socialist news] (Tokyo: Nihon Shakaitō), February 11, 1968.

76. See Eda faction's journal, *Shakaishugi Undō* [Socialist movement] (Tokyo), June 1967, pp. 3-4, July 1967, p. 3, and August 1967, pp. 50-60; and ex-Kawakami faction's journal, *Undō to Seisaku* [Movement and policy] (Tokyo), August 1967, p. 12.

77. See Katsumata faction's journal, *Seisaku Kenkyu* [Policy research] (Tokyo), August 1967, pp. 6-8.

78. They included Yamamoto Kōichi, Ōshiba Shigeo, Nonoyama Ichizō, Matsumoto Shichirō, Ioka Daiji, Morimoto Yasushi, and Narazaki Yanosuke. *Asahi Shimbun*, December 12, 1968.

79. *Peking Review*, January 6, 1967, p. 15, and April 21, 1967, p. 20.

80. *Japan Times*, April 13, 1968.

81. See Donald W. Klein, "The State Council and the Cultural Revolution," in *Party Leadership and Revolutionary Power in China*, ed. John Wilson Lewis (London: Cambridge University Press, 1970), pp. 351-72.

82. See *Tsusan Hakusho: Soron* [White paper on trade: general parts] (Tokyo: Ministry of International Trade and Industry, 1968), pp. 290-94.

83. See, for example, Melvin Gurtov, *The Foreign Ministry and Foreign Affairs in China's "Cultural Revolution"* (Santa Monica: Rand Corporation, March 1969).

84. See Furui's report in *Asahi Jānaru* [Asahi journal], April 7, 1968, p. 107.

85. *Asahi Shimbun*, March 10-12, 1968.

86. Ibid., July 13, 1968.

87. Ibid., September 25, 1968.

88. Ibid., June 10, 1968.

89. *Free China Weekly*, October 13, 1968.

90. *Tōzaibōeki Repōto*, Spring 1970, pp. 9-10.

91. See *Waga gaikō no kinkyō* [Recent state of our diplomacy] (Tokyo: Gaimushō, 1970), pp. 10, 89.

92. *Nihon to chūgoku*, p. 114.

93. Minister of International Trade and Industry Ōhira Masayoshi used the COCOM regulations in January 1969 to prevent the Japanese Association for Promotion of International Trade from exhibiting 19 items in China and from selling another 19 items to China. Asked by the Japanese Association, the Tokyo District Court handed down such a decision, but dismissed the Japanese Association's request for compensation from the Japanese government. For the COCOM list of 153 items, as of 1969, which were divided into three categories—weapons and ammunition, nuclear-related equipment and machinery, and sensitive industrial products, see Hirai, *Nitchu bōeki no kisochishiki*, pp. 107-110.

94. *Yomiuri Shimbun*, May 31, 1970. For the release of additional information, I am grateful to Sakai Yukio, chief of the Opinion Research Section of *Yomiuri Shimbun*.

95. *Asahi Shimbun*, April 29, 1970.

96. *Shiryōshū*, pp. 315-17.

97. *Tōzaibōeki Repōto*, Autumn 1970, pp. 10-11.

98. For the full text of this statement, see Suga Eiichi, Yamamoto Tsuyoshi, and Shiranishi Shinichirō, *Nitchū mondai* [Japan-China problems] (Tokyo: Sanseidō, 1971), appendix, pp. 50-51.

99. *People's Daily* editorial of November 28, 1969.

100. For a discussion of Sino-Japanese rivalry over Korea, see Chae-Jin Lee, "The Development of Sino-Japanese Competition over Korea," in *Foreign Policies of Korea*, ed. Young C. Kim (Washington, D.C.: Institute for Asian Studies, 1974), pp. 37-53.

101. See *People's Daily*, October 1-4, 1969.

102. See *Ajiyakeizai Jumpō*, March 11, 1971, p. 1.

103. *Asahi Shimbun*, May 22, 1970.

104. *Asahi Shimbun*, May 15, 1970.

105. Upon returning from his visit to South Korea, Ishii conferred with Satō, and both also agreed that Chou's four conditions would have no adverse effect upon Japanese-South Korean economic cooperation. *Nihonkeizai Shimbun*, May 29, 1970. For Miyazawa's statement, see *Nihon to chūgoku*, pp. 118-19.

106. Yatsugi was standing director of the *Kokusaku kenkyūkai* (National Policy Research Association) and a key member of both committees.

107. It was reported that about 100 Japanese companies were invited to the session, but only 36 companies were represented. 87 Japanese and 36 Nationalist Chinese members were present; the South Korean group was headed by Chung Il-kwon (ex-prime minister), who was the South Korean chairman of the Committee on Japan-(South) Korea Cooperation. His Japanese counterpart was Kishi, and Ishii was adviser to the committee.

108. For the full text, see Suga, Yamamoto, and Shiranishi, *Nitchū mondai*, appendix, pp. 51-52.

109. For Uemura's statement, see *Nihonkeizai Shimbun*, October 14, 1970; Japanese auto makers noted that the "big three" U.S. auto makers, General Motors, Ford, and Chrysler, had their subsidiaries in Canada, *Ajiyakeizai Jumpō*, March 11, 1971, pp. 13-19.

110. *Asahi Shimbun*, January 19, 1971.

111. Fujiyama was chairman of the Japan Chamber of Commerce in 1957 when Prime Minister Kishi appointed him foreign minister, ibid., January 31, 1971.

112. Frank Langdon, *Politics in Japan* (Boston: Little, Brown, 1967) pp. 106-8. For a discussion of Japanese business leaders—their backgrounds, associations, rivalries, and person-alities, see Akimoto Hideo, *Keidanren* [Federation of economic organizations] (Tokyo: Sekkasha, 1968).

113. For the list of Japanese companies accepting Chou's conditions as of April 1971, see Watanabe Tamao and Ogawa Kazuo, *Nitchū bōeki nyūmon* [Introduction to Japan-China trade] (Tokyo: Nihonkeizai shimbunsha, 1972), pp. 303-4. For Chou's talks with Sasaki and other Japanese visitors, see *Chūgokukenkyū Geppō* [Monthly research on China], March 1971, pp. 23-31, and *Tōzaibōeki Repōto*, Spring 1971, pp. A 1-3.

114. See Chou's talks with Kimura Ichizō, managing director of the Kansai Chapter of the Japanese Association for Promotion of International Trade, on February 24, 1971, in *Ajiyakeizai Jumpō*, April 1, 1971, pp. 1-12; and with Fujiyama on February 23, and March 3, 1971, in *Chūgokukenkyū Geppō*, March 1971, pp. 32-35.

115. For Chou's intense interest in the post-Satō development, see Tagawa, *Nitchū kōsho hiroku*, p. 298.

116. *Peking Review*, April 10, 1970, pp. 36, 38, and April 24, 1970, pp. 21, 38.

117. Tagawa, *Nitchū kōsho hiroku*, pp. 267-302.

118. *Peking Review*, March 12, 1971, pp. 24-25.

119. *Asahi Shimbun*, March 2 and 16, 1971.

120. Ibid., March 2, 1971.

121. *Seron Chōsa* [Public opinion survey], Mary 1971, p. 99.

122. Ibid., January 1972, pp. 78-81.

123. The secret Takeiri-Wang meeting in a Fukuoka hotel, arranged by LDP Dietman Kawasaki Hideji, set the stage for the CGP's official mission to China. See Kawasaki Hideji, *Nitchū fukkōgo no sekai* [The world after Japan-China diplomatic restoration] (Tokyo: Nyu saiensusha, 1972), p. 71. Wang visited the JSP Headquarters, *Shakai Shimpō*, May 5, 1971.

124. *Asahi Shimbun*, April 14, 1971.

125. Ibid., April 24, 1971.

126. On April 14, 1971, the White House announced a relaxation of a 20-year embargo on trade against China: (1) U.S. currency control (imposed in 1950) would be softened so that China could use dollars to pay for exports; (2) U.S. oil companies would be allowed to provide fuel to ships or plans going to or from Chinese ports; and (3) U.S. vessels would be permitted to carry Chinese cargo between non-Chinese ports, etc. A further relaxation of trade restrictions was announced on June 10, 1971; U.S. companies would be able to export to China fertilizers, chemicals, textiles, metals, equipment, etc. See

China and U.S. Foreign Policy (Washington, D.C.: Congressional Quarterly, 2d ed., 1973), pp. 10–11.

127. *Asahi Shimbun*, July 17, 1971.
128. Ibid., October 2, 1971.
129. Maiya Kenichirō, ed., *Shu Onlai: Nihon o kataru* [Chou En-lai: speaks on Japan] (Tokyo: Jitsugyōno nihonsha, 1972), pp. 165–83.
130. Kuo Mo-jo and Nagano Shigeo, as alumni of a prewar Okayama higher school, renewed their friendship at Peking; thereafter, Kuo sent a collection of Chinese poems to Nagano, while Nagano mailed the Okayama alumni association directory and other old school memorabilia to Kuo. (Kuroda Hisao, too attended the same higher school.)
131. For Chou's talks, see *Asahi Shimbun*, November 19, 1971, Maiya, *Shu Onlai*, pp. 225–29 (a summary of his conversation with the Tokyo group), and Kawasaki, *Nitchū fukkō*, pp. 34–36 (Nagano's recollection).
132. See Shiranishi Shinichirō's (a long-time participant in Sino-Japanese trade) report in *Shūkan Asahi* [Asahi weekly], September 22, 1972, p. 130.
133. They also met Liao Cheng-chih at Peking for the first time in several years. For a moving scene of their reunion, see Tagawa, *Nitchū kōshō hiroku*, pp. 317–19.
134. *Asahi Shimbun*, December 22, 1971.
135. *Shakai Shimpō*, December 29, 1971.
136. For examples of these activities, see *Asahi Shimbun*, March 4, and 26, 1972.
137. Ibid., May 24, 1972.
138. For the list of COCOM regulations as of June 1971, see Watanabe and Ogawa, *Nitchū bōeki nyūmon*, pp. 199–247.
139. Asahi Shimbun, June 14 and 15, 1972.
140. This interpretation is based on Shiranishi Shinichirō's report in *Shūkan Asahi*, p. 131.
141. Ibid., pp. 128–29.
142. Ibid., October 20, 1972, pp. 116–17.
143. *Asahi Shimbun*, October 30, 1972.
144. Ibid., October 19 and November 22, 1972.
145. For Sasaki's recollection, see *Shakai Shimpō*, July 30, 1972. As of 1971, the total number of Japanese companies engaged in Sino-Japanese trade reached 295—238 friendship companies, 14 banks, 6 insurance agencies, 5 inspection firms, 22 marine transportation companies, 6 storage firms, and 4 travel agencies; 118 friendship companies were located in Tokyo, 47 in Osaka, and the rest in other cities. See Hirai, *Nitchū bōeki no kisochishiki*, p. 188.
146. See Tagawa, *Nitchū kōshō hiroku*, pp. 364–66, and *Tōzaibōeki Repōto*, Spring 1973, p. A 3. This was a familiar quotation repeated many times in Chinese documents and statements thereafter.
147. See Brown, "Chinese Economic Leverage," p. 756, and Richard Ellingsworth, *Japanese Economic Policies and Security* (London: International Institute for Strategic Studies, October 1972, Adelphi Papers, no. 90), pp. 22–24.
148. For Chou's explanation of Chinese trade policy to Fujiyama Aiichirō, Tagawa Seiichi, and other Japanese leaders in April 1970, see Tagawa, *Nitchū kōshō hiroku*, pp. 260–261.
149. *Nitchū bōeki techō* [Notebook on Japan-China trade] (Tokyo: JETRO, 1971), pp. 6–7.
150. Grossman, "International Economic Relations," p. 790.
151. See *Chōsa Geppō*, January 1973, pp. 41–60.
152. China seeks to produce the largest quantity of coal in the world by the end of its fourth Five-Year Economic Plan and to increase oil production substantially during this period. Japan was anxious to obtain both of these energy resources from China. For a detailed discussion, see ibid.
153. As quoted in ibid., p. 54.
154. *Chūgoko Yoran* [China almanac] (Tokyo: Jiji tsūshinsha, 1973), pp. 242–43.
155. See Kawasaki, *Nitchū fukkō*, pp. 179–81.

Index